D0831037

The Political Organization of Bolivia

N. ANDREW N. CLEVEN

Professor of History, University of Pittsburgh
Sometime Research Associate in History,
Carnegie Institution of Washington

PUBLISHED BY CARNEGIE INSTITUTION OF WASHINGTON
WASHINGTON, D. C.
1940

CARNEGIE INSTITUTION OF WASHINGTON PUBLICATION NO. 510

NEW YORK MONOTYPE COMPOSITION CO. INC., NEW YORK, N. Y.
LANMAN ENGRAVING CO., WASHINGTON, D. C.

FOREWORD

This study was authorized by the Board of Trustees of the Carnegie Institution of Washington in May 1930. The author was appointed a Research Associate in History for the year 1930–1931, and was instructed to make a study of the political organization of Bolivia. He spent several months of that year in the Republic of Bolivia gathering data for a written report on the subject under investigation. As the footnotes and the bibliography will show, much of the information was culled from published works, secondary as well as primary sources. It is believed, however, that the information is reliable.

The author has had in view throughout the preparation of this work something more than the political organization, in the more restricted sense, of the Republic of Bolivia. The emphasis, obviously, has been on the nature and organization of the constitutionalism of the country. But he has kept in mind the sage admonition of the celebrated Argentine jurisconsult Rufino de Elizalde, given to Domingo F. Sarmiento, that the constitutional history of a country must be dealt with as an integral part of the whole history of that country. In other words, the political organization of a country is only a part of the whole history of that country, and cannot be fully understood outside and apart from that history. The author has sought, in the first place, to lay emphasis upon the fact that Bolivia is a mediterranean land, and is composed of three distinct physical regions: the Andean, the Amazonian, and the La Platan. The problem of the decentralization of the national government, the development of the means of communication and transportation, and the development of the natural resources are largely determined by geographical factors. The fact that Bolivia has always had a unitary form of government is primarily due to the size, the location, the topography, the climate, and above all else to the ethnological makeup of the country.

The treatment of the geographical background is followed by a study of the important phases of the history of the colonial period and the establishment of the republic. The foundations of the country were laid in these periods, and have continued with but few essential modifications to the present day. The national government and local government receive, quite naturally, the largest share of attention. These chapters might well have terminated the study but for the fact that the relation between Church and State has been a determining influence in the political organization of the republic. No single institution has had a more powerful influence upon the life of the Bolivian people than the Roman Catholic Church. To ignore that fact would be to ignore an essential.

The study is based upon the fact that the history of Bolivia is complex, and that its political organization cannot adequately be understood in any other light. Bolivia is not only fundamentally an Indian but also a Spanish country. It is with these two racial elements as a foundation that the Bolivians have sought to maintain an independent republican political government. The study comes to a rather abrupt end with the year 1931. Since there had to be an end, it was felt that the period which marked the readoption of the Constitution would be a fitting close.

The author is naturally under heavy obligations to a large number of people. First and foremost is the eminent and distinguished head of the Pan American Union. History alone will deal adequately with the larger services which Dr. L. S. Rowe has rendered to the cause of Pan Americanism. The author is under great obligation to Dr. Rowe not only for inspiration but also for the rare opportunity of studying Bolivian life in Bolivia. He is also under great obligation to the President Emeritus of the Carnegie Institution of Washington, the distinguished administrator and scholar Dr. John C. Merriam, who has given him inspiration and encouragement throughout the preparation of this study. He is especially grateful to Dr. Merriam for the patience he has always shown during the preparation of the work and the faith he has had in its ultimate conclusion. He is also under obligation to Dr. A. V. Kidder, Director of the Division of Historical Research of the Carnegie Institution, for the larger emphasis upon political history; and to Chancellor John G. Bowman of the University of Pittsburgh, and Dr. John W. Oliver, Head of the Department of History of that institution, for granting him a leave of absence under favorable circumstances.

The number of those from whom the author received aid, in sundry and various forms, in Bolivia is of course very large. Only those who rendered him the most important services need be mentioned here, however. First on the list come the former United States Minister to Bolivia, Mr. Edward F. Feely, and his able assistant Mr. Henry Winston Boltz. He received invaluable aid from both of these men, especially from Mr. Feely, who was able to put him in contact with the men at the head of the national government at the time. He is under great obligation to General Blanco Galindo, President of the Governmental Military Junta (*Presidente de la Junta Militar de Gobierno*); the late Dr. Daniel Salamanca, Constitutional President of Bolivia (*Presidente Constitucional de Bolivia*); Dr. José Luis Tejada Sorzano, Vice-President of Bolivia (*Vice-Presidente de Bolivia*), and later president of the republic upon the resignation of President Salamanca; Colonel Filiberto Osorio, Minister of Foreign Relations and Religion (*Ministro de Relaciones Exteriores y Culto*), and later Chief of the Mayor General Staff (*la Jefatura de Estado Mayor General*); the late Dr. Daniel Sánchez Bustamante, Minister of Foreign Relations and Religion; Dr. Juan de la Cruz Delgado, President of the Supreme Court, and the Ministers of the Supreme Court: Dr. Mariano Zambrana, Dr. Angel Sandoval, Dr. Manuel Ordóñez López, Dr. S. J. Agreda, and Dr. Anibal Calvo; Dr. Agustín Iturricha, Attorney General of Bolivia; Dr. José de

Gutiérrez, Secretary of the Governmental Military Junta, and Dean of the Faculty of Law of the University of San Andrés in La Paz; Don Agustín Mendieta, Prefect of the Department of Potosí; Monseñor Carlo Chiarlo, Archbishop of Amida, Papal Nuncio; Fray Francisco Pierini, Archbishop of La Plata; Dr. Victor Muñoz Reyes, Consul General of Japan in La Paz, and former Minister of State; Mr. William N. Pickwood, General Administrator of the Antofagasta Railway to Bolivia; Dr. Casto Rojas; Dr. León M. Loza, former Minister of State, former member of Congress; the late Dr. Ricardo Mujía; Dr. Juan Bedegral, Rector of the University of San Andrés, and Minister of Public Instruction and Agriculture; Dr. Luis Subieta Sagárnaga, Rector of the University of Tomás Frías in Potosí; Dr. Ezequiel L. Osorio, Rector of the University of San Xavier in Sucre; Dr. Vicente Donoso Torres, Director of the Normal School of the University of San Xavier; Dr. Enrique Sánchez de Lozada, Professor of International Law in the University of San Andrés; Dr. José Antonio Arze; Mr. H. J. D. Penhale, of Potosí; the Director General of the National Archives; the General Editor of *El Diario* of La Paz; Señorita Rebeca Salazar Brito, Assistant in the National Archives; Dr. Benjamín Calvo, President of the Supreme National Tribunal of Accounts; and General Oscar de Santa-Cruz, son of Marshal Andrés Santa Cruz. To all these, and to those whom he has not named here, the author expresses his deepest appreciation. All were unfailing in their courtesy and consideration and represented their country and people with rare skill and ability.

N. Andrew N. Cleven

University of Pittsburgh
August 10, 1938

CONTENTS

THE POLITICAL ORGANIZATION OF BOLIVIA

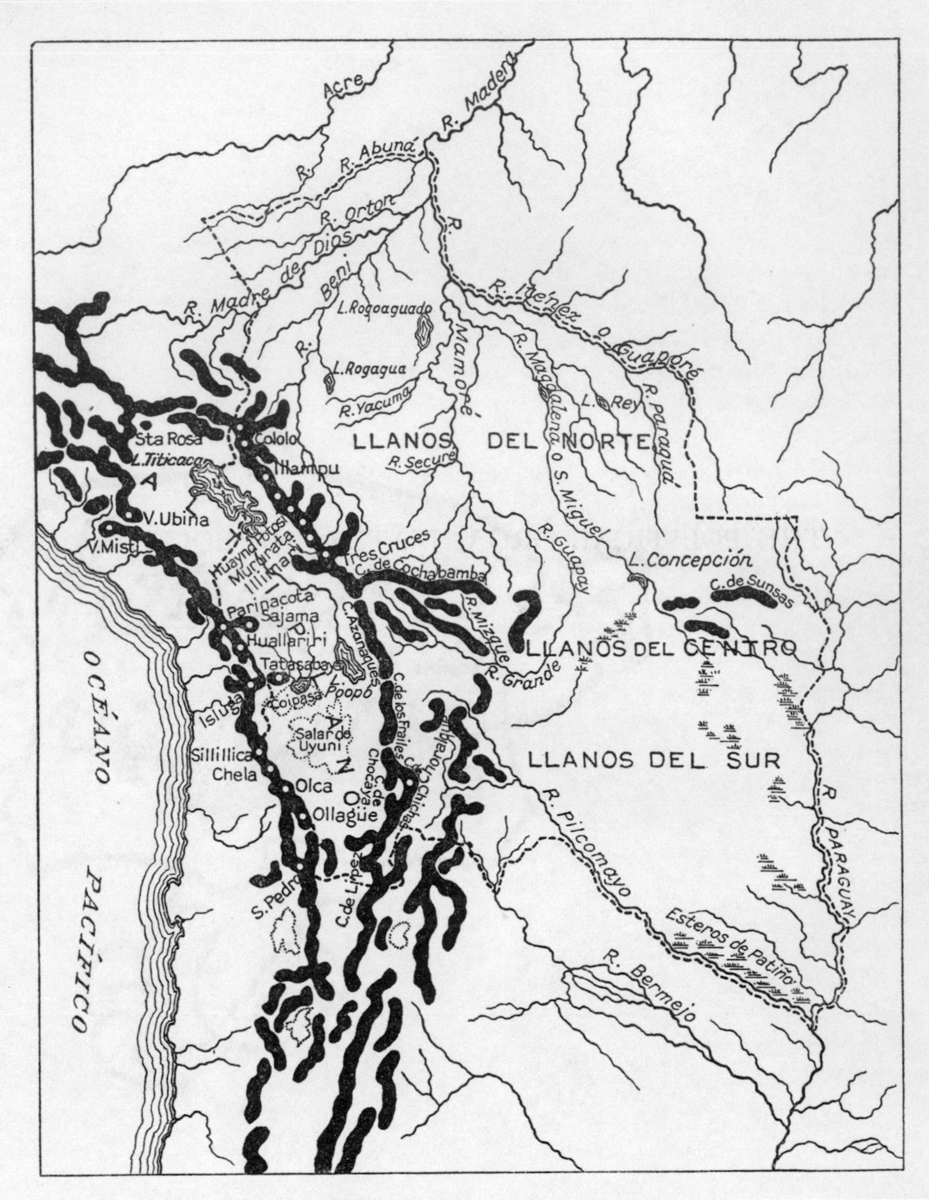

Physical Map of Bolivia
(Courtesy of Arnó Hnos., La Paz, Bolivia)

THE GEOGRAPHIC BACKGROUND

Bolivia lies in the heart of South America.[1] It may be likened, roughly, to a lady's fan, the pivot of which is the Andean tableland, and the open, sector-like section, the plains (*llanuras*) of the Amazonian and the La Platan regions. The land is a veritable mediterranean country, and thoroughly isolated from the rest of the world. On the north and the northeast lies the United States of Brazil, on the southeast Paraguay, on the south Argentina, and on the west Chile and Peru. When Bolivia became independent it had an area of 2,151,264 square kilometers. This area, however, has been reduced by cessions and by war to 1,332,808 square kilometers, the total loss amounting to 818,456 square kilometers. Of that amount, 337,836 square kilometers were ceded to Brazil, 157,000 to Argentina, 81,950 to Peru, and 66,456 to Chile, while 175,000 square kilometers have been in dispute with Paraguay.[2] In spite of these losses, Bolivia is still the third largest country in South America, the fourth in Latin America, and the sixth in the New World. Brazil, Canada, the United States of America, Argentina, and Mexico alone are larger.[3] Bolivia is 1700 kilometers long and 1000 kilometers wide.

Bolivia is one of the most remarkable countries in the world topographically. Within its boundaries are found every known topographical feature: vast mountain passes, lofty plateaus (*mesetas* or *punas*), gigantic mountain peaks, mighty gorges, large valleys, and bleak, inhospitable deserts. The Andean Cordillera is the most extensive mountain range in the world and the second in elevation. Sorata peak (Illampu) is the highest in the Andes, more than 400 meters higher than Aconcagua, popularly considered the highest in South America. About two-fifths of the area of Bolivia lies within the Andean zone, usually called the Andes del Centro, or the Andes Bolivianos. The Andes divide into two distinct sections before they enter Bolivia and remain separated until they leave the country. The western range is called the Cordillera Occidental, and forms a large part of the boundary between Bolivia and Chile, between Bolivia and Peru, and between Chile and Peru. The eastern range is

[1] Bolivia lies between 57° 29′ 40″ and 69° 35′ 36″ west longitude, and between 9° 34′ 50″ and 25° 13′ south latitude on the east, and 10° 56′ 40″ and 25° 0′ 05″ south latitude on the west.

[2] Alfredo Guillén Pinto and Heriberto Guillén Pinto, *Geografía-atlas escolar de Bolivia*, pp. 25–26.

[3] Colombia has an area of 1,114,800 square kilometers, Peru 1,135,000 square kilometers, and Venezuela 1,025,000 square kilometers.

called the Cordillera Oriental.[1] Between these two ranges lies the immense tableland (*meseta*, *puna*, or *planicie*), with an elevation of about 3800 meters in the north and about 2800 meters in the south. This tableland is obviously the former bed of a large inland sea with an outlet through the La Paz gorge. Lake Titicaca and Lake Poopó and the large saline tracts between them and about them are the present remains of that sea.

The total area of the *puna* is 81,000 square kilometers. Lake Titicaca has an elevation of 3812 meters above the level of the sea, and an area of 8300 square kilometers. It is 160 kilometers long and 60 wide, and has a depth of from 100 to 270 meters.[2] Of the many islands in the lake, those of Intikarka and Coati are important in the history of the Titicaca region. On Intikarka are the ruins of the Palace of the Inca and on Coati is the Santuario de las Ñustas. The principal peninsulas are those of Copacabana, Achacachi, and Yunguyo (in Peru). The last is the site of the terminus of the Mollendo-Puno Railroad. Important, too, are the Strait of Tiquina, dividing the lake into two unequal parts, and the Cape of Taraco. The leading ports on Lake Titicaca are: Guaqui, the western terminus of the La Paz-Guaqui Railroad; Puno (in Peru), the southern terminus of the Cuzco-Puno Railroad; Copacabana, Puerto Pérez, Puerto Acosta, and Ancoraimes. Lake Poopó, or the Pampa Aullagas, is smaller than Lake Titicaca, but is large enough to be important. It has an elevation of 3700 meters and an area of 2700 square kilometers. It is 99 kilometers long and 50 wide, but its waters are shallow (only 5 meters) and salty. Its largest islands

[1] The Cordillera Occidental contains four important *serranías:* that of the Norte between the Acayali River and Peru and the Bolivian branches of the Amazon; that of Tata Savaya between the Savaya River and Coipasa; that of Sillilica; and that of Los Volcanes. The Cordillera Real or Oriental contains three cordilleras: that of the Cololo; that of Illampu or Ancohuma, which contains the two highest peaks in Bolivia: Illampu or Sorata, 6645 meters elevation, and Illimani, 6619 meters; and that of Tres Cruces. East of the city of Oruro is the Cordillera de los Asanaques. East of Lake Poopó is the Cordillera de Corregidores. In the south of Bolivia is the Cordillera de Atacama. The Department of Potosí has the Cordillera de Charcas y Chayana, in the north; the Cordillera de Lípez, in the southeast; the Cordilleras de Chichas, in the east and southeast; and the Cordillera de Livichuco or Toro and the Cordillera de Huaina-Potosí. The Department of Chuquisaca has three *serranías:* those of Sopachui y Tomina, Tarabuco, and Los Naranjos. These lie between the Pilcomayo and Guapay Rivers, which separate the waters of the Amazon from those of the Plata River. Between the Departments of Chuquisaca and Santa Cruz lies the Serranía de Incahuasi. The Serranía de Charagua y Aguaragué lies in the Chaco Boreal. The Serranía de Caiza lies in the Department of Tarija between the Bermejo and the Pilcomayo Rivers. The Serranía Agoapey lies between the Guaporé and Juarú Rivers. The Serranía de San Simón and the Serranía de Franco lie in the Amazonian zone of the Departments of El Beni and Santa Cruz. The three *serranías* of La Concepción, San José, and Santiago separate the waters of the Madera from those of the Plata River. In addition to Illampu and Illimani there are the peaks of Misti and Sajama, each with an elevation of 6463 meters, both in the Cordillera Occidental; and Huayna Potosí, 6220 meters, and Chachacomani, 6403 meters, both in the Cordillera Real or Oriental.

[2] The following rivers flow into Lake Titicaca: the Colorado, Suches, Escoma, Huaicho, Sehuenca, Keka, and others.

are Panza and Filomena. Lake Poopó receives the waters of the streams of the cordilleras, but has no visible outlet. To the south of Lake Poopó are the *salares* (salt pans) of Coipasa, Lípez, and Uyuni. Lake Poopó is connected with Lake Titicaca by the Desaguadero, a river as famous in the history of Bolivia and Peru as was the Rubicon in that of ancient Rome. The Desaguadero is a short river of only 320 meters, and is about 6 meters deep at its deepest point.[1]

The Bolivian Andean region has a large number of valleys, many of which are large, fertile, and picturesque. Mighty erosive processes are constantly at work; water and wind play havoc with mountain side, plain, and valley. The melting snows of the mountain peaks cause an ever flowing volume of waters, wearing for itself deeply grooved beds, forming cascades and waterfalls, and possessing great potential hydraulic power, which may yet be the economic salvation of the Bolivian people. The grandeur of the mountain scenery and the great and varied beauty of the valleys combine to make this highland region the veritable "Switzerland of South America."

The other three-fifths of Bolivia is, topographically, of a very different character. This is the woodland (*montaña*) region of the republic and forms the irregular longitudinal strip of country east of the Cordillera Oriental. The region is the celebrated "eyebrow of the woodlands" (*ceja de la montaña*), as the Indians call it. It is the damp, hot, river-veined sylvan wilderness of the Amazonian and La Platan regions of the republic. It is a region where Nature "takes on terrifying proportions—terrifying luxuriance of vegetation, terrifying onrush of rivers, terrifying animal life."[2] This region constitutes the whole of

[1] Among the rivers flowing into the Poopó is the Mauri, a stream of no mean importance. The other rivers, outside of the Desaguadero, are smaller. It should be borne in mind, however, that the streams of this tableland are all of much importance in the life of its people.

[2] Philip A. Means, *Ancient civilizations of the Andes*, p. 22. Means declares that such regions as those of eastern Bolivia have never been the seat of important civilizations. To quote his exact words: "Never, at any rate so far as we now know, have either the lower portions of the *ceja de montaña* or the *montaña* itself been the seat of any stable and advanced community; on the contrary, they are properly the habitat of arboreal man in an archaic stage of culture beyond which progress is not possible save under very definite suasion from the outside world. Nevertheless, to certain highland folk—notably the Incas—the *montaña* was always at once alluring and inimical. Guided by the water-courses pouring into it from their homelands, they sought repeatedly to penetrate its mysteries and to establish some kind of dominion over it. But invariably a force, invisible but irresistible, threw their acquisitive plans awry, preventing prolonged residence amid the humid tangle of the woodland world" (*ibid.*, pp. 22–23; quoted by permission of the publisher, Charles Scribner's Sons, New York). One need not take issue with Means, but merely point out that much of the success of man in his endeavors in the cultural fields has been due to some "very definite suasion from the outside world." And the point which should be stressed is that Bolivia possesses in these sylvan wildernesses a challenge to herself as well as to the outside world. These wildernesses may some day prove, through the efforts of her own people as well as of others, to be the granary of the whole world. But obviously her people must learn to place less emphasis on the political and more on the economic if they wish to develop these wildernesses, a feat by no means impossible if the will to do so is there.

the eastern part of Bolivia, from the Andes to the Brazilian, the Paraguayan, and the Argentine frontiers. This zone of *llanuras* (plains) consists of three unequal parts: the northern, the central, and the southern *llanos*. The *llanos* of the north include Caupolicán, Territorios de Colonias, and El Beni. These *llanos* have an elevation of 200 meters above the level of the sea, and a large number of rivers, all belonging to the Amazonian system. The Abuná is a short stream flowing into the Madera, and forms a part of the northwestern boundary of the republic. The Madre de Dios River rises near Vilcañota, flows in a northeasterly direction, crosses the northeastern part of the Territorios de Colonias, is joined by the Orton and the Madidi Rivers, and empties into the Beni River. The Madre de Dios is 1500 kilometers long and, at the junction with the Beni, is 715 meters wide. The Beni rises in the heights of Chacaltaya (La Paz) and, under the name of Choqeyapu, joins with the Bopi and the Madre de Dios to form the Gran Beni, which empties into the Mamoré River. The Mamoré rises in the Cordillera de Cochabamba under the name of Grande, later taking the name of Guapay, gathers to itself the waters of the Piray, the Chapare, the Chimoré, the Securé, the Isiboro, and the Yacuma Rivers, and the waters of Lake Mojos, finally taking the name of Mamoré, and empties into the Madera. The Iténez or Guaporé River rises in the Serranía de Matto Grosso, flows in a northwesterly direction, receives the waters of the Paraguá, the Magdalena, the Baures, the Itonamas, and other streams, and unites with the Mamoré to form the Gran Mamoré.[1] The Gran Beni and the Gran Mamoré then unite to form the Madera, which in turn, flowing in a northeasterly direction, empties into the Amazon River. The Madera is the chief tributary of the Amazon, and has a number of waterfalls. A branch of the Acre River forms a part of the northwestern boundary of Bolivia; on it lies the important port of Cobija. There are also important lakes in these *llanos* of the north, the principal ones being Lake Rogoaguado and Lake Rogagua. The former has an area of 150 square kilometers.

The *llanos del centro* lie between those of the north and the south, and comprise the Department of Santa Cruz and the Province of Azero in the Department of Chuquisaca. These *llanos* have an elevation of 500 meters, but are undulating, and are broken up still further by the Serranías de Matto Grosso and de Incahuasi. The *llanos del centro* contain some very important rivers. The largest of these is the Paraguay, which rises in Matto Grosso, Brazil, flows southward, collecting the waters of many streams and of Lake Uberaba, Lake Cáceres, and other lakes, and finally empties into the Paraná River, which in turn empties into the Río de la Plata. The Parapeti River rises in the Serranía de Chuquisaca, flows into Lake Concepción, thence continues under the name of San Miguel or Magdalena, and empties into the Mamoré River.

[1] The principal ports on the Mamoré and its branches are: Cuatro Ojos on the Piray, Ichilo on the Ichilo, Todosantos on the Chapare, and Santa Ana on the Yacuma.

The *llanos del sur* embrace the Chaco Boreal, between the Pilcomayo and Paraguay Rivers. They lie lower than the *llanos del centro*, and during the heavy rainy season are the scenes of great inundations.[1] There are several important rivers. The Pilcomayo rises in the Andean cordillera, near Sucre, receives the waters of the Cachimayo and Pilaya Rivers, and empties into the Paraguay River, near Asunción, Paraguay. It has many waterfalls, which makes the navigation of its waters very difficult. Through the Plata the waters of the *llanos del sur* flow into the Atlantic Ocean, while the waters of the *llanos del norte* flow into the Atlantic through the Amazon River. These two systems, the Plata and the Amazon, are the main outlet of this vast territory of eastern Bolivia. But as their most important parts lie in foreign countries, their value to Bolivia as routes of travel is greatly lessened.

The climatic conditions of Bolivia are, naturally enough, no less varied than her topographical features. There are several temperature zones. The region ranging in elevation from sea level to about 1300 meters is the zone of the *llanos* and the *yungas* (valleys). It is the region of perpetual summertime. The rainfall is excessively heavy, electrical storms are unusually violent, and the exuberance of the vegetation is terrifying. In the *llanuras* of the north the climate is excessively hot. During the months of December, January, and February the rains are torrential, 250 centimeters in depth. The rivers rise, overflow their banks, and form an inland sea, since the drainage is very slow. As the rivers recede they leave very rich deposits, making the soils unusually fertile. One of the most pronounced phenomena of Nature here are the *surazos*, violent winds from the south. Diseases, such as the *ehujcho*, take a large toll of human lives. And yet the region is extremely picturesque, the landscape of incomparable beauty, with a wealth and a variety of colors possible only in the tropical regions.

The climate of the *llanuras* of the center is temperate but with an abundance of rainfall. The terrible winds from the south, the *surazos*, also visit these regions with the usual ill effects. The climate of the *llanuras* of the south is but little different from that of the *llanuras* of the north and the center. The elevation is greater and hence the rainfall is lighter, the temperature lower, and the wet season shorter.

The next climatic zone is that of the *valles*, or valleys. This zone contains the lands lying at an elevation from 1500 to 2000 meters above the level of the sea.

[1] The author had occasion to observe the importance of these inundations on a visit to Asunción in May 1931. The floods of that year were those which come at intervals of about 25 years and which are of very great extent. The country to the north and east of Asunción was covered for miles and miles with the waters which sought an outlet to the sea. It took weeks for the waters to recede, and as they did so they left in their wake much sediment which went to enrich further the soils in that region. The railroad between Rio de Janeiro and Corumbá was under water for about a hundred kilometers from the latter city, making it necessary to use water transportation for that distance.

The *valles* have a tropical climate, abundant rainfall, large rivers, and fertile soils. Hydraulic power is especially abundant. The region is also one of great natural beauty, with numerous cascades, mighty waterfalls, not infrequent avalanches, steep granite mountains, and lofty peaks with coats of eternal ice and snow. This is the region of perpetual springtime, in which are found such cities as Sucre and Cochabamba, veritable centers of beauty, charm, and intellectuality. These two cities are, together with the city of Tarija, the cultural centers of Bolivia, and the hope of her future.

The region with an elevation of 3000 or 4000 meters is known as the *puna*. The climate is dry and cold, exacting but stimulating. It is the home of the larger part of the population of the republic, the center of its industrial and commercial life, and the seat of ancient civilizations. It is a region of particular grandeur: mighty ranges of mountains, lofty peaks covered with eternal ice and snow, and great and terrific electrical disturbances. Earthquakes, too, add to the awe and the splendor of the region. It is strangely challenging, a place in which man rises to his greatest stature and power.

The variety and quantity of the natural resources of Bolivia are obviously no less remarkable than the topographical and climatic features. The flora of the *llanuras* is especially rich. Rubber trees are found in large numbers in the valleys of the Acre, Abuná, Orton, Madre de Dios, Beni, Madidi, Iténez, Mamoré, Champore, and Magdalena and their tributaries. Cotton is grown extensively in the Territorios de Colonias, and in the Departments of El Beni, La Paz, Cochabamba, Santa Cruz, and Tarija. Forest products are conspicuous not only for their variety but also for the immense quantities found throughout the region of the *llanuras*. Tobacco is also grown extensively in the Departments of Santa Cruz, Tarija, El Beni, Cochabamba, and La Paz, and in the Territorios de Colonias. The *quina*, from the bark of which quinine is made, is found in the forests of the Departments of La Paz, El Beni, Santa Cruz, Cochabamba, and Tarija. The coca, from the juice of which cocaine is made,[1] is grown in large quantities in the *yungas* of the Departments of La Paz and Cochabamba. Coffee of excellent quality is grown in large quantities in all the *yunga* regions and also in the Departments of El Beni and Santa Cruz. Cacao of good quality is grown in large quantities in the *yungas* of the Departments of La Paz and El Beni. Rice is grown in large quantities in the *yungas* of the Departments of La Paz, Santa Cruz, and Chuquisaca. The sugar cane, from which honey, sugar, and alcohol are made, is grown in the river valleys of the Departments of El Beni, Santa Cruz, Cochabamba, and Chuquisaca. In addition, large quantities and varieties of fruits, medicinal plants and herbs, dye plants, textile fibers, and grasses are found in different parts of the republic. The wealth

[1] The coca has a variety of uses. It is a plant of which the native peoples are very fond. The juice is both a stimulant and a beverage. The leaves are chewed much after the fashion of tobacco. Its use becomes a habit, creating an appetite for itself. The combination of the narcotic, the cocaine, and the alimentary juices of the coca makes it a very important plant.

of the flora of the *llanuras* is very great, and enables one to say that the economic future of the country lies in Bolivia Oriental. The great problem is of course transportation, a means whereby Bolivia may exchange the products of the *llanuras* for the products of other countries. No solution of Bolivia's transportation problem can be permanent which does not provide a coast for the republic. Any solution short of that objective must merely invite to wars and rumors of wars.

The flora of the *montaña* region is more varied and more abundant. The vine is cultivated extensively in the valleys of Cinti, Luribay, Mizque, and Méndez. Maize is grown in the Departments of Chuquisaca, La Paz, Potosí, Tarija, and Cochabamba. It is not known whether maize is native to Bolivia, or whether it was brought down from the *montaña* regions of northern South America or southwestern North America. In any event, maize has long been a staple food product among the peoples of Bolivia, white as well as Indian. The amount of maize grown in the Department of Cochabamba is large, making it the "granary of Bolivia." Potatoes, too, are grown extensively in the Department of Cochabamba, as well as many different kinds of fruit trees, fodder crops, including alfalfa, and the more important cereals, including wheat.

The flora of the *puna* region is scanty as compared with those of the other regions, but nevertheless it contains some of the most important plants known to man. The tuber family is represented by a fairly large variety. The most important is undoubtedly the potato, both the white and yellow varieties, forming a staple food product for the native peoples of the *puna* region. It is not known whether the potato is native to Bolivia, but it is native to the vast Andean regions of South America, in which it would seem natural to include at least the Andean portions of Bolivia. The potato is grown in abundance, and is used in different forms. The *chuño* (a kind of potato cake) and the *tunta* (a frozen potato, or *patata helada*, as the Spaniards call it) form a large part of the food of the Indians of the *puna* region. The *oca* and other plants belonging to the tuber family are also cultivated extensively, as is the *quínua* (a cereal). Other useful plants are the *ichu* or *ychu* grass, which is eaten by the llamas and the vicuñas, and is used for roofing and matting; the *totora* reed, used for weaving baskets and boats, especially the balsas, which are used extensively on Lake Titicaca; the *tola* bush, the *llareta* or *yareta*, and the *quínua* or *queñua* tree, used for fuel. Of importance, too, is the *quishuar* tree, resembling the olive tree, with lovely orange-colored flowers. This tree is used by the *puna* Indians for making their *tacllas* or plows.[1] The sierra region of the *puna* produces the *kantuta*, a valuable flowering plant.

The fauna of Bolivia is also of great importance in the national economy.

[1] Means, *Ancient civilizations of the Andes*, p. 21. Means describes in great detail the geographic background of the Andean regions, and should be consulted for a more detailed account of the geographic features than has here been possible.

The fauna of the *llanuras* is of course gorgeously varied and noisily plentiful: monkeys, pumas, jaguars, leopards, armadillos, squirrels, and an infinite number of birds of rich plumage, ostriches, numerous fish, boas, other reptiles, and insects innumerable, among them the butterflies, mosquitos, and ants. The fauna of the *montaña* region is less varied than that of the *llanuras*, but animal life is still abundant. Deer are numerous, and goats, sheep, horses, mules, cattle, swine, and poultry are raised in large numbers. There is a great variety of birds, the *aves de corral* and the parrots being especially plentiful; there are also many insects. The fauna of the *puna* region is richer than at first glance would seem to be the case. The llama, alpaca, vicuña, and guanaco are only a few of the better-known animals. There are also many others, such as the vizcacha, the chinchilla, the ostrich, the condor, the *ave de corral*, the *cui* (edible guinea pig), the *yutu* (a kind of partridge), and many different kinds of fish.

The mineral resources of Bolivia are, of course, both varied and plentiful. *Cori*, or *curi* (Quechua for gold), is found throughout the Andean and the *montaña* regions of the republic. This metal has been mined from time immemorial in these regions. Great quantities were mined even in the pre-Incaic periods, and in the Incaic, the Spanish, and the republican periods a large amount of gold has been produced. Despite that fact a great amount of gold is still to be found in the republic. It is found in the Departments of La Paz, Cochabamba, El Beni, Santa Cruz, and Chuquisaca, and in the Territorios de Colonias. *Collque* (Quechua for silver) is found in greater quantities than gold; and like gold, silver is written all over the history of Bolivia. It, too, has been mined from time immemorial, and still exists in large quantities. The production of both gold and silver has decreased in recent years, and has given way to the production of tin, or *chayanta*, as it is called in the Quechua language. Tin is mined throughout the Cordillera Oriental region, between 14° and 21° south latitude. The greatest amount is produced in the Departments of Oruro, La Paz, Potosí, and Chuquisaca. The tin industry is an important source of the natural wealth of the country, for Bolivia leads the world, as well as the Americas, in the production of this metal.[1] Copper is also mined in large quantities. It was known as *anta* by the Quechuas, and was known to the Incas and used by them. Copper is mined in Corocoro, Omasuyos, Muñecas, Caupolicán (La Paz), Oruro, Salinas, Poopó, Carangas, Chayanta, Charcas, and Cinti. Lead, known as *titi* in the Quechua, is also mined extensively in different places in the Departments of La Paz and Potosí, and in the Province of Cinti. Bolivia is the largest producer in the world of bismuth, which is found in large quan-

[1] The tin industry has made it possible for one man to acquire great wealth: Sr. José Patiño. Sr. Patiño has been able to render his country valuable services. Recently he has given a considerable amount of money for cultural purposes, the gift to the University of San Andrés being of unusual importance. It is to be hoped that wealthy citizens will come to the aid of other educational institutions in Bolivia. Her educational problem is a pressing one, and public-spirited men and women can do much to help solve it.

tities in Huayna Potosí, Sorata, Palca, Chacaltaya (La Paz), Antequera, Poopó (Oruro), Chorolque, Chichas, Lípez, Chocaya, San Vicente (Potosí). Wolfram, antimony, borax, *hulla* (coal), zinc, salt, and saltpeter are also produced in large quantities. Petroleum has recently been produced in increasingly large quantities. It is found in the region between the Yacuba and Santa, and more particularly in Aguarague, Charagua, Azero, on the Parapeti, in Chapare, Ayopaya, Arque, Caupolicán, Yungas, and Pacajes.

The part that man has played in these several regions of the republic is obviously of very great importance. This holds true of the ancient as well as the modern age. Bolivia has been the home of man for countless centuries. And the problem of man's activities in this region of the world is exceptionally difficult and complex for the historian as well as the ethnologist and the archaeologist. There is no space here for even a superficial treatment of this phase of our subject.[1] A brief statement should be made, however, concerning the presence in Bolivia of remarkable ruins of works of antiquity. The most important of these ruins are those at Tiahuanaco, situated some eight miles southeast of Lake Titicaca. Whatever may be the true story of the people, or peoples, who built the marvelous city of Tiahuanaco, the fact remains that they must have been among the great of antiquity.[2] It is to the eternal honor of the Bolivian people that the

[1] There is no more perplexing problem than that of the origin of man in the Americas and his rise to power in that section of the world. Able scientists like Ales Hrdlicka, Max Uhle, Julio Tello, and Philip A. Means have worked with intelligence and zeal to unravel the mysteries surrounding man's appearance in the New World. But the larger story is still very nebulous and is likely to remain so for many a year. Of the several theories of the origin of man in the Americas, the Asiatic is proving increasingly popular. Despite that fact, the Polynesian and the African theories will not down. Nor is the theory of the autochthonous origin of man in America without its staunch supporters. If man was not autochthonous to America, whence came he to Bolivia? Here again the answer is conjectural. There are several possible routes by which he may have come. He may have come from Central America along the northern coast of South America into the Guianas and Brazil, and then into Bolivia. Interesting discoveries have been made in Bolivia Oriental, particularly in the Gran Chaco region, which may have a bearing on the question. He may have come along the Pacific coast routes into Colombia, Ecuador, and Peru and thence on into Bolivia. Or he may have come along the Cauca and the Magdalena river valleys to the Plateau of Cundinamarca and then into Bolivia. Or he may have come to the coastal regions of Peru and then worked his way up into Bolivia. The latter theory has many supporters, since it is believed that there have been several different cultural periods in the coastal as well as in the Andean regions of South America. Whatever may be the true story of man's arrival in what is now Bolivia, the thing that concerns us here is that the Bolivian people of today are conscious of an important past. Obviously this interest is keenest among the native peoples, especially among the Quechuas and Aymaras. And since Bolivia is predominantly an Indian country, the present population, as in the colonial period, being overwhelmingly Indian, this interest in the past is a factor of no mean importance.

[2] Means, *Ancient civilizations of the Andes*, pp. 117–118. Means was greatly impressed, as countless others have been, with the ruins at Tiahuanaco. He expresses himself in these words: "Tiahuanaco, perhaps the most important archaeological site in South America, is clearly the metropolis of the mountains so far as the period here under consideration is concerned. It lies

ruins of this city have been made national property. These ruins have become a national shrine, and rightly so, because they are in themselves an emblem of glory as well as of greatness.

The history of the Incas can be traced with more accuracy, although the beginnings of these peoples also lie deeply hidden in the distant past. The origins and the culture of the peoples whom the Spaniards conquered are described with singular interest in the writings of the Chroniclers. The Bolivia of that day

in a wide, flat-bottomed valley that drains into the southernmost part of Lake Titicaca. The site has been occupied by a people sufficiently advanced culturally to know how to hew stone and to lay out huge buildings of a crude sort, a people who lived and wrought in that locality during the Tiahuanaco I period mentioned in the previous chapter. They were a people who, on their own initiative, had been able to make decided progress and who were in need only of directional stimulus from outside that would push their progress still further, enabling it to attain to civilization of no mean worth in some respects." Means is of the opinion that the culture of the Tiahuanaco I period came in contact with the early Nasca culture to produce the Tiahuanaco II cultural period. Tiahuanaco was called Taypicala in ancient times. Viracocha, the supreme deity among the Incas, lived for a time at Tiahuanaco, according to the legends of these people.

Means was also very much impressed, as all travelers must be who view it, with the environment of Tiahuanaco, declaring: "Lake Titicaca is beautiful, particularly at the hour of sunset, with the tall reeds along its margins swaying in the evening wind, and with the all too rapidly passing glory of the sky mirrored in the water. Here and there a reed balsa with a sail of matting floats with an air of immeasurable antiquity, and quaintly clad modern Indians go silently and patiently about their mysterious affairs. Far off to the west and south snow-clad peaks of the Eastern Cordillera—Sorata, Huayna Potosí, and Illampu—bite into the sky with glistening white teeth. The traveller looks upon it all and sees the keynote of that land is majesty, distinctly cold and grim, but majesty all the same, and very seldom tempered by any softer or more genial note" (*ibid.*, p. 130; quotations from this work by permission of the publisher, Charles Scribner's Sons, New York). He adds: "The art of the region corresponds well with the quality of the country which saw its rise. Its media include stone, pottery, metal, and textiles, and in whichever one of them it appears the Tiahuanaco II art invariably displays a style so highly individual that it is a relatively easy matter to trace, by its means, the spread of great Tiahuanaco's intellectual and aesthetic influence, if not of its political paramountcy."

The Spanish writers, too, found these ruins of Tiahuanaco of great interest. Padre Miguel Cabello de Balboa studied the folklore of the Indians for ten years, 1576–1586, during which time he traveled in that region. He came to the conclusion that the coastal people came from the mountain regions, and not from the Pacific coast. This would indicate a Cauca-Magdalena route of entry into Bolivia. Friar Jerónimo de Román y Zamora wrote of the two cultural zones. Friar Reginaldo de Lizárraga traveled in Peru between 1555 and 1599 and was much impressed with Tiahuanaco and its culture. Padre Fernando Montesinos gave the results of the labors of Padre Blas Valera in his *Memorias antiguas historicales del Perú*. Padre Valera had visited Tiahuanaco in his travels between 1571 and 1590 in Peru. Padre Bernabé Cabo, Pedro de Cieza de León, Inca Garcilaso de la Vega, Pedro Mercado de Peñalosa, and many other Spaniards also wrote about Tiahuanaco and its culture. The student of the history of Inca land will find a wealth of interesting data about this "City of the Dead" in the writings of these Chroniclers. It is as the heirs of this and other cultures of the Andean regions that the Inca peoples deserve careful study. The "Egypt of the New World" has a value, historically, no whit less than that of the Egypt of Africa. The Bolivians have a rich heritage indeed.

extended to the Pacific and hence had a coastal as well as an Andean cultural zone. The Chroniclers, therefore, divided the country into two cultural zones. The scientific work of Max Uhle, Julio Tello, Philip A. Means, and others supports a similar division. The Chroniclers, however, were divided in their opinion as to the origin of the Incas and the development of the Inca Empire. The Toledan school, named for the powerful viceroy Francisco de Toledo, pictured the Incas as a line of "usurpers, tyrants, and murderers" and discounted the Incaic accounts. The Garcilasan school, named for Inca Garcilaso de la Vega, "undoubtedly the greatest and most authoritative of the Chroniclers," held that the Sun created the Incas on an island in Lake Titicaca. The Incas thus became the first rulers of a great empire. From these beginnings grew the empire conquered by the Spaniards.

The Inca régime, which came to an end with this conquest, had economic, social, ecclesiastical, and political institutions of no mean importance.[1] The basic unit of organization was the *ayllu*, or tribe, under the rule of an officer called *sinchi*, or chieftain. The more advanced groups had a higher type of gov-

[1] The first rulers of the country were, according to tradition, Inca Manco Cápac and Coya (Queen) Mama Ocllo. These may have been merely overlords of "llama-tending, potato-growing mountaineers," to use Means' term, who came into prominence during or after the decline of the Tiahuanaco cultural periods. Manco Cápac was merely more able and successful than his contemporaries. Whatever may be the true account of these peoples, the fact remains that from these beginnings came one of the "most amazing empires the world has ever seen," to quote Means again. The Inca Sinchi Roca was evidently the first historical ruler of this empire. He was at the head of the state in the valley of Cuzco about A. D. 1105. He was followed by Inca Lloque Yupanqui, who began to rule about 1140. The next ruler was Inca Mayta Cápac, in power from about 1195 to 1230. He appears to have been the first Inca to cross the Desaguadero River, and was thus the first of these rulers to come into what is now Bolivia. He is said to have added much of the country to the southeast of Lake Titicaca to his empire. He was followed by Inca Cápac Yupanqui, who ruled from about 1230 to 1250, and who added the country about Lake Poopó and the Cochabamba Valley to his domain. Inca Viracocha, ruling from about 1347 to 1400, undertook the conquest of Charcas. Inca Tupac Yupanqui, ruling from about 1449 to 1482, undertook the conquest of the Madre de Dios River country. He defeated the Chiriguanos and did much to enlarge the boundaries of his empire in what is now Bolivia Oriental. His successor was Inca Huayna Cápac, ruling from about 1482 to 1529. He conquered most of present-day Ecuador. His marriage with the Princess of Quito was of momentous consequence to his people. His wife bore him a son, the ill-fated Atahualpa, and urged that the empire be divided into two parts so as to provide an empire for her son. The heir to the Inca Empire was Huáscar, the half-brother of Atahualpa. Inca Huayna Cápac accordingly divided the empire into two unequal parts, giving the northern and smaller part, with Quito as the capital, to Atahualpa, and the southern and larger part, with Cuzco as the capital, to Huáscar. After the death of Inca Huayna Cápac the two half-brothers began a struggle for the control of the whole of the empire. Atahualpa was able to bring about the death of Huáscar and have his rule recognized throughout the empire. There was much discontent with his rule, more particularly in the southern section, over which Huáscar had ruled. This was the state of affairs when the Spaniards arrived upon the scene. The conquest of the Inca Empire, like the conquest of the Aztec Empire, was thus made relatively easy. The people themselves were really the destroyers of their own rulers and ultimately of their own countries.

ernment in the *ayllu-cuna*, under the rule of a *curaca*, or permanent chieftain, whose authority was hereditary. The third group was the *curaca*-dom, composed of a number of *ayllu-cuna* units.[1] But the fundamental unit throughout the empire was the *ayllu*, which must have been evolved long before the Inca Empire was thought of. The Incas were thus, like the Spaniards, the adapters of a social polity which had been developed long before their arrival. The people of the *ayllu* appear to have had a pretty good understanding of government. In any event they appear to have been rather easily ruled.

The Inca peoples appear to have had a notion of the value of property, for they engaged freely in the interchange of commodities. This practice appears to have been of pre-Incaic origin. The land system among them was particularly important. The land was owned by the *ayllu;* there was no private ownership in land. This notion of ownership of land by the *ayllu* was also of pre-Incaic origin. The land was divided into three parts, one part belonging to the Sun, another to the Inca, and a third to the *ayllu*. The Inca rulers are said to have established the idea that the land belonged to the ruler, to be shared by him with the Sun and the people. The land of the *ayllu* did not belong to the people individually, as we have noted above, but was merely rented to them.[2] The produce of the land, however, belonged to the people who tilled it.

The Incas had a real genius for political government. They had, for one thing, a very effective administrative system, under which the people were divided into symmetrical units for administrative purposes.[3] They also had a very

[1] The best examples of the *curaca*-doms were the groupings known as the Colla Confederacy in the Lake Titicaca valley; the Chanca Confederacy in Andahuayllas; and the Chincha Confederacy on the Pacific coast.

[2] The land was allotted in the following fashion: Every married man received a *tupu* of land, measuring about 60 by 50 paces, to be cultivated by him. For every male child born to his wife, an additional *tupu* was allotted to him, but with the birth of a female child only half a *tupu* was given him. When the young man married, the father turned over a *tupu* to him, but when the young woman was married, no land was turned over to her. No land was bought or sold, since it belonged to the Inca as the head of the state. The allotment of the land was an annual affair and was made by the chieftains. As the population grew, lands were taken away from the portion set aside for the Inca. All able-bodied men of the *ayllu* helped to cultivate the land belonging to the Sun, and the land of those unable to cultivate it, such as widows, orphans, the aged, the sick, and the absent. The work was supervised by *ayllu* officials called *llacta-camayoc*. The able-bodied men also tilled the lands belonging to the *curacas* and the Inca. The land can thus be said to have been the basis of the social and economic structure of the Incaic state. This accounts for the fact that the Indians of Bolivia are passionately fond of the land, and definitely attached to the soil. This love of the land is one of the most important phases of the traditions of the Indian population of present-day Bolivia, especially among the Quechuas and the Aymaras. It also accounts for their interest in the communal form of land ownership, which is still so pronounced among them.

[3] Means, *Ancient civilizations of the Andes*, pp. 292–293.

Means arranges the hierarchy of administrative units in this wise: the *chunca*, composed of 10 households, and ruled by the *chunca-camayu-cuna;* the *pichca-chunca*, of 50 households,

effective method of furthering the amalgamation of conquered peoples. The chief of the conquered peoples was not infrequently made to serve that process. He was usually given a position of importance, such as that of *pachaca-camayu* or *huaranca-camayu*. The conquered king might be made a *tucuiricuc-cuna*. The process of amalgamation was made more intensive in the case of conquered peoples by a system of colonization. The *mitimaes* were especially important for that purpose. Colonists were taken from the older and more densely populated districts and from among the newly conquered peoples. These colonists were placed in the more important parts of the empire to prepare the people for their place in the governmental scheme. This was also an effective means of preventing insurrections as well as of spreading Incaic culture and control.

---

under the *pichca-chunca-camayu-cuna;* the *pachaca*, of 100 households, under the *pachaca-camayu-cuna;* the *pichca-pachaca*, of 500 households, under the *pichca-pachaca-camayu-cuna;* the *huaranca*, of 1000 households, under the *huaranca-camayu-cuna;* the *hunu*, of 10,000 households, under the *hunu-camayu-cuna;* and the *guamán*, of 40,000 households, under the *tucuircuc-cuna*. The *guamán* was really a province. The empire, known as *Ttahua-ntin-suyu*, was divided into four quarters, each of which was called a *suyu-cuna*, and was governed by an *apu-cuna*, or *hatun apu-cuna*. The *apu-cuna* was really a viceroy or governor general. The four *apu-cuna* formed an imperial council and resided much of the time at the court of the Inca.

While the household was the administrative unit and the individual subordinated to it, notice was also taken of the individual as such. Means presents this series of categories of persons based on their capacity to work: the *mosoc-caparic* ("Babe newly born and still in arms"); the *saya-huamrac* ("Child able to stand, about one year old"); the *macta-puric* ("Child between one and six years old"); the *ttanta-raquizic* ("Bread-receiver, a child six to eight years old"); the *pucllac-huamrac* ("Boy playing about, eight to sixteen years old"); the *cuca-pallac* ("Coca-picker, doing light manual labor, sixteen to twenty years old"); the *ima-huayna* ("Almost a youth, aiding his elders in their tasks, twenty to twenty-five years old"); the *puric* ("The able-bodied man, head of a household and payer of tribute, from twenty-five to fifty years old"); the *chaupi-rucu* ("Half old, doing light work, fifty to sixty"); and the *puñuc-rucu* ("Old man sleeping, sixty and upwards") (*ibid*., p. 294).

An estimate of the total population of the Inca Empire at the height of its power can be had from the number of people in the households. The *puric* household must have had from five to ten members; the *chunca*, from fifty to a hundred; the *pachaca* (Incaized *ayllu*), from five hundred to one thousand; the *huaranca*, from five thousand to ten thousand; the *hunu*, from fifty thousand to one hundred thousand; and the *guamán*, or province, from two hundred thousand to four hundred thousand people. Ttahua-ntin-suyu must thus have had, at the height of its power, between sixteen million and thirty-two million inhabitants. Means is of the opinion that the population of the Inca Empire in 1532 was twice as large as the present total population of the countries which were carved out of that empire (*ibid*., p. 296).

THE SPANISH PERIOD

The capture of Inca Atahualpa, November 16, 1532, in the plaza of Cajamarca, was the beginning of the end of the Inca Empire. The strangulation of Atahualpa, August 29, 1533, made the conquest of the empire less difficult, and the surrender of Cuzco, the Inca capital, November 15, 1533, was of even greater significance.[1] There was still very much to be done before Spain could successfully establish her power in the empire. This account, however, is concerned primarily with the conquest of Kollasuyu, or that part which today bears the name of Bolivia.

The expedition of Diego de Almagro into the land of the Araucanians brought the Spaniards into Kollasuyu for the first time. It was in 1535 that Juan de Saavedra, a member of this expedition, entered the country and founded Paría in the valley of the Copiapó. The Almagro forces followed the Inca road across the *meseta* of Kollasuyu. The failure of the Almagro Chilean expedition, the return of the forces to take part in the war for Cuzco, the defeat of Almagro the Elder in the battle of Salinas, April 6, 1538, and the execution of Almagro belong to the history of Peru. The war between the Almagristas and the Pizarristas over Cuzco delayed the conquest of Kollasuyu, but the success of the Pizarristas gave Gonzalo Pizarro, half-brother of Francisco Pizarro, the opportunity to undertake this project. He left Cuzco, accordingly, in April 1538, in command of a small force, in search of the "Land of Cinnamon," as the region of the Río Napo was then thought to be. He met with stubborn resist-

[1] Cuzco was always an object of the greatest interest to the *conquistadores* and to their descendants, even aside from its strategic importance. They were deeply impressed with the manner in which the city had been built, and more particularly with the exquisite stone work of the public buildings. The most remarkable example of this stone work was the Temple of the Sun. While the Spaniards found the gold ornamentation of this edifice of immediate value, they did not fail to appreciate the beauty of its architecture. They used the building throughout the colonial period as a religious sanctuary. It has also remained throughout the independence period as an example of rarely beautiful stone work. There were also many other buildings of great interest to the Spaniards, the foundations of which still stand. Of particular interest was the powerful fortress of Sacsahuamán, lying a short distance north of the city. It was a constant source of wonderment to them, and constitutes a remarkable ruin even to this day. For reasons yet to be explained, the Spaniards appear never to have found the most sacred of all the Inca cities, Machu Picchu. It was left for Hiram Bingham to discover this city and to immortalize it. Consult his great work, entitled *Machu Picchu*, for an exhaustive account of the city and its environs. It is especially illuminating because of its many and rare pictures.

ance, and was disastrously defeated at the Inca stronghold Kirpin-chaca by Cacique Titu.[1]

An important result of this expedition was the exploration of the Amazon River by Francisco de Orellana and his men in 1540–1541.[2] Gonzalo Pizarro secured new enforcements and set out to conquer the fierce Chiriguanos of the Gran Chaco. Though he met with determined opposition, he took possession of Chuki-chaca without much delay. He organized the political government of the newly conquered region and called it the District of Charcas. He was governor (*gobernador*) and chief judge (*justicia mayor*) of the district. He granted *encomiendas* in the name of Francisco Pizarro, governor and captain general (*capitán general*) of Nuevo Toledo, as Peru was then called.[3] In the meantime, Fray Tomás de San Martín, a Dominican, crossed the Desaguadero, and is reputed to have been the first Spaniard to cross that celebrated river. On September 29, 1538, La Plata was founded by Pedro de Anzúres on the site of Guayacacha, today Gero, in the Province of Charcas, in the Territory of Chuki-chaca (*Comarca de Chuki-chaca*). This was the beginning of the City of the Four Names (Charcas, La Plata, Chuquisaca, and Sucre), the seat of the government of the District of Charcas throughout the Spanish period, and the *de jure* capital of Bolivia since its establishment as an independent nation. Gonzalo Pizarro spent considerable time in the new municipality, seeking to establish the Spanish power on a firm basis. He was particularly interested in the welfare of the *encomenderos*, and came to be called the Lord of the Land of the Charcas (*Señor del País de los Charcas*). At the same time he and the deputy governor (*lugar teniente*) Diego de Rojas acquired some of the richest *encomiendas* for themselves. They are accused of having reserved for themselves the richest lands in the district. Gonzalo Pizarro was recalled and returned to Lima. Francisco Pizarro appointed Pedro de Anzúres to succeed him, and made Francisco de Almendras and Diego de Zúñiga councilmen (*regidores*), Garcilaso de la Vega and Luis Pardono mayors (*alcaldes*), and Antonio Alvarez high constable (*aguacil mayor*) of La Plata.

The assassination of Francisco Pizarro, the result of a *coup* by Almagro the Lad, the son of Almagro the Elder, June 26, 1541, had a profound effect upon

[1] It is claimed that Gonzalo Pizarro returned with only three men, namely, Juan de Figueroa, Garcilaso de la Vega, and Gaspar de Lara. Consult the excellent work by Alfredo Jáuregui Rosquellas, entitled *La ciudad de los cuatro nombres*, for the beginnings of Bolivia, as well as for much of its later history.

[2] Consult Friar Gaspar de Carvajal's work on *The discovery of the Amazon* (trans. Bertram T. Lee, ed. H. C. Heaton; American Geographical Society, New York, 1934) for a detailed account of this remarkable expedition.

[3] The Inca Empire was divided by a royal decree (*real cédula*) of 1542 into Nueva Castilla, the northern section, and Nuevo Toledo, the southern section. The name of the present section in which Sucre is located is Chuquisaca, a name derived from the Inca name Chuki-chaca. The city of Sucre also bore this same name for some time.

the life of the District of Charcas. As soon as the news of the murder of the Marqués de Pizarro came to La Plata, the citizens (*vecinos*) of that city displayed the degree of loyalty to Spain for which they were famous throughout the colonial period. Anzúres took up the cause of the Pizarristas, as the legal representatives of the cause of Spain. Diego Méndez, *maestro de campo* of Almagro the Younger, turned on La Plata, captured it, and treated its inhabitants with great cruelty. He levied heavy tribute in money, arms, and horses. On September 16, 1542, the Almagristas were defeated in the battle of Chupas, and Almagro the Younger was executed. The men of La Plata had rendered valuable services in the battle of Chupas and were duly rewarded by the new ruler, the *pacificador* Vaca de Castro. Soon after this battle, Anzúres returned to La Plata to begin a campaign against the Mojos, the Indians of Paraguay and the Gran Chaco. This entry into the mythical lands of the orient was of profound importance to Bolivia, for it marked the beginning of the controversy over that region which has continued between her and Brazil, Paraguay, and Argentina to the present day.

Gonzalo Pizarro had become the most powerful man in the viceroyalty of Peru after the assassination of the Marqués de Pizarro, and especially after the defeat of the Almagristas. As such he became an object of suspicion to the home government. It was feared that he might establish an independent government with himself as the ruler. Unfortunately for the home government, the struggle between the supporters and the opponents of its Indian policy took a very serious turn at this time. The efforts of the reformers, under the leadership of Bartolomé de Las Casas, to improve the lot of the Indian had borne fruit. Las Casas had resolved, as early as 1511, to oppose the Indian policy of the home government as one which the government could not afford to continue. He had induced King Ferdinand to begin much-needed reforms, and had been appointed official General Protector of the Indians as early as 1516. The King-Emperor Charles had been friendly toward the reforms proposed by Las Casas from the beginning of his reign. In 1520 he had granted Las Casas the right to establish a model colony, but the effort proved a humiliating failure. But Las Casas did not give up his great idea of reform even though he became a Dominican monk. He urged his reforms with much success. The first important result of his labors was the pronouncement of Pope Paul III of June 17, 1537, in the famous bull *Sublimis Deus sic dilexit*. The Pope laid down the famous principle that the Indian was a human being and should be treated as such. He was not to be enslaved or deprived of his possessions. He was to enjoy "freely and lawfully of said liberty and possession" and was to be immediately liberated from slavery.[1]

The next logical step was the legislation known as the New Laws, promul-

[1] L. A. Dutto, *The life of Bartolomé de Las Casas*, pp. 383–384. Also N. Andrew N. Cleven, *Readings in Hispanic American history*, pp. 225–226.

gated by the King-Emperor on November 20, 1542. The New Laws had for their purpose the good treatment and preservation of the native peoples of the Indies. The Royal Audiencia (*Real Audiencia*) was to take special care of the Indians. The *encomiendas* were to be abolished and steps taken to end the practices which led to ill treatment of the Indians. Vaca de Castro, who brought the New Laws with him to Peru, was instructed to proclaim them in force in the viceroyalty. The vested interests in the country were determined, however, to prevent their enforcement. In this they were only following the example of the vested interests throughout the other colonies and in old Spain itself. The story of the opposition to the New Laws forms one of the most illuminating pages in the history of Spain in the Old World as well as in the New. The New Laws struck at the very heart of the politico-economic system of the country. The very foundations of the Spanish colonial system in the Americas were based upon the *encomienda* régime, with its control over the rich lands and the labor of the native peoples. An attack upon the New Laws was not to be averted, and became one of the most formidable with which the King-Emperor had to deal.

Gonzalo Pizarro made use of the opposition to the New Laws in Peru to further his own ambitious designs. He became the champion not only of those who opposed these laws but also of those who desired to see Peru independent of Spain. He accordingly took up arms against the home government, defeating Vaca de Castro, and also made war against the new viceroy Blasco Núñez de Vela. He was in Chaqui, interested in the mining developments of that region, at the time of the arrival of the new ruler. The city council (*ayuntamiento*) of La Plata sent two commissioners to the viceroy to induce him not to enforce the New Laws until he had heard the views of those opposed to their enforcement in Peru.[1] But in this they failed. Gonzalo Pizarro also went to the viceroy, not as a private citizen, but as commander of the armed forces and with the title of chief judge, district attorney (*procurador*), and captain general of Peru. He, too, failed to dissuade the viceroy from enforcing the New Laws. He then turned traitor to the King-Emperor, striving by force of arms to prevent the viceroy from ruling the country. The people of La Plata, much as they opposed the New Laws, could not condone the actions of Gonzalo Pizarro, and, accordingly, took up arms against him and in support of the King-Emperor. The people of Lima, Cuzco, and Guamango, however, received Gonzalo Pizarro as governor general of Peru, and as the real heir to the Marqués de Pizarro. The viceroy left Lima and took up his headquarters in Cuzco. This meant that the colonial authorities were, for the time being, compelled to take orders from Gonzalo Pizarro. The latter appointed Francisco de Almendras

[1] The commissioners were Diego Centeno and Pedro Alonso de Hinojosa. They represented the interests of the *encomenderos* of the District of Charcas, who, in common with the *encomenderos* in other parts of the Indies, could not look with indifference upon measures that were directed against the source of their wealth.

governor of Charcas. Almendras was cruel and vindictive, and a man of evil antecedents. Diego Centeno, learning of the designs of Gonzalo Pizarro, returned to La Plata and began openly to oppose him. Centeno set himself against the rule of Almendras, and took the title of chief judge and captain general of Charcas; he was ably assisted by the *vecinos* of La Plata, who conducted themselves as loyal and enthusiastic supporters of their king and country. He marched with a strong force against Gonzalo Pizarro in Cuzco. The city was defended by the forces of Alonso de Toro, which were easily defeated. Toro then marched against La Plata. Negotiations between Toro and Centeno for the return of Cuzco failed, and Centeno returned to La Plata. He set about repairing the damages inflicted upon it by the Pizarristas. Gonzalo Pizarro then sent Carbajal, justly known as the Devil of the Andes (*el demonio de los Andes*), to take control of Charcas. Carbajal took La Plata and began a merciless persecution of its people and destruction of their property.

Centeno had, in the meantime, again gone to conquer Cuzco. Gonzalo Pizarro sought to negotiate with Centeno, but the ravages of Carbajal precluded any hope of success. On October 20, 1547, Gonzalo Pizarro defeated Centeno in the battle of Huarina. Centeno escaped, however, and joined the Royalists in Lima. La Plata was made to suffer for the support it had given the Royalist cause, Gonzalo Pizarro taking reprisals with a heavy hand. The days of the Pizarristas, however, especially those of Gonzalo Pizarro, were numbered. The New Laws had been abrogated in 1545, and could no longer be given as a reason for continuing the opposition to the home government.[1] Finally the troops of President de la Gasca and Gonzalo Pizarro met on April 9, 1548, on the plains of Sacsahuamán, near Cuzco. The victory was with the Royalists. Gonzalo Pizarro was taken prisoner, was tried and condemned, and was executed on July 8, 1548. He was only forty-two years of age, and died with the courage and dignity becoming a Spanish *hidalgo*.

Centeno, who had rendered his King-Emperor and his country great services, was duly rewarded by de la Gasca. He was made Permanent Captain of La Plata (*Capitán Permanente de la Ilustre y Leal Ciudad de La Plata*), and given several *encomiendas*. In addition he was commissioned to discover, conquer, and colonize the regions about the Río de la Plata. Death overtook him, however, before he could enter upon his new duties. He died in La Plata, the city for which he had done so much.[2]

[1] Pedro de Cieza de León, *Civil wars of Peru. The war of Chupas*, vol. CXLII, pp. 340–360 (trans. Sir Clements R. Markham; Hakluyt Society, London). Also in Cleven, *Readings in Hispanic American history*, pp. 226–233.

[2] Jáuregui Rosquellas, *La ciudad de los cuatro nombres*, pp. 115–116. This writer maintains that the founders of La Plata and the Province of Charcas were not merely warriors but builders as well. "Los fundadores y primeros pobladores de La Plata no pertenecen a esa mesa enorme de guerreros que no sabiendo en emplear la espada ni en dónde hallar productivas aventuras y peligrosas correrías " he contended, and added: "se lanzaron al Nuevo Mundo en

The defeat of the Pizarristas gave the Province of Charcas a period of peace.[1]

---

pos de nueva vida y en busca de oro. La mayoría de ellos era gente de pro, hijodalgos segundones y lanzas de primera clase, que perseguían aventuras, es verdad, pero de orden superior, bizarramente romanesco y encuadrado al idealismo batallador de la época. Obtuvieron el oro como una justa compensación de sus esfuerzos, pero una vez obtenido y colmadas sus aspiraciones de gloria y lucro, lejos de tornar a la península a alardear de las fortunas adquiridas, quedáronse en tierras de América, colonizando los vastos territorios, civilizando a los pobladores, roturando los campos y fundando ciudades que más tarde habían de ser orgullo de madre patria. Y La Plata, más de otras, fué el asilo de los cruzados sobresalientes de la expedición de Panamá, que siguiendo las huellas de los de la Isla del Gallo se adentraron valerosamente en países desconocidos, hasta dar con las tierras de los charcas en cuyo centro, atraídos por el dulzor de las aguas y la esplendidez del clima fundaron la villa más castellana de cuantas hubieron en el Perú, pronto trocada en ciudad de primera clase, gracias, justamente, a la índole progresista y al espíritu altivo y leal de sus pobladores."

[1] In the meantime the Spaniards had continued their advance into the eastern lands of Peru. In 1540 Francisco Pizarro visited La Plata and remained for several days. He granted many *encomiendas* and in other ways rewarded those who had rendered important services to the cause of Spain. In 1545 the Cuzqueño Indian Diego Huallpa informed his *patrón*, Juan de Villarroel, of his discovery of silver on the hillside of the Cerro de Potosí. Diego Centeno and Luis de Santandía, captains in the service of Gonzalo Pizarro, took formal possession of the Mountain of Silver on January 1, 1546, and in April of the same year they laid the foundations of the city of Potosí. They had defeated the Indians of the *parcialidades* of Urinsayas and Anasayas, the owners of this region. The city grew rapidly from the very first, thanks to its wealth in minerals. No strike for mining stakes in modern times has attracted greater attention, and none has had more sinister consequences. In 1547 Potosí had two thousand five hundred houses and fourteen thousand inhabitants. In that year the King-Emperor gave the city a coat of arms. On September 8, 1548, La Paz was founded by Alonso de Mendoza on the site of the Inca city of Chuquisayapu. It was called Pueblo Nuevo, and was located midway between La Plata and Cuzco. It lies more than 4000 meters above sea level, and in a large canyon. In 1553 the King-Emperor gave Potosí the name of Villa Imperial de Potosí. Consult the work by Bartolomé Martínez y Vela on the *Anales de Villa Imperial de Potosí* for interesting and useful information about life in this famous city in the colonial period. In 1555 the King-Emperor gave a coat of arms to La Paz. In 1570, under orders of Viceroy Toledo, Jerónimo de Osorio and Ruy de Melgarejo founded the Villa de Oropeza, later Cochabamba, in the valley of Koto-pankara. On July 4, 1574, Luis de Fuentes, under instructions from Viceroy Toledo, founded the city of Tarija, then known as San Bernardo de Tarija, on the banks of the Taruxa River; later the name was again changed to Tarija, the name which it still retains. The name is also given to the department in which the city of Tarija is located. The celebrated city of Santa Cruz de la Sierra was first founded by Ñuflo de Chávez at the foothills of the Cerro San José de Chiquitos in 1560. Thirty-five years later, May 21, 1595, the city was moved to the site it now occupies. It was removed to the ruins of Apu-phirapis by Suárez de Figueroa, Hoguín, Juan de Urrutia, and many other notables, and later became the capital of the department in which it is located. In 1601 a fortlet (*presidio*) was founded on the site that later was called Villa de San Felipe de Asturia, and still later Oruro. It was made a city on November 1, 1606, by Manuel de Padilla, the senior judge (*oidor decano*) of the Royal Audiencia of Charcas, in compliance with the royal orders (*reales órdenes*) issued for that purpose. Thus by the early part of the seventeenth century the principal cities of modern Bolivia had been founded: La Plata (Sucre), Potosí, La Paz, Cochabamba, Tarija, Santa Cruz de la Sierra, and Oruro. This is an example of the constructive work of Spain which Jáuregui Rosquellas emphasizes in his writings. It is indeed high time that the work of Spain in the Americas should be evaluated from that point of view.

Mining and agriculture were developed and much wealth was accumulated. But the peace was of short duration. The high-handed acts of the Royal Audiencia of Lima caused much discontent. On November 12, 1553, Francisco Hernández Girón began the famous revolt which bears his name. Girón was defeated in the battle of Chuquingua, and the revolt was at an end. The revolt, however, had dire results. It had destroyed a large part of the best people of La Plata. Juan de Sandoval, the new *corregidor* and chief judge of Charcas, spent much of his time repairing the damages done by the Girón Revolt. The new viceroy of Peru, García Hurtado de Mendoza, the Marqués de Cañete, removed Sandoval and put Altamirano in his place. Viceroy Mendoza soon brought peace to the whole viceroyalty. He improved the condition of the Indians by making changes in the original allotments of *encomiendas*. The wealth of Potosí and La Plata was increased, making Charcas famous throughout the Indies.[1]

The conquest and settlement of Kollasuyu was, of course, a part of the general movement to establish the power of Spain in the New World. The men who penetrated into the Altiplanicie, the Andean region of South America, were actuated, in their service to God and king, by the same motives that actuated the other Spaniards who sought to penetrate the vast resources of the western hemisphere. The insatiably ambitious Portuguese had to be restricted to the lands allotted them by the Treaty of Tordesillas of 1494. The native peoples were to be Christianized and civilized, the natural resources of the country developed, permanent settlements made, and the love of adventure, power, and glory nurtured. Gonzalo Pizarro was bent upon the same errand as Pedro de Mendoza, Álvar Núñez Cabeza de Vaca, and Domingo Martínez de Irala in the southeast, and Sebastián de Benalcázar, Nikolaus Federmann, and Gonzalo Jiménez de Quesada in the north. They were all pawns in the great game of curbing the advance of the Portuguese. Spain and Portugal were struggling for world domination. It was necessary that Spain should guard against infringements upon her territories by the Portuguese. Not knowing the full extent of their ambitions, and fearing that these might include the greater part of South America, she was determined to curb their activities in the continent.

Spain was also gravely concerned about the activities of the Portuguese in the Pacific and Indian Oceans, of which the Magalhães–El Cano expedition of 1519–1522 had made her aware. Antonio Pigafetta's intriguing account of

[1] Some idea of the richness of the mines of Bolivia can be gotten from the report of Escalona and Friar Tomás de Argüello. The former estimated the silver mined in Potosí between 1556 and 1576 as amounting to 29,140,000 pesos, with the Crown's share at 6,061,000 pesos. The figures of de Argüello are for the period between 1546 and 1674 and are 957,320,500 pesos, the royal fifth amounting to 191,464,100 pesos. Escalona declared that the amount of silver produced between 1579 and 1638 amounted to 236,128,000 pesos, with the king's share at 53,451,000 pesos. In addition there was the yield of gold, which was also large, although these two authorities do not give figures on that point. The Crown also received large revenues from the Province of Charcas in other forms, such as the *tributo* from the Indians, and imposts and other taxes. The amount of the *tributo* was of course large.

that expedition further emphasized the importance of the rivalry of Portugal.[1] The complicated and delicate diplomatic controversy which grew out of this expedition, resulting in the celebrated Treaty of Saragossa of 1529, further convinced Spain of the need of an ever watchful policy toward her powerful rival. The fact to be kept in mind, therefore, is that the effects of the bitter rivalry between Spain and Portugal in the sixteenth century were not ended by these diplomatic arrangements, but continued throughout the colonial period, and down to the present day; the great struggle between Bolivia and Paraguay is also a phase of that contest. The Spaniards were determined to curb the activities of the Portuguese in South America. This is the larger significance of the feverish activities of the Spaniards on the coastal plains of the Pacific, on the Caribbean islands, on the coastal plains north and south of Brazil, and in the heart of the continent, which resulted in the conquest and settlement of Kollasuyu in the hectic second half of the sixteenth century.

The difficulty of quelling the civil wars in Peru had impressed the home government with the need of a more centralized control of the Province of Charcas. The great distance between Lima and the Atlantic made control over the administrative affairs of Charcas very difficult. The Royal Audiencia of Lima had recommended, as early as 1551, the establishment of another such tribunal in the viceroyalty. It was not until 1559, however, that the home government acted upon this recommendation. Philip II issued his famous royal decree of June 12, 1559, at Valladolid, creating the Royal Audiencia of Charcas. But it was not until September 7, 1561, that the tribunal was actually established. The judges (*oidores*) appointed were Pedro Ramírez de Quiñones, Antonio López de Haro, Pedro de Ortíz, and Nicholás de Recalde. Ramírez de Quiñones was chosen regent (*regente*) and Ravanal Empero attorney (*fiscal*). To this body was later added the celebrated jurisconsult Juan Matienzo, of the Royal Audiencia of Lima.

The jurisdiction of the Royal Audiencia of Charcas extended, at first, over a territory circular in shape and one hundred leagues in diameter, with La Plata as the center. On August 29, 1563, the territories of Tucumán, Juries y Diaguitas, and Mojos, and the Indians and lands of Chávez (*Chunchos y tierras de Chávez*) and Manso were added. On the north the jurisdiction extended to the boundary of the District of Cuzco.[2] In the same year a change was made in the internal organization of the tribunal. A president (*presidente*)

[1] Consult *Magellan's voyage around the world, by Antonio Pigafetta*, translated by James A. Robertson, and also the monumental work on *The Philippine Islands, 1493–1898*, by Helen Blair and James A. Robertson, for detailed information on this whole subject.

[2] The Royal Audiencia of Charcas was one of fourteen such tribunals established in the Indies: Santo Domingo, 1526; Mexico City, 1527; Panamá, 1535; Lima, 1542; Guatemala, 1543; Guadalajara, 1548; Bogotá, 1549; Quito, 1563; Manila, 1583; Santiago de Chile, 1609 (succeeding that established at Concepción, 1565); Buenos Aires, 1663; Caracas, 1786; and Cuzco, 1787. Other such tribunals were established, but these were the important ones.

was placed at its head in the person of Juan Matienzo.[1] He was also made captain general of La Plata. Justice was administered in the name of the king of Spain in accordance with the *Recopilación de las leyes de las Indias*. In case this code did not cover the points at issue, justice was administered in conformity with the laws of Castile. The Audiencia had a variety of duties to perform besides its purely judicial function. It had to protect the frontiers and religious missions, settle differences between the civil and the ecclesiastical authorities, establish military zones, and preserve peace throughout the Presidency of Charcas (*Presidencia de Charcas*), as the country under the jurisdiction of the Audiencia came to be called. The situation in the Province of Tucumán soon made the labors of the Royal Audiencia of Charcas more arduous, as will be explained in the next two paragraphs.

The defeat of the Pizarristas in 1548, which put an end to the civil wars in Peru, made it necessary for President de la Gasca to look about for suitable rewards for the men who had served Spain in that conflict. These rewards might be in lands or in high governmental positions, or both. De la Gasca selected the territory which was to form the Province of Tucumán for that purpose. He sent Juan Núñez de Prado at the head of an expedition to conquer and settle that region. Núñez de Prado made a settlement at Barco near the Escaba River. His entry into this district brought on a conflict with Pedro de Valdivia, the governor of Chile, who with Francisco de Aguirre had established the power of Spain in that region.[2] Aguirre was appointed governor of Chile in 1552, and was ordered to take Núñez de Prado prisoner. He carried out his orders, brought Núñez de Prado prisoner to Chile, and placed the people of Barco under the rule of Chile. He then began to have revolts on his hands. The *encomenderos* treated the Indians so harshly that a revolt of the natives broke out. The people of Barco were forced to the northern side of the Dulce River, where they founded Santiago del Estero in 1553. García Hurtado de Mendoza, governor of Chile, appointed Juan Pérez de Zurita governor of Tucumán. Pérez de Zurita changed the name of the province to Nueva Inglaterra, in honor of the marriage of Philip, Prince of the Asturias, to Queen Mary of England. He founded three small municipalities which he named London, Cañete, and Córdova.[3]

Viceroy López de Zúñiga y Velasco arrived at his new post in 1560 determined

[1] Roberto Levillier, *La Audiencia de Charcas: correspondencia de presidentes y oidores*. Documentos del Archivo de Indias, vol. II, p. xiv.

[2] Valdivia and Aguirre had taken part in the expedition in the Valley of Cochabamba before they went to Chile. After the establishment of Santiago de Chile, Aguirre was elected the first *alcalde* in 1540, and proved himself a very able administrator.

[3] Córdova was destined to have a brilliant career, becoming the intellectual center of the Province of Tucumán and of the southeastern section of South America, and continuing as such for more than two hundred and fifty years. The fame of the city, and more especially of its celebrated university, has continued to the present day.

to make the Province of Tucumán independent of all governments other than that of Peru. The people of Tucumán were opposed to the rule of Peru and wished to remain under the rule of Chile. In 1562 the Province of Tucumán was placed under the jurisdiction of the Royal Audiencia of Charcas, but with a separate government (*gobierno*). In 1563 Philip II confirmed the appointment of Aguirre as governor of the Province of Tucumán, thereby approving the act of the viceroy of Peru. Aguirre soon began to have trouble with the Royal Audiencia of Charcas. He was ordered by the Audiencia to surrender the government, but refused to do so. A force was sent against him. He was defeated, arrested, and taken prisoner to Santiago del Estero. Later he was taken to La Plata, where he was duly tried and found guilty of heresy.[1] He was finally freed, however, and was permitted to continue to govern the Province of Tucumán. But he was soon in trouble, for he sought to avenge himself upon his former accusers. He was arrested a second time and sent to Lima for trial by the Holy Office. He was acquitted but not allowed to govern Tucumán.[2] In 1570 Arana still found the people of the Province of Tucumán very much opposed to the rule of the Audiencia of Charcas, and troubles continued. It was not until near the end of the century that the rule of the Audiencia of Charcas was firmly established in the province.

The exploration and colonization of Kollasuyu was a matter of great concern to the Spaniards in other parts of the Americas. As early as 1515–1516 Juan de Solís had discovered the mouth of the Río de la Plata. He had come in search of a strait, but had also heard rumors of the great wealth of the interior of the continent. In 1526 Sebastián Cabot may have come to the region of the estuary of the Río de la Plata. Again it is to be noted that these explorations were connected with the activities of the Portuguese. Both Spain and Portugal were anxious to explore and settle the eastern coast of South America, particularly because of the data gathered by the Magalhães–El Cano expedition, which had learned much about the coast line of the continent. Portugal began, about 1529, to turn her serious attention to the settlement of Brazil. She divided the colony into captaincies (*capitanías*), granting them to *donatorios*, with the

[1] José Toribio Medina, *Historia del tribunal del Santo Oficio de la Inquisición en Chile*, vol. I, pp. 118–121. Also in Bernard Moses, *The Spanish dependencies in South America*, vol. II, pp. 31–33. Aguirre was accused of believing that faith alone was sufficient to man's salvation and that it was unnecessary to hear mass; of having little confidence in prayer, of desiring to banish the priests and retain the blacksmiths, and of absolving the Indians so that they might work on feast days.

[2] Aguirre returned to Tucumán in 1569. In 1570 Viceroy Toledo sent Diego de Arana to take over the government of the province under the jurisdiction of the Royal Audiencia of Charcas. He was also instructed to arrest Aguirre and have him sent to La Plata for a second trial. Aguirre was accordingly arrested and taken to La Plata and then to Lima. His trial there began in May 1571 and lasted for five years. He was acquitted, as we have already noted, but was permanently banished from the Province of Tucumán. He died in 1581.

injunction that they form permanent settlements in their captaincies.[1] These movements only tended to convince the Spaniards of the need of making settlements on the east coast of the continent. The result was a series of very important movements to explore and settle the region of the Río de la Plata in the next three decades. And since these movements vitally affected the history of the country with which we are dealing, they deserve attention here.

Almost contemporaneously with the activities of the Spaniards in Peru came the efforts of Mendoza, Ayollas, Irala, and Cabeza de Vaca to colonize what is now Argentina, Uruguay, Paraguay, and Bolivia Oriental. The Spanish government realized that it was necessary to settle the country lying between the Atlantic and the highlands of Peru. In 1534 Simón de Alcazaba was appointed governor of the Province of León, and ordered to settle that country.[2] In the same year Pedro de Mendoza was appointed *adelantado* of Río de la Plata. Mendoza left Bonanza, Spain, August 24, 1535, and arrived at the mouth of the Río de la Plata on February 2, 1536, with instructions to search for the gold and silver of Peru, as well as to protect the region of the Río de la Plata against the Portuguese. He established headquarters at Riachuelo de los Navíos, which was the beginning of the great city of Buenos Aires, then called Nuestra Señora Santa María del Buen Aire.[3] It was a precarious beginning, for Mendoza and his men were bent upon getting to Peru to share the wealth of that region. Juan de Ayollas was commissioned to lead an expedition up the rivers of Río de la Plata, and to blaze a trail to the Peruvian highlands. He was to present himself to the *conquistadores* of Peru, Francisco Pizarro and Diego de Almagro, and to ask for their support.[4] He was to insist upon the right of Pedro de Mendoza to the territory of the Río de la Plata. Ayollas traveled on into Nuevo Toledo,[5] but he, too, was bent upon reaching Peru and not on making settlements. He was accompanied on this expedition by Domingo Martínez de Irala, one of the most ambitious of the Spanish *conquistadores*. They reached the present site of Asunción, where, on August 15, 1536, they founded Nuestra Señora de la Asunción.

[1] J. B. Hafkemeyer, "Determinação da área conhecida do Brasil do Norte até fins do século XVII. Principaes elementos que contribuiram para a sua exploração," *Revista do Instituto Histórico e Geográphico Brasiléiro*, tomo especiál, Congresso Internacionál de História da América, vol. V, pp. 9–27.

[2] Medardo Chávez S., *Los adelantados del Río de la Plata*, pp. 45–52.

[3] *Ibid.*, pp. 56, 74–80. The date of the exact founding of Buenos Aires is in doubt. In a document dated June 3, 1538, Buenos Aires is called Nuestra Señora Santa María del Buen Aire (*ibid.*, p. 79).

[4] *Ibid.*, pp. 81–83. Ayollas was to inform Francisco Pizarro or Diego de Almagro, or both, that the *adelantado* Pedro de Mendoza was *adelantado* and captain general of all of the south of Peru (*de todo el Sur del Perú*).

[5] This was the land given to Diego de Almagro and claimed by him.

Martínez de Irala was determined to establish the right of Spain to Paraguay, while the Portuguese were equally determined to prevent him from doing so. The founding of Asunción brought a solemn protest from the Portuguese government, which claimed that the city was founded on territory belonging to Portugal. The controversy was temporarily settled by the King-Emperor Charles on June 13, 1554, by a royal decree in which he declared that Asunción had been founded on territory belonging to Spain. Martínez de Irala set up a government in Asunción in August 1538, and made it the capital of the Adelantamiento of Río de la Plata. On June 15, 1540, the King-Emperor Charles had complicated the situation by entering into a capitulation with the notorious Álvar Núñez Cabeza de Vaca, the second *adelantado* of the Río de la Plata. On arriving, Cabeza de Vaca took the overland route and arrived in Asunción on March 12, 1542.

The city of Asunción had already become important as the gateway to the Cerro de la Plata in the Andean region. Although he had been appointed to assist Pedro de Mendoza in founding settlements, Cabeza de Vaca was determined to find the route to the wealth of Peru. He sailed up the Río Paraguay to the Puerto de los Reyes, and founded the town of Reyes on January 6, 1544. He sent Hernando de Ribera to proceed as far as possible toward Peru, while he returned to Asunción.[1] On April 25, 1544, Martínez de Irala led a revolution which gave him control of the government of the Adelantamiento of Río de la Plata. He was proclaimed governor by the people, and proceeded to take full charge of the government. Ñuflo de Chávez, one of the ablest figures in the conquest of Río de la Plata, entered the service of Martínez de Irala, despite the fact that he had come over with Núñez Cabeza de Vaca. Chávez was directed to reach the rich uplands of Potosí (*sierras ricas de Potosí*), and began his expedition on the Río Pilcomayo at Asunción in 1546. He was interested in the wealth of Peru and not in Río de la Plata, Asunción, or the Río Paraguay. He reached the foothills of the Andes and returned to Asunción. His expedition was the first to explore the region about the Pilcomayo, one of the most important rivers in Bolivia; he found the Pilcomayo valley inhabited by Indians who were well along in their cultural life. He was also the first Spaniard to reach the foothills of the Andes from the Río de la Plata.

A second expedition by Chávez was begun in 1548 in company with Martínez

[1] Chávez S., *Los adelantados del Río de la Plata*, p. 109. Chávez declares that the urge to get to Perú "era la fiebre y la ambición de todos los exploradores españoles, que palpitaba en las masas y quería hacerse realidad." Núñez Cabeza de Vaca declared in his instructions to Ribera: "Nuestro destino es el oro y la plata: eso prometimos buscar y eso esperan de nuestra diligencia nuestros conciudadanos en la Asunción. Si lo hallásemos, la fortuna será común y la felicidad para todos. Si no lo encontramos, tendremos el consuelo de haber trabajado para la patria, y el desconsuelo de no haber medio de mejorar su fortuna." And Chávez adds: "Al constituir la exploración este segundo Adelantado, demostró sus únicas miras, que eran el oro y la plata de Potosí. Nada de poblamiento a fundaciones de pueblos, ni siquiera reducciones de indígenas."

de Irala. They reached the Río Guapay and learned that Potosí had been discovered, and that the country was already in possession of the Spaniards. Martínez de Irala returned to Asunción, while Chávez went on to Lima over what is known as the Horcas de Chávez. He gave an account of the lands through which he had traveled and asked President de la Gasca's permission to establish a government over the region which he had explored. He also asked the president to appoint someone to rule over Paraguay. Chávez was cordially received but he was not made governor of Paraguay, that honor going to Diego Centeno. De la Gasca had heard of the revolution in Paraguay and wrote Martínez de Irala a stern rebuke, reminding him of the need of establishing a government in accordance with the laws of Spain. The news of the appointment of Centeno caused consternation among the loyalists (*leales*) as well as the rebels (*comuneros*). Centeno, however, died on July 9, 1549, before he could assume the duties of his new position. Martínez de Irala was recognized later as the legal governor of Paraguay, and continued to rule in that capacity until 1557.

Martínez de Irala continued his efforts to reach Peru. He appointed Ñuflo de Chávez commander of an expedition which reached the Gran Paititi, or El Dorado, the land of diamonds, silver, and gold (*el país de los diamantes, de la plata y del oro*).[1] Chávez reached the land of the Gran Mojos, where he learned of the death of Martínez de Irala. In the meantime, Viceroy Hurtado de Mendoza, the Marqués de Cañete, had sent Andrés Manso to explore the country between Upper Peru (*Alto Perú*) and the Adelantamiento of Río de la Plata. Manso was to settle the entire region between the Paraguay, the Pilcomayo, and the Bermejo Rivers. He began his work but soon came into conflict with Chávez, who was operating in the same territory.[2] There were now two forces at work in Bolivia Oriental: Ñuflo de Chávez from Asunción, and Andrés Manso from La Plata in Upper Peru. Chávez took his case before the viceroy in Lima.[3] He was fortunate in that the viceroy was a relative of his wife, and granted all that he asked. The viceroy recognized the territory which Chávez had explored, organized it into a separate government, and appointed his son García Hutardo de Mendoza governor and Chávez lieutenant governor. Later Hurtado de Mendoza resigned in favor of Chávez. The controversy between

[1] Chávez had followed the lure of the tale of El Dorado, the magnet of all the Spaniards: "los del Paraguay pensaban encontrarlo hacia el Perú, los del Perú llegaron en su persecución hasta el Río de la Plata." This region became known as La Gran Noticia, La Tierra Rica, El Paititi, Laguna del Sol, Reino del Sol, Laguna Dorada, etc.

[2] A direct result of this search for El Dorado was the establishment of the cities of Buenos Aires, Corpus Christi, Buena Esperanza, and Asunción.

[3] Chávez founded settlements as he went along. On February 26, 1560, he laid the foundations, as we have already noted, of Santa Cruz de la Sierra, named in honor of his native town, near Trujillo, Spain. On August 1, 1560, he founded the Pueblo de la Nueva Asunción on the Rio Guapay, later called La Barranca.

Chávez and Manso, however, was not to be settled so easily. Viceroy Diego López de Zúñiga y Velasco, the Conde de Nieva, who had displaced Mendoza, sent Juan de Medina Avellaneda to mediate the differences between Chávez and Manso. The agreement which was reached provided for a division of the territory between the two men, each to govern in his own section. Manso died, however, before the agreement was concluded.[1] In 1565 Chávez took charge of the new government. A veritable exodus of people of quality from Asunción followed him to Santa Cruz de la Sierra. But ill fortune also followed Chávez. The Indians gave a great deal of trouble despite efforts to treat them kindly. In one of the engagements which followed, Chávez was killed. This brought an end to the controversy between the two men who had striven valiantly to further the work of Spain in Bolivia Oriental.[2]

Conditions in the Presidency of Charcas continued peaceful. The next event of great importance was the tour of inspection (*visita*) of Viceroy Toledo.[3] Few men have had more interesting careers in the Spanish New World than Francisco Álvarez de Toledo y Figueroa, the Marqués de Oropesa. It is the mature judgment of reputable historians that the rule of Toledo was of profound importance for more than two hundred and fifty years. Naturally his work for the District of Charcas was of fundamental importance.[4] Toledo arrived in La

[1] The *llanos* between the Pilcomayo and the Bermejo Rivers have since been named in honor of Manso.

[2] Chávez S., *Los adelantados del Río de la Plata*, p. 177. Chávez was accompanied by his wife and children to his new post. He was killed on the banks of the Paraguay River in 1568. The importance of the work of Chávez and Manso can hardly be overestimated. Chávez was the first Spaniard to find a route from Asunción to Lower Peru (*Bajo Perú*); and he also worked successfully for the reduction and settlement of Bolivia Oriental. He strove to establish, as Chávez S. points out, "el principio de autoridad, y después laborar la mina y el suelo para acrecentar la riqueza de las colonias y de la madre patria." And the brilliant and erudite writer of Sucre, Jaime Mendoza, declares: "Así murió el gran conquistador, el soldado de bronce, el político sutil que había realizado portentosas hazañas."

[3] During the period from 1542 to 1776 when Upper Peru was under the rule of a viceroy of Peru, more than thirty different rulers occupied the viceregal throne. The celebrated Antonio de Mendoza, the first viceroy of New Spain, ruled over Peru for a short time, and spent some little time in Chuquisaca and Potosí. Melchor Portocarrero Lazo de la Vega ruled from 1690 to 1706, or more than fifteen years. It was during the rule of Manuel Guirior that the Viceroyalty of Río de la Plata was founded, by the royal decree of August 8, 1776. During the period between 1776 and the fall of the Viceroyalty of Río de la Plata in 1810, twelve men served as viceroys of the new kingdom.

[4] Toledo was appointed viceroy and captain general of Peru in July 1568. He left San Lucar de Barrameda on March 19, 1569, arrived in Santo Domingo on April 28, touched at Cartagena on May 8, and arrived on June 1 at Nombre de Dios, where he remained until June 20. Arriving at Panama on June 23, he remained in that city until August 12, when he proceeded on his journey to Lima. He arrived at Manta on September 2, where he met the *corregidor* of Guayaquil and distinguished *vecinos* of that region. He then went on to Paita, where he ordered the port reconstructed, giving it the name of Francisco de la Buena Esperanza de

Plata in November 1573. His entry into the city was a solemn event, celebrated in appropriate fashion. The judges Quiñones, Haro, and Ravanal of the Audiencia performed the honors of the occasion. The viceroy established headquarters in the palace of the archbishop, facing the Cathedral. Toledo set about his work of strengthening the government of the presidency. On the day of the patron saint of Charcas, San Miguel, he decreed the final nature of the flag of the city,[1] gave the city the title of Valiant City of La Plata (*Valerosa Villa de La Plata*), and spoke of it in glowing terms.

Paita. He had clearly shown that mania for personal inspection of the affairs of the viceroyalty for which he was to be noted throughout his rule of Peru. He arrived in Trujillo on October 15, 1569, where he also made important investigations. He made his formal entry into Lima on November 1, beginning a rule that was to last until September 23, 1581. He remained in Lima only until October 30, 1570. During that time the Inquisition was established in Lima, and an expedition sent to establish a more effective control over Chile. He then decided to make a tour of inspection to the more important parts of the viceroyalty in order to overhaul the political and financial structure of the country. He left the government of northern Peru in the hands of the judges of the Royal Audiencia of Lima and traveled to Cuzco by way of Jauja, Huencavélica, and Huamanga, arriving in Cuzco early in January 1571. In Cuzco he learned of the refusal of the young Inca Tupac Amaru I to accept the rule of Philip II, and at once determined to destroy the whole Inca dynasty. Toledo had come to establish the absolute rule of his king, and worked to that end during the entire period of his rule in Peru. The whole of the viceregal system was predicated upon the cardinal fact that the king of Spain was the absolute ruler of Peru. Hence there could be no room for a rebellious Inca, or for any other ruler in the viceroyalty. Inca Tupac Amaru I was easily captured. He was duly tried, convicted, and executed in the plaza of Cuzco with all the barbarity of a savage age. But Toledo was not satisfied with the destruction of the young Inca. He was determined to root out the entire dynasty and came very near doing so. In addition he took steps to have the history of the Incas written so as to make them out "a set of ruffians, blackguards, bastards, and usurpers." This task was assigned to Pedro Sarmiento de Gamboa, who wrote the *History of the Incas*, and thereby helped to give currency to the thesis of the Toledo-Sarmiento school of thought on that subject. The work was translated by Sir Clements R. Markham and published by the Hakluyt Society of London in 1907. This destruction of the Inca was the one dark spot on the character of this famous administrator, and the one for which he suffered the most. Toledo returned to Lima early in 1576 by way of Arequipa. He never returned to La Plata. On his return to Spain in 1581 he found that Philip II did not approve of his harsh treatment of the Inca, and he was very coldly received in Spain. He died soon after of a broken heart. The more important work done for the Presidency of Charcas will be dealt with in some detail in the course of this study.

[1] Jáuregui Rosquellas, *La ciudad de los cuatro nombres*, p. 185. Toledo declared that the city was "una de las repúblicas que más efectos y mayor ha aventurado las vidas y haciendas de sus moradores, es esta ciudad de La Plata, en todo lo que se ha ofrecido, con tanto celo y determinación y limpios servicios, que qualquier premio que se diera teneis bestante merecidos." He also gave voice to his appreciation of the importance of the city as the home of a people truly worthy of the highest praise. The city grew in importance with the achievements of the viceroyalty, and became in reality a second capital. Toledo desired a new capital for the viceroyalty because of the rivalry between Lima and Cuzco. He thus contributed to the fierce rivalry between the leaders of the municipalities in Lower as well as in Upper Peru, a rivalry which has continued to this day, and is intensely bitter even now. The large rôle of Sucre (as Charcas, La Plata, and Chuquisaca) in this formative period of the history of

Toledo labored incessantly throughout his entire sojourn in La Plata. No phase of the administration of the presidency was overlooked or ignored. One may state accordingly that the real basis of the Toledan administrative system for the Viceroyalty of Peru was largely worked out in La Plata. The legislation known as the Ordinances (*Ordenanzas*), which dealt with almost every phase of the administrative system, was drawn up in Charcas. That the *Ordenanzas* were very important is proved by the fact that many of them were incorporated in the *Recopilación de leyes de las Indias*.[1] The *Ordenanzas* prescribed,

Bolivia made her the first choice for the capital of the Republic of Bolivia in 1825, although this honor did not come to her without an intense contest between her and the other cities of the newly created nation-state. Bolívar contributed, as we shall see later, to this contest by openly favoring Cochabamba for the capital of the new nation.

There is need, in this connection, to point out that each of the major cities of Bolivia, including Sucre, La Paz, Potosí, Cochabamba, Tarija, Oruro, and Santa Cruz, is the center of a peculiarly powerful sectionalism. Each of the seven cities is, of course, different from the others and each has its peculiar characteristics. Geographical factors largely account for this difference, although ethnological elements are also a powerful factor. Sucre, Cochabamba, and Tarija, blessed with a very charming climate, reflect that cardinal fact in the life of their people. Sucre, with the eternal springtime of its climate, makes of the Sucreños a people apart, with a wealth of tradition and romance. Cochabamba, with its eternal summertime, makes the Cochabambinos a people fully as distinctive as the Sucreños. Cochabamba is the Athens of modern Bolivia, the home of scholars and thinkers. Tarija, with its charmingly invigorating climate and its isolation, makes of the Tarijeños also a people apart. Nowhere in all Bolivia is the Castilian language spoken with greater purity, and nowhere are the mentality and character of the people more definitely Spanish. Even more distinctly different from the people of these cities and from one another are the Pazeños, the Orureños, and the Cruzeños. La Paz, the great metropolitan center of Bolivia, located in the very heart of the Andean region, is the heart of present-day industrial and commercial Bolivia. Oruro, the most cosmopolitan of the Bolivian cities, the home of more foreigners than any other city in the republic, is the industrial center *par excellence*. Potosí, located at the base of the great Mountain of Silver, is uniquely important, for its tradition of great wealth and as a great mining center makes the Potosiños one of the most powerful groups in the whole country. And Santa Cruz, located in the heart of Bolivia Oriental, is of course a city quite apart from all others. The Cruzeños, too, have a great pride in their past and ambition for the future. Each of these seven cities is the center of a fierce localism that tends to become more and more intense with age. Herein lies one good reason for the failure of federalism to make any very great headway in Bolivia. Herein lies also a cause for the eternal fierceness of the untamed *caudillismo*, or *caudillaje*, which is so characteristic of the modern as well as of the colonial period. For colonial as well as modern independent Bolivia is a child of *caudillismo*, or dictatorship. The Pizarristas and the Almagristas, both of which groups had such a large share in the reduction and colonization of Bolivia, were the first Spanish *caudillos*, dictators, examplars for those of a later period. The Bolivians seem never able to live down that fact, or its baneful influence.

[1] The *Ordenanzas* were dictated in the *cabildo* of La Plata; and the book in which they were entered is preserved in the Archivo de la Nación in Sucre. Toledo had the assistance of Acosta, Matienzo, and Polo de Ondegardo of La Plata in drafting these *Ordenanzas*. The *Recopilación de leyes de los reynos de las Indias* was first published in Madrid in 1681. There were also later editions, published in Madrid in 1756, 1774, 1791, and 1841. Each new edition, as was to be expected, added new materials or made alterations in the preceding edition.

among other things, the boundaries of the cities of Lima, Arequipa, Cuzco, La Paz, La Plata, Potosí, Cochabamba, Tarija, and the smaller municipalities. They also described in detail the government of the native peoples. In many respects this attention to the government of the Indians was Toledo's most important work in Peru. He had perceived from the outset the need of a more satisfactory form of government for these people. In order better to organize such a government, a survey was made of the Incaic institutions. Out of this survey, which continued from 1570 to 1575, or for more than five years, grew the viceroy's idea for a bipartite system of local government.

The superior, or major, government was wholly Spanish in character, and was of course transplanted from Spain. It was, as a matter of fact, the *corregidor* system, which had been in operation in Spain for centuries. The features of this system were simple enough. A certain section of the viceroyalty was organized into a *corregimiento*, at the head of which was the *corregidor*. He was the officer who came into closest contact with the Indians. This was due to the nature of his office, for he was charged with the collection of the *tributo* and other taxes, with the supervision of the personal labor of the natives, and with the supervision of local trade. There were two classes of *corregidores:* the Spanish royal *corregidores* (*corregidores españoles*, or *corregidores reales*), and *corregidores* of the Indians (*corregidores de Indios*). The first were appointed by the king and lived in the larger towns and cities. The second were appointed by the viceroy and lived in the smaller towns and villages. The *corregidores* of the Indians also presided over the *cabildos* of the smaller municipalities.

Toledo took the feudal régime of Spain, known as the *repartimiento* or *encomienda*, and combined it with the Incaic system. The *encomienda* was a tract of land granted by the Crown, as the absolute owner of the land, to those subjects who had rendered important services to the state. The land so granted carried with it the Indians on the land. These Indians then came under the special care of the *encomenderos*, or those to whom *encomiendas* were granted. Not only were the Indians on the *encomiendas* under obligation to work for the *encomendero*, but every male Indian between the ages of eighteen and fifty years was also obliged to pay the personal tax known as the *tributo*. The *encomendero* was under obligation to the Crown to Christianize and civilize the natives on his *encomienda*, and to treat them kindly and humanely, a fact already noted in connection with the New Laws of 1542–1545. Under Toledo, the territory divided into *encomiendas* was in two divisions: the upper division (*hanan-suyu*) and the lower division (*hurín-suyu*). At the head of each division was a chieftain (*curaca*), but the chieftain of the upper division was above the chieftain of the lower division in rank. Under the *curaca* were other officials, the first persons (*primeras personas*) and the second persons (*segundas personas*), and under each of these were officers known as bosses (*mandones*). Toledo took this system over, but called the *curacas* caciques. It is estimated that about half of the land of the Presidency of Charcas was divided into *encomiendas*.

The other feature of the Toledan system was that which provided for the town or village life of the Indians. Here again Toledo built upon the Incaic system, for there were many municipalities which were taken over from before the Pizarran conquest. In case no municipality existed, a new one was established. Toledo was only carrying out his instructions, for the king had become convinced that the Indians could be taken care of much better in towns and villages than outside such settlements. The king was anxious to have the Indians remain pure in blood, which meant that they had to be protected from admixture with the Spaniards and the Negroes. No Spaniard or Negro, not even the *encomendero* or his sons, was allowed to live in Indian towns and villages. This applied also to *mestizos*, mulattoes, and *zambos* (offspring of the union of Negro and Indian). Toledo laid down detailed instructions for the building of towns, especially Indian towns. The houses in the Indian towns were to be larger for the caciques than for the Indians; and the houses for both the caciques and the Indians were to be built in such a manner as to provide privacy.[1]

The Indians became objects of oppression under the Toledan régime. In fact it may be said that the object of the entire plan was to make the Indians feel that they were a subject people. The Spaniards believed that the Indians should be driven mercilessly in order to make them work. Toledo drew up a

[1] Zelia Nuttall, "Royal ordinances concerning the laying out of new towns," *Hispanic American Historical Review*, vol. V, pp. 249–254; also in Cleven, *Readings in Hispanic American history*, pp. 331–336. Means in *The fall of the Inca Empire and the Spanish rule in Peru, 1530–1780*, pp. 156–157, gives the instructions for founding Indian towns. These excerpts (quoted by permission of the publisher, Charles Scribner's Sons, New York) give in essence the idea that Toledo had in mind:

"You will trace the houses of the Indians in such a way that they shall have their doors upon the public streets, the house of each Indian being separate and without any door leading into the house of any other Indian.

"You will trace the house of the principal chief with a greater degree of spaciousness and with somewhat more of an air of authority than the houses of private Indians. This shall be done in such a way that there shall be a patio and an apartment large enough to permit the chief to assemble there the principal Indians, and the Indians of the repartimiento in general, whenever he has to discuss with them matters touching the public good and the government of the repartimiento. And, in addition to the said patio and apartment, you will endeavor to plan so that there shall be a parlor wherein the said chief may eat and be at his convenience. And on one side of the said parlor there shall be a chamber and an inner chamber, so that the chief and wife may sleep in that chamber, whilst in the inner chamber their daughters and other women who serve the wife of the said chief will sleep. And on the other side of the parlor there shall be two rooms for the sons of the said chief and for the other Indians in his service; and there shall be no connection between these rooms and the apartments of the chief. And you will try to arrange so that, in addition to the rooms mentioned already, there shall be a kitchen and such yards as may be necessary for the services of the house.

"And you will try to arrange so that in the houses of the private Indians the apartment of the wife, the daughters, and women servants of the Indians shall be separate from the apartment of the sons and other Indian men who may be in said house."

book of tax rates (*Libro de tasas*) in which the amount of the *tributo* which each male Indian had to pay was prescribed in detail. For example, the *encomienda* of Sipe-Sipe, in the Presidency of Charcas, contained 819 men who paid *tributo*. In addition it had 112 old Indian men, 846 Indian boys under eighteen years of age, and 1814 Indian women and female children. These 3591 Indians were settled by Toledo in the village of Talavera de Sipe-Sipe. The *tributo* amounted to 5255 pesos, or about 7 pesos to a man, and 450 pesos' worth of seed corn a year. The abuse came in connection with the plan to raise more money, rather than more produce. This meant that more laborers were needed for the mines. Toledo forced the Indians to cease paying *tributo* in produce and to pay in silver instead. It was done, as Friar Rodrigo de Loaysa declared, to force the Indians to go to work in the "accursed hill" of Potosí for silver.

The Indians were divided into several classes of laborers. There were among the unattached Indians (*hatunrunas*) the class of laborers known as *tindarunas*, who could be hired out for work on public buildings, state undertakings, or private enterprises. The application for such laborers was made to the Spanish *corregidores*, who gave orders to the caciques to supply the required number of laborers. The most pernicious form of forced labor was, of course, the *mita*, or the system of *corvées*. This was not new, for a similar system was in operation under Inca rule. It was another feature which Toledo took over from the Incaic régime. Toledo ordered that from one-seventh to one-fifth of the *hatunrunas* should work in the mines. Under the cruel and greedy management of the *corregidores*, the *mita* became utterly unbearable. No phase of the whole Spanish colonial administration has been more justly condemned; and no group of colonial officials has been more justly condemned than the *corregidores*.[1] It is true that the priests (*curas*) also came in for well-deserved condemnation, especially where they cooperated with the *corregidores*, which they did altogether too often. In fact the *curas* deserve even more severe condemnation, for they were those who should have behaved more humanely. They were charged, after all, with the care of the souls of the unfortunate Indians.

The whole country from within twenty-five miles southwest of Cuzco to and around Lake Titicaca, and thence in a broad strip running southeastwardly along the shores of Lake Poopó, down to and around Villa Imperial de Potosí, was drained of its Indian population for *mitayos* (laborers) for the silver mines of Potosí. The caciques were notified to have the *mitayos* ready to be collected at a given date. The *corregidor* sent the captain of the *mita* to each town of a

[1] The classic work on the whole corregidoral system, including the *mita*, is of course that by Jorge Juan y Santacilia and Antonio de Ulloa, called *Noticias secretas de América* (1826). These two men also published the work which was translated into English under the title of *A voyage to South America, etc.*, in two volumes (2d ed., Dublin, 1765). They had come to the Indies in 1535 and had had an excellent opportunity to study conditions at first hand. They were members of the Royal Academy of Spain and of the navy and were thus well prepared for their task.

province to collect the *mitayos* in gangs to be taken to the mines. The *mitayo* might, it is true, secure exemption by purchase, the usual amount being 350 pesos. A *cura* sometimes paid the exemption fee out of sympathy for some certain *mitayo* in whom he might be interested. Many of those who could not buy exemption ran away into the wilds of Bolivia Oriental to escape the dreaded work in the mines.[1] Juan de Carvajal y Sandi, the president and *visitador* of the Royal Audiencia of Charcas, introduced reforms in the Indian régime in 1633. He forced a number of the mine owners to give up their Indian laborers and to close their mines because of their cruel treatment of their *mitayos*. In 1684 the viceroy, the Duque de la Plata, sought to improve upon the *mita* system, but with little success. There was too much at stake. The vested interests were successful then, as they had been in 1542–1545 in opposing the New Laws, in preventing the government from curbing their control over such a lucrative source of wealth.

The work of Toledo was of very great importance to the two Perus, for it was he who really established the *sistema español* in those colonies.[2] He was of

[1] Luis Subieta Sagárnaga, in his very interesting and illuminating pamphlet *La mita* (Potosí, 1917), has given important data on the origin and development of this system. He describes the corral of the *mitayos* (*corral de los mitayos*), where the laborers were kept for distribution, and gives much emphasis to the "dark legend" (*leyenda negra*) which has had such a powerful hold upon the Indian mind for centuries. He describes the work of Alonso de Ibáñez for the abolition of the *mita* and for good treatment of the Indians. There is a monument to Ibáñez in Potosí on which are to be found some evidences of his idealism. The rôle of the *mita* in the tradition of the native peoples of Bolivia is shown in the attention paid it in the literature of the country. "La canción de los mitayos" is still popular among the laborers (*punta*) of the country. The *yaraví*, a song of the mines, is also sung to the accompaniment of a rustic flute (*quena*). Subieta Sagárnaga's own views on the *mita* are shown in these excerpts:

"¡Mita! . . . Ved ahí una palabra extraña, de muy mal significación, ligeramente descrita por los señores Jorge Juan y Antonio de Ulloa, en las 'Noticias Secretas de América' y usada hasta hoy únicamente en las minas del Potosí.

"Esas cuatro letras, con todo su laconismo, encierran en sí la historia del coloniaje y son un epitafio de una raza entera.

"¡Mita! . . . Voz horrible de la que no pueden tener idea los que no han visitado las minas de este rico y legendario cerro que se destaca majestuoso, como emblema de riqueza, en el escudo nacional de Bolivia."

[2] No account of the sojourn of Toledo in the Presidency of Charcas would be complete without a brief notice of his military encounter with the Chiriguanos. These fierce Indians had insulted some of the religious rites of the Spaniards. The Chiriguanos were determined to keep the conquerors of the Incas from conquering them. Toledo was determined to punish these people for their insult to the Roman Catholic religion, and organized an expedition against them. He invaded their country, only to have the whole affair turn out a complete fiasco. He himself barely escaped serious personal injury. The net result of the expedition was that the Spaniards refrained from any serious efforts to conquer the Chiriguanos for many decades. Bolivia Oriental has continued ever since a great frontier land for the Bolivians, and is even to this day very much of a virgin land. The heroic efforts of Andrés Manso, Ñuflo de Chávez, and Juan de Baños had greatly impressed Toledo and had induced him to found

that group of men who helped make the work of Spain in the Americas great. It has long been the fashion of writers, following the Creoles of the revolutionary period, to belabor and berate Spain for the evils of her colonial system. There were many evils in that system of course; but these have been emphasized at the expense of the great work which Spain performed in establishing her institutional life in the western world. She laid the foundations of the eighteen independent republics of Spanish America, a feat no whit less remarkable than that accomplished by England. The institutional life of these republics is still fundamentally Spanish. Spanish America has an area of more than five million square miles, and a population of over fifty million. Of late these people have been drawn much closer to old Spain, a *rapprochement* that betokens almost a renaissance in the life of the Spaniards in the two hemispheres.

The Presidency of Charcas continued to play a very important rôle in the history of the Viceroyalty of Peru long after the departure of Toledo. Her cities, especially La Plata and Potosí, grew in wealth and cultural achievement. The great mineral wealth of the latter city helped to give grandeur to the former. By the end of the sixteenth century La Plata was among the greatest cities of the Indies. None was really superior to her. In South America she was easily the peer of Lima and Buenos Aires. In 1615 the Principe de Esquilache, the viceroy of Peru, visited La Plata and made the occasion an exceptionally important one. He was greatly impressed with the city, and praised it highly. In 1624 the famous University of San Francisco Xavier was founded under the auspices of the Order of Jesus. This university gradually came to be recognized throughout the Indies as one of the greatest institutions of learning in the Americas.[1] The

settlements in these unconquered lands. We have already noted that it was through his efforts that Cochabamba and Tarija were founded. Thus, as noted above, Toledo did much of permanent value for Spain, a fact which Alfredo Jáuregui Rosquellas has done much to popularize. The latter is the leader among the increasing group of scholars who see much good, as well as much that was not good, in the Spanish colonial system. His work on *La España heroica en el Nuevo Mundo* has justly won for him much renown.

[1] On the occasion of the anniversary of the founding of the University of Charcas, as it is now called, the institution came in for much attention. The fecund writer of Bolivia, Jaime Mendoza, wrote a booklet entitled *La Universidad de Charcas y la idea revolucionaria: ensayo histórico*, which contains much useful information. The University of Charcas was the seventh university to be founded by Spain in the New World; all were modeled upon the celebrated University of Salamanca, founded in 1223. The demand for a university for La Plata began shortly after the city had been founded. The king of Spain was repeatedly importuned to grant permission for the founding of such an institution, but it was not until 1622 that Philip III issued a royal decree by which the university was founded. It was not opened for business until March 27, 1624. In time the university became pontifical (*pontificia*) and royal (*regia*), and was given the name of San Francisco Xavier. It was founded "para mayor exaltación de la fé católica y triunfo de la justicia en el nuevo mundo" and "para la mayor exaltación del dominio de España y triunfo de sus métodos en el nuevo mundo, etc." It was natural that the university should be founded in La Plata because that city was "el núcleo de población más selecto por su calidad en esta parte de la América," as Jaime Mendoza

Royal Audiencia of Charcas also grew in importance and in reputation, as did the *ayuntamiento* of La Plata. Ecclesiastically La Plata was especially influential, having been raised to an archbishopric as early as 1575. Other cities increased in importance also. Potosí, to which the mint had been moved from Lima, became increasingly influential. As the most powerful mining center in South America, she became, along with La Plata, a great cultural center. It was the mining centers that became, in Upper Peru as in other parts of the Indies, early centers of civilization, while the municipalities which relied on agriculture and pastoral industry grew slowly or almost not at all. The first census of Potosí was taken in 1574 and revealed a population of about 120,000 inhabitants. In 1611 she had a population of about 114,000, of whom 65,000 were Indians, 42,000 Spaniards, and the remainder Negroes and mulattoes. In 1650 her population was about 160,000; but by 1825 it had decreased to about 8000.[1]

The population of other parts of the Presidency of Charcas was of course less fluctuating. After all, the migrations from Spain were not large, owing to the restrictions placed upon them. No one might migrate to the Indies without definite permission from the king's government. This meant further that the people who were allowed to migrate to the Indies were of the approved classes. From 1540 on, converts to Roman Catholicism from Islamism or from Judaism and their descendants, heretics and their descendants, unmarried women unless accompanied by their parents or a close relative, foreigners (*extranjeros*), all persons not subjects of Castile, Aragon, Navarre, Catalonia, or Valencia were forbidden to migrate to the colonies. A profoundly important result of the small number of women allowed to migrate from these kingdoms was the biological one. In Upper Peru, as elsewhere in the Indies, this meant the mating of Spaniards with native women, and later also with Negro women. The extensive intermixture between the Spaniards and Indian women produced the *mestizos*, or *cholos* as they are called in Bolivia, a class of people which has had a profound influence upon the life of the people throughout most of its history. The inter-

states it. He adds: "Su situación, por último, hacíale el punto céntrico de la enorme circunscripción colonial llamada Audiencia de Charcas que, como se sabe, en esos tiempos se extendía 'de mar a mar' por el Este y Oeste, y desde el Cuzco hasta Tucumán por el Norte y el Sur." He finds that the university deserved its fame because "La Plata tenía desde luego a su favor el factor natural. No parecía sino que la Naturaleza la hubiese hecho expresamente para ser una ciudad universitaria. Diríase de su clima, un clima propiamente intelectual" (*ibid.*, pp. 5–9). We shall later point out how this institution evolved the revolutionary idea, of which Jaime Mendoza has so much to say.

[1] Philip II took frequent censuses. The *censo de población* of 1594 gave Spain a population of 9,034,410. This was twice as large as the population of England at the time. Consult Tomás Gonzáles, *Censo de población de las provincias y partidos de la Corona de Castilla en el siglo XVI* (Madrid, 1829). This population was divided among the kingdoms of Iberia as follows: Old and New Castile, 6,020,915; Murcia and Andalusía, 1,656,790; Aragon, 378,710; Valencia, 486,860; and Navarre, 154,165. This meant, by the way, strong proof of the Castilianization of the Iberian Peninsula, and also of the influence of Castile in the Indies.

mixture between the Spaniards and the Negro women was of less importance only because of the small number of Negro women in the country. The proximity of Upper Peru to Brazil brought a relatively large number of Negroes into Upper Peru. Again, the climate of Bolivia Oriental was suitable to Negro labor. The result has been that the percentage of negroid blood in the population has been by no means unimportant. There was also further mixture of races. Intermixture between the Indian and the Negro produced the *zambo*, an ethnical element of some importance. The mulattoes, the *mestizos*, and the *zambos* have intermixed, and the offspring of all these have in turn carried on the process until the mixed caste has become a highly mongrel people. All of which tends to emphasize the fact that the ethnological composition of the Bolivian people is a very important factor in its national life.[1]

The seventeenth century was a turbulent one in Upper Peru. The era of *conquistadores* had closed, or had, at least, lost much of its glamor. The Presidency of Charcas was primarily concerned with the affairs growing out of disputes over jurisdiction. The Royal Audiencia became involved with the Mamelukes (*mamelucos*), who were especially interested in slave-raiding expeditions, and became particularly obnoxious under the leadership of Luis de Céspedes. They made incursions into Charcas for Indian slaves for the markets of Rio de Janeiro, Brazil. There were also many Indian uprisings, of which the one under Cacique Rodrigo Yaguariguay and Bohorquez was particularly formidable. Then there was the revolt of Buenos Aires against the rule of Paraguay, with the ultimate separation of Buenos Aires from Paraguay, and its incorporation within the Royal Audiencia of Charcas. In 1663 the Spanish government created the Royal Audiencia of Buenos Aires in order to relieve the Royal Audiencia of Charcas of the rule over that vast territory. But the Royal Audiencia of Buenos Aires was abolished in 1672; it was not finally established until 1782, and even then it did not begin to function until 1785. In the meantime the whole region was again placed under the Royal Audiencia of Charcas.

Paraguay and Tucumán were also under its jurisdiction. At the beginning of the seventeenth century southeastern Spanish America was, accordingly, divided into three provinces: the Province of Buenos Aires, the Province of Paraguay, and the Province of Tucumán; and all three of them were under the jurisdiction of the Royal Audiencia of Charcas. After the restoration of the Braganza monarchy in Portugal there was renewed trouble between the Spanish and the Portuguese in the Río de la Plata countries. The Portuguese were a constant source of danger in the Banda Oriental del Uruguay. Toward the end of the century the controversy took on a formidable international aspect. England, France, and Holland caused Spain great concern, for they supported the

[1] Bolivia is fundamentally an Indian country to this day. Only about a sixth of the total population of about 3,000,000 is white. This makes the ethnological problem of the country one of fundamental importance. No study of its complex life can afford to ignore that cardinal factor.

Portuguese in their efforts to establish a foothold in the disputed territory. The Portuguese were determined to establish themselves at the mouth of the Río de la Plata. The Colonia del Sacramento, or Colonia, on the Río de la Plata itself, in present-day Uruguay, became an object of special concern to the Portuguese.[1] By the end of the century Portugal had been recognized in her possession of Colonia by the three great powers, Great Britain, France, and Holland.[2] The contest continued on into the eighteenth century, and will be dealt with later.

The internal affairs of the Presidency of Charcas continued unsettled. Life in Potosí was especially turbulent. There was almost constant strife between the Basques (*Vicuñas*) and the Castilians. In 1623 Felipe Manrique strove to put down the trouble between them. The Vicuñas retired to the valley of the Ulti, whence they attacked La Plata and Potosí. Peace was finally restored, but economic life had been greatly demoralized.[3] Some effort was made to improve the lot of the Indians. On November 24, 1601, the king decreed reforms, the purpose of which was to release the Indians from their obligations to the *encomenderos*.[4] The king forbade personal service in lieu of the money *tributo*. No Indian might be forced to labor as a penalty for crime, or be employed in the fisheries, or as a beast of burden, or in the cultivation of the coca, or in the factories belonging to the Spaniards, or in the sugar mills, or in any other establishment. No Indian might be taken away from the community in which he lived to work in another community. The Indians were to be given time off for work on their own small farms. The *yanaconas* (Indians in the personal service of Spaniards) were no longer to remain in servitude on the *encomiendas*, but were at liberty to leave one *encomienda* to seek work on another. The *mita* was to be gradually abolished. But the opposition to these reforms was much too strong, and they again proved a failure.[5] The Ordinances of 1612 provided that the

[1] The Colonia del Sacramento had been founded in 1680 by the Portuguese, opposite Buenos Aires. It was destroyed by the Spaniards almost immediately, but was restored by the Portuguese in 1683. From that time to 1763 Colonia was a pawn in the international rivalries in which South America was involved in that critical period.

[2] Francisco Bauzá, *Historia de la dominación española en el Uruguay*, deals with these facts in detail. Vol. I, pp. 171–208 is especially good.

[3] But there was still much mineral wealth in the Cerro de Potosí. The city of Potosí "continued to be the centre of the gayest, the most extravagant, and the most reckless society in the kingdom. No other city was as rich as Potosí."

[4] The *encomendero* took an oath, feudal in character, before he could take over the control of the *encomienda*. Consult Amunátegui y Solar, *Las encomiendas de indíjenas en Chile*, vol. I, p. 70, for a typical oath.

[5] Consult Ricardo Palma, *Tradiciones peruanas*, for detailed information on these and many other matters.

tributo should be accepted in lieu of personal service;[1] but this legislation also proved too idealistic, and failed. The Indian policy continued with but little change for the remainder of the colonial period. In fact, new mines tended to make the labor of the Indians all the more exacting.[2] Graft and corruption increased among the administrative officials, and made the lot of the Indian more and more difficult.[3]

The eighteenth century was of momentous importance to the people of the Presidency of Charcas. Only the more important events need be noted here. The Revolution of 1720 in Paraguay, in reality a contest between the Jesuits and the civil authorities, brought the Royal Audiencia of Charcas into open opposition to the viceroy of Peru. The people of Paraguay were opposed to the rule of Governor Diego de los Reyes and appealed to the Audiencia of Charcas. The Audiencia appointed José de Antequera to the governorship and removed de los Reyes. De los Reyes refused, however, to surrender the office, and civil war began. The viceroy of Peru ordered the Audiencia of Charcas, February 26, 1723, to recall Antequera and to restore de los Reyes in Paraguay. He informed the Audiencia that it had overreached its authority, and that sovereignty was vested solely in the king of Spain, and not in any tribunal or judge, no matter how exalted.[4] The controversy between the viceroy and the Audiencia continued, but in the end the king upheld the viceroy, and ordered Antequera taken to Lima to stand trial for his treasonable activities. He was found guilty, condemned to death, and executed in the plaza of Lima on July 5, 1731. He had fought the Jesuits in Paraguay and, because the Jesuits were still very powerful in Peru, he was made to suffer for his opposition to the Order of Jesus. The people of Paraguay, however, continued their opposition to the Jesuits,

[1] The Royal Audiencia of Charcas appointed Judge Francisco de Alfaro *visitador* with powers to make a careful survey of the condition of the Indians in the presidency. One of the results of this survey was these Ordinances of 1612.

[2] The labor of Indians was especially needed for the mines of Laicocota, discovered in 1657. They were the property of José and Gaspar Salcedo. These mines were not in Upper Peru, but Indians of Upper Peru were used as *mitayos* in them.

[3] A good example of the corruption and graft in the colonial administration of this period was the case of the treasurer of La Paz. He was convicted in 1675 of embezzling 400,000 pesos, and was hanged for that crime.

[4] Consult Lozano, *Revoluciones*, for a detailed account of this case. Antequera had been in the service of the king of Spain for upwards of forty years, much of which time he had been a judge of the Royal Audiencia of Charcas. The viceroy of Peru wrote a letter to the Audiencia on May 26, 1723, further emphasizing the importance of the illegal position it had taken in the controversy. On June 7, 1723, he ordered the removal of Antequera and the restoration of de los Reyes to the governorship of Paraguay. Antequera then left Asunción, but did not go to Lima as he had been ordered to do, going to Córdova instead. His property was confiscated and the measures which he had taken against the Jesuits annulled. On April 11, 1726, the king ordered his trial in Lima. In the meantime he had come to La Plata, but was taken to Potosí and thrown into prison at the orders of the Audiencia.

and as rebels (*comuneros*) they helped to bring on the expulsion of that order. After the Jesuits had been expelled Charles III made amends for the injustice done to Antequera. The king declared that Antequera had been a loyal and honorable minister, and ordered that pensions should be paid to the members of the Antequera family from the goods taken from the Jesuits.

The difficulties with the Portuguese increased with the advance of the Spaniards and the Portuguese into the frontier regions. The problem was aggravated, as we have seen, by the support which the English, the French, and the Dutch gave to the Portuguese. The latter had been determined from the outset of their interest in South America to seize control of the country drained by the Río de la Plata. They continued to strengthen their hold on the Colonia del Sacramento and the Plata coast. The Treaty of Madrid of 1750 was very distasteful to the Jesuits of Paraguay. They protested the provisions of the treaty dealing with their reductions, or settlements, in Paraguay. The seven reductions in the territory which Spain promised to return to Portugal involved some sixty thousand Guarani Indians.[1] The Jesuits appealed to the Royal Audiencia of Charcas, but without success. The Indians opposed the exchange of masters and war began between them and the Spaniards. Nicholas Nanguirú became the leader and continued the war until 1757.[2] In 1761 Charles III annulled the Treaty of Madrid; and the next year the Spanish again captured Colonia, and the twenty-seven English ships involved in the war. But in 1763 Colonia was again returned to Portugal by the Treaty of Paris. The Marquis de Pombal, the strong man of Portugal, was determined to enlarge the territory of his country at the expense of Spain. He took an active part in European affairs, enjoying the support of the English government up to the time of the outbreak of the British American Revolution. The treaties of 1777 and 1778 with Portugal gave Spain possession of Colonia. The efforts of the Portuguese had again been temporarily checked; and the Audiencia of Charcas was in a position to devote its attention to the internal affairs of the presidency.

The activities of the Jesuits during the period when Spain was striving to adjust her differences with Portugal intensified the opposition of the Spanish civil authorities to the Order of Jesus. The Order had acquired great material

[1] The reductions were San Miguel, San Angel, San Lorenzo, San Luis, San Nicolás, San Juan, and La Concepción. The revolt of the Indians in the so-called Guarani War, 1752–1756, is an excellent example of the influence of the Jesuits upon the Indians. Consult Cárlos Calvo, *América latina. Colección histórica completa de los tratados, etc.*, vol. II, pp. 241–260, for the treaty in question.

[2] Nanguirú took the title of Nicholas I, King of Paraguay and Emperor of the Mamelucos. Much mystery still surrounds the life of this man. Consult Martín Dobrizhoffer, *Account of the Abipones*, for the story of his life and activities. The achievements of Pedro Ceballos in this war showed him to be a very able military leader as well as administrator. It was he who brought the war to a successful close in 1757. We shall have more to say about him in the account of the establishment of the Viceroyalty of Río de la Plata.

wealth in its career, and enjoyed much political and social power, which brought upon it the jealous eye of monarchs and statesmen. In the struggle over the enforcement of the Treaty of Madrid of 1750, the Jesuits had taken the side of the Indians, and brought on the War of the Seven Reductions, referred to above. This intensified the opposition of the *encomenderos*, who had been against the growth of the reductions from the beginning. The Indians on the reductions were under the political and economic control of the Jesuits, and were exempt from the payment of the *tributo* and from the performance of personal service. The number of Indians decreased on the *encomiendas* and increased on the reductions. The *encomenderos* saw the whole *encomienda* régime threatened with ultimate extinction, and made vigorous protests to the home government.

Charles III had been suspicious of the Order of Jesus from the beginning of his reign in Spain. He was convinced that the Order was a menace to the state and that it ought to be abolished. The War of the Seven Reductions and the policy of the Order in the relations between Spain and Portugal gave him a good excuse for action. He sent José Moñino, later the Conde de Floridablanca, as minister to the Vatican with instructions to lay before the Holy Father the grievances of his government against the Jesuits, and to urge him to suppress the Order.[1] In the meantime, Charles III prepared his celebrated royal edict

[1] Gayetano Alcázar Molino, *Los hombres del despotismo ilustrado en España. El Conde de Floridablanca: su vida y su obra*, pp. 42 ff. The Conde de Floridablanca became one of the ablest ministers of state that Spain has produced. He was born on October 21, 1728, in Murcia. He received a good education and soon rose to power in the service of the government. After his success with the Holy Father in the matter of the suppression of the Order of Jesus, Moñino was created Conde de Floridablanca by his grateful sovereign. In 1777 he was appointed first minister of state and served his king with rare intelligence and fortitude throughout the remainder of his reign, up to 1788. He was continued in the same office by the new King Charles IV until 1792, but was forced out of office by Manuel Godoy, the queen's paramour. He then went into retirement, but had the satisfaction of seeing his rival defeated in the fateful year 1808. He came back into public life long enough to preside at a meeting of his fellow countrymen in Seville in that year. Floridablanca was opposed to the imperialistic and warlike activities of Spain, and as minister, deliberately set about to turn the energies of the Spanish people to the upbuilding of the country from within. He was unable to prevent the war with England, 1779–1783, but was able to prevent Spain from taking sides in the French Revolution and to settle the controversy with England over the Nootka Sound question, 1790–1793, without war. The contests with England during his ministry were of fundamental importance to both countries. The territorial gains from the war with England, great though they were, could not offset the danger to Spain from the establishment of the United States of America, to which Spain had been, at least indirectly, a party. The Nootka Sound controversy was of even greater importance, for it meant the beginning of the end of Spain's power in the Americas. Floridablanca was always a loyal son of Murcia. After his fall from office he returned to his native city, where he lived his life in retirement. From February 28, 1792, the day on which he was driven from office, the fortunes of his country began to decline. To quote Alcázar Molino: "El proceso de esta crisis de 1792 señala en la historia española el comienzo de una serie sucesiva de desventuras. Al abandonar el gobierno Floridablanca, el prestigio exterior de España, hasta entonces noblemente mantenido, comenzó a sufrir grandes vaivenes." He died in 1808, having served his country for twenty-six years.

(*real cédula*) for the expulsion of the Jesuits from his dominions in Europe and in the Americas as elsewhere. On March 1, 1767, the Conde de Aranda, the able minister of Charles III, issued instructions to the viceroys, presidents, and governors in the Indies for the execution of the royal edict of February 7, 1767. On March 20, Aranda sent a circular letter to the magistrates of the localities in which there were Jesuits with orders to arrest them. The whole affair was to be carried out with the utmost secrecy and with the utmost dispatch. The houses and colleges, the archives, the libraries, and all other kinds of property, except a few personal effects which the members of the Order were allowed to take with them, were to be seized and turned over to the state.

The execution of the edict of expulsion in the Presidency of Charcas did not differ materially from the manner in which it was enforced in other parts of the Indies. Victoriano Martínez de Tineo, president *ad interim* of the Audiencia, received Aranda's instructions from the governor of Buenos Aires. Martínez de Tineo enforced the edict with zeal and with a degree of cruelty like that of his fellow officers throughout the Indies. The total number of Jesuits expelled from the Presidency of Charcas is not definitely known, but there may have been three hundred all told.[1] There was a great deal of opposition to the decree of expulsion, however, among the people of the presidency. There were many who questioned the wisdom of the course pursued by the home government. Charles III may have been actuated by the best of motives. He intended to carry on an enlightened administration throughout his dominions and felt that the Jesuits were determined to thwart him in that endeavor. The Jesuits had, it must be remembered, but little regard for the civil administration of any country. They wanted a theocracy in which the civil authorities were definitely subordinated to the ecclesiastical authorities. It was not to be expected that so powerful a monarch as Charles III would brook any opposition to his policies, even from them. The Jesuits had been a powerful factor in the cultural as well as the ecclesiastical life of the colony. The removal of this body of influential men left a void which was never really filled. No one could take the place of the Jesuits as educators, perverted as much of their instruction may have been

[1] The Jesuits expelled from the presidency ultimately joined the six thousand Jesuits expelled from the Spanish lands and sent to the Papal States. Consult the *Colección general de las provincias hasta aquí tomadas por el gobierno sobre el estrañamiento y ocupación de temporalidades de los regulares de la Compañía, que existían en los dominios de S. M. de España, Indias, é Islas Filipinas* (Madrid, 1767) for the *real decreto de ejecución* and other documents dealing with the expulsion of the Order of Jesus. The Order itself was suppressed on July 21, 1773. The document was in the form of a *breve* by Pope Clement XIV called *Dominus ac Redemptor*. Consult also the work by Enrique Pacheco y Leyva on *La intervención de Floridablanca en la redacción del breve para la supresión de los jesuítas*. The Order was restored by Pope Pius VII in 1814 by the document *Solicitudo omnium ecclesiarum*. Ferdinand VII restored the Order in Spain and its colonies in the same year. It was expelled again in 1823 and again restored by Ferdinand VII. In 1835 it was again expelled from Spain and has had no legal status there since that year.

when judged by scientific standards.[1] It was a stunning blow to the old order, for it helped to prepare the way for the order which was to end in the loss to Spain of the greater part of the Indies. The Jesuits became, very naturally, the bitter enemies of the Spanish monarchs, and figured conspicuously among the precursors of the movement for independence in the colonies. The Indians, too, lost their good protectors and well-wishers. On the whole, therefore, it may be accurate to conclude that the expulsion of the Jesuits from the Spanish dominions was by no means an unmixed blessing, and that it was one of the least enlightened of the many acts of Charles III as a ruler.

Another event of profound importance to the Presidency of Charcas, in the reign of Charles III, was the establishment of the Viceroyalty of Río de la Plata. In many respects it was to have the most important effect of any act of that monarch. The viceroyalty was created by the royal decree of August 8, 1776. The territory of the new viceroyalty included all the lands under the jurisdiction of the Royal Audiencia of Charcas. For more than two hundred years the Audiencia had exercised jurisdiction over most of the territory of the new viceroyalty. It had wielded almost sovereign power, and had even set itself, as we have seen, against the viceroy of Peru.[2] The Audiencia had remained serene and unmoved by the agitations which disturbed Lima, Asunción, Potosí, Buenos Aires, and other cities in the Indies. It had even served as a training school for positions in the Audiencia of Lima. But it was not the proper body to govern so vast a territory.

The creation of the new viceroyalty was the result of several years of agitation for such an organization.[3] The king did not act favorably until

[1] Jáuregui Rosquellas describes in some detail the effect upon Charcas of the expulsion of the Jesuits. He found that the twenty-one missions which they had founded in the presidency were allowed to fall into ruins and finally disappear altogether. With the disappearance of these and the master minds that had directed them, there remained only the *poesía de las ruinas* and the traditions of the greatness of the Order in the field of civilized endeavors. He adds: "Las instalaciones, fábricas que allí tenían los padres jesuítas, las magníficas escuelas, las plantaciones modelo, las fábricas de cordelería, tejidas fuertes, sombreros y trajes de lana abatanada; el tallado en madera, la pintura en colores impermeables y sin aceite; la primera imprenta con tipos de madera que sirvieron para imprimir allí mismo, en prensas combinadas de éllos, un vocabulario guaranino español; el superior tallada en piedra, cuyos restos aun se pueden contemplar con admiración, y tanta labor reveladora del esfuerzo de que eran capaces los misionarios, todo se vino abajo, todo es perdido cincuenta años después" (*La ciudad de los cuatro nombres*, pp. 147–149).

[2] Gabriel René-Moreno, *Bolivia y Perú: notas históricas y bibliográficas*. The essay on "La Audiencia de Charcas, 1559–1809" is found on pages 201–325. Consult also Vicente Gaspar Quesada, *Vireinato del Río de la Plata 1776–1810*, for much useful information on this subject.

[3] Tomás Álvarez de Acevedo, *fiscal* of the Royal Audiencia of Charcas, had advocated the establishment of the Viceroyalty of Río de la Plata for many years. On January 12, 1771, the Audiencia communicated the views of Álvarez de Acevedo to the king, but without any immediate favorable results.

1776,[1] and it was not until October 27, 1777, that Charles III issued the royal decree from San Lorenzo that made the viceroyalty a permanent one. The viceroyalty was divided into the provinces of Montevideo, Tucumán, Paraguay, Charcas, Potosí, La Paz, Chucuito, Santa Cruz de la Sierra, Mojos, Chiquitos, and the Missions of the Guarani Indians (*Misiones de Indios Guaranis*). The Presidency of Charcas contained the four provinces of Charcas, Potosí, La Paz, and Santa Cruz de la Sierra, with the governments of Mojos and Chiquitos. The Presidency of Charcas was thenceforth called Upper Peru, a name which it retained until the creation of the republic in 1825. Charles III took another important step when he established freedom of trade between Spain and the Indies by the famous Regulation of Free Commerce between Spain and the Indies (*Reglamento para el comercio libre de España á Indias*) on October 12, 1778. This policy was still further emphasized by the royal decree of August 5, 1784. This latter measure was taken because of fear of loss of the colonies. The success of the British American Revolution was not considered in a favorable light by Spain. It might have been well for Charles III to have adopted the proposal of the Conde de Aranda in 1783 for the division of the Indies into three kingdoms with an *infante* as king over each, the whole to form, together with Spain, an empire with Charles III as emperor. Aranda saw clearly, as did Floridablanca and other statesmen, that the rôle of Spain in the British American Revolution was likely to lead to the loss of her own colonies.

Another event of great importance to the Presidency of Charcas in this period was the powerful protest against the corregidoral system, which had become more and more oppressive with age and was by this time well-nigh unbearable. The collection of the hated *tributo* was a constant source of grievance. The question of the status of the *tributo*-paying individual was becoming increasingly important. In the first place, it was necessary to determine when an Indian was an Indian and not a *mestizo*, since a *mestizo* was exempt from the payment of the *tributo*. The *corregidores* often solved the problem in very arbitrary manner, classing the *mestizos* as Indians in order to increase the amount of the *tributo*, with dire results in the form of open revolt.[2] The most important

[1] The first viceroy was Pedro Ceballos, who had been governor of Buenos Aires from 1756 to 1766. He had proved himself an able administrator and was no stranger among the people of the new viceroyalty. He had also served, as we have noted above, with much distinction in the War of the Seven Reductions. He made an excellent beginning by decreeing freedom of trade for the city of Buenos Aires early in 1777. Ceballos was naturally very much concerned with the activities of the Portuguese. He knew the "Portuguese problem" and could be counted upon to handle it intelligently. Fortunately for him and for Spain, the thirteen British American Colonies had broken with England, thereby depriving the Portuguese of the support of the English. The result we have already noted in another place.

[2] The *mestizos* of Cochabamba, under the leadership of Alejo Calatayud, rose in rebellion. They failed and Calatayud was executed. *Mestizos* in other parts of the Presidency of Charcas had an even greater excuse for revolt. This situation prepared the ground for the Revolt of Tupac Amaru II, and accounts, in large measure, for the initial success of this uprising.

of the revolts was that of 1780–1781 under the leadership of Tupac Amaru II, a man of superior powers and much practical political experience.[1] Tupac Amaru II was the cacique of Tungasuca in the Province of Tinta. In 1770 the Royal Audiencia of Charcas recognized his claims to the marquisate of Orepesa. This victory gave him the impression that he was destined to do much for his native people, and he began to dream of great power and prestige. Believing that he was destined to revive the Inca Empire, he began to assert his rights to the Inca throne. He was especially concerned about the oppressive rule of the *corregidor* of Tinta, Antonio Aliaga, and took upon himself the task of ridding the province of the rule of *corregidores*. In a controversy with Aliaga, he caused the latter to be arrested, tried, condemned, and executed. This high-handed act brought about the revolt, which spread with great rapidity. It was a social revolution, an effort to bring about relief from the corregidoral system, and, in general, a reform in the whole colonial régime. At first, therefore, many of the *mestizos* and even Spaniards took part in the preparation for the revolt. Almost the whole of the Indian population of the Peruvian and Bolivian Andean regions supported Tupac Amaru II and the cause for which he was fighting. The Indians believed that the time had come for them to reassert their right to govern themselves and their countries. It was a dream which the Indians of Peru and Bolivia had nurtured since the fall of the Inca Empire, and one, by the way, which many of them still dream.

The excesses committed by the supporters of Tupac Amaru II quickly caused the *mestizos* and Spaniards to desert the cause and to turn against him. The revolt developed into a war of the races, and caused consternation in the viceregal capitals involved. The Spaniards of the region about Sorata and La Paz were especially hard pressed by the followers of the Inca, and sought refuge within those cities. The two viceroys sent military expeditions to put down the revolt. La Paz was besieged for one hundred and nine days by more than forty thousand Indians. Troops came from Buenos Aires, Tucumán, and Cochabamba to help La Paz. Sebastián Segurola was in charge of the defense of the city and was able to raise the siege.[2] The revolt was finally crushed, but not until Tupac Amaru II had been betrayed by some of his own men. Zunuario de Castro and Ventura Landeata were especially active in the plot against him. The Inca was taken prisoner, tried, and condemned to be executed. The *visitador* José Antonio Arecha pronounced the sentence against him on May 15,

[1] Tupac Amaru II was born in Tinta and baptized José Gabriel Condorcanqui. He was educated by Padre Antonio López of Pampamarca and Padre Carlos Rodríguez of Yanacona in Upper Peru. He was a lineal descendant of Inca Tupac Amaru I, put to death by Toledo in 1571. The revolt began on November 4, 1780, and continued on even after the death of Tupac Amaru II.

[2] Vicente de Ballivián y Rojas (ed.), *Diario de los sucesos del cercò de la ciudad de la Paz en 1781, hasta la total pacificación de la rebelión general del Perú*, gives an excellent account of the siege.

1781. It was carried out in all its barbarity on May 18, 1781, in the main plaza of Cuzco.[1] The revolt continued in various parts of the Presidency of Charcas, however, for almost two years after the death of Tupac Amaru II. There was, of course, no hope of success for the movement begun by him. On the other hand, the Indians were neither wholly defeated nor placated by the defeat of the leader. The Revolt of Tupac Amaru II was the most powerful Indian uprising in the whole of Spanish America, and one the effects of which have not been fully obliterated even to the present day. More than a hundred thousand lives were lost in the great struggle, and an untold amount of damage was inflicted upon Spaniards and Indians alike. It was just one more link in the chain of events which ultimately brought about the independence of Upper Peru from the rule of the mother country.

One of the immediate results of the Tupac Amaru II Revolt was a further emphasis upon the system of intendencies which had been introduced in the Viceroyalty of Río de la Plata by the royal decree of October 27, 1777. By this act the control of financial affairs was taken out of the hands of the viceroy and placed in the hands of the general superintendent of the army and the treasury. In 1782 the Royal Ordinance for the Establishment and Instruction of the Intendents of the Viceroyalty of Bueno Aires (*Real ordenanza para el establecimiento e instrucción de intendentes de exército y providencia en el virreinato de Buenos Aires*) was issued. One of the purposes of the establishment of the intendency system was the removal of the abuses practiced by the *encomenderos* and *corregidores*.[2] The Viceroyalty of Río de la Plata was divided into the eight intendencies of Buenos Aires, Asunción, Tucumán, Santa Cruz de la Sierra, La Paz, Mendoza, La Plata, and Potosí. The Intendency of Santa Cruz de la Sierra also included Mojos and Chiquitos. By the supplemental royal decree of August 5, 1783, the Audiencia of Buenos Aires was henceforth confined to the region it had controlled at the end of the sixteenth century.

[1] The charges against the Inca were that he had rebelled against Spain, abolished the *mita*, caused his portrait to be painted in imitation of the Incas of old, and caused his victory at Sangarara to be represented in pictures. The Inca was compelled to witness the execution of his wife, a son, his uncle, his brother-in-law Antonio Bastidas, and his captains. He then had his tongue cut out and was torn to pieces by horses hitched to his arms and legs. His body was burned and his head and legs were stuck up in different places that had been loyal to him. His houses were demolished, his goods confiscated, his relatives declared infamous, and all the documents relating to his descent burned by the hangman. This destruction of important documents is a rather common practice in the country in great crises, and is one of the reasons for the glaring gaps in the history of Bolivia. Mendiburu gives a letter (vol. VIII, p. 137) in which Tupac Amaru II called himself "Don José I, by the grace of God, Inca, King of Perú, Quito, Chile, Buenos Aires, and the continents of the South Sea, Lord of the River of Amazons, with dominion over the Grand Paiti." It also sets forth the crimes which the king of Spain had committed against the people of the Perus. Many historians are inclined to believe that the letter was the work of Spaniards and not of the Inca, and was written for use against him.

[2] V. F. López, *Historia de Argentina* (Buenos Aires, 1883), vol. I, p. 403. Consult also Quesada, *Vireinato del Río de la Plata 1776–1810*, p. 574.

Spain had again demonstrated her desire to give Upper Peru a separate existence. Upper Peru had been separated first from Lower Peru and now from Buenos Aires. It was indeed rapidly becoming a separate political entity, and a new nationality was being formed. It may be concluded, accordingly, that Upper Peru enjoyed an almost independent existence from August 5, 1783. In 1810 Upper Peru, or the Presidency of Charcas, contained the Intendency of La Paz, the Intendency of Cochabamba, the Intendency of La Plata, the Intendency of Potosí, the Government of Mojos, and the Government of Chiquitos. The Intendency of Tarija continued to be a part of the Royal Audiencia of Buenos Aires up to 1810, when it became a part of the United Provinces of Río de la Plata.[1] In 1796 Upper Peru lost certain districts northwest of Lake Titicaca to the Viceroyalty of Peru. During the momentous years closing the eighteenth century, the Presidency of Charcas, or Upper Peru, was a loyal member of the Viceroyalty of Río de la Plata. It was keenly interested in the events of Europe and apprehensive of their outcome.

[1] The movement came to a head, as we shall see, on May 25, 1810, resulting in the establishment of an independent nation, known as the United Provinces of Río de la Plata. That nation has remained independent since that time. The movement for independence began, however, in Chuquisaca in Upper Peru on May 25, 1809. For this haste in taking up the cause of independence, and because of her mediterranean location, Upper Peru was to pay dearly, for her independence was not achieved until 1825. This Fifteen Years' War (*Guerra de Quince Años*) was to have a profound influence upon the people of Upper Peru, a fact which will be dealt with in detail in the following chapter.

THE ESTABLISHMENT OF THE REPUBLIC

The death of Charles III in 1788 was a serious loss to the Spanish people, and brought to an end a really great period in the history of the Presidency of Charcas. The new ruler, Charles IV, began his rule auspiciously. The Conde de Floridablanca was continued as first minister of state. Queen María Luisa had no intention, however, of permitting Floridablanca to remain in power longer than she could help it. She found in Manuel Godoy,[1] a member of the king's bodyguard, an able assistant. In 1792 Godoy and a group of men removed Floridablanca. In a few months Godoy was placed in an important position in the ministry, and in a short space of time he became the most powerful man in Spain. In this position he remained until the March 1808 Revolution. It was hardly to be expected that Godoy would further the interests of Spain and her colonies. In fact, Spain decreased in importance in the counsels of Europe and the Indies in proportion as the Prince of Peace grew in power at the court of Charles IV.

The internal affairs of the Presidency of Charcas were shaped for the final break with the mother country during the reign of Charles IV under the guidance of Godoy. The Audiencia continued to exert a powerful influence upon the political life of the colony. The Academia Carolina, which was composed of men of the legal profession, and which had been established in 1776, was of even greater importance as a school of theoretical and practical politics. The Academia was open to Creoles as well as Peninsulars, and became a powerful factor in the forthcoming struggle. Of still greater importance was the University of San Xavier, for it was detached from the government to a greater degree than either of the other two institutions. Together the three institutions prepared the ground for independence. Chuquisaca was, in reality, the Athens of America, in which learning as well as elegance of life flourished during the two decades of the

[1] Manuel Godoy was one of those men who rise to dizzy heights of power in the state through the ability to gain and retain the affections of women in high positions. As such he was one of the most remarkable of his class. He was born in Badajoz of parents of only mediocre social and financial position in 1767, and died in poverty and oblivion in Paris in 1851. He entered the service of the king of Spain as a member of his bodyguard, and soon attracted the attention of the queen, who seized upon him as the object of her affections. He rose from position to position of power and responsibility until he became the Prince of Peace (*el Príncipe de la Paz*), a title given him because of his success in the war with Portugal. The disastrous effects of his rule in the Presidency of Charcas will be told briefly in this narrative.

reign of Charles IV.[1] But the people could have but little respect for the monarch who permitted the paramour of the queen to exercise such great power in the state.

The immediate cause of the break with Spain was of course the Napoleonic invasion of Iberia in 1807 and 1808. In the interest of Napoleon I in Spain lay the hope of regenerating the Spanish people in the Old World as well as in the New, for there was little to be hoped for from the Prince of Asturias. Not only was Ferdinand in opposition to his parents, but he was a tool and a dupe in the hands of the enemies of his country. Above all, he was known to have all the weaknesses of his father the king. The Creoles (*criollos*) or Spaniards of America (*españoles de América*) became greatly concerned with the future of the Presidency of Charcas and the whole of the Indies. They openly criticized the Spaniards of Spain (the *godos*, or *españoles de España*) for their unwillingness to help bring about reforms in the government of the colonies. The *mestizos* supported the Creoles in their opposition to the *chapetones*, as the Peninsulars were

[1] Mendoza, *La Universidad de Charcas y la idea revolucionaria: ensayo histórico*, p. 11. In this work Mendoza expresses the opinion that in Chuquisaca "plantificaron el primer centro intelectual que debía hacerles los supremos directores de la personalidad humana en su más elevado atributo: la razón." In the first place, the students were the heirs in 1768–1808 of the great Jesuit teachings. With the expulsion of the Order of Jesus came the age of the jurists, with its logical center in the Academia Carolina. It was then that the study of law became very important. Chuquisaca became a veritable Mecca for "los peregrinos de la idea, los buscadores del saber y de la ciencia." The University was the one institution needed in Upper Peru. Mendoza explains: "En la etapa revolucionaria, el papel de la Universidad es tan transcendental, tan eficiente como lo es el funcionamiento cerebral en la económia humana." It was the doctors (*doctores*) that were the "autores de la revolución." They had little or no financial power: "Ni tenían ejércitos, ni armas, ni municiones, ni vituales, ni cuarteles, . . . —Sólo tenían su intelecto sutil, su verbo copioso, su astucia incomparable. . . . Sólo con eso fué que hicieron la revolución los doctores.—Bonaparte no tenía según los doctores ningún derecho al imperio colonial hispánico. . . . El único rey legítimo era Fernando VII." It was in this sense that the people took up the cry "¡Viva Fernando VII!" with such success on May 25, 1809, in Chuquisaca. Mendoza points to the existence of secret *juntas de libertad e independencia* in Chuquisaca and to the fact that they were well attended. Then there was also developed the other cry, "¡abajo el tirano!" Gabriel René-Moreno divides the doctors into two groups: "los doctores jurídicos y los doctores radicales." The first group wanted independence through legal means, the second wanted direct action, if necessary. Mendoza declares that the country was, of course, not ready for independence. The doctors acted more in keeping with their ancestral heritage: "Recuérdese a los Almagros, los Pizarros [Gonzalo], los Carvajal y sus secuaces, que apenas llegados a estas alturas andinas, hace cerca de cuatrocientos años, ya pensaron en rebelarse contra su rey." He calls attention also to the truth of the title of Benjamín Vicuña Mackenna's work, *La revolución de la independencia del Perú desde 1809 a 1819*. Vicuña Mackenna calls Chuquisaca "la cuna volcánica de la revolución americana." Mendoza concludes that the *idea revolucionaria* began with the Jesuits of the seventeenth century, then became more powerful through legal studies in the eighteenth century, and then in the nineteenth century took form in action. He adds: "La España obró contra sí misma al crear la Universidad de San Francisco Xavier.—Políticamente, la Universidad fué el ariete más formidable contra el grueso muro del poder español en el Alto Perú."

vulgarly called. The *mestizos* were, however, in a better position than the Creoles, for the latter were studiously kept out of the highest and most important positions in the government of the colony. These lucrative positions usually went to the Peninsulars, for the Spanish government felt that the Creoles were an inferior class, as compared with the people of the mother country. There was even greater opposition to this policy in Charcas than elsewhere because of the higher degree of learning among the Creoles of that colony.

The effect of the information concerning the Napoleonic activities in the Iberian Peninsula was to bring the conservatives and the liberals of the Presidency of Charcas into open conflict. There was a very sharp difference of opinion over the best methods to pursue in the crisis. The leaders of the conservative group were Benito María de Moxó y Francoli,[1] archbishop of La Plata, and Ramón García de León y Pizarro,[2] the president of the Audiencia of Charcas. Moxó and Pizarro were the guardians of the old order, and occupied a precarious position because of the liberal influences in the colony. The people had become increasingly concerned with questions concerning reforms. They were especially apprehensive of conditions in old Spain. In the period from 1800 to 1808 Napoleon I had conquered powerful countries, overthrown dynasties, and created new ones. What ought Upper Peru to do in case a like calamity were to befall Spain? Should they sever relations with the mother country? These and other questions were freely discussed in intellectual circles throughout the Presidency of Charcas.[3] Moxó and Pizarro believed that the people did not

[1] Archbishop Moxó was born on April 10, 1763, in Cervera-Cataluña, Spain. He was the natural son of Charles IV, and was given an excellent education. He became professor in the Real Universidad de Cataluña, a deputy in the Cortes, poet laureate in 1803, bishop of Asura in 1805, and archbishop of La Plata in the same year. He was a man of great power and prestige in Charcas, not merely because of the high position which he held, but because of his native charm and learning and ability. He exerted, as archbishop, a powerful influence throughout the entire Viceroyalty of Río de la Plata, for the archbishopric of La Plata included the whole of the viceroyalty. He was, as archbishop, next to the viceroy the most powerful man in the viceroyalty. Owing his high office to the king of Spain and to the pope, it was natural that he should be the defender of the old conservative order.

[2] Ramón García de León y Pizarro was born in Oran, Africa. Soon after his arrival in the Indies he became a very active leader. In 1793 he founded the city of Nueva Oran. He was much interested in agriculture, and did much to improve that industry in the Presidency of Quito as well as in the Presidency of Charcas. He became president of the latter in 1797 as successor to Joaquín del Pino. He was a member of the Order of Calatrava, and was made *mariscal de campo* in 1795. The latter position made him the highest ranking military officer in Upper Peru. Taborga, in his *Relaciones*, holds Pizarro in very high esteem, considering him one of the ablest men in the Presidency of Charcas. Pizarro remained at the head of the presidency until forced out of that office in May 1809. The Spanish rule in Bolivia began with a Pizarro and ended with a Pizarro. Ramón García de León y Pizarro has been called the first ruler of Upper Peru, a great compliment to his ability as an administrator.

[3] The discussion was especially heated in university circles, and particularly in the Academia Carolina. There is something in the tang of the atmosphere of Sucre that makes for disputa-

fully realize what it all meant, and they strove to quiet and calm the people's agitated minds. One of the gravest obstacles to a peaceful solution of the many problems was the ignorance of the court of Spain concerning the real situation in the Indies.

The overthrow of the Bourbon dynasty and the establishment of the Bonapartist dynasty in Spain brought consternation to the people of Charcas. The rebellion of Elio in Montevideo against the rule of Viceroy Liniers was a sign of the spirit of the age. The rise of Santiago de Liniers to the dizzy heights of viceregal power was in itself a strange proceeding. It was true that Liniers had rendered the inhabitants of Buenos Aires (the *Porteños*) very great services during the British invasion of 1806 and 1807, but he was a foreigner, which in itself was a great handicap. Liniers had become even more objectionable after his rise to power because he had turned against the liberals.[1] The news of the arrival of

---

tion, and the young men of that age, like the men of earlier ages, took great delight in such intellectual exercise. Napoleon I was a suitable subject for discussion at all times, and particularly so at that time. The liberals of the Indies had given much thought to the more important events of the previous half-century. The British American Revolution, the French Revolution, and the French American Revolution had had a powerful influence upon them, and especially the first and the last of the three, because they were efforts of colonial peoples to break away from the rule of the mother country. The French Revolution supplied them with catchwords and phrases by which to arouse enthusiasm. The Principles of Eighty-nine were the spark which set off the flame of the Spanish American Revolution. The revolutionary teachings of the French, the English, and the United States philosophers had made a fertile soil for these principles in the Presidency of Charcas. Events nearer home, such as the Revolt of Tupac Amaru II, emphasized the defects in the Spanish colonial system and the urgency of the need of reforms. The gigantic struggle between Great Britain and France, intensified by the genius of Napoleon I, forced these liberals of Charcas to consider fundamental issues. The activities of the British in Buenos Aires in 1806 and 1807 gave the people of the presidency grave concern. The support given to Francisco de Miranda for more than a score of years by the British government was not unknown to them, and awakened in them the hope for a change in the colonial régime. The invasion of Portugal by France late in 1807 and the flight of the court of Portugal to Brazil brought home to the liberals the importance of the events in western Europe. With the court of Portugal in Brazil, the fear of renewed efforts by the Portuguese against the territorial possessions of Spain was intensified. The victories of the Porteños in those momentous crises were an object lesson of the utmost importance to the Upper Peruvians (*Altoperuanos*). It showed them the potential power of the colonists. It is essential here to keep in mind the wide interests of the intellectuals of Upper Peru during these formative periods. The point is not that the people of this colony were the only ones who thought about these things. There was no important center in any part of the Indies which did not have its intellectual liberals. One of the gravest errors of the uninformed is the notion that all the people of Spanish America were steeped in ignorance, superstition, and inexperience. On the contrary, every country had a group of men, small to be sure, that were exceptionally well versed in the ideology of the times. The point here made, however, is that of the Spanish American liberals those of Upper Peru were among the best informed and most intellectual. That they should be fully alive to the larger significance of the events of their age was inevitable. Such interest had its results, as this study will demonstrate.

[1] Santiago de Liniers was a Frenchman born in France in 1756. He had been forced to leave

the Marquis Bernardo de Sassenay in Montevideo on August 11, 1808, as the representative of the new French régime in Spain, did not improve matters. The arrival of the Peruvian General José Manuel de Goyeneche in Buenos Aires on August 19, 1808, as the agent of the Central Junta of Seville, was of even greater importance, because of the great rôle he was to play in the Presidency of Charcas.[1] Goyeneche had come by way of Rio de Janeiro, Brazil. While in the latter city he had become interested in the movement to place Carlota, the wife of Prince Regent John of Portugal and the oldest sister of the deposed King Ferdinand VII, on the Spanish throne. The claims of Carlota would probably have been received with greater favor had she renounced her rights to the throne of Portugal, but she had no desire to relinquish that claim, and really desired to annex Spain and its colonies to Portugal. Goyeneche was instrumental in arousing interest in the claims of Carlota immediately upon his arrival in Buenos

his country during its revolution and had come to Spain to enter her military service. He had previously come to Spain as early as 1775, but had returned to France only to leave it again. He saw in the British invasion of Buenos Aires an opportunity for service. With the aid of troops from Montevideo he forced Beresford to surrender in 1807. This made him the hero of the hour to the Porteños, who, in an open town meeting (*cabildo abierto*) of Buenos Aires, elected him viceroy of Río de la Plata after deposing Rafael Sobremonte from that office. Liniers continued in the office because the act of the *cabildo abierto* of Buenos Aires was approved by the government of Spain during the turbulent period of 1809–1810. He was opposed to the radical measures of the Porteños in 1810, and was deposed, arrested, and executed in that same year by the very people whom he had saved from the yoke of the British in 1806–1807. This act, for which Mariano Moreno was primarily to blame, has been condemned as well as praised. Liniers belongs to that interesting group of men in Spanish America who turn conservative after they get into power. It is, however, probably not correct to say that Liniers had turned conservative, for he probably had not, but he refrained from going along with the radicals who gradually came to assume control of the government of the viceroyalty, especially after the revolutionists had taken control of the government of the country.

[1] José Manuel de Goyeneche was born in Arequipa, Peru, of a prominent family. The rôle he played in the Presidency of Charcas will be narrated briefly later. The cruel vindictive manner of the man is well illustrated in his proceedings in La Paz. He was duly rewarded by a grateful monarch for having reduced the revolt throughout the Altiplanicie; he was made Conde de Haqui and accumulated great riches. He is very naturally hated with all the fervor of an outraged people. Jáuregui Rosquellas calls him "el feroz Goyeneche" who "demostró sus instintos de hiena," and adds: "Cuando ya había obtenido el título de Conde de Guaqui, que fué premio de una traición, y cuando ya tenía enorme fortuna acumulada que le permitía vivir con los humos de un gran guerrero, de un ilustre prócer y de un paladín, como él pensaba serlo, pidió su retiro y fué substituído por Pezuela." That he was treated much after the fashion in which Benedict Arnold was treated in England is indicated by this statement from the same author: "En España asilé su grandeza ensangrentada y traidora, él hizo alarde de sus glorias. Pero sus acciones fueron conocidas y la opinión le señaló como a un miserable, no obstante el esplendor de que estaba rodeado." On the other hand, he was, according to the historian López of Argentina, a rather handsome but haughty man, and one who loved to dress in the fashion of the day, and with much show. He was, in many respects, a very distinguished son of Arequipa, and of Spain in the Americas.

Aires. A powerful party was organized to establish an empire in Spanish America with Carlota as ruler. Goyeneche found a lively supporter in Viceroy Liniers. Liniers sought to induce Carlota to come to Buenos Aires to take over the government of the viceroyalty. He wanted her to govern Spain and the Indies from Buenos Aires as she and her husband were governing Portugal and Brazil from Rio de Janeiro. Many historians, including Bartolomé Mitre, are of the opinion that had Carlota come in person to Buenos Aires she could easily have become the ruler of Argentina, and possibly of the whole Spanish Empire.

The events in Buenos Aires intensified the gravity of the situation in the Presidency of Charcas. The Chuquiseños discussed with more warmth than ever the delicacy of the situation. They discussed fundamentals. Many believed in the doctrines of St. Thomas Aquinas. They held that the sovereignty of the people reverted to the people when a king had been deposed. They believed that since the Bourbon dynasty had been overthrown the people had the right to choose another dynasty, or to establish another form of government, if they so desired. Moxó and Pizarro, on the other hand, were staunch supporters of the deposed king, and they were determined to save Upper Peru for him at any cost. Many of the men learned in the law argued that the whole question should be discussed in a *cabildo abierto*, and urged Pizarro to call such a meeting. The judges of the Royal Audiencia favored this idea; but the support of the judges was not due to any favor for the plan, but rather to the fact that they opposed Pizarro, and saw in it an opportunity to force him out of office. In the midst of these discussions Goyeneche came to Chuquisaca demanding to be received as the official representative of the Central Junta of Seville.

The Audiencia met on September 18, 1808, to consider his claims. The commission presented by Goyeneche was found to be irregular, and was rejected. Goyeneche protested this action, but decided to await new instructions. These arrived soon afterward, and on September 23 the Audiencia met to consider the new credentials, and found them also unacceptable. Moxó supported the viceroy in his refusal to accept the position of the Audiencia, and demanded a reconsideration of the whole problem. Another meeting was held by the Audiencia for this purpose on November 12. The conduct of Goyeneche, however, was so offensive that the position of Moxó and Pizarro became more precarious. What did Goyeneche want? He represented three different bodies: the Central Junta of Seville, Joseph I, and Carlota. The correspondence of Carlota was turned over to the University of San Xavier, and was found to be irregular. She was duly informed of that fact. The first period of reform had come to an end with a victory for the liberal forces.

The second period, or phase, of the movement for independence began in May 1809. Moxó and the viceroy resolved upon a more drastic course of action. On May 21 the liberals brought the crisis to an abrupt head. Judge José Agustín Ussoz accused Pizarro of treason in the session of the Audiencia because of the support he was giving to the Carlotinos, as the supporters of the claims of

Carlota were called. This was the beginning of the end of Spanish rule in Upper Peru, for the sentiment against the conservatives grew in strength rapidly. But there was still a great deal of sympathy for the deposed king. The leaders of the liberal forces decided to follow the example of liberal leaders in other parts of the Indies, notably of those in Montevideo, Buenos Aires, Caracas, Bogotá, and Mexico City, and take over the government. The *cabildo abierto* of Chuquisaca, however, was primarily juridical, while those of the other cities were primarily military in character. Pizarro had no armed forces at hand. He had sent urgent orders on May 23 to Francisco de Paula Sanz, intendent of Potosí, to bring armed forces to aid him. But Sanz failed to do so, and Pizarro was left powerless to deal with the situation in Chuquisaca. Juan Antonio Álvarez de Arenales, a military officer in Buenos Aires, gave support to the Chuquiseños then as well as later.

The situation in Chuquisaca became hourly more critical. Pizarro failed to realize the dangerous position that he was in, and acted tyrannically. On the morning of May 25, 1809, he gave orders for the arrest of the judges of the Royal Audiencia. All of them had gotten beyond his reach, except Jaime Zudáñez, who was promptly taken and cast into prison. This act enraged the people and caused the liberal leaders to put an end to an intolerable situation. The people gathered in the Plaza Mayor of Chuquisaca on this day and demanded the release of Zudáñez and the overthrow of Pizarro. They took the law into their own hands, immediately released Zudáñez, arrested Pizarro,[1] and forced Moxó to flee to Siccha for safety. The people then proceeded to set up their own government. They had immortalized May 25, 1809, by launching a movement for independence from Spain. It was a movement not merely against an oppressive government in the Presidency of Charcas but in favor of complete political independence. The Chuquiseños deserve, accordingly, the honor of having taken the first overt action for Spanish American independence. It was the logical result of years of intelligent agitation for a share in a government of their own making.

The Audiencia took over the government and selected Álvarez de Arenales

[1] Jáuregui Rosquellas gives the names of the men who took an active part in the events of the memorable twenty-fifth of May, 1809: Bernardo Monteagudo, José Joaquin de Lemoine, Jaime and Manuel Zudañes, Domingo de Anivarro, Mariano Michel, Juan Antonio Fernandez, José Antonio Álvarez de Arenales, Pedro Ignacio del Rivero, Juan Antonio Paredes, Vicente Rodriguez Romano, Angel Mariano Toro, Angel de Alonso y Gutiérrez, José Sivilat, Fermín Cueto, Luis Mariano Terrazas, Antonio Anava y Zárate, Tomas de Alcérreca, Manuel Gil, Gabriel Argüelles, Pedro Antonio Cabezas Vargas, Mariano Fariñas, Marcos Miranda, Manuel Corcuera, Juan Lorenzo Mirabal, Manuel de Entrambasaguas, José Mariano Serrano, Juan Bautista Villegas, Manuel Mercado, José Benito Alcérreca, José Patricio Malavia, Manuel Eusebio Ruiz, Fortunato Lemoine, José Manuel de Lemoine, Toribio Salinas, Pedro Carvajal, Diego Ruiz, Miguel Monteagudo, Francisco Cecilio, Lorenzo Saavedra, Pedro Dorado, Francisco de Entrambasaguas, José Sotomayor, Mariano Guzmán, and Nicolas Larrazabal (*La ciudad de los cuatro nombres*, p. 179, note 1).

to take charge of the administration of the presidency. It gave him valiant support, furnished the people with arms, and urged support of the independence movement throughout the country. Missions were sent to the other cities of the presidency to urge them to take action similar to that taken in Chuquisaca.[1] The missions did good work. As early as July 16, 1809, the people of La Paz overthrew the government and set up the Defensive Junta of the Rights of the King and of the People (*Junta Tuitiva de los Derechos del Rei i del Pueblo*). Governor Dávilla, Bishop La Santa, and other authorities were forced to resign.[2]

The course of events in La Paz brought on a serious conflict with the viceregal authorities at Lima as well as at Buenos Aires. Viceroy Abascal of Peru sent Goyeneche with a force of some five thousand men to put down the uprising in La Paz. Goyeneche was the man for the task. He was astute, ambitious, courageous, intriguing, crafty, and cruel, one of the most formidable enemies of the Patriot cause in Spanish America. He went about his task with zeal and perseverance. He was able to reduce the revolution more easily because of traitorous defection in the Patriot ranks. Indaburú went over to the Royalists, but was killed in a counter-revolution under Murillo on October 18. On October 25 Goyeneche attacked Murillo at Chacaltaya and defeated him after a brief engagement. Domingo Tristan was sent by Goyeneche to defeat the Patriots under Victoria Lanza. The Patriots were defeated in the Yungas of La Paz, and were made to pay the penalty of rebellion. Goyeneche took a heavy toll of his enemies. Examples had to be made of the leaders. Accordingly Murillo, Catacora, Jaime, Jiménez, Granero, Sagárnaga, Figuero, and Bueno were executed in La Paz. The movement for independence had been crushed, for the time, in the Province of La Paz.

Viceroy Liniers of Río de La Plata sent General Vicente Nieto to put down the revolt in Chuquisaca. He was given the title of president and pacifier of Chuquisaca, and entered that city formally on December 24. He took possession of the government, but followed a more conciliatory course than Goyeneche, the Tiger of Arequipa (*el Tigre de Arequipa*). The Chuquiseños, however, were a very formidable group of opponents. They had governed them-

[1] Juan Manuel Mercado, Mariano Michel, and Francisco Rios were sent to La Paz; Benito Alcérreca and a little later Manuel Zudañes were sent to Cochabamba; and Bernardo Monteagudo was sent to Potosí and Chichas. Bernardo Monteagudo was also sent later to Lima. Antonio Paredes was sent to Puno, Arequipa, and Cuzco; and Joaquin de Lemoine and others were sent to Oruro (Jáuregui Rosquellas, *La ciudad de los cuatro nombres*, pp. 181–182).

[2] Pedro Domingo Murillo was placed in command of the troops. Later he was elected president of the Defensive Junta of the Rights of the King and the People. He was a native of La Paz, and a very able man. An interesting feature of the government of La Paz was the treatment of the Indians. An Indian was chosen to the Junta from each of the *partidos* of the province. The Junta also issued a proclamation to the people urging them to support the cause of independence.

selves for more than seven months, or from May 25 to December 24, 1809, and had become conscious of their power as well as of their rights. They might be expected to put up a very stubborn resistance to any effort to reduce them to a colonial status.

The revolutionary activities in the Viceroyalty of Río de la Plata next broke out in Buenos Aires. A veritable exodus of Patriots had moved upon the port city from Chuquisaca. Among the men who migrated to Buenos Aires to aid in the movement for independence were Cornelio Saavedra, Mariano Moreno, Juan José Castelli, Bernardo Monteagudo, and Manuel Belgrano.[1] Many of these were alumni of the University of San Xavier and members of the Academia Carolina. These men helped to bring about the overthrow of the government of Baltasar de Cisneros. On May 25, 1810, a new government was sworn in as the Provisional Junta of the Provinces of Río de la Plata. One of the main objectives of this Junta was to establish its power over the whole of the former Viceroyalty of Río de la Plata. It was this larger purpose of the Porteños that brought about a new phase of the independence movement in Upper Peru.

The movement in Upper Peru had not, however, been suppressed. On the contrary it spread to the other centers of the presidency. On September 14, 1810, the people of Cochabamba revolted against the rule of Spain, Francisco Rivero, Estevan Arce, and Melchor Guzmán Quitón taking the lead. The Cochabambinos won an immortal battle at Aroma, and did noble service in the cause of independence. The people of Oruro followed shortly, setting up an independent government under the leadership of Tomás Barrón. In November of the same year, Potosí revolted against Spain and set up a governmental junta with Matos, Molina, Ascárrate, Eguivar, Nogales, Quintana, and Millares as members. Later the people of Santa Cruz de la Sierra also revolted and set up an independent government. During the remaining years of the Fifteen Years' War (*Guerra de Quince Años*), Upper Peru played a very interesting but a less important rôle. The Porteños continued for several years their efforts to drive the Royalists out of Upper Peru, but failed to do so. The liberation of Upper Peru was to come from Lower Peru and not from Buenos Aires, as was to be expected.[2]

[1] Jáuregui Rosquellas adds these others to the list: Araoz, Bustamante, Andrade, Madrano, Molina, Gorriti, Zapiola, Gazcón, Gómez, Agrelo, Medina, Boedo, Castro, Aldao, Frías, and Pedriel.

[2] General Nieto was replaced by General Juan José Castelli in 1810 as the representative of the Supreme Junta of Buenos Aires in Chuquisaca. Castelli was able to collect a considerable amount of money for the Patriot cause in Potosí as well as Chuquisaca and other municipalities. Following Castelli came General Juan Ramírez y Orosco and General Manuel Belgrano. The latter spent some time in Potosí. He went north to meet the Royalists and was disastrously defeated by them at Vilcapujki and Ayoma, and forced to retire. These defeats were followed by a large migration from Chuquisaca and Potosí to Jujui, Salta, and Tucumán. General José Randeau then came with an army, but he was defeated by Viceroy Pezuela at

The situation in Europe had, in the period under consideration, made the success of the Royalists in Spanish America very difficult. The situation in Spain itself had undergone several important changes. As early as January 22, 1809, the Central Junta of Seville had declared, in a moment of patriotic fervor, that the Spaniards of the New World and the Old were equal, and that the old division line between them had been forever removed. In the organization of the Cortes, which was to meet in Cadiz, the Indies were to have a part. The difficulty of holding elections in the Indies for deputies to the Cortes made the selection almost impossible. Many of the deputies were thus chosen from among the Americans in Spain. But the men selected in that manner proved to be a very able group. The American delegation (*delegación Americana*) never swerved from its loyalty to the *causa santa*, as the American cause has been called. Perhaps the most important achievement of the Cortes of 1810–1813 was the political constitution which it adopted. The instrument is known as the Constitution of 1812, and was adopted on March 18 of that year. Despite the ridicule which has been heaped upon it, the Constitution was a remarkable document. It was sworn to throughout the Indies and, in the period of constitution-making in the newly created states, became a prototype. The Constitution of 1812 was, in the first place, drawn from the fundamental laws then in existence, or from those which had served as fundamental laws up to that time. The influence of the political thought of Great Britain, France, and the United States was very great. Greater in importance was the influence of the political thought of Spain herself, especially of the Spain of the periods of her greatest political achievement.

There is nothing more illuminating to the student of constitutional government in Spain and Spanish America than the manner in which the men of the Cortes of 1810–1813 searched the annals of their own people for the ideas and forms which they felt they needed for the establishment of an independent political régime. The French in their eagerness to regain the political soul of France never sought more strenuously for it, during the period 1798–1800, than did the Spaniards of 1810–1813.[1] The Cortes of Cadiz sought to draw up a

---

Lipilipi and Viloma in 1815. Only partially successful was the army under command of General La Madrid. In the meantime, the guerrilla warfare was kept up, and the *guerreros*, like Padilla and Warne, did good work for the Patriots, especially against the ferocious Miguel Tacón. These several attempts to liberate Upper Peru, and through it Lower Peru, illustrate the futility of the efforts from Buenos Aires. Since 1812, the campaigns in Upper Peru had been growing less popular, owing to the pronounced opposition of General José de San Martín. He had returned in 1812 and had not hesitated in denouncing these campaigns and refusing to accept the command of them. His wish was respected and he was appointed governor of the Province of Cuyo in order that he might be able to organize an expedition against Lima by way of Chile and the Pacific later.

[1] Consult Cleven, "Modern political life in Hispanic America," *in* A. Curtis Wilgus (ed.), *Modern Hispanic America*, pp. 70–138.

fundamental law that should best meet the needs of the Spanish people in both hemispheres. In the first place, the members of the Cortes represented a new age. Representatives of the third estate were in the majority, and more particularly men influenced by the ideas of the age. Most of the members, it must be admitted, were lacking in practical political experience, and experimented with untried theories. Nevertheless the fundamental law prepared by them has had a larger influence upon later political life in Spanish America than is generally believed. A rather detailed digest of the document is, therefore, in place here.

The document began with the statement that Ferdinand VII was "by the grace of God and the Constitution of the Spanish Monarchy, King of the Spains, and in his absence and captivity, the Regency of the Realm, nominated by the General and Extraordinary Cortes." The Constitution declared that the Spanish nation was free and independent, and that it was not and never could become the patrimony of any family or person.[1] The nation was a "union of all the Spanish people in both hemispheres."[2] The sovereignty was declared to be vested in the nation, which alone had the exclusive power to make the fundamental laws.[3] The territorial possessions of the monarchy in the four continents were given in detail.[4] The religion of the state was the Apostolic Roman Catholic, to the utter exclusion of the public worship of all others.[5] The object of government was declared to be the "happiness of the Nation since the main purpose of all political societies is the care and wellbeing of those that compose them."[6] The Cortes, as the national legislature, was to assemble once a year, and was to consist of representatives from both hemispheres.[7] The representation was proportional: one deputy for each 70,000 inhabitants. In case there were less than 140,000 and more than 105,000 two deputies were to be chosen.[8] The deputies were to be chosen in parochial, county, and provincial elections.[9] The manner of conducting the three types of election was explained in great detail.[10]

[1] Cleven (trans.), *The constitutions of Spain of 1808 and 1812*, pp. 1–2, art. 2.

[2] *Ibid.*, p. 1, art. 1.

[3] *Ibid.*, p. 2, art. 3.

[4] *Ibid.*, p. 3, art. 10.

[5] *Ibid.*, p. 3, art. 12.

[6] *Ibid.*, p. 4, art. 13.

[7] *Ibid.*, pp. 6–7, arts. 28–29.

[8] *Ibid.*, p. 7, arts. 32–33.

[9] *Ibid.*, p. 7, art. 34.

[10] *Ibid.*, pp. 7–21, arts. 35–103.

The annual sessions of the Cortes were to be held in the capital of the kingdom but might be held in another place if conditions demanded it.[1] The latter provision is of interest because a like provision will be found in the political constitutions of Bolivia. The sessions of the Cortes were to be opened and closed in the presence of the king, who was to deliver an address on the state of the monarchy at the opening session.[2] The deputies were to enjoy the usual immunities guaranteed members of legislative assemblies, but they were not allowed to accept or to solicit appointments from the king.[3] The powers of the Cortes were of course to be many and were given in detail.[4] The Cortes had final control of legislation in that an act passed over the veto of the king became a law.[5] The Cortes had the right to choose the Permanent Commission, composed of seven members, three from the European, three from the overseas provinces, and one of two deputies, one from the European and another from the overseas provinces, chosen by lot.[6] This body will be found to have its counterpart in several of the Bolivian constitutions. The Cortes could be called in special session by the king or by the Permanent Commission.[7]

The person of the king was sacred and inviolable and he could do no wrong.[8] The powers of the king were many, as were the things which he might not do.[9] He could not prevent the Cortes from meeting, nor could he suspend or dismiss it, or interfere in its affairs.[10] The oath which the king had to take was in keeping with the ideas of the hour, binding him to the very letter of the Constitution and the laws.[11] The Cortes had the right to prevent the heir to the throne from succeeding to it if it considered him incapable of ruling, or for crimes committed.[12] Of the seven secretaries of state, one was to be secretary of the interior for the overseas provinces.[13] The secretaries of state were responsible for the acts

[1] Cleven (trans.), *The constitutions of Spain of 1808 and 1812*, p. 21, arts. 104–105.

[2] *Ibid.*, p. 24, art. 121.

[3] *Ibid.*, p. 25, arts. 128–129.

[4] *Ibid.*, pp. 26–28, art. 131.

[5] *Ibid.*, pp. 29–31, arts. 142–153.

[6] *Ibid.*, p. 32, art. 157.

[7] *Ibid.*, pp. 33–34, arts. 161–167.

[8] *Ibid.*, p. 34, art. 168.

[9] *Ibid.*, pp. 34–36, art. 171.

[10] *Ibid.*, pp. 36–37, art. 172.

[11] *Ibid.*, pp. 37–38, art. 173.

[12] *Ibid.*, pp. 39–40, art. 181.

[13] *Ibid.*, p. 45, art. 222.

which they committed contrary to the Constitution and the laws.[1] All the orders of the king had to be countersigned by a secretary of state.[2] Of the forty members composing the Council of State, twelve had to have been born in the overseas provinces.[3]

The judiciary was given large powers, in the explanation of which the Constitution laid down certain rights to which all Spaniards were entitled.[4] There were also provisions for the government of local units, the municipalities and the provinces having the right to hold deliberative councils. The provision governing taxation was a modern one, taxation in proportion to wealth, and without exemption or privilege. There were to be customs offices only at the seaports and on the frontiers.[5] In addition to the regular army there was to be a national militia.[6] Much attention was also given to public education, provision being made for primary schools in all the municipalities, and for secondary schools and universities.[7] All Spaniards on assuming public office, civil, military, or ecclesiastical, were to take an oath to observe the Constitution, to be loyal to the king, and to perform the duties of the office to which they had been elected or appointed.[8] The document also provided means for amending the Constitution. The right to amend lay in the Cortes, and was to be carried out in the manner of making laws.[9] The Constitution might not be amended, however, until eight years had elapsed after its adoption.[10]

The Constitution of 1812 remained in force only until the return of Ferdinand VII to the throne in 1814. During the period between 1814 and 1821 Ferdinand ruled without benefit of the Constitution. But with the overthrow of the absolutist régime in 1821, the Constitution of 1812 was again in force. King Ferdinand VII took an oath to support it, though it was merely lip service. When he again regained control of the reins of government he reestablished the nonconstitutional régime. It was during this second brief period of liberal rule in Spain that the Cortes again sought to conciliate the overseas Spaniards. On

[1] Cleven (trans.), *The constitutions of Spain of 1808 and 1812*, p. 46, art. 226.

[2] *Ibid.*, pp. 45–46, art. 225.

[3] *Ibid.*, p. 47, art. 232.

[4] *Ibid.*, pp. 48–49, arts. 243–308.

[5] *Ibid.*, pp. 65–68, arts. 338–355.

[6] *Ibid.*, pp. 68–69, arts. 356–361.

[7] *Ibid.*, pp. 69–70, arts. 366–371.

[8] *Ibid.*, p. 70, art. 374.

[9] *Ibid.*, pp. 70–71, arts. 375–384.

[10] *Ibid.*, p. 70, art. 375. The Constitution was signed by Francisco López Lisperguer, Manuel Rodrigo, and Luis de Velasco from Buenos Aires.

June 24, 1821, the Cortes adopted a plan for the selection of the members of the American deputation (*deputación Americana*).[1] The chaotic conditions in Upper Peru, however, prevented the Upper Peruvians (*Altoperuanos*) from taking advantage of this plan. Nor had it been possible to make use of the legislation for the abolition of the Negro slave trade.[2] Ferdinand VII issued his famous decree forbidding this trade in 1817, but had difficulty in enforcing the decree. The proximity of Upper Peru to Brazil made the question of the traffic in Negro slaves a complicated one for the Altoperuanos.

The Fifteen Years' War, which had seemed doomed to become an eternal war (*una guerra eterna*), continued on even after all the countries of Spanish America had been liberated from the rule of Spain.[3] San Martín and Bolívar had done their great work as liberators before Upper Peru was given the aid she so richly deserved. Despite all the interest that San Martín may have had in the ultimate liberation of this region, he failed to take the steps that might have liberated it along with Lower Peru and the Presidency of Quito three years earlier.[4]

General Pedro de Olañeta took over the control of Upper Peru during the last years of the colonial period. After 1821 he was still a loyal supporter of

[1] Cleven, *Readings in Hispanic American history*, pp. 444–446.

[2] *Ibid.*, pp. 429–433. The *British and foreign state papers*, vol. IV, pp. 536–543, contains the report of the Council of the Indies on this whole slave question. Of especial importance was the opinion of the minority opposing the immediate emancipation of the Negro slaves, found on pp. 543–549 in the same volume.

[3] This does not include, of course, either Cuba or Panama, both of which became independent later: Cuba in 1898, Panama in 1903.

[4] Wilgus (ed.), *South American dictators*. Consult Cleven on "The dictators of Peru, Bolivia, and Ecuador" in that work, pp. 215–288, for the work of San Martín and Bolívar in Peru. In regard to Cuba it should be said that there were plans for her liberation in the Bolivarian period. The United States of America, however, wished otherwise. The men at the head of the government of our country between 1822 and 1850 supported Spain in her possession of Cuba, as the best all-around arrangement for the Caribbean and for the United States. Cuba has always been of the utmost importance to our country, or rather the United States has always felt that way about the island. The thing to bear in mind, however, is that while the United States was interested in the Congress of 1826 at Panama, and provided for a diplomatic mission to that historic body, she was determined that no one country or group of countries should control the destinies of Cuba. Believing that the people of Cuba were incapable of governing themselves, and unwilling that either Great Colombia or Mexico, or both, should either aid Cuba in that delicate task or annex her, the United States government preferred to have the island remain in the possession of Spain. After 1850 the policy changed. The government of the United States wanted Cuba to break with Spain. If she could not be induced to seek annexation to the United States, she might at least become independent. By 1898 the situation had become intolerable in Cuba and the United States fought Spain for the independence of the island, which since that time has been free of the rule of Spain. As for Panama, the great interest in the Isthmian routes led the United States to aid her in liberating herself from the rule of Colombia in 1903.

Ferdinand VII, the absolutist monarch, and refused to assist either the Royalists of liberal Spain or the Patriots of Upper Peru. He carried on a war for the establishment of an independent kingdom in Upper Peru in order to preserve it for Ferdinand VII. It was not, however, until the Spanish forces had been defeated in Lower Peru in 1824 that the Patriots turned upon Pedro de Olañeta in real earnest.[1] The glorious victory of Ayacucho left the Liberating Army free to turn its attention to Upper Peru. After several efforts to induce Olañeta to join the Patriot forces, Bolívar determined to crush him. Bolívar explained in a letter to Santander of Great Colombia of January 23, 1825, that if he did not destroy Olañeta, Olañeta would destroy him and the whole of Spanish America "assisted by the Prince of Brazil and all the *godos* of this world."[2]

Bolívar was also concerned about the interest that the United Provinces of Río de la Plata was taking in the situation in Upper Peru. He was aware of the chaotic conditions in European countries and feared the effects of these upon the situation in the Americas. The assassination of Bernardo Monteagudo in Lima he believed to be the work of agents of the Holy Alliance.[3] He believed also that

[1] The liberation of Lower Peru was achieved in the second year of the dictatorship of Bolívar in Peru. It took famous battles to bring this about, however: the battle of Junín on August 6, 1824, and the battle of Ayacucho on December 9 of the same year. The former was won by Simón Bolívar, as commander of the Liberating Army, the latter by the immortal Antonio José de Sucre. The battle of Junín has been selected by the Fathers of the Republic of Bolivia for special commemoration, as will be emphasized in this study. Had Bolívar won the battle of Ayacucho it is not unlikely that that battle, rather than Junín, would have had the larger place in the lives of the Bolivian people.

[2] Vicente Lecuna, *Cartas del Libertador*, vol. IV, pp. 250–252. Simón Bolívar was a voluminous writer and left excellent accounts of many of his actions as well as of his views. Lecuna has made a valuable collection of his writings. In this letter to Santander Bolívar dealt with the world situation in considerable detail, as he was wont to do with other events of this fateful period. These *Cartas* should be read and reread in order to get an idea of what Bolívar had on his mind at this time. The year 1825 was, as we shall see, of the greatest importance to Bolívar, to the peoples of South America, and to the whole of the Americas at that time. Bolívar began his third year as dictator of Peru in that year and was determined to work out the larger ideas which he had hatched for the Americas and the world. These ideas will be found expressed in detail in the letters contained in the volumes covering this period in the Lecuna collection.

[3] Monteagudo had been one of the most important as well as the most powerful ministers of the Supreme Protector San Martín of Peru. He had made himself thoroughly obnoxious and utterly impossible to the people of Lima. He was overthrown and exiled during the absence of San Martín in Guayaquil in 1822 for the famous interview with Bolívar. Since that time he had spent much of his time with Bolívar in Ecuador and had, as was natural, made a great impression upon him. At the time that Bolívar learned to know him personally, Monteagudo had become quite definitely convinced of the need of a highly centralized government for the people of Spanish America, and had worked to that end as minister of state under San Martín. In 1825 he returned to Lima, and was pounced upon by the infuriated Limeños and killed like a dog.

The career of Monteagudo is one of the most spectacular in all the history of Spanish

Brazil was becoming more dangerous to Spanish America, primarily because of her close relation with the Holy Alliance, and that General Olañeta was a tool of the Holy Alliance, actually in its service. Hence he was determined to have him destroyed.[1] He did not want to undertake the task himself, but he would send an army to bring Upper Peru under his control. He was of the opinion that Upper Peru was a region coveted by all its neighbors because of the great wealth of Potosí, one of the richest cities of the world. Bolívar also understood that he was in a very difficult position in relation to these countries, especially those that had achieved independence without his direct aid. The leaders of those countries looked upon him as a grave potential danger, as great as, if not greater than, that from either Brazil or the Holy Alliance. It was this delicate situation in South America itself that made the year 1825 so important in American history.

Bolívar selected Sucre to command the Liberating Army in Upper Peru and ordered him to liberate that region from the control of its enemies. Sucre crossed the Desaguadero River early in 1825 and began earnestly to study the entire situation in Upper Peru. He soon became aware of the existence of a militant nationality, a nationality seeking expression. By the time he arrived in La Paz, February 7, 1825, he came to see the need of giving the people of the country an opportunity to determine for themselves their future political status. On February 9, 1825, he issued his famous decree convoking a deliberative assembly for the provinces of Upper Peru. In the preface to the decree he declared that the Liberating Army had crossed the Desaguadero for the sole purpose of freeing the provinces of Upper Peru from Spanish oppression and of restoring their political rights. He declared that the Liberating Army would not interfere with their domestic affairs, but would, of course, maintain order and prevent anarchy and disorder. He further declared that it was the wish of the United Provinces of Río de La Plata to let the people of Upper Peru determine their own political future. He ordered the election of deputies for such

America. From Chuquisaca he went in 1810 to Buenos Aires, where he took a prominent part in the overthrow of the Spanish power and later in the internal government of the United Provinces of Río de la Plata. He made himself so obnoxious with his egoistic radicalism that he was forced into exile. While in Europe he underwent a complete change of thought, going over into the most conservative circles. On his return to Argentina, in 1816, he joined the Army of the Andes under San Martín. He became most valuable to the latter and doubtless had a great deal to do with his efforts to set up an aristocratic government in Peru. He was a very able journalist and exercised great influence through the press. He is a conspicuous example of the rôle of the mulatto in the history of Spanish America.

[1] Lecuna, *Cartas del Libertador*, vol. IV, pp. 252–253, 255–258, letter to Juan Pay del Castillo of January 23, 1825, and to Santander of February 9, 1825. To the former he declared that no one knew just what General Olañeta might do. Hence he had ordered Sucre into Upper Peru with ten thousand troops to induce him to join the Patriot cause or to drive him out of the country. And to Santander Bolívar declared that there was no room in America for Olañeta as long as he continued to oppose the Patriot cause.

an assembly. The votes were to be counted in the *partidos* on March 18, and in the capitals of the departments on March 31, 1825. He named the five larger provinces departments: the Department of La Paz, the Department of Cochabamba, the Department of Chuquisaca, the Department of Potosí, and the Department of Santa Cruz. He gave the number of deputies to be selected in the several cantons (*cantones*) of each department, and prescribed the qualifications for each deputy.[1] The deputies were to assemble in Oruro on April 15, 1825, for a preparatory meeting. The General Assembly of Upper Peru (*Asamblea General del Alto Perú*) was to begin its formal sessions on April 19, 1825. In order to give the people perfect freedom of action in the assembly, the Liberating Army was to be kept away from the city where the assembly was to meet. He concluded the decree by declaring that the governments of Lower Peru and the United Provinces of Río de la Plata would be formally informed of the proceedings of the assembly, and that the Liberating Army had no desire whatever to impose its will upon the people of Upper Peru. The step was being taken solely in the interest of their freedom and well-being.[2]

Sucre had taken a very serious step without due deliberation. Bolívar's reaction was instant and severe. On February 21, 1825, he wrote his famous letter from Lima in which he took Sucre to task because he had acted without the necessary authority. He sharply reminded him of the task he had been sent into Upper Peru to perform, and informed him that he was still serving under him as dictator of Peru. For while Sucre was in command of the troops of Great Colombia, he was not an officer of that country, nor under Bolívar as dictator of that country, because he was no longer its dictator, but under him as dictator of Peru. He declared that neither he nor Sucre, nor the Congress of Peru, nor that of Colombia, had a right to violate the basic public law of America.

He pointed out that the republican governments that had been formed in Spanish America had been formed out of units within viceroyalties, captaincies general, and presidencies like that of Chile. Upper Peru, on the other hand, was, he declared, an immediate dependency of the Viceroyalty of Buenos Aires, as

[1] The naming of these divisions was of great significance, for the larger divisions of the republic have continued to be called departments and not states or commonwealths. The decree provided that a deputy to the assembly must be at least twenty-five years of age, a native of the department or resident therein for four years, a supporter of the cause of independence, public-spirited, and of known moral integrity. No man might refuse to serve in the office to which he had been elected. Those illegally elected were to be expelled from the assembly and declared "indignas de la confianza del pueblo." Herein Sucre gave form to a practice which has been used throughout the period of the republic as a favorite way of expressing hatred of acts unworthy of a citizen of the state.

[2] *Colección oficial de leyes, decretos, órdenes, resoluciones, de la República Boliviana, años 1825 y 1826*, pp. 1–5. (Hereinafter to be cited as *Colección oficial, años 1825 y 1826.*) The decree explained, as was to be expected, the manner of conducting the elections in great detail. Sucre was laying down a mode of procedure that might be used as an example for later elections.

Quito de Santa Fé was of Great Colombia. Chile and Guatemala, he admitted, had become independent, although they had been parts of viceroyalties: the one of the Viceroyalty of Peru, the other of the Viceroyalty of New Spain. But neither Ecuador nor Upper Peru could be constituted an independent nation without a treaty between the parties concerned, or as a result of war, or by action of the congresses which had jurisdiction over them. He declared that Sucre's decree of February 9, convoking an assembly, was in itself an act of sovereignty, inviting the people of Upper Peru to sever their relations with the United Provinces of Río de la Plata. At the same time the act was offensive to Colombia, Peru, and Río de la Plata, none of which could look upon it with indifference. In any event, an assembly could only be called after the nations concerned had given their permission. Bolívar added that no one desired greater glory for Sucre than he did, but declared that Sucre's acts would have to be performed in strict conformity with the laws governing such proceedings. And since Bolívar had no other course, he was compelled to declare the Decree of February 9, 1825, null and void.[1] The receipt of this letter was a heavy blow not only to Sucre but to the leaders of Upper Peru who had urged him to act without due deliberation and sagacity. There was nothing for him to do but to await further orders from Bolívar.

Sucre sought, in the meantime, to reduce General Olañeta to submission, for the latter stubbornly refused all overtures. The two armies met in the battle of Tumusla, April 2, 1825. The result was an easy victory for Sucre and the death of Olañeta, who died two days later from wounds received in the battle. The passing of General Olañeta was the passing of Spanish power in Spanish South America. Authorities differ in their estimate of Olañeta's services to Upper Peru. He did not bring the Bolivian nationality into being, for it was already in existence before his arrival. The nationality had been in the process of development throughout the entire colonial period. Lying between Lima and Buenos Aires, it was geographically a mediterranean land, and had developed as such. Its cities of Chuquisaca, Potosí, Cochabamba, La Paz, Tarija, Santa Cruz, and Oruro had early become, as already noted, centers of wealth and culture. It was to be expected that a nationality distinctly separate from that of any other part of the Indies would be developed in Upper Peru. The separation of the Presidency of Charcas from the Viceroyalty of Peru in 1776 and its incorporation with that of Río de la Plata merely tended to intensify that nationality. Whatever may have been the factors in this silent process of creating it, the fact remains that in 1825 there was already a nationality in Upper Peru clamoring for expression. General Olañeta may not have done much for that nationality ex-

[1] Lecuna, *Cartas del Libertador*, vol. IV, pp. 263–265. The letter was written with true Bolivarian force and style. There could be no excuse for failure to understand him. Sucre had, indeed, committed a serious mistake, and one that required a severe reprimand. He was, however, big enough to accept the consequences and to await new instructions.

cept to help develop a leadership ready and willing to give it concrete expression.[1]

Bolívar was anxious to inspect southern Peru and Upper Peru. After the Congress of Peru had renewed his dictatorship for one more year, February 10, 1825, he determined to make a tour of inspection of these regions. He delegated his authority to a council of government (*consejo de gobierno*)[2] and began the tour on April 10.[3] In Arequipa he issued, on May 16, the celebrated decree approving Sucre's decree of February 9, 1825, convoking an assembly. He explained in the preamble to that decree that the Congress of Peru had authorized such action, that the United Provinces of Río de la Plata had given Álvarez de Arenales [4] powers to deal with the authorities of Upper Peru, and that since the

[1] Cleven, "The dictators of Peru, Bolivia, and Ecuador," *in* Wilgus (ed.), *South American dictators*, p. 271.

[2] The *consejo* was composed of José de La Mar, Sánchez Carrión, and José Hipólito Unánue. It was installed on April 3, 1825, with La Mar as president. Later Salazar and Larrera y Loredo were added to the *consejo*, while General Héres acted in an advisory capacity.

[3] Lecuna, *Cartas del Libertador*, vol. IV, pp. 316–319. Bolívar went from Lima to Arequipa and remained there from May 15 to June 10. From Arequipa he went to Cuzco. On May 15 he had written a long letter to Sucre from Arequipa in which he informed him that he approved the policy which Sucre had inaugurated in Upper Peru. As early as February 23 the Congress had, in a *resolución* of that date, given Bolívar permission to send the Liberating Army to any part of the country to destroy its enemies. He was authorized to establish a provisional government in Upper Peru if circumstances demanded such action. In the event that Upper Peru was separated from the United Provinces of Río de la Plata, the new state was to indemnify Peru for the cost of the emancipatory expedition. He declared that it was no more than right and just that the people should be given an opportunity to choose their own form of government. In order to keep out of the picture, Bolívar declared that he would not go into Upper Peru until the assembly had taken some final action in the matter of its government. He would thus be in a better position to deal with Argentina. He ordered Sucre to use great care in keeping the military out of politics. The military was to be kept away from the voting places and the troops were to be kept at least twenty leagues away from the meeting place of the assembly. He would visit Cuzco, Puno, and La Paz, and would remain away from Chuquisaca until after the assembly had taken action on the future of Upper Peru. On May 20 he wrote a long letter to Santander from Arequipa. He took note of the article in the *Morning Chronicle* by Mollien, who stated that Bolívar was not well versed in political philosophy, and that his education in general had been very limited. Bolívar declared that while he had not studied the philosophy of Aristotle he had studied Locke, Condillac, Buffon, Dalambert, Helvetius, Montesquieu, Voltaire, Malby, Filangieri, Lalande, Rousseau, Rollin, Berthot, "y todos los clásicos de antigüedad, así filósofos, historiadores, oradores y poetas; y todos los clásicos modernos de España, Francia, Italia y gran parte de los ingleses." But he added: "Yo multiplico las ideas en muy pocas palabras, aunque sin orden ni concierto."

[4] The Congress of the United Provinces of Río de la Plata had decreed, on May 9, 1825, authority to the executive power to send within as short a space as possible a mission to Upper Peru to thank Bolívar, in the name of the Argentine nation, for the distinguished services he had rendered "a la causa del nuevo mundo, cuya libertad e independencia acaba de afianzar irrevocablemente." He was to be thanked especially for having established order and

object of both Great Colombia and Peru was to liberate the people of the Americas in order to enable them to resume their functions of sovereignty and decide their own political future, he had decided to convoke an assembly of the people of Upper Peru in accordance with the decree issued by Sucre on February 9, 1825. He declared that he wanted the people to express their desires freely concerning the form of the government they might want, and in agreement with the wishes of the United Provinces of Río de la Plata. He declared, also, that the deliberations of the assembly would receive no sanction from him until the Congress of Peru had authorized such action. In the meantime the Provinces of Upper Peru were to remain under the immediate authority of Sucre, commander in chief of the Liberating Army, and must recognize no other authority until the Congress of Peru had taken some definite action about the form of their government.[1]

The people of Upper Peru were naturally highly pleased with this act of the Liberator, and set about preparing for the election of the deputies for the assembly. On June 3, 1825, Bolívar issued an order for the meeting of the assembly on June 24 in Chuquisaca. He urged the deputies to leave early in order to be on hand for the opening session, for no excuses would be accepted for absences from the meetings of that body.[2]

Bolívar continued his journey. He spent considerable time in Cuzco. It was while in that city that he again gave his serious attention to reforms in the Indian policy. He was fully determined to improve the lot of the native peoples.[3] The result was a series of decrees issued from Cuzco. The Decree of July 4, 1825, abolished the title and powers of the caciques.[4] Another decree of the

stability in Upper Peru. Juan Antonio Álvarez de Arenales was to negotiate with Peru the boundaries between the United Provinces of Río de la Plata and Upper Peru. While the Provinces of Upper Peru belonged to the United Provinces of Río de la Plata, the Congress declared that it was willing to give the people of those provinces the right to determine for themselves what their future political status should be (*Colección oficial, años 1825 y 1826*, pp. 10–11).

[1] *Colección oficial, años 1825 y 1826*, pp. 11–12.

[2] *Ibid.*, p. 13.

[3] Lecuna, *Cartas del Libertador*, vol. V, pp. 11–14, letter to Santander from Cuzco, June 25, 1825. Bolívar was greatly impressed with the sacred city of the Incas, and was very busy during his visit to that city studying the evidences of the genius of the Incas as shown in the ruins in and about the city. It was natural that his sensitive, highly imaginative soul should respond sympathetically amid the evidences of the grandeur of these peoples. Letters written from Cuzco prove that fact.

[4] *Colección oficial, años 1825 y 1826*, p. 30. The Decree of July 4, 1825, was a duplicate of that issued by Bolívar from Trujillo on April 8, 1824 (*ibid.*, pp. 34–35). The preamble of the Decree of July 4, 1825, declared that since the Constitution of Peru did not recognize inequality among the people and since all hereditary titles had been abolished, there was no reason why the title and powers of the caciques should any longer be recognized. In the future, therefore, there would be no such distinctions, and the functions which had been performed by the caciques would be performed by local civil authorities.

same date abolished the personal service of the Indians.[1] A third dealt with the tenure of land among the Indians, declaring the Decree of April 8, 1824, redividing the lands taken from the Indians, in force in Upper Peru.[2] These were laudable efforts of a great reformer, but they were immature and doomed to failure. One may admire Bolívar for his view that the ills of Bolivia would never be removed until the Indian question had been solved and solved right. But one cannot help but marvel at his failure to realize that the reforms he decreed were utterly impossible of realization at the time. Bolivia was then, as she had been for centuries, and still is, an Indian land. To have given the Indians full rights with the non-Indians in 1825 would have been to court one of the greatest race wars of history. For it is not to be supposed that the Indians would have remained quietly enduring the rule of the whites, or even of the *cholos*. A nation in which whites constitute only about one-sixth of the total population could hardly be expected to continue an Indian's country under white man's rule. All these decrees were soon repealed, except that which abolished the rank and office of the caciques.[3]

The elections for the General Assembly had been held and preparations were made for the first meeting in Chuquisaca. On July 2, 1825, Sucre left

[1] *Colección oficial, años 1825 y 1826*, pp. 31–32. This decree was also based upon the fundamental principle of equality as laid down in the Constitution. Since the Indians were on an equal footing, legally, with the other people of the state, they could not be forced to render personal services. A contract for such services was necessary with the distinct provision that a definite and fixed salary or wage would be paid. Even the government was forbidden to exact labor from the Indians for public works. The political authorities were also forbidden to demand of the Indians any labor in connection with the army without payment for such services; nor could this latter type of labor be required of the Indians without their consent. All prefects of departments, intendents, governors, judges, ecclesiastical prelates, curates and their lieutenants, *hacendados*, and owners of mines were strictly forbidden to employ Indians contrary to their wishes in *faenas*, *sétimas*, *mitas*, *pongueajes*, or any other domestic or rural labor.

[2] *Ibid*, pp. 32–34. The preamble of this decree declared that the lands of the Indians had never been divided proportionally, that the great number of Indians had been deprived of most of their best lands, that much of the land which had been left in their possession had been illegally taken away from them by the Spaniards, that the small amount of land left to the Indians had been detrimental to agriculture and to the general prosperity of the state, and that the Constitution of the state did not recognize the authority of the caciques. It was therefore ordered that the Decree of April 8, 1824, issued from Trujillo, should be enforced throughout Upper Peru. The lands were to be redivided upon a more equitable basis, the redivision to be done by honest and intelligent officials appointed by the prefect of the department. The lands which belonged to the caciques were not to be disturbed, and the caciques who had no lands were to be given lands. The Indians who had no land were to be given lands. Lands which had been taken away from the Indians in 1814 and given to the king were to be returned to them, plus a third more than they had had before it was taken away. Finally, the Indians were to be recognized as having a right to private ownership in land.

[3] The third decree was repealed by the Law of September 20, 1826, and the Law of September 28, 1831. The second decree was repealed by the Law of July 2, 1829.

that city in order to be away from it when the Assembly began its sessions. He placed the command of the city in the hands of Andrés Santa Cruz,[1] who

[1] Andrés Santa Cruz was one of Bolivia's greatest sons. No other man, not even the two who created Bolivia, Bolívar and Sucre, brought greater renown to the republic. He was a *cholo*, a fact of much significance, and was born November 30, 1792, in Huarina, near the city of La Paz. The exact date of his birth has been and still is a subject of dispute among historians. The date 1795 is frequently given, and such a noted scholar as Jorge Basadre of the University of San Marcos holds that view; his work on *La iniciación de la república* gives a very good analysis of the life and work of Santa Cruz. We have, on the other hand, come to the conclusion that his son, General Oscar de Santa-Cruz, knows the exact date of his father's birth. He discusses this phase of the subject in detail in his work entitled *El general Andrés de Santa-Cruz, gran mariscal de Zepita y del Gran Perú*. Andrés Santa Cruz was the son of José Santa Cruz, a Spaniard, and María Calahuma, *cacica* of Huarina, an Inca princess, a lineal descendant of the last ruling Inca. The family was a prominent one. Not a little of the success of this distinguished son was due to the advantage of birth and social position. His mother exercised a singularly powerful influence upon him throughout her life. She indoctrinated him with a fire of soul for things Incaic. There can be no question that Andrés Santa Cruz dreamed of resurrecting the Inca Empire, with himself at its head; and next to Bolívar he came nearer doing so than any other man since the fall of that remarkable empire. He did not receive a classical education, but did acquire a good style of writing, an achievement which stood him in good stead throughout his later life. His political philosophy appears to have been learned through experience rather than from any scholarly theories of political government.

He chose the army as a career and entered the armies of Spain at an early age. In 1817, while he was still in the military service of Spain, he was captured by the Patriot army and imprisoned in the city of Tarija. He made his escape and visited Rio de Janeiro, Brazil, but soon returned to Peru to reenter the Royalist army. He was again taken prisoner by Arenales in the celebrated battle of Cerro de Pasco on December 6, 1820, and was released on promise that he would join the Patriot cause. He was greatly impressed with José de San Martín and became very active in the Patriot army. It was the beginning of his political as well as his military career in the Patriot cause. He had the ability to ingratiate himself with men in high positions, and was always held in the highest esteem by both San Martín and Bolívar, both of whom gave him an opportunity to demonstrate his ability and advance his own personal ambition. He did not succeed, however, with Antonio José de Sucre, for the two men took a dislike to each other from the first. Santa Cruz took an active part in the Patriot cause from 1820 on. He rendered very important services in the celebrated battle of Pichincha on May 25, 1822, as commander of the Peruvian Division under orders from the Supreme Protector of Peru, José de San Martín, with the result that Pichincha is considered by many Peruvians as more of a Peruvian than a Colombian victory. At the one hundredth anniversary of the battle of Pichincha the Peruvian government took due notice of this fact, and incorporated it in the inscription upon the monument erected in his honor. Santa Cruz was not so fortunate, however, in the campaign in the south of Peru, for while the battle of Zepita was a victory for him, he made no real use of it at the time. Later he was made grand marshal of Zepita and was very much pleased with that title. Bolívar made him prefect of the Department of Lima, and later president of the Council of Government of Peru. It was in the latter position that he made the Bolivarian Constitution the Constitution of Peru. After his defeat in the presidential campaign of 1827 he was sent by La Mar as Peruvian minister to Chile. He was elected president of Bolivia in 1828 but did not assume that office until 1829.

Santa Cruz served as president of Bolivia for almost ten years with great ability and left an indelible impression upon his native country. In many respects the most remarkable

represented La Paz in the Assembly. Owing to the late arrival of many of the deputies, the Assembly did not begin its sessions until July 10, 1825. The leading lights of this gathering were Casimiro Olañeta, José María Serrano, Manuel María Urcullu, Eusebio Gutiérrez, José María Pérez de Urdininea, Juan Manuel Velarde, and José Miguel Lanza. They were all able men. Serrano was elected president of the Assembly, a position for which he was well prepared, having taken a conspicuous part in public affairs for many years. He had been a prominent member of the Congress of Tucumán in 1816 and had proved himself a parliamentarian of much ability. José María Mendizábal was elected vice-president of the Assembly.[1]

---

work done during that period was the establishment of the Peru-Bolivian Confederation. The details of this phase of the history of Bolivia and Peru would take too much space and cannot be given here. The aim of Santa Cruz was to reunite the two countries and to make the Confederation a means through which the people might make the greatest progress. The chaotic situation in Peru, coupled with the grave dangers from Chile, impelled him to accede to a request from Luis José Orbegoso to come into Peru to reestablish peace and order there and to deal with Chile. In Peru he was able to defeat Agustín Gamarra and Santiago Felipe de Salaverry in the battles of Yanacocha on August 13, 1835, and Socobaya on February 7, 1836. On October 28, 1836, he proclaimed the Peru-Bolivian Confederation, composed of the State of North Peru, the State of South Peru (which had come into being upon the dissolution of the Republic of Peru as a result of the defeat of Gamarra and Salaverry), and Bolivia. The Pact of Tacna (*Pacto de Tacna*) of 1837 became the political constitution of the Confederation, as will be noted later. Chile, Argentina, and Brazil considered the Confederation dangerous to the future welfare of South America, and more especially to their own countries, and were able to bring about the defeat of Santa Cruz in the celebrated battle of Yungay, on January 20, 1839. It was Chile who bore the brunt of the attack upon Santa Cruz and the Peru-Bolivian Confederation, which may be said to have been the beginning of the famous War of the Pacific, which proved so disastrous to both Peru and Bolivia. Santa Cruz resigned as Supreme Protector of the Confederation and as president of Bolivia and fled from Bolivia into exile. He went to Ecuador, where he was befriended by Juan José Flores, but was unable to stage a comeback in Bolivia. In 1845, through joint action of Peru, Bolivia, and Chile, he was banished to Europe. While he did come to Argentina, he was never permitted to return to Bolivia, and died in Nantes, France, on September 23, 1865; he was buried in Versailles, where his mortal remains still rest.

Santa Cruz has been and still is the subject of controversy. We cannot help but own to a very high appreciation of the man and his work. His faults were many and grievous, but he did great work for Bolivia. In the final analysis he must accept the verdict of unimpassioned history. One of the best ways to show this esteem in which he is held would be to have his remains brought back to his country and placed in a monument in La Paz. Bolivia owes that much, and much more, to the memory and honor of her most celebrated son.

There are several works on Santa Cruz. Agustín Iturricha, *Historia de Bolivia bajo la administración del mariscal Andrés Santa Cruz*, is an excellent account. Jorge Basadre deals admirably with him and his work in his two volumes on *La iniciación de la república*. Santa Cruz' own volume, *El general Santa-Cruz explica su conducta pública y los móviles de su política en la presidencia de Bolivia y en el protectorado de la Confederación Perú-Boliviana*, is also very good.

[1] República de Bolivia, *Libro menor de sesiones secretas, etc.*, pp. 1–2.

The Assembly took the position, as early as July 17, 1825, that it had the unquestioned right to declare Upper Peru free and independent, and to form a government of its own. It held that the people had a right to independence because of the geographical location of the country, the variety and richness of its natural resources, and the ability of its people. But there were differences of opinion as to the best manner of proceeding. There were, as a matter of fact, three parties, each of which had its supporters in the Assembly, as well as outside that body. Gutiérrez was the leader of the party that wanted Upper Peru to join Lower Peru, believing the Upper Peruvians unable to govern themselves as an independent state. There was another party which favored union with the United Provinces of Río de la Plata. The third party favored complete independence. This group was by far the largest of the three.

The Assembly decided that before any definite action was taken it should consult Bolívar. Upon motion of Mendizábal, the Assembly created a mission to wait upon the Liberator in order to ascertain his wishes and to obtain his advice. The mission was to thank the Liberator for his great services to Upper Peru and to America, and to request him to explain his decree of May 16, 1825, and to suggest the course which the Assembly ought to follow.[1] Olañeta and Mendizábal were appointed on this mission, with Hilarión Fernández as secretary. The mission was also instructed to ask Bolívar to present a project for a political constitution for the new republic. They were also to ask him to settle the boundary question between Peru and Upper Peru, and at the same time to declare that the people of Upper Peru desired to have the boundary line run along the Desaguadero River.

The Assembly, after receiving the permission of Bolívar, took up the question of the future political status of Upper Peru. On the question of a union with Argentina, the vote was unanimously against it. On the question of a union with Peru, the vote was overwhelmingly against such a union, only Gutiérrez and Velarde favoring it. On the last great question, of the independence of Upper Peru from Spain and from every other nation, the vote was unanimous. The die had been cast and a new nation had formally come into being. On August 6, 1825, the declaration of independence was adopted and proclaimed. It was known as the Acta de Independencia[2] and was a very interesting document.

[1] The motion was passed on August 5, 1825, in a secret session.

[2] *Colección oficial, años 1825 y 1826*, pp. 14–18. Also in the booklet *Constitución política de la República de Bolivia*, pp. i–viii. The bombastic nature of the document may be judged from these paragraphs:

"The Lion of Iberia, hurling itself furiously from the Pillars of Hercules to the empires of Moctezuma and Atahualpa, has for many centuries torn into pieces the unfortunate body of America and has fed upon its substance. All the nations of the continent can point the world to their deep wounds to give evidence of the laceration they have suffered; but Upper

The story of Bolívar in Upper Peru would be incomplete without an account of the attitude of the Assembly toward him. On August 11, 1825, the Assembly passed an act which has justly been called the "deification of the Liberator." It declared that the new nation should bear the name of Republic of Bolívar (*República de Bolívar*); declared Bolívar the Father and Protector of the

---

Peru has suffered even more enormous ones, and the blood it has shed is the most authentic monument of the ferocity of that monster.

"After sixteen years in which America has been a battlefield, and in which throughout this period the cries of liberty, repeated by its sons, have met another crisis, without leaving a single corner in all the land where this sacred name has not been the enchantment of the American and the rage of the Spaniard, after which, in extensive fighting, the nations of the world have received different reports concerning the justice and legality with which the regions of America have had recourse, in order to save themselves, to sacred revolution; when, in fine, great nations have recognized already the independence of Mexico, Colombia, and Buenos Aires, whose complaints and grievances have not been greater than those of Upper Peru: it would be needless to present a new manifesto in justification of the resolution we have made.

"The world knows that Upper Peru has been, on the continent of America, the altar whereon was spilt the first blood of the free, and the land wherein exists the tomb of the last of the tyrants: that Charcas, Potosí, Cochabamba, La Paz, and Santa Cruz have made constant efforts to throw off the peninsular yoke; and that the irretractability of its vows against the domination of Spain, its heroic opposition, have arrested a thousand times the impetuous marches of the enemy in regions which, without this, would have been enchained, or would have saved themselves only by the most heroic and prodigious efforts.

"The world knows also that, located in the heart of the continent, destitute of arms, of all kinds of implements of war, without opportunity which the other states had to obtain them in the nations overseas, the Altoperuanos have torn down the standards of despots in Aroma and in Florida, in Chuquitos, Tarabuco, Sinti, in the valleys of the Sicasica and Ayopaya, Tumusla, and at many other different points; that the barbaric burning of more than a hundred towns, the sacking of the cities, scaffolds by the hundreds erected against the free, the blood of thousands of martyrs of the fatherland brought to an end by atrocious tortures which would make the Caribs shudder, tribute, taxes, and arbitrary and inhuman levies, the absolute insecurity of honor, of the life of the people, and of property, and a system, in fine, which was inquisitorial, atrocious and savage, have not been able to extinguish in Upper Peru the sacred fire of liberty, the holy wrath that destroyed the power of Iberia."

There were forty-eight signers of this Acta de Independencia, representing the five departments: From Chuquisaca: José María Serrano, president of the Assembly; Manuel María Urcullu, José María Francisco Palazuelas, Ambrosio Mariano Hidalgo, Angel Mariano Moscoso, secretary. From La Paz: José María Mendizábal, vice-president; José María Azin, Miguel Fermín Aparicio, José Miguel Lanza, Fermín Eyzaguirre, José Ballivián, Martín Cardón, Juan Manuel Velarde, Francisco María Pineda, José Indalecio Calderón y Sanjinés, Rafael Monje, Eusebio Gutiérrez. From Cochabamba: Miguel José Cabrera, José Manuel Pérez, Nicolás Cabrera, Manuel Mariano Centeno, Dinisio de la Borda, José Manuel Tames, Pedro Terrazas, Melchor Paz, Marcos Escudero, Mariano Méndez, Manuel Cabello. From Potosí: Melchor Daza, Manuel José Calderón, Manuel Antonio Arellano, Manuel Anselmo de Tapia, Manuel Argote, José Antonio Pallares, José Eustaquio Gareca, Manuel María García, José Mariano Enríquez, Isidoro Trujillo, J. Manuel Montoya, Martiniano Vargas, José Ignacio de Sanjinés, secretary. From Santa Cruz: Antonio Vicente Soane, Vicente Caballero.

country; conferred upon him the supreme executive power, to be exercised as long as he remained within its borders; proclaimed that his birthday should be a national holiday and observed as such, that his picture should be hung in all the tribunals, the *cabildos*, the universities, the colleges, the schools, and the houses of public instruction of the state, that a statue was to be erected to him in the capital of every department, and that a gold medal, set in brilliants, was to be made for him. A million pesos were voted to him as a gift from a grateful people, but he declined to accept them.[1] Honors were also paid to Sucre only a little different from those paid to the Liberator.[2] The Liberating Army also came in for attention and honors.[3]

Bolívar entered the city of La Paz on August 18, 1825, and was received with the pomp and ceremony becoming his position. He took delight in showering honors upon Sucre, who had come to La Paz from Chuquisaca to welcome him.[4] But toward the people he was less gracious. He did not conceal his conviction that they were unprepared for self-government. He had no sooner entered La Paz than he dissolved the Governmental Junta, fearing that its deliberations might prove embarrassing in a delicate international situation. This act has been criticized as high-handed and directly contradictory to Bolívar's oft-repeated statements about the rights of the people. At the banquet to the delegation from the General Deliberative Assembly he declared that the Bolivian people were not prepared to govern themselves and that they were not

[1] *Colección oficial, años 1825 y 1826*, pp. 20–22. The medal which was struck had this inscription on it: "La República Bolívar agradecida al héroe cuyo nombre lleva." It was characteristic of Bolívar not to accept moneys appropriated for him in this wise.

[2] The birthday of Sucre was also to be a national civic holiday and celebrated annually as such. His picture was to be hung to the left of that of Bolívar in all the places in which the latter was to be displayed. Sucre was to be known as the first general of Bolivia and was also to have the title of captain general until the exact title of the ranking military officer of the republic had been determined. He was also to have the title of Defender and Grand Citizen of the Republic. The name of the capital of the country was to be changed to Sucre in his honor. The president of the Department of Chuquisaca was ordered to have a gold medal, set in diamonds, made for Sucre with the inscription on it: "La República de Bolívar á su defensor héroe de Ayacucho." A statue was to be erected in his honor in every capital of every department in the republic. In the picture which was to be painted of a scene in which Bolívar and Sucre were to be represented, he was to have a place of honor next to Bolívar. This picture was to be hung in the Halls of the Congress of Bolivia.

[3] A million pesos were appropriated for the victors of Junín and Ayacucho. This was to be a small reward for the services rendered by them in behalf of America in general and Bolivia in particular. It was declared that every man who had fought in these two battles was to be considered a citizen of Bolivia. August 6 and December 9, the dates on which the two battles had been fought, were to be celebrated every year as national holidays.

[4] At the reception a group of ladies placed a crown of gold on Bolívar's head. He took it off and placed it on the head of Sucre. He was lavish toward Sucre, and well he might be, for Sucre had done much for him.

worthy of independence.[1] He declined to accept the honors conferred upon him by the Assembly on the ground that he had not been authorized by the Congress of Peru to accept the Acta de Independencia. He insisted upon the fact that Upper Peru was still under the rule of Peru and would have to remain under that rule until the Congress of Peru had recognized her independence. Bolívar was keenly alive to the dangers of the position to which the activities of Sucre had committed him in Upper Peru, further seriously complicated by the activities of the Assembly in Chuquisaca. The tone of the press in the several countries of South America, especially in Argentina and Brazil, was hostile to him. The press was very critical of his proceedings in Ecuador, Peru, and Bolivia and denounced him as a grave menace to democratic institutions. It saw in him a danger to the independence of these countries and frankly declared that it did not know what he planned to do with Bolivia and Peru. He was the most powerful figure at the time in the New World, ambitious for the success of his larger plans for the political government of the countries of the continent. Bolívar gave great thought, accordingly, to the whole situation. He was loud in proclaiming the need of training for self-government. The Bolivians had so many things to learn, he pointed out, before they could hope to govern themselves. They would have to learn the need of developing the natural resources of their country. It was necessary that the whites should also do manual labor. Only in this way could they ever hope to emancipate themselves from the slavery of the Indians. It was the Indians who did the major work of the country, and not the whites. It was, in the true sense of the word, the whites who were the slaves of an antiquated economic system. That system was out of date for a free country, the future of which demanded the modernization of its whole life. There was a great need, he insisted, for a new type of education, an education that should prepare the people to make the new nation a success.

Bolívar was lavish in dispensing the wisdom which he had gained through extensive experience. He displayed then, as he had before, a real understanding of the needs of the Spaniards in the Americas. No one knew better than he the need of emancipation from the thralldom of the past. He had no illusions about the work to be done in Bolivia, for the Bolivians were no more prepared for his great ideals than the Colombians and Peruvians were. It is only with this in mind that one can understand what he strove to do on this tour of inspection of 1825. The history of Bolivia, and especially of the period of its creation, is different from that of the other Spanish American countries. The years of the Bolivarian rule were a period of real transition. Not only was Bolivia made to order, as it were, as a state, but her governmental institutions were made to order also, and by the man who had liberated her. It was because of this need

[1] The mission from the General Deliberative Assembly, composed, as we have already noted, of Olañeta and Mendizábal, arrived in La Paz on September 25, 1825, to perform the duty which had been assigned it.

that Bolívar decided to spend several months in Bolivia, as he had in Ecuador, while her institutions were taking shape through his guidance.

The General Deliberative Assembly had, in the meantime, continued its labors.[1] On August 13, 1825, it decreed that the national government should be representative republican and unitarian in form. The administration was to be exercised through a legislative, an executive, and a judicial department.[2] On August 17, the Assembly decreed a flag for the republic.[3] On the same date it adopted a coat of arms, and prescribed it in detail.[4] Another decree of the same date prescribed the monetary system of the new state.[5] On August 23, Sucre ordered that the postal system should be duly protected and organized.[6] On August 29, Bolívar found it necessary to seize, on account of the republic, the property of Julián Noboa, who was living in Spain.[7] On the same date Bolívar decreed that the mines that were not in operation should be the property of the state.[8] On the same date also he ordered that the decree which he had issued

[1] On August 8, 1825, the Assembly decreed that its members should receive compensation for their labors. Each deputy was to receive 2000 pesos a year for *dietas;* and the deputies from La Paz and Santa Cruz were to receive 200 pesos, and the others 100 pesos, for *viáticos*, to cover the expenses of the journey to and from Chuquisaca.

[2] *Colección oficial*, *años 1825 y 1826*, p. 23.

[3] *Ibid.*, pp. 23–24. The flag was to be bicolored, green and orange (*punzó*). The arrangement was to indicate the territorial composition of the republic. The foundation color was *punzó*. On it were placed five ovals (*óvales*), one in the middle and four around it, and all around this group "se colocará una estrella color de oro."

[4] *Ibid.*, pp. 24–25. This decree was modified by the Law of July 26, 1826, and has remained in force since that date. The coat of arms incorporates some of the tradition of the past as well as some of the more important topographical features and natural resources of the country.

[5] *Ibid.*, pp. 25–26. The coins were to be in gold and silver, but in different denominations. They were to be, however, those that were then in use in the country; that is, the basic coin was still the peso.

[6] *Ibid.*, pp. 26–27. The postal service was still in a rather primitive condition. The problem of delivering the mail to the distant parts of the republic was a very serious one, especially in view of the great size of the country. New roads had to be built, and the old ones repaired. The postman was the man on horseback, or muleback, and has continued to be so in many parts of the republic even up to the present time. The credit for beginning improvements in the postal system of Bolivia must go, however, to Sucre.

[7] *Ibid.*, p. 27. The need for more revenue for the state made it easy to attack absentee owners of property in the republic, as the case of Noboa illustrates.

[8] *Ibid.*, pp. 28–29. Bolívar had issued a decree on August 2, 1825, from Pucará, in which he made provision for increasing the revenues of the republic. He declared that "sobre el gobierno de la República gravita una inmensa deuda"; that it was necessary to provide money to pay that debt; and that the abandoned mines should be taken over by the state, since "las minas abandonadas pertenecen de derecho al Estado." He then explained in detail the manner in which these properties were to be taken over by the state and the manner

from Cuzco on July 4, 1824, should be put into force also in Bolivia.[1] This decree, and those based upon it, dealt with reforms in the Indian policy of the national government, already explained. On October 3 the General Assembly decreed that in the event that Bolívar should find it necessary to leave the republic, the supreme power in the state should be given to Sucre, to be exercised by him during the absence of the Liberator.[2] On the same date the General Assembly decreed the appointment of envoys to be sent to Argentina, Colombia, and Peru to secure recognition of the independence of the republic, and to express the gratitude of the Bolivian people for the aid given them in achieving that independence. The envoy to Colombia was also to ask the government to permit Sucre to remain in Bolivia as long as his services were necessary. This envoy was to attend the Congress of Panama to ask that body also to recognize the independence of Bolivia.[3] On October 4 the General Assembly decreed that the Colombian troops to the number of two thousand should remain permanently in Bolivia.[4] On October 6 the Assembly requested Bolívar to invite the oppressed of the world to come to Bolivia. The only condition laid down was that they should be worthy of the invitation.[5] The Assembly then adjourned on October 6. Before adjournment it created a Permanent Deputation of five members, selected from its own membership, one from each of the five departments. The Deputation was to sit in the capital of the republic and work for the welfare of the people, and was to continue in office until the meeting of the Congress on May 25, 1826.[6] Bolívar decreed, October 17, that no Spaniard might contract

in which they were to be managed. Above all, the properties must be secured in accordance with the laws governing such confiscation, for no person was to be defrauded of his property. A careful examination of the whole subject was ordered, and the enforcement of the decree placed in the hands of Secretary General Felipe Santiago Estenós.

[1] *Colección oficial, años 1825 y 1826*, pp. 29–35. The decree proper is short and is given on pp. 29–30. Then follow the four decrees issued from Cuzco and from Trujillo on April 8, 1824, as noted above. The third and fourth decrees were repealed in 1831.

[2] *Ibid.*, pp. 37–38. It will be recalled that Bolívar had been elected president of Bolivia for life, and that this provision was for the government of the country only during his absence from the republic.

[3] *Ibid.*, pp. 38–39. An envoy was later appointed to represent Bolivia in the Congress of Panama.

[4] *Ibid.*, pp. 39–40. The General Assembly was especially concerned about the condition of the country during this trying period. They wanted to be sure that it would not be left to the tender mercies of its own ambitious chieftains, as well as of its neighbors.

[5] *Ibid.*, p. 40.

[6] *Ibid.*, p. 41. The Assembly still called itself "la Asamblea general de Alto Perú," and declared in the decree of dissolution that it had come into being through the decrees of February 9 and May 16, 1825, issued by Sucre and Bolívar respectively.

matrimony in Bolivia without formal permission of the government.[1] The Liberator continued to govern Bolivia during the remainder of the year. He did so, however, not as president, to which office he had been elected by the General Assembly on August 11, 1825, but as dictator of Peru and conqueror of Upper Peru, under instructions from the Congress of Peru.[2]

Bolívar continued to take measures for the more perfect government of the republic. In a *resolución* of November 8 he informed the presidents of the departments and the governors of provinces that they did not have the right to exercise judicial power.[3] On the same day in an *orden* he ordered that no one but a native should be appointed to public office or employment.[4] On the same date he also ordered that in the administration of the communal lands (*tierras de comunidad*) the decree of July 4, 1824, should apply.[5] In this *resolución* he ordered that the surplus communal lands (*tierras sobrantes de comunidad*) should be sold for the benefit of the state. In the decree of November 16 he forbade the introduction into the Provinces of Upper Peru of all obscene printed materials because of the evil effects that such materials have upon society.[6] On November 26 he issued a *reglamento* for the election of deputies to the General Constituent Assembly, prescribing the procedure in great detail. The elections were to be conducted with great care. Only men of known probity and good morals were to be permitted to run for office. The elections were to be public, and were to be held in places where full publicity could be given them.[7] It was to be expected

[1] *Colección oficial, años 1825 y 1826*, pp. 42–43. Bolívar declared that he favored marriages between Bolivians and foreigners, "á excepción de los españoles que deben obtener permiso especial de la autoridad suprema para verificarlo."

[2] Bolívar was careful to state in the decrees which he issued in Upper Peru that he performed those acts as "Libertador Presidente de Colombia, Libertador de la del Perú, y encargado del supremo mando de ella, etc." He also continued to call the country Alto Perú and not Bolivia. These formalities were of course necessary under the conditions under which he was operating.

[3] *Colección oficial, años 1825 y 1826*, p. 45.

[4] *Ibid.*, pp. 45–46. This was a measure intended to put foreigners in their place in Bolivia. After all, it was the Bolivians, and not the foreigners, who should have their interests taken care of.

[5] *Ibid.*, p. 46. Bolívar experienced great opposition in Bolivia to his Indian policy, and while he was temporarily successful he was to see this policy changed as soon as Sucre was out of the country. The people of Bolivia would no doubt have changed it as soon as Bolívar was gone had it not been for the presence of Sucre. The reforms were far too idealistic to be successful at the time.

[6] *Ibid.*, pp. 46–47. He forbade the introduction into the "provincias del Alto Perú de estampas, cajas, sellos y abanicos obcenos, y folletos impuros" because their introduction was detrimental to "la conservación y prosperidad de la moral pública contribuyen esencialmente a la de la sociedad."

[7] *Ibid.*, pp. 48–52. The *reglamento* had a preamble, four chapters, and thirty-five articles.

that Bolívar would emphasize the selection of men who were equipped for the office to which they were to be elected. The selection of the right kind of deputies was to be made through the right kind of electors, who, in turn, were to choose the right kind of men for the Assembly.

The interest of the Liberator in public education was shown in the means he took to improve it. On December 11, he decreed the establishment of primary schools and colleges of science in the capitals of all the departments of the republic. A military school was also to be established. A general director of public instruction was to have charge of these institutions. The military school was to be established in the capital of the republic. The college of the sciences and the arts was to be named San Juan de Chuquisaca. Revenues were also provided for these educational establishments.[1] On December 12, in an *orden*, Bolívar ordered that the postal administration of Chuquisaca should be placed

---

The first chapter dealt with the elections in the parochial districts (*parroquía*), which were to be held on Sunday, January 15, 1826. Chapter two dealt with the electoral juntas of the *partido*, which were to be held on Sunday, January 29, 1826, in the capitals of the depart ments. The number of electors of the *partidos* was to be: for the Department of La Paz, 30 Department of Cochabamba, 27; Department of Potosí, 24; Department of Chuquisaca, 24; and Department of Santa Cruz, 15. Chapter three dealt with the departmental elections, which were to be held on February 26, 1826, in the capital of the department and under the presidency of the president of the department. After the credentials had been verified and approved, all were to go to the Cathedral, where a solemn mass was to be sung. The ecclesiastic *de más dignidad* was then to deliver an address appropriate to the occasion, after which the electors were to return to the polling place where the deputies were to be elected. There was to be one deputy for every 25,000 inhabitants. The Department of La Paz was to have ten, Cochabamba nine, Potosí eight, Chuquisaca five, Santa Cruz five, and Oruro three deputies. Alternates, or *suplentes*, were also to be elected at the same time, as follows: for La Paz three, Cochabamba three, Chuquisaca two, Santa Cruz two, and Oruro one. "Estos," that is, the alternates, "serán llamados en lugar de los propietarios en caso de muerte ó imposibilidad á juicio de la asamblea." The deputies and alternates were to be given certificates of election, and their election was to be reported to the national government, after which the results were to be published in the newspapers. No man was to be chosen deputy or alternate who had not attained the age of twenty-five, and who did not have a good reputation *y luces*. He was to be a native of Bolivia or a naturalized citizen of the republic with seven years' residence in the country. These instructions are of interest since they will be found to have been used in the Bolivarian constitution, and also in later instructions for elections.

[1] *Colección oficial, años 1825 y 1826*, pp. 64–65. The preamble declared that "el primer deber del gobierno es dar educación al pueblo," that "esta educación debe ser uniforme y general," that "los establecimientos de este género deben ponerse de acuerdo con las leyes del Estado," and that "la salud de una república depende de la moral que por la educación adquieren los ciudadanos en infancia." On the same day Bolívar also decreed the establishment of schools for orphans. He declared that schools for "los niños varones huérfanos" should be established because "una gran parte de los males de que adolece la sociedad, proviene del abandono en que se crian muchos individuos, por haber perdido en su infancia el apoyo de sus padres" (*ibid.*, p. 66).

under control of the national government.[1] On December 15, he ordered the establishment of a superior court of justice in La Paz. This court was to have the same powers as the old *audiencias*. It was to have four justices and an attorney (*fiscal*), and was to have jurisdiction over the Departments of La Paz and Cochabamba, together with the Provinces of Oruro, Paría, and Carangas.[2]

Bolívar continued to issue legislative acts for the improvement of conditions in Bolivia. On December 18 he ordered roads to be constructed between Chuquisaca and Oruro, Cochabamba and Santa Cruz, Oruro and Tacna, Potosí and Atacama, and from Potosí to the frontiers of Salta. He ordered that the existing roads should be repaired, and that a plan should be developed by which all the important places in the republic should be connected by roads. He ordered that all the departmental authorities should concern themselves with this matter.[3] On December 20 he ordered the establishment of a general accountant's office (*contaduría general de hacienda*) in the capital of the republic. It was to be composed of three general accountants and other officers.[4] On the same date he made many changes in the Colegio Seminario de Chuquisaca. Its name was to be changed to Colegio General de Ordenanzas de toda República. It was to be placed under government control, and was to offer instruction only in the subjects approved by the government. He also ordered that later schools of the sciences and the arts, with courses of instruction specified in the decree, should be established in the capital of each department of the republic.[5] On December 21 he ordered that the proceedings of the judicial tribunals in the country should be in accordance with the Law of the Cortes of Spain of October 9, 1812. This was to apply in civil as well as criminal cases.[6] On December 22 he decreed the abolition of the *tributo*, and the payment of other taxes in proportion to the ability to pay. The government was to appoint the officers for the collection of the new taxes.[7] In a supplemental decree of the same date he specified the salaries to be paid to these new officials.[8]

[1] *Colección oficial, años 1825 y 1826*, p. 69. On December 13, 1825, Bolívar decreed the establishment in Chuquisaca of the *compañía de alumnos militares*, because "la instrucción es la base de la organización de los ejércitos," and such instruction was not possible without "un método uniforme constante y regular," and also because it was necessary "proporcionar á los jóvenes que se dedican á la carrera de las armas una brillante educación." This was a good beginning, for the young men of Bolivia, below the officers' class, usually get no other education than that which they receive while in the military service.

[2] *Ibid.*, p. 74.

[3] *Ibid.*, pp. 78–79.

[4] *Ibid.*, pp. 79–80.

[5] *Ibid.*, pp. 80–83. This decree gave minute attention to the nature of the instruction as well as to the courses to be given.

[6] *Ibid.*, pp. 83–84.

[7] *Ibid.*, pp. 85–88. Bolívar declared that the *tributo* was unjust because it fell upon "la clase más miserable de la sociedad."

[8] *Ibid.*, pp. 88–89.

There was still much to do and Bolívar continued to issue legislative measures. On December 24 he decreed the establishment of an economic society in Chuquisaca to study the economic life of the country.[1] On December 28 he decreed that Cobija should be made a major port, to be known as Puerto de la Mar.[2] On December 29 he decreed that the opening of the General Constituent Assembly should be changed from April 19 to May 25, 1826.[3] On the same day he also decreed that the executive power in Bolivia should be exercised by Sucre, and, in the event of Sucre's inability to serve, by Andrés Santa Cruz.[4] On December 31 he decreed the separation of the *curates* of Sicasica and others from the Archbishopric of La Plata and their incorporation with the Bishopric of La Paz.[5] This was an unusually high-handed act even for a dictator, but was in no wise unusual in the rule of Bolívar. Throughout his rule in Peru and Upper Peru he allowed no interference from ecclesiastical authorities in the affairs of state.[6]

Bolívar issued his famous decree on January 1, 1826, in which he promised that Upper Peru would be recognized as an independent nation by the Congress of Peru.[7] He then left Chuquisaca for Cochabamba, and returned to

[1] *Colección oficial, años 1825 y 1826*, p. 92.

[2] *Ibid.*, p. 93.

[3] *Ibid.*, p. 94.

[4] *Ibid.*, p. 95.

[5] *Ibid.*, p. 96.

[6] *Ibid.* Bolívar had taken pains to curb the power of the clergy on this tour of inspection. On August 7, 1825, from Puno, he declared the separation of the Provinces of Chucuito and Huancane from the Bishopric of La Paz and their incorporation with the Bishopric of Cuzco. On June 25, 1825, he declared in a letter to La Fuente from Cuzco that if the bishop of Cuzco did not issue a pastoral letter to his people La Fuente was to send him out of the country and to embargo the goods belonging to the brother of the bishop in Spain. Consult Lecuna, *Cartas del Libertador*, vol. V, pp. 4–5. In a letter to Anánue, July 22, 1825, from Cuzco, Bolívar declared that the ecclesiastical authorities ought to help finance public education. In Cuzco he took the income of rich *padres* and gave it to the colleges and hospitals which he founded. On November 14, 1825, the bishop of La Paz refused to take the oath of allegiance to the new government of Upper Peru. He was removed from his office by Bolívar. Bolívar also exiled Friar Andrés de los Remedios and Friar Manuel del Tránsito for the murder of Friar Cristóval de la Magdalena, prefect of the Bethlehemites, and ordered the establishment of a school in the monastery of the Bethlehemites in Cuzco. The clergy of Cuzco opposed this measure strenuously, but Bolívar ordered the president of the Department of Cuzco to write a strong letter to the bishop of Cuzco on this subject. This was done and the clergy calmed down. Bolívar also founded two hospitals, one in Cuzco and another in Urabamba. He ordered that the convents of Cuzco should pay for the upkeep of these new hospitals. Consult Vargas, *Participación de Colombia en la independencia del Perú*.

[7] *Colección oficial, años 1825 y 1826*, p. 97. The preamble declared it was necessary for Bolívar to return to Lima to give an account of his administration to the Congress of Peru,

Lima.[1] While on his way to Lima, he refused a request of the people of Arica to be incorporated with Upper Peru. He has been very severely criticized for this act. It was in his power to establish the boundaries of Bolivia with much fairness to its people. Had he arranged these boundaries more in keeping with the needs of the Bolivian people he might have changed profoundly the course of the history of their country. Such great crises as the War of the Pacific and the War with Paraguay could hardly have been avoided, but a more friendly policy toward Chile and Paraguay in this formative period might have enabled Bolivia to make a more rational beginning. Those who criticize the Liberator for his acts as dictator find in his failure to permit the incorporation of Tarija and Arica painful proof of the fact that Bolívar had but little real consideration for the wishes of a people who he felt stood in his way, whatever might be his ultimate plans.

Sucre began his rule in Upper Peru as soon as Bolívar had left Chuquisaca. On January 13 he decreed the creation of two departments of the executive branch of the national government. One was to have charge of government and the treasury, and was to have Facundo Infante at its head. The other was to have charge of the military, and to have Agustín Jeraldino in charge. These two officers were known as secretaries and were authorized to sign all orders and resolutions of the national government concerning their respective departments.[2] On January 16 Sucre decreed a change in the postal system.[3] On January 23 he decreed the division of the five Departments of Chuquisaca, Potosí, La Paz, Cochabamba, and Santa Cruz into provinces. The provinces were to be divided into cantons. At the head of each department there was a prefect, at the head of each province a governor, subordinate to the prefect, and at the head of the canton a *corregidor*, under the immediate supervision of the governor.

The prefect was appointed by the national government. The governor was appointed by the national government upon nomination of the prefect. The *corregidor* was elected by the people of the canton. These officers were forbidden,

---

which was to meet on February 10, 1826. It further declared that Bolívar delegated his authority in Upper Peru to Sucre by virtue of the acts of the Peruvian Congress of February 10, February 23, and March 10, 1825.

[1] *Colección oficial, años 1825 y 1826*, p. 97. Bolívar left Chuquisaca on January 3, 1826. At Tacna he embarked on the *Chimborazo* for Chorillos, Peru, and arrived in Lima on the day of the opening of the Peruvian Congress, February 10. He delivered his message to that Congress and was reelected dictator of Peru. He took time in deciding what to do, but finally declined the reelection and returned to Great Colombia in September 1826. Like San Martín, he had remained too long as dictator, and like him, too, he must take much blame for many of the malpractices in the political government of Peru during the next half-century. Both San Martín and Bolívar helped train the people of Peru and Bolivia in the fine art of dictatorship.

[2] *Ibid.*, p. 98.

[3] *Ibid.*, p. 99. He ordered that the mails should be delivered more often.

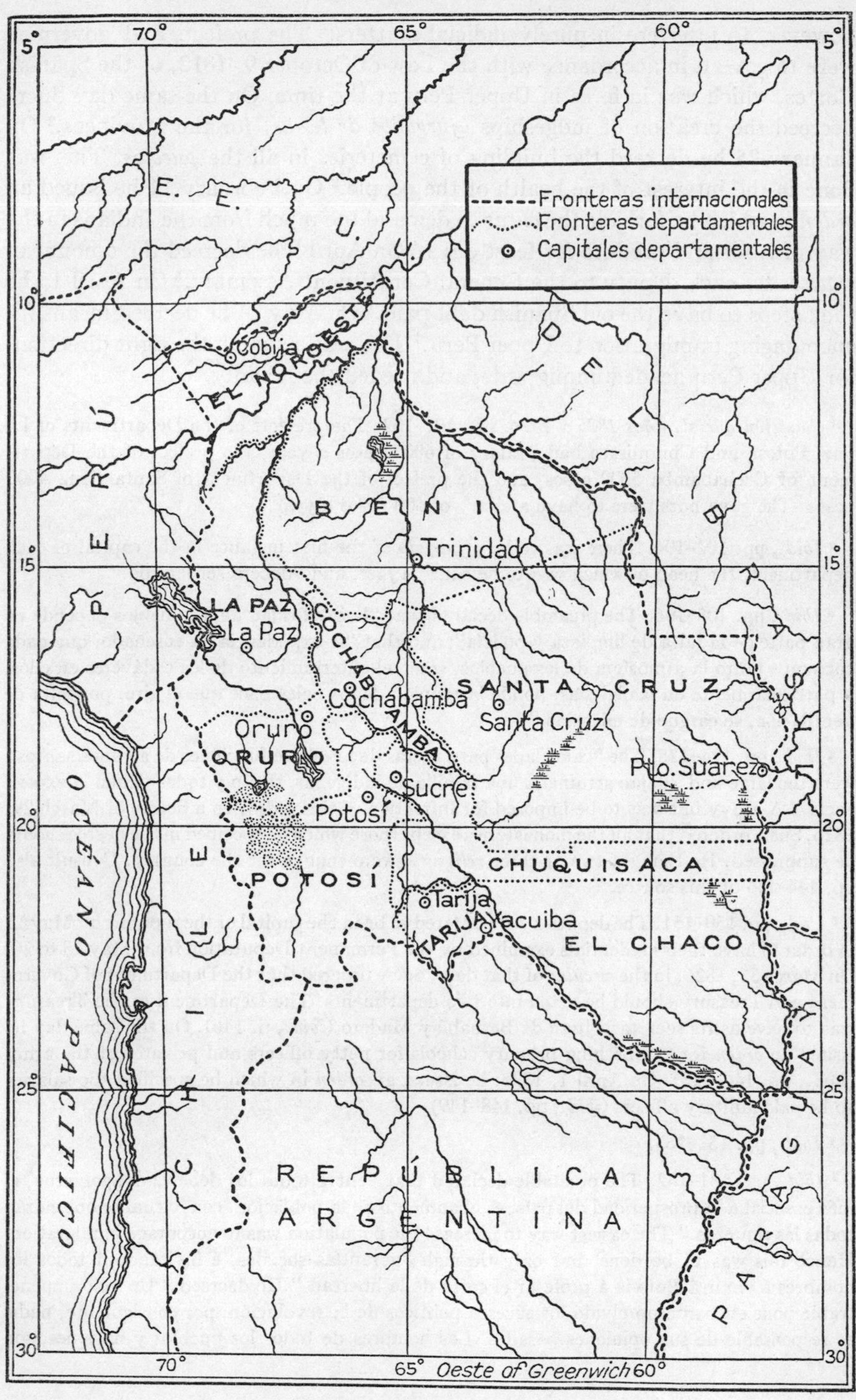

Political Map of Bolivia
(Courtesy of Arnó Hnos., La Paz, Bolivia)

however, to interfere in purely judicial matters.[1] The prefects and governors were to govern in accordance with the Law of October 9, 1812, of the Spanish Cortes, which was in force in Upper Peru at the time. On the same day Sucre decreed the creation of judgeships (*juzgados de letras*) for the provinces.[2] On January 25 he decreed the building of cemeteries in all the *pueblos*. This was done in the interest of the health of the people.[3] On February 11 he issued an *orden* in which he forbade the *curas* to demand too much from the Indians in the way of labor and produce for feast days.[4] On April 9 he decreed the amount of *viáticos* for each deputy to the General Constituent Assembly.[5] On April 13 he took steps to have the old Spanish debt paid.[6] On May 24 he decreed means for encouraging immigration to Upper Peru.[7] This was a step in the right direction, for Upper Peru needed immigrants, and needed them badly.

[1] *Colección oficial, años 1825 y 1826*, pp. 101–102. The prefects of the Departments of La Paz, Potosí, and Chuquisaca had a salary of 6000 pesos a year, the prefect of the Department of Cochabamba 5000 pesos, and the prefect of the Department of Santa Cruz 4000 pesos. The governors were to have a salary of 600 pesos a year.

[2] *Ibid.*, pp. 102–104. There was to be a *juzgado* of the first instance in the capital of each department, the head of which was to be called a *juez*, and "deberá ser letrado."

[3] *Ibid.*, pp. 105–106. The preamble declared that "la salubridad de los pueblos depende en gran parte de la falta de limpieza y policía"; and that "la experiencia ha enseñado, que nada corrompe tanto la atmósfera de los pueblos, como el enterramiento de los cadáveres en ellos, y particularmente en las iglesias, donde la reunión de los fieles hace que el aire, por falta de ventilación, se cargue de miasmas."

[4] *Ibid.*, pp. 124–125. The "cantidades para fiestas de iglesias ó funciones de algunos santos" were too large and "dejan arruinada una familia de indígenas, según y todos tienen la experiencia." A heavy fine was to be imposed for infraction of this *orden*. In a decree of March 29, 1826, Sucre ordered that all the monasteries except those which he specified in the decree should be suppressed. He thought two or three *religiosos* were enough for the country. Consult also pp. 144–146 of this source.

[5] *Ibid.*, pp. 150–151. The deputies were ordered to be in the capital of the republic on May 15 in order to have their credentials examined by the Permanent Deputation from May 15 to 20. On March 31, 1826, in the *circular* of that date, Sucre ordered that the Department of Government and Treasury should be made into two departments. The Department of the Treasury was to have as its secretary Juan de Bernabé y Madero (*ibid.*, p. 146). On the same day he issued an *orden* for establishing primary schools for petty officers and privates of the army (*ibid.*, pp. 146–148). On April 1, 1826, he issued an *orden* in which he specified the salaries to be paid military officers (*ibid.*, pp. 148–149).

[6] *Ibid.*, pp. 151–153.

[7] *Ibid.*, pp. 181–182. The preamble declared that "entre todos los deberes del gobierno, el más esencial á la prosperidad del país, es el aumento de la población, con lo cual se obtendrán todas las riquezas." The easiest way to increase the population was to encourage immigration. Hence this was to be done, but only through "garantías sociales, é invitando á todos los hombres á venir á Bolivia á profesar el culto de la libertad." He decreed: "Un velo impenetrable pone en perpetuo olvido los sucesos políticos de la revolución: por consiguiente, nadie es responsable de sus opiniones pasadas. Los hombres de todos los pueblos y naciones, son

The General Constituent Assembly began its formal sessions on May 26, 1826. One of its first acts was to continue Sucre in the presidency of the republic until a political constitution had been adopted.[1] Sucre was, accordingly, installed on May 28 before the session of the General Constituent Assembly.[2] He delivered an address in which he urged the people to help him in his efforts to govern the country. On June 15 Facundo Infante, secretary of government, informed the prefects of the departments of the republic that the Peruvian government had recognized the independence of Bolivia on May 18.[3] In a Law of June 19, the General Constituent Assembly described the position of the chief executive of the republic. He was to have the title of President of the Republic and was to be addressed as Excellency. He was declared to be inviolable and without any responsibility for the acts of his administration. He was charged with the administration of the country and was to use the necessary means to preserve order within and security from without. He was to have three ministers of state (*ministros del despacho*): one for domestic and foreign relations, another for the treasury (*hacienda*), and a third for war. These ministers of state were responsible for the acts of the administration. The president was to have a salary of 30,000 pesos a year, to be paid from January 1, 1826.[4]

---

invitados á venir á Bolivia, donde su libertad civil tiene todas las garantías que den las leyes á los bolivianos. . . . El derecho de propiedad y seguridad, es sagrado en la república. Bolivia no reconoce otros enemigos exteriores, que los de su libertad, su integridad é independencia; ni enemigos interiores, sino los de su prosperidad y sus leyes." Equally interesting was this declaration: "La república no reconoce ningún poder humano con intervención sobre la conciencia de los habitantes de Bolivia, cuando éstos observen las leyes establecidas para conservar el culto, la buena moral y sanas costumbres." This was extremely important in view of the position which Bolívar was to take on this same subject in his project for a political constitution for the republic, as we shall see later.

[1] *Colección oficial, años 1825 y 1826*, p. 183. A committee was appointed by the General Constituent Assembly to escort Sucre to the *sala* in which the Assembly met. After he had been escorted to the seat reserved for him, and after a brief address by the president of the Assembly, he took the following oath: "¿Juráis por Dios y estos santos evangelios, respetar y hacer respetar la religión católica, observar y hacer observar las leyes de la república, proteger la libertad individual, la propiedad y demás derechos del ciudadano, y gobernar con sólo el objeto de la felicidad y gloria de Bolivia?" "Yo lo prometo," was Sucre's reply, and his official duties had begun anew. All then went to the Cathedral, where a solemn *Te Deum* was sung, after which Sucre was escorted to his home. The inauguration had begun at high noon.

[2] *Ibid.*, pp. 183–184. This was the Law of May 27, 1826, which prescribed in detail the ceremony to be performed, as explained above. This has been the practice in Bolivia from that time to the present. The Congress has the duty as well as the power of determining who has been elected to the high office of president of the republic, and makes its decision known in the form of a law. The day, the hour, and the place where the oath is to be taken are also prescribed in a law of Congress. Further details will be given later.

[3] *Ibid.*, pp. 186–188.

[4] *Ibid.*, pp. 191–192. The president was given a great many powers. He was given full power to appoint and dismiss his ministers of state, and he was given the power to nominate

The year 1826 was a very important one for the people of Bolivia. The Fathers of the Republic continued to enact important legislative measures in the General Constituent Assembly. On June 21 the Assembly passed an act suppressing the municipalities throughout the republic. Their moneys (*fundos* and *rentas*) were to be transferred to the national treasury. The duties which had been performed by the mayors (*alcaldes*) were henceforth to be performed by the judges of the first instance (*jueces de primera instancia*).[1] On June 24 an act was passed creating the office of intendent and commissioner of police for the departments.[2] On June 28 an act was passed authorizing the president of the republic to appoint deputies to the General Congress of Panama.[3] On July 1 an act was passed making Chuquisaca the provisional capital of the republic with the name of Sucre.[4] On August 2 an act was passed reimposing the *tributo* on the Indians.[5] On August 5 an act was passed abolishing the sales tax (*alcabalas*).[6] On September 5 an act was passed making Oruro into a department.[7] On September 20 the decree of July 4, 1825, was repealed, and the lands of the Indians were ordered divided. The decree of April 8, 1824, was also repealed.[8] On October 3, 1826, an act was passed declaring that the Province of Tarija was a part of Upper Peru and hence a part of Bolivia, and the deputies from that province were, accordingly, seated in the Assembly.[9] On October 28 an act

---

to all the ecclesiastical positions in the republic. The right of the *patronato nacional* was accordingly exercised as a right inhering in sovereignty and lodged in the national government.

[1] *Colección oficial, años 1825 y 1826*, p. 195. "Se suprimen los ayuntamientos en el territorio de la República." This act was no doubt taken to please the Liberator, whose well-known opposition to municipalities made this act politic at the time.

[2] *Ibid.*, pp. 196–201.

[3] *Ibid.*, p. 201. These deputies never reached the Congress of Panama, since that body began its sessions on July 15 and closed them on July 22, 1826.

[4] *Ibid.*, pp. 204–205. On July 25 an act was passed adding a third color to the national flag, yellow (*amarilla*), in place of the star of gold (*ibid.*, p. 210).

[5] *Ibid.*, pp. 213–215.

[6] *Ibid.*, p. 215.

[7] *Ibid.*, pp. 223–224. The Department of Oruro was composed of the Provinces of Oruro, Paría, and Carangas, with the capital at the city of Oruro.

[8] *Ibid.*, pp. 230–231. These were, it will be remembered, measures which Bolívar had put into effect in Upper Peru for a new Indian policy.

[9] *Ibid.*, pp. 238–239. This was, therefore, the final solution of the Tarija question, which we have already discussed. By this act the movement for separatism in the Viceroyalty of Río de la Plata came temporarily to an end. The separatist movement has been pronounced in Argentina since that date, although less so than it had been in the period 1810–1826. Even the nationalization of the national capital, Buenos Aires, in 1881 can hardly be said to have put an end to the movement in that country. On the other hand, the movement for division of that viceroyalty into separate nations had come to a definite end, for Argentina, Paraguay,

was passed designating December 9 as the day on which President-elect Sucre was to take the oath of office before the General Constituent Assembly.[1] On November 3 an act was passed fixing August 6, 1828, as the day on which the new national legislature was to begin its regular session.[2] And on November 6 the political Constitution of Bolivia was adopted.[3] The draft of this document was sent to the Assembly by Bolívar at the request of the leaders for a fundamental law. Because it was the first political constitution, its main provisions will be given here in some detail.

The instrument began with the words "In the Name of God" (*En el Nombre de Dios*), and declared that the General Constituent Congress had been elected by the people to draft a political constitution, and that it had performed that task. It was declared that the Bolivian nation was a union of all Bolivians, and that Bolivia was, and always should be, independent of all foreign domination. It was never to become the patrimony of any person or family. The republic was divided into six departments, the departments into provinces, and the provinces into cantons. The religion of the state was the Roman Catholic Apostolic, to the utter exclusion of all other religions. The principle was recognized that there is no human power over a man's conscience.[4] The government was to be popular and representative, the sovereignty emanating from the people, and exercised in accordance with the provisions of the political Constitution. The government was divided into four branches: the electoral, the legislative, the executive, and the judicial. These several branches were to be co-

---

Uruguay, and Bolivia had been carved out of the viceroyalty by the incorporation of Tarija with Bolivia. It is true that Bolivia was obliged to cede some of her territory to Argentina, as has been noted.

[1] *Colección oficial, años 1825 y 1826*, pp. 250–251. Sucre was duly inaugurated on December 9, 1826, taking the following oath: "Yo Antonio José de Sucre, Presidente Constitucional de Bolivia, juro por Dios y estos santos Evangelios, cumplir y hacer cumplir la Constitución Política y las leyes de la República; conservar su soberanía é independencia, y la integridad de sus territorios; velar por la seguridad interior y exterior del Estado; y proteger la religión católica, apostólica, romana. Así, Dios me ayude y sea en mi defensa; y si no me lo demande, y la posteridad execre mi memoria."

[2] *Ibid.*, p. 251.

[3] *Ibid.*, pp. 253–275. The celebrated first constitution of Bolivia is here given in full. It was signed in the *sala de sesiones* in Chuquisaca by Eusebio Gutiérrez, president of the General Constituent Assembly; Mariano Collejo, vice-president; José María Pérez de Urdininea, vice-president; Mariano Calvimonte and José María Salinas, secretaries; and by forty deputies, all told. As promulgated it was signed by Antonio José de Sucre, as president of the republic; Facundo Infante, as *el ministro del interior y relaciones exteriores;* Agustín Jeraldino, as *el ministro de guerra;* and Juan de Bernabé y Madero, as *el ministro de hacienda*. It was promulgated on November 19, 1826.

[4] The religious phase of the Constitution of 1826 will be discussed in the chapter on "The Church and the State."

ordinate, and there was to be no infringement by any branch upon another's rights.

Every Bolivian had certain duties to perform. He was to live in conformity with the Constitution and the laws, respect and obey constituted authorities, contribute to the public expenses (*gastos públicos*), sacrifice his property and even his life for the welfare of the state, and help conserve the public liberties. Citizenship was to be suspended for insanity, for fraudulent indebtedness, for implication in crimes, for drunkenness, gambling, and begging, and for buying or selling votes at elections, or for disturbing the peace on election days. Citizenship was to be lost for treason, for naturalization in a foreign country, for criminal condemnation, and for accepting employment, titles, or emoluments from foreign governments without formal permission of the Chamber of Censors.

The electoral power was to be exercised by the citizens in the enjoyment of political rights. One hundred citizens were to elect one elector. The magistrates were to renew the body of electors whenever necessary. The electoral body was thus composed of the electors chosen by the total citizenry of the republic. No person was eligible to serve as an elector who was not in full possession of the rights of citizenship and who did not know how to read and write. Each electoral body was to meet every year in its province, and was to continue as an electoral body for four years. It was to meet on April 1, 2, 3, 4, 5, and 6 of each year for the purpose of passing upon the qualifications of prospective candidates for public office, for electing, for the first time, the members of the different chambers of the national legislature, and for filling vacancies in the Congress, in the courts, in the prefectures of the departments, and in the office of the justice of the peace. The electoral body was to nominate from six to ten candidates for the office of prefect of a department, for the offices in the provinces and the cantons, and for the ecclesiastical positions in the republic. It was to examine the results of the popular elections, and to remind the members of the different chambers of the government of their duties to the country whenever the electoral body should think that necessary.

The legislative branch was divided into three branches: the tribunes, the senators, and the censors. Each chamber was to be composed of twenty members, and was to meet on August 6 of each year, even though it had not been formally convoked.[1] Jointly the national legislature was to:[2]

[1] Members of the chambers might be elected to the office of vice-president of the republic or to the ministry of state. When selected for such office they were to resign their seat in the Congress. No member of the chambers might absent himself from a session of the Congress without permission of the chamber of which he was a member. Members might not be criticized for opinions expressed in the sessions while in performance of their duties. Each legislature was to continue for four years and each session was to last for two months, all the chambers to open and close their session at the same time. The Congress was to be opened in the presence of the president of the republic, the vice-president, and the ministers of state. The sessions

[2] *Colección oficial, años 1825 y 1826*, p. 257.

1) elect the president of the republic and confirm the appointment of his successor by an absolute plurality of votes;

2) ratify the nomination for vice-president of the republic;

3) select the seat of the national government and change this whenever necessary;

4) impeach the vice-president of the republic, the ministers of state, and the members of the judiciary;

5) invest the president of the republic, in time of war, with dictatorial powers, or confer upon him powers that are indispensable for the salvation of the state (*facultades que se juzguen indispensables para la salvación del Estado*);

6) elect from among the nominees of the electoral bodies to vacancies in any one of the chambers.

The Chamber of Tribunes was composed of men with the same qualifications as the electors.[1] This Chamber had power to:[2]

1) arrange for the division of the territory of the republic;

2) levy taxes and determine public expenses;

3) authorize the president of the republic to negotiate concessions and means for paying the public debt;

4) coin money and supervise the public finances;

5) open ports, and construct roads, highways (*calzadas*), bridges, and public buildings;

6) suggest improvement in industry;

7) determine the salaries of public employees;

8) urge reforms in the management of the public finances and war;

9) help make war and negotiate peace;

10) make alliances with foreign powers;

11) grant permission (*pase*) for foreign troops to pass through Bolivia;

12) determine the size of the armed forces on land and sea;

13) make rules and regulations for the marine, the army, and the national militia;

14) grant citizenship rights and naturalization papers.

The Chamber of Senators was composed of men with the same qualifications

---

were to be public, and only such matters as demanded consideration in secret were to be so considered. A majority vote of the members present was necessary to transact business. Employees of the state, when elected to a seat in the legislature, were to resign from the position with the national government. No chamber was to conduct business unless two-thirds of its members were present. No chamber had the right to initiate legislation which the Constitution assigned to another chamber. The legislature might meet in extra session, but was not permitted to consider any question other than that for which it had been called.

[1] That is, a tribune must be a native of Bolivia or a naturalized citizen with six years' residence in the republic; he must not have been legally convicted of a crime, and must be at least twenty-five years of age. The term of office was four years. The Chamber of Tribunes was renewed every two years by halves; the division for the first time was decided by lot (*suerte*). The members of this Chamber might be reelected.

[2] *Colección oficial, años 1825 y 1826*, pp. 259–260.

as the tribunes, except that the age was fixed at thirty years.[1] This Chamber had the power to:[2]

1) codify civil and criminal law;

2) codify laws of judicial procedure (*procedimientos*) and commerce;

3) make regulations for the transaction of eccelesiastical business;

4) initiate reforms in the judiciary;

5) initiate laws against infringement of the Constitution and the laws by magistrates, judges, and ecclesiastics;

6) pass on the guilt of members of the superior tribunals of justice, prefects, and magistrates of the inferior courts (*subalternos jueces);*

7) nominate members for the Supreme Court, and for the offices of archbishop, bishop, dignity (*dignidad*), canon (*canónigo*), and prebend (*prebendado*) in the cathedralis;

8) ratfy or refuse to ratify the appointments of prefects, governors, and *corregidores* made to the national government by the electoral bodies;

9) elect from among the nominees of the ecclesiastical bodies members of the district courts and all the inferior officers in the department of justice;

10) determine the nature and right of patronage;

11) prepare projects for laws governing all ecclesiastical matters which concern the government of the state;

12) examine conciliar decisions, papal bulls, rescripts, and briefs (*breves*), and accept or reject them as they may determine.

The Chamber of Censors was composed of members with the same qualifications as for the other two chambers, except that they must be at least thirty-five years of age.[3] The censors were to:[4]

1) see that the national government enforced the Constitution, the laws, and the public treaties;

2) impeach the chief executive before the Chamber of Senators for infringements of the Constitution, the laws, and the public treaties;

[1] The term of office for the senators was eight years, the membership of the Chamber to be renewed by halves every four years. The first renewal was to be determined by lot in the first session of the first legislature. The senators might be reelected.

[2] *Colección oficial, años 1825 y 1826*, pp. 260–261.

[3] *Ibid.*, p. 261.

[4] *Ibid.*, pp. 261–262. In case the Chamber of Senators found charges against the vice-president of the republic or a minister of state to be well founded, it was to order a national trial (*juicio nacional*) to be held. If the Chamber of Tribunes concurred in the decision of the Chamber of Senators, the three chambers were to meet as a body to try the accused officials. If the three chambers found the officials guilty of the charges preferred against them, the officials were to be deposed from office and turned over to the Supreme Court for trial. The Supreme Court alone had the right to try these officials and its decision was final. As soon as these officials had been suspended from office, the president of the republic was to fill the vacancies. The term of office of the censors was to be for life.

3) request the Chamber of Senators to suspend the vice-president of the republic and the ministers of state, if the good of the state demanded such action;

4) elect from among the nominees of the Chamber of Senators members of the Supreme Court, archbishops, and bishops, and fill vacancies in the canonries (*canonjías*) and prebendaries (*prebendas*);

5) approve the laws for regulation of the press and for the national economy, and the plans of study and methods to be used in public instruction;

6) propose rules for regulating work in the arts and the sciences;

7) award premiums and national prizes for those who have served the state with distinction;

8) decree public honors to the memory of great men, and rewards for the virtues and services of citizens;

9) condemn to eternal opprobium (*opobrio eterno*) traitors and notorious criminals (*criminales insignes*);

10) grant permission for employment, titles, and emoluments proffered to Bolivians by foreign governments, if thought advisable.

The executive power (*poder ejecutivo*) was vested in a president elected for life, a vice-president, and three ministers of state. The president was to be elected for the first time by the Constituent Congress upon nomination by the electoral colleges (*á propuesta de los colegios electorales*). In order to be eligible to this high office it was necessary to be in the enjoyment of full citizenship rights and a native of Bolivia. The candidate must profess the religion of the state, be at least thirty-five years of age, have rendered important services to the state, possess proved administrative ability, and never have been convicted of crime by any tribunal, *ni aun por faltas de leyes*. The president of the republic was the chief of the administration of the state, but without any responsibility for the acts of that administration. In case of death, disability, resignation, or absence from the country of the president of the republic, the vice-president of the republic was to succeed to the presidency of the republic. In case there was neither a president nor a vice-president of the republic, the administration of the state was to be performed *ad interim* by the ministers of state. The minister who had been in the service longest was to preside. This arrangement was to continue in force until the next legislature had chosen a successor to the presidency.[1] The president of the republic was to:[2]

[1] *Colección oficial, años 1825 y 1826*, p. 265.

[2] *Ibid.*, pp. 265–267. The process of law-making was explained in detail. The national government had the right to present the proposal for any law which it believed necessary. The vice-president of the republic and the ministers of state might attend the sessions of the chambers and take part in the debates or in the explanation of the laws, but they could neither vote nor be present when the vote was taken. In order to become a law a bill had to be passed by the three chambers and signed by the president of the republic. In case the president of the republic vetoed a bill, the chambers could, by a plurality vote, repass it, after which it automatically became a law.

1) open the sessions of the chambers and present a message on the state of the republic;

2) present to the chambers a nominee for the vice-presidency of the republic;

3) appoint and dismiss, in his own right, the ministers of state;

4) order the laws published, circulated, and respected;

5) authorize the regulations and orders for the best enforcement of the Constitution, the laws, and the public treaties;

6) execute and cause to be executed the decisions of the tribunals of justice;

7) request the chambers to adjourn their sessions for a period not to exceed thirty days;

8) call special sessions of the chambers whenever such sessions should be necessary;

9) order the standing army in its service on land or on the sea in defense of the republic;

10) command the army of the republic in peace and in war, in person, if necessary. But when he took over the personal command of the armed forces, the vice-president of the republic was to take charge of the administration. When in command of the armed forces, the president of the republic might reside in any part of the republic occupied by the national forces;

11) order the national militia to serve anywhere in the departments, or outside the departments, but only with the consent of the chambers, whenever the safety of the state should demand such services;

12) appoint the employees of the army, the navy, and the marine;

13) establish military and nautical schools;

14) order the establishment of military hospitals and homes for invalids;

15) grant leaves of absence, or retirements;

16) grant pensions to the military and their families;

17) administer the affairs of the military department;

18) declare war in the name of the republic, when authorized to do so by the chambers;

19) grant patents *de corso;*

20) collect the taxes either by *recaudación* or by *inversion;*

21) appoint the employees of the treasury (*hacienda*);

22) direct diplomatic negotiations, enter into truces (*treguas*) and treaties of peace, friendship, federation, alliance, neutrality, military alliance (*armada*), commerce, and of whatever other kind deemed necessary, but always with the approval of the chambers;

23) appoint diplomatic agents, consuls, and subordinates of the department of foreign relations;

24) receive foreign ministers;

25) grant the *pase* or suspend conciliar decisions, papal bulls, briefs (*breves*), and rescripts, with the authority of the chambers;

26) present the nominees of the electoral bodies for prefects, governors, and *corregidores* to the Chamber of Senators;

27) present the nominees of the electoral bodies for priests (*curas*) and vicars (*vicarios*) of the provinces to the Chamber of Senators;

28) suspend public employees for three months, if that was deemed necessary for the welfare of the state;

29) commute capital sentences to exile for ten years, or to perpetual exile from Bolivian territory;

30) confer, in the name of the republic, titles or appointments on all employees of the republic; and

31) govern the country in the best interest of its people.

There were also restrictions upon the powers of the president of the republic. He could not deprive an individual of his liberty or impose upon him any punishment. In case the welfare of the state demanded the arrest and detention of an individual, such arrest and detention could be made by the president of the republic, but in no case might the detention exceed forty-eight hours without trial by a competent tribunal. The president of the republic could not deprive an individual of his property, except in the interest of the public weal, and then only with a proper indemnification to its owner or owners. He might not legally interfere with elections, or with public functionaries who were performing the duties of their office in accordance with the law. And finally he might not absent himself from the republic without formal permission of the chambers.[1]

The vice-president of the republic was appointed by the president of the republic and approved by the chambers, as already noted. The qualifications for the office of vice-president of the republic were the same as for the office of president of the republic. The vice-president was the chief of the ministry (*ministerio*), responsible for the administration of the republic, together with the ministers *del despacho* in their respective ministries. He was to sign and confirm, in the name of the president of the republic, all acts of the administration, with the minister of the ministry concerned. He could not leave the republic without formal permission of the chambers.[2]

There was a minister *del despacho* for the ministry of the interior and foreign relations, another for that of the treasury, and a third for that of war and the navy. These three ministers were to serve under the immediate orders of the vice-president of the republic. No tribunal and no public official had the right to enforce any orders of the ministers which were not countersigned by the vice-president of the republic and the minister of the ministry concerned. In case of incapacity of the vice-president of the republic, the acts were to be signed by the president of the republic. The ministers *del despacho* were responsible, together with the vice-president, for all orders which they issued contrary to the Constitution, the laws, and the public treaties. The ministers were to prepare the budget for the year for the several ministries, and give an account of the expenditures for the year. In order to be a minister of state it was necessary to be in the enjoyment of full citizenship rights, to be at least thirty years of age, and never to have been convicted of a crime by a competent judicial tribunal.[3]

[1] *Colección oficial, años 1825 y 1826*, pp. 266–267.

[2] *Ibid.*, p. 267.

[3] *Ibid.*, p. 268.

The right to render judgments at law belonged exclusively to the judicial tribunals established by law. The term of office for magistrates and judges was for good behavior. Magistrates and judges could be removed from office only for causes prescribed by law. They were personally responsible for their acts, in accordance with the laws governing that subject. Neither the national government nor the judicial authorities had the right to modify the laws in any case whatsoever, nor had they a right to change the manner in which the laws of the republic were to be enforced. No Bolivian was to be judged in civil or in criminal matters except by competent judicial tribunals established by law for that purpose. Law was to be administered in the name of the Bolivian nation, and the decisions and judgments of the superior tribunals were to be enforced in the name of the nation. The supreme judicial authority resided in the Supreme Court of Justice, composed of a president, six justices (*vocales*), and an attorney (*fiscal*), divided into two chambers. To be a member of the Supreme Court it was necessary to have reached the age of thirty-five years, to be in full possession of the rights of citizenship, and to have been a member of one of the district courts, or, in lieu of that experience, to have practiced law successfully for ten years.[1] The Supreme Court was to:[2]

1) take cognizance of criminal suits in which the vice-president of the republic, the ministers of state, or members of the chambers were involved, whenever the national legislature had ordered such officials to be tried;

2) try cases arising out of infringements of the national patronage (*patronato nacional*);

3) examine bulls, briefs, and rescripts whenever these dealt with civil matters;

4) try cases involving ambassadors, resident ministers, consuls, and diplomatic agents;

5) try cases involving magistrates of the district courts and prefects of departments;

6) determine the competence of the district courts in judgments arising out of differences between public authorities;

7) try, in the third instance, the verdicts of the courts of inquiry into conduct while in office (or the *residencia*) of all public officials;

8) hear petitions from all the tribunals on the interpretation of the law;

9) consult with the chief executive of the republic on matters of interpretation of law in a given question or questions;

10) take cognizance of reversal of decisions of lower courts by the district courts;

11) examine civil and criminal cases pending in the district courts, as prescribed by law;

12) supervise the directive powers, economic as well as correctional, over the tribunals and judgeships (*juzgados*) in the republic.

District courts were to be established whenever the national government

[1] *Colección oficial, años 1825 y 1826*, p. 269.

[2] *Ibid.*, pp. 269–270.

should deem necessary. The qualifications for membership in these courts were also prescribed. To be a member (*vocal*) in these courts it was necessary to have reached the age of thirty years, to be a citizen in the enjoyment of full citizenship rights, and to have been graduated from a law school (*juez de letras*), or to have practiced law successfully for eight years. Judicial districts (*partidos*) were also to be established in the capital of each department of the republic. In the capital of the district there was to be a *juez de letras*. To be a *juez de letras* it was necessary to have attained the age of twenty-five years, to be a citizen in the enjoyment of full citizenship rights, to have the right to practice in any of the tribunals of the republic, and to have practiced law successfully for six years. There was to be a justice of the peace in each *pueblo* to have charge of legal conciliatory methods. There could be no complaint in the courts of a civil or criminal nature until efforts at conciliation had failed. The courts of conciliators had the right to hear both sides to a controversy, to instruct the parties to the controversy in their rights in the case at issue, and to seek to find a practical solution of the issues involved. There was to be no persecution without just trial before a competent judicial tribunal. No person was to be kept in prison more than forty-eight hours without trial. All persons caught committing a crime (*en fragante*) could be arrested by any person and taken before a judge (*juez*). Every case must be tried in public and before a jury. The laws were to be administered by the justices. There was to be neither torture nor forced confessions. All the practices of confiscation or alienation of property were to be abolished, and all cruel and infamous punishments were to cease. The criminal code was to prevent capital punishment whenever that was possible.[1]

The political government of each department was vested in a prefect, and each province was to have a governor. To be a prefect or governor it was necessary to have attained the age of thirty years, to be a citizen in the enjoyment of full citizenship rights, and never to have been convicted of a crime. In each canton there was to be a *corregidor*. The prefects, governors, and *corregidores* were to serve for a term of four years, and might serve for only one more term of equal length. Each *pueblo* with a population of less than two thousand was to have a justice of the peace, who was to serve for one year. The justice of the peace might be reelected but not until after the end of two years. The duties and powers of the prefects, governors, and *corregidores* were to be prescribed by a special law, but these officers were not to exercise judicial powers unless the welfare of the state demanded it. All public officials were to be held strictly accountable for any infractions of the law, or for failure to perform satisfactorily the duties of their office.[2]

There was to be a standing army and a navy and a national militia in every department, composed of the inhabitants of the department. There was also

[1] *Colección oficial, años 1825 y 1826*, pp. 270–272.

[2] *Ibid.*, pp. 272–273.

to be a special armed force, the military police (*resguardo militar*), whose duty was to prevent all illicit commerce and trade.

The Constitution might be amended but not until a period of ten years had elapsed. The amendment was to be presented in writing, signed by at least a third of the members of the Chamber of Tribunes and proposed by a two-thirds vote of that Chamber. The amendment was to be read three different times, with six days between readings, and then discussed after the third reading. If adopted by the three chambers, a law was to be passed declaring the amendment a part of the Constitution. Such a law could not be enacted, however, until the ensuing session of the national legislature.[1]

The Constitution also laid down definite guaranties. All Bolivians were to enjoy liberty, individual security, protection of property, and equality before the law. All persons were to have the right to communicate their ideas by word of mouth or in writing, and might publish the same, without previous censorship, but in conformity with the law. Every Bolivian had the right to enter and leave the republic freely, but had, of course, to observe all police regulations governing such movements. The domicile was a sacredly inviolable asylum. It might not be entered at night except by consent of the owner, nor by day except by a warrant issued by a proper authority and in the manner prescribed by law. Taxes were to be paid by all and in proportion to their ability to pay, and without any privilege to anyone whatsoever. All hereditary employments and privileges (*vinculaciones*) were abolished. No work or industry or commerce was to be prohibited unless it was contrary to public customs or against the security and health of the people. Inventions were to be protected by a special law. Mortmain was abolished.[2] Finally, all constitutional authorities were prohibited from suspending the Constitution or the rights which belonged to every Bolivian, except in the manner prescribed by the Constitution, and then only for a period deemed indispensable for that purpose.[3]

The Constituent Congress declared, in a law of November 13, 1826, that nationals of all countries which had not recognized the independence of Bolivia would be considered foreigners after January 1, 1827. All nationals of such countries were to pay the taxes paid by foreigners. Those who had married Bolivians or who had resided in the republic for four years were not classed as foreigners.

[1] *Colección oficial, años 1825 y 1826*, pp. 273–274.

[2] All properties "aunque pertenezcan á obras pías, á religiones, ó á otros objetos" were to be declared *enajenables*. This is another example of the policy of the Liberator of subordinating the Church to the State.

[3] Then followed the signatures of the deputies of the Constituent Congress. Many of the signers of this instrument had also signed the Acta de Independencia. Many of these signers played important rôles in the later history of the country. Not one of them, however, was ever elected to the presidency of the republic, though many served as ministers of state and members of the Supreme Court.

The executive power was forbidden to employ any foreigner in the service of the government, unless he had lived in the republic for five years if single, or four years if married to a Bolivian.[1] On November 16, 1826, the Constituent Congress authorized the president of the republic to negotiate a loan (*empréstito*) for two million pesos, a million of which was to go to the Liberating Army, and the other million to defray the cost of the Peruvian Expedition.[2] On November 19 the Congress fixed December 9 as the day on which the public authorities were to take the oath to support the Constitution, and prescribed the ceremonies in connection with this act. The members of the national legislature were to take this oath on December 8, 1826.[3] On November 22 the Constituent Congress finally incorporated the Province of Tarija with the Archbishopric of La Plata.[4] The ceremonies to be observed in connection with the administering of the oath on December 9 were also prescribed in detail.[5] On December 7 the Constituent

[1] *Colección oficial, años 1825 y 1826*, pp. 278–279.

[2] *Ibid.*, p. 280. This legislation was required, it will be remembered, by the agreement under which Peru granted independence to Bolivia. The other part of the act was in fulfilment of the act honoring Bolívar and Sucre, of August 11, 1825.

[3] *Ibid.*, pp. 281–282. A *misa solemne* was to be sung on December 9, 1826, at which the Constitution of the republic was to be read before the *ofertorio*, after which the oath to the Constitution was to be taken. All the authorities, ecclesiastical as well as others, were obliged to swear to *guardar y hacer guardar* the fundamental law.

[4] *Ibid.*, p. 284.

[5] *Ibid.*, pp. 289–291. These ceremonies were prescribed in an *orden* issued by Facundo Infante on November 28, 1826. This *orden* concerned primarily the ceremonies to be observed when the public authorities and corporations attended religious functions. The national government, he declared, would attend the religious ceremonies in the Cathedral on Sundays, holy Thursdays and Fridays, Thursdays of the Corpus, August 6, and December 9; and, after the death of Bolívar and Sucre, on July 23 and February 3, the birthdays of the two men. When the national government attended the religious services it was to be accompanied by all public authorities of every rank without exception. The seating in the Cathedral was to be as follows: The president of the republic was to have the seat of honor in the Cathedral, and was to be attended by two chaplains (*capellanes*), one of whom had to be a canon (*canónigo*) or prebend (*prebendado*). To the right of the president were to be seated the ministers of state, the foreign ministers, the members of the Supreme Court, and the members of the district courts. On the left of the president were to be seated the departmental officials, headed by the prefect of the department. The president was to be received by the clergy on arriving and was to be escorted by the clergy to the main door on leaving. The ministers of state, the members of the diplomatic corps, the ministers of the Supreme Court, the prefect of the department, the president of the district court, and the captain general of the armies were to be supplied with a chair and cushion (*silla y cojín*). The ministers and attorneys (*fiscales*) of the district court and the generals of the army were to have chairs without cushions. All the others were merely to have benches. This is an example of the importance of a state religion and a state church.

On December 7, 1826, Infante issued an *orden* forbidding the judge of the first instance to leave the capital of the province in which he was located without formal permission of the Supreme Court. He also forbade governors to leave the territory of their provinces without special permission from the national government (*ibid.*, pp. 298–299).

Congress passed an act governing the conduct of the free press.[1] Several other important acts were passed by the Constituent Congress before the end of the year, in addition to important instructions issued by the ministers of state.[2]

[1] *Colección oficial, años 1825 y 1826*, pp. 299–302. While there was to be freedom of the press, the management of the press was to be carefully controlled. The punishment for the infringement of the law was severe. Everyone who abused the freedom of the press by attacking the government in such a way as to induce to actions against the fundamental laws of the state, by writing against morals and public decency, or by publishing derogatory material concerning the private life of any person, was liable to severe punishment. No person might publish a paper without first giving to the police the name of the paper, the place of publication, and the day on which it was to be published. The publisher was also obliged to have all the articles published in his paper signed by the authors, and to give to the police the names of the subscribers to the paper. Every Bolivian had the right to accuse the publisher for infringing this law. In the trial of such cases there was to be a jury, *el juicio por jurados*. The Constituent Congress was to appoint twenty-five jurors and five alternates at its first session, and after that the jurors were to be chosen by the Chamber of Censors. The juror was to be a citizen in the enjoyment of full citizenship rights, and at least twenty-five years of age. He was to serve for one year. In the trial of cases against this law the court was to recognize no special privilege whatever (*fuero alguno*). The jurors were to keep a record of all the cases that came before them. This was freedom of the press with a vengeance!

[2] On December 15, 1826, the Constituent Congress passed an act consolidating the Spanish debt which was due on May 25, 1809, and ordered its payment beginning January 1, 1827 (*ibid.*, pp. 310–311). On December 19 the Congress passed an act compelling liberated slaves to remain in the employ of their former masters until they had paid for themselves by their labor, the amount to be paid being equal to the amount for which the slaves were last sold. The slave was to pay in addition, if a domestic servant, 30 pesos a year for board and clothing, and if a *peón*, 50 pesos a year (*ibid.*, pp. 315–317). The freed slave might work for someone other than his former master, in which case he was to apply his earnings to the payment of his debt. If the debt was not paid by the time the freed slave was fifty-five years of age, he was to be considered in full possession of his liberty. All traffic in human beings was of course forever abolished, and all contracts for such traffic were also abolished. The masters of slaves who had not been paid were to be paid by the state. On December 21 the Congress passed an act prescribing the dress to be worn by the president of the republic. He was to wear the uniform of his military rank, with the three-colored band, and the insignia (*insignia del bastón*). If he did not belong to the military, he was to wear the dress of a diplomat, with the band and the *bastón*. He was to be addressed as Excellency. In turn the president of the republic was to prescribe the dress to be worn by the vice-president of the republic, the ministers of state, the members of the judicial tribunals, and other functionaries of the government (*ibid.*, p. 321). On December 29 Bernabé y Madero issued, as minister of the treasury (*ministro de hacienda*), an *orden* forbidding the governors of the provinces to receive more than *cinco por cinco* for the collection of the *tributo* (*ibid.*, p. 331). On December 26 an act was passed by the Congress prescribing the amount of income tax to be paid (*ibid.*, pp. 323–325). On December 27 an act was passed by the Congress exempting the Indians from payment of the income tax on their communal lands and on the cattle of the natives (*ganados de indígenas*). The Indians were only to pay the ordinary *tributo*. They might, if they so desired, acquire title to the lands that they possessed, or to parts of the public lands (*tierras baldías*). It was ordered that the proceedings in the matter of securing title to such lands should be as simple as possible (*ibid.*, pp. 325–326). On December 28 the Congress passed an act naming the classes that were to pay the commission (*patente*) and the amount to be paid by each member of the class. There were to be seven

And finally on December 31, 1826, the Constituent Congress passed an act by which the national government recognized, as a national debt, damages due to the citizens of Bolivia in the claims against the Spanish government prior to 1809.[1]

The Bolivian nation had been established on a fairly sound basis by the end of the year 1826. Between February 9, 1825, and December 31, 1826, the constitutional government had been established, the governments of the United Provinces of Río de la Plata and Peru had recognized the independence of the republic, and the internal condition of the country had been improved. The greatest work done by Bolívar and Sucre, with the aid of the Liberating Army, was in establishing and maintaining peace and order in the republic. While this is to their eternal credit, the fact that they remained too long after their work was done greatly detracts from that glory. They developed a feeling among the Bolivian people that Bolivia was merely an appendage of Great Colombia, and that, in the end, Bolivia would lose her independence and her sovereignty and become a part of Colombia. The intense bitterness of feeling toward both men that was thus engendered made the overthrow of the Bolivarian régime in Bolivia inevitable. Sucre was forced to resign in 1828, and left the country.[2]

---

classes of *patentes*, each of which was to pay a fixed sum. One class was to pay 52 pesos a year, another 28 pesos, another 12 pesos, and another only 2 pesos a year. The whole matter was described in detail (*ibid.*, pp. 327–329). On December 30 the Congress passed an act recognizing the services which certain army officers had rendered in the establishment of the republic. Generals of Brigade José Miguel Lanza and José María Pérez de Urdininea were each to be paid 15,000 pesos for services rendered on February 9, 1825, and in general for such services as they had rendered the state (*ibid.*, pp. 331–332).

[1] *Colección oficial, años 1825 y 1826*, pp. 332–333.

[2] The machinations of Agustín Gamarra, the notorious *caudillo* dictator of Peru, brought about the *motín militar* of April 18, 1828, which led to the end of the rule of Sucre. Sucre was so severely wounded in suppressing that revolt that he was unable adequately to care for the affairs of state. At any rate he was obliged to intrust the government of the country to the Council of Ministers (*Consejo de Ministros*) with Urdininea at the head. This body failed to prepare the country for defense against Gamarra, with the result that Gamarra invaded Bolivia and forced its government to sign the hated Treaty of Piquiza on July 6, 1828. Gamarra was able to force Bolivia to drive out the Colombian influence. The terms of the treaty required that Sucre resign the presidency and a new government be established. The Congress of Bolivia met for that purpose. But before it met Sucre had already resigned, on August 1, 1828, and left the Bolivian people an excellent legacy in the shape of his farewell address to the Congress. On August 2, 1828, Sucre left Chuquisaca for Colombia, a forlorn and pathetic figure, a victim of intrigue and the sins of Bolívar. In this crisis the remarkable and sinister figure of Casimiro Olañeta played one of his characteristic rôles. He was one of those who were convinced that Bolivia would never really come into its own until it had broken completely with the Bolivarian régime, for which reason he worked against Sucre and in favor of his overthrow and the establishment of a new government. Olañeta is best known in this crisis for the brilliant note of October 11, 1828, in which he denounced Bolívar and his policy toward Bolivia. Olañeta declared that Bolívar had forced upon the Bolivian people an impossible government, and that the Bolivarian constitution was "la vergüenza de la especie humana,

The Colombian troops also left the republic in the same year. Both Bolivia and Peru made war upon Great Colombia, and won what is called the second independence for Bolivia. The whole is a sad commentary on the ingratitude of peoples, and on the consequences of dictatorship.

---

porque es el pacto de los opresores de los pueblos con cuatro parásitos." He declared that, thanks to the aid given Bolivia by Peru through Gamarra, Bolivia had been liberated from this abominable domination, and had erected an appropriate new government, which the Bolivian people were determined to defend at any cost. He grew eloquent and sarcastic in describing the actual state of affairs in Bolivia under the rule of Great Colombia, declaring: "Ya no quiere ser el patrimonio de personas, la colonia de otro Estado americano, la esclava de su política, el pedestal de sus aspiraciones, i aborrece el título de la HIJA QUERIDA. Bolivia habría reconocido un padre si sacada de la esclavitud no se la encadenara de nuevo, i se la hubiese dejado disponer libremente de sus destinos i suerte. . . . Bolivia renuncia para siempre, una, mil i millones de veces a tal dictado. No tiene otra madre que la libertad, otros hermanos que las naciones que obren por los principios de justicia universal, ni más parientes que la razón." He concluded by declaring that Bolivia could not remain indifferent in case of a war between Peru and Great Colombia. In the war that followed Bolívar and Sucre were victorious, but the result was that Bolivia remained independent of the rule of Great Colombia. The appearance upon the scene in Bolivia of Andrés Santa Cruz in 1829, to remain her ruler for almost ten years, sealed the doom of Colombia in Bolivia. This whole phase of the history of Bolivia is, of course, dealt with in great detail by many important writers. Agustín Iturricha, in his excellent *Historia de Bolivia bajo la administración del mariscal Andrés Santa Cruz*, is very critical of Bolívar and his policy toward Bolivia. He declares that Bolívar was one of those men who believe that because they have rendered some service to the state they are entitled to be raised to the supreme power in the state, and to remain there. He declares that Bolívar lacked modesty, that he always wanted to bask in the sunshine of public popularity, and that he sought the ovations of men. He declares that the great Liberator refused to immolate himself for the sacredness of the cause for which he labored. Nor did Bolívar crown his great work with permanency. The greatest error of his whole career was, according to Iturricha, that he did not curb the military, but made it an instrument to keep him perpetually in power. Hence his legacy to Bolivia is the militant *caudillaje*, the bane of the political life of the republic. Consult Iturricha, pp. 53–55. For the view of J. Fred Rippy and that of the present author on dictatorship, with emphasis upon Bolívar as a dictator, consult Wilgus (ed.), *South American dictators*, pp. 22–35, 255–289. Also see Basadre, *La iniciación de la república*. For Bolívar's own views on Bolivia, consult Lecuna's *Cartas del Libertador*, vols. III, IV, V, VI; and the most recent work defending Bolívar, by Enrique Finot, *Bolívar pacifista* (New York, 1926).

THE NATIONAL GOVERNMENT: THE LEGISLATURE

THE Republic of Bolivia adopted her present, the thirteenth, political Constitution on September 26, 1931.[1] The legislative power (*poder legislativo*) is vested in a National Congress (*Congreso Nacional*), composed of a Chamber of Deputies (*Cámara de Diputados*) and a Chamber of Senators (*Cámara de Senadores*). The Congress meets in regular annual sessions, beginning on August 6. The regular session continues for sixty days, and may be prolonged by action of the Congress itself, or by the chief executive, for thirty days. The Congress may also be convened in extra session whenever the chief executive shall deem such a session necessary. The regular and special sessions of the Congress are held in the capital of the republic unless otherwise specified in the call for the session.[2] The Congress may meet in a place other than the

[1] The *Constitución política de la República de Bolivia* is the source used here, and is a pamphlet authorized by the Chamber of Deputies on September 26, 1931. It contains, in addition to the Constitution proper, the *Acta de Independencia*, or Declaration of Independence, adopted on August 6, 1825. The first political constitution of Bolivia was adopted, as we have already noted, on November 6 and promulgated on November 19, 1826. The second constitution was promulgated August 14, 1831; the third October 20, 1834; the fourth May 1, 1839 (the *Pacto de la Confederación Perú-Boliviana*, or Constitution of the Peru-Bolivian Confederation); the fifth October 26, 1839; the sixth June 17, 1843; the seventh September 21, 1851; the eighth August 5, 1861; the ninth October 1, 1868; the tenth October 18, 1871; the eleventh February 15, 1878; and the twelfth on October 28, 1880. These data are from the indispensable three-volume work by Mario C. Araoz, *Nuevo digesto de legislación boliviana*, vol. I, p. 29. The first twelve fundamental laws are also given in Manuel Ordóñez López, *Constitución política de la República de Bolivia: leyes y disposiciones más usuales*, vol. II, pp. 285–454, except that of 1880, which is given in Araoz, *op. cit.*, vol. I, pp. 1–21. The Constitution of 1880 was readopted by the Convención Nacional of 1899, with some important changes, and remained in force until July 12, 1920. The Law of January 24, 1921, enacted by the Convención Nacional, again readopted the Constitution of 1880, with certain changes. It was continued in force until June 1930, when it was suspended as a result of the Revolution of June of that year. The Constitution of 1931 is in reality the Constitution of 1880, amended, to be sure, in several important respects. These changes will be noted later. The political organization of the present national government will be discussed in the light of these several fundamental laws. We have already set forth in detail the main provisions of the *Constitución vitalicia*, as the Bolivarian Constitution of 1826 was called. The plan is first to give the set-up as at present in force, and then to call attention to the differences between that set-up and those under the other fundamental laws. It is necessary to have in mind that the term "political constitution" is used to distinguish a political constitution from an ecclesiastical constitution, a universal practice in Bolivia.

[2] Bolivia has, as is well known, really two capitals. Sucre is still the *de jure* capital. The Supreme Court, the National Archives, the National Tribunal of Accounts, and the National Library are located in Sucre. The *de facto* capital is at La Paz.

capital city if the chief executive deems that the condition of the country demands it. As a matter of fact the national legislature has met in several different places. In the period between 1825 and 1925 it held exactly one hundred different sessions, of which twenty-nine were in Sucre, sixty in La Paz, fifty-eight in Oruro, two in Cochabamba, and one in Tapacari.[1] The national legislature was also known by different names during that period. The first was called the General Deliberative Assembly, four were called Constituent Congresses, one the National Assembly, seven Constitutional Congresses, twenty-four Extraordinary Congresses, six National Conventions, one Extraordinary Constituent Congress, forty-three Ordinary Congresses, four Constituent Assemblies, two Extraordinary Assemblies, two Ordinary Assemblies, two Ordinary Legislatures, and one simply a Legislature. These national legislatures sanctioned twelve political constitutions and elected, or approved the election of, twenty-five presidents of the republic.[2] Since 1925 the Congress has met in La Paz. Only one of the political constitutions, that of 1868, specifically mentions the capital by name.[3] The Constitution of 1826 began the practice by stating that the Congress should meet in the capital of the republic, but without mentioning the capital by name. The omission may have been intentional, for it is a well-known fact that Bolívar wanted the capital located in Cochabamba and not in Sucre.

The right to convoke the Congress in regular or special session belongs to the chief executive. The people have insisted, however, upon the right to meet in Congress even without authorization by the executive. All the constitutions except those of 1831 and 1834 have the provision, accordingly, that the Congress shall meet even though the chief executive has not formally called it. The Constitution of 1868 made provision, however, for only one session of the Congress in two years.[4] The Constitutions of 1831,[5] 1834,[6] 1839,[7] 1843,[8] 1851,[9] 1868,[10]

[1] *Historia parlamentaria de Bolivia desde 1825 hasta 1925*. This publication, which was issued in connection with the hundredth anniversary (1925) of the founding of the republic, contains a great amount of very useful factual information.

[2] *Ibid.*

[3] Manuel Ordóñez López, *Constitución política de la República de Bolivia: leyes y disposiciones más usuales*, vol. II, p. 407. (Hereinafter to be cited as Ordóñez López, *Constitución política*.) The location of the national capital has always been, and still is, one of the most complex questions in Bolivia. As was pointed out earlier, Bolivia is a land of sectionalism. The leading cities, such as La Paz, Cochabamba, Sucre, Potosí, Oruro, Santa Cruz, and Tarija, are deeply concerned about this important question. Perhaps the most dangerous movement to force the capital away from Sucre was the Revolution of 1898–1899. In that event, which will be described later, the question of the federal form of the national government also played an important part. Though the efforts to change the government from a unitarian to a federal form failed, the movement did result in making La Paz the *de facto* capital, although there has been no legislation depriving Sucre of the title.

[4] *Ibid.*, p. 407, art. 32.

[5] *Ibid.*, pp. 305–306, art. 17.

[6] *Ibid.*, p. 324, art. 17.

[7] *Ibid.*, p. 344, art. 19.

[8] *Ibid.*, p. 365, art. 14.

[9] *Ibid.*, p. 379, art. 28.

[10] *Ibid.*, p. 406, art. 28.

1878,[1] and 1880[2] divided the Congress into two houses. The Constitutions of 1861[3] and 1871,[4] on the other hand, provided only for one chamber, which was called the Assembly (*Asamblea*). The lower house was called the Chamber of Representatives (*Câmara de Representantes*) in the Constitutions of 1831,[5] 1834,[6] 1839,[7] 1843,[8] 1851,[9] and 1868.[10] It was called the Chamber of Deputies (*Câmara de Diputados*) in the Constitutions of 1878[11] and 1880.[12] The upper house has always been called the Chamber of Senators (*Câmara de Senadores*).

The members of the Congress enjoy the rights, privileges, and immunities usually enjoyed by members of legislative bodies in other constitutional régimes. There is immunity from accusation, persecution, and arrest, except in case of crime *en fragante*, on the way to and from the sessions of the Congress. Any member may, however, be arrested by order of the chamber of which he is a member.[13] No member may be molested for opinions expressed in the performance of his legislative functions.[14] Members of the Congress may be appointed ministers of state, diplomatic representatives, or military officers in time of war, and they may be elected president or vice-president of the republic, but members chosen to such positions must resign their seat in the Congress.[15] Members may not accept any public employment which is controlled by the chief executive; and no civil, ecclesiastical, or military functionaries may be elected to the Congress. Nor may other public functionaries be elected to the Congress from the electoral districts in which they exercise jurisdiction or authority.[16] All the members of the Congress have the right, during their term of

[1] Ordóñez López, *Constitución política*, vol. II, p. 438, art. 39.

[2] Mario C. Araoz, *Nuevo digesto de legislación boliviana*, vol. I, p. 6, art. 39. (Hereinafter to be cited as Araoz, *Nuevo digesto*.)

[3] Ordóñez López, *Constitución política*, vol. II, p. 392, art. 21.

[4] *Ibid.*, p. 421, art. 36.

[5] *Ibid.*, pp. 305–306, art. 17.

[6] *Ibid.*, p. 324, art. 17.

[7] *Ibid.*, p. 344, art. 21.

[8] *Ibid.*, p. 366, art. 20.

[9] *Ibid.*, p. 379, art. 28.

[10] *Ibid.*, p. 406, art. 28.

[11] *Ibid.*, p. 438, art. 39.

[12] Araoz, *Nuevo digesto*, vol. I, p. 6, art. 39.

[13] *Constitución política de la República de Bolivia*, p. 23, art. 53. (Hereinafter to be cited as *Constitución política*.)

[14] *Ibid.*, pp. 22–23, art. 52.

[15] *Ibid.*, p. 22, art. 50.

[16] *Ibid.*, p. 22, art. 51.

office, to make observations on the manner of enforcing legislation, and to make suggestions to the chief executive for improvement in the administration.[1] The sessions of the Congress are public except in cases where the welfare of the state demands that they be secret.[2] When a citizen is elected to both chambers of the Congress, he must choose the Senate,[3] but may choose the department or district which he wishes to represent.[4] A member may resign his seat in the Congress. Every member receives a salary (*dietas*) for each session; the salary is fixed by law, and may not be changed until after two years after such a change has been authorized.[5] The Congress has the power to:[6]

1) make, repeal, amend, and interpret the laws;

2) levy taxes, abolish old ones, and determine, when necessary, the amount of taxes to be allocated to the departments and the provinces;

3) fix the budget for the public administration, at every session of the regular Congress;

4) determine the strength of the standing army in every regular session of the Congress in time of peace; but appropriations for the upkeep of the armed forces of the republic shall only be for eighteen months at a time, and the size of the standing army shall be determined for a like period of time;

5) authorize the chief executive to make loans (*contratar empréstitos*) for purposes of raising funds, specifying the use to be made of the funds so raised; and recognize the public debts and arrange means for their payment;

6) create new departments and provinces, fixing their boundaries; and provide for major ports and establish customhouses;

7) coin money, and determine the weight, value, type, and denomination thereof; authorize the issuance and circulation of bank notes; and regulate the system of weights and measures;

8) grant subsidies, or provide means of support, for the construction of railways, canals, roads, and other means of transportation;

9) permit the transit of foreign troops across the territory of the republic, and determine the time during which they may remain in the territory;

10) permit bodies of the permanent army to be stationed in the place where the Congress holds its sessions or within a radius of ten leagues;

11) permit the national troops to leave the territory of the republic, and determine when they must return;

12) create and abolish public offices, fix or modify their powers, and fix the salaries of public officials;

[1] *Constitución política*, p. 23, art. 53.

[2] *Ibid.*, p. 24, art. 54.

[3] *Ibid.*, p. 24, art. 55.

[4] *Ibid.*, p. 24, art. 56.

[5] *Ibid.*, p. 24, art. 58.

[6] *Ibid.*, pp. 24–26, art. 59.

13) declare amnesties and grant pardons to specified persons, but only with the permission of the Supreme Court;

14) ratify or refuse to ratify treaties and conventions of all kinds.

Each chamber is the sole judge of the election of its members, with the right to refuse to seat a member, temporarily or permanently. It may punish all infringements of its rules, organize its secretariat, appoint all the employees dependent upon it, determine the expenses of the chamber and provide means to defray such expenses, and attend to all that which concerns its formal government.[1]

The two chambers meet in joint session to:[2]

1) open and close the sessions;

2) verify the votes, or *actas*, in the elections for the president and the vice-president of the republic; and elect these officers in case no one has been elected to these offices, as provided in articles 91, 92, 93, and 94 of the Constitution;

3) receive the oath of office of the officers named in the preceding paragraph;

4) accept or refuse to accept the resignations of these officers;

5) ratify or refuse to ratify public treaties and conventions negotiated by the chief executive;

6) reconsider bills vetoed by the executive;

7) resolve upon a declaration of war, upon request of the chief executive;

8) approve or disapprove the report of the treasury (*la cuenta de hacienda*), which the chief executive is obliged to present to the Congress;

9) determine the strength of the armed forces of the republic;

10) decide the conflicts of jurisdiction between it and the executive or the Supreme Court of Justice, by a two-thirds vote; and by an absolute majority of votes the conflicts of these powers with each other, or between the district courts and the Court of Cassation;

11) grant, by a two-thirds vote, financial rewards (*premios pecuniarios*);

12) examine the account of the use made of the state of siege by the chief executive and the authority for the exercise of the power to declare a state of siege (*estado de sitio*);

13) elect the president and the ministers of the Supreme Court.

The Congress has no power to delegate to one of its members or to a group of its members, or to any other power, the powers (*atribuciones*) which have been granted to it by the Constitution.[3]

The Chamber of Deputies is composed of deputies elected by a direct vote of the citizens by a simple plurality of votes.[4] To be a deputy a citizen must have his name duly inscribed in the national register of voters, must be over twenty-

[1] *Constitución política*, pp. 26–27, art. 60.

[2] *Ibid.*, pp. 27–28, art. 61.

[3] *Ibid.*, p. 28, art. 62.

[4] *Ibid.*, pp. 28–29, art. 63.

five years of age, a native-born or naturalized citizen with a residence of five years in the country, and must have an annual income of Bs.[1] 400 from a profession, a trade, or real property. He must never have been condemned to corporal punishment by the regular courts.[2] The term of office is four years. The membership of the Chamber of Deputies is renewed by halves every two years.[3] The Chamber of Deputies has the sole power to:[4]

1) originate the measures explained in clauses 2, 3, 4, and 5 of article 59;

2) impeach the president and the vice-president of the republic, the ministers of state, the ministers of the Supreme Court, and the diplomatic agents before the Chamber of Senators for crimes committed by them in the performance of the functions of their offices;

3) elect, from a list of nominees presented by the Chamber of Senators, the members of the National Tribunal of Accounts (*vocales del Tribunal Nacional de Cuentas*).

The Chamber of Senators is composed of two senators from each department of the republic. To be a senator it is necessary to be a native-born or naturalized citizen, with a residence of five years in the republic, and duly inscribed in the national register. The candidate must be over thirty-five years of age, and have an annual income of Bs. 800 from real property, trade, or a profession. He must never have been condemned to corporal punishment by a regularly constituted judicial tribunal.[5] The term of office of the senator is six years. The membership of the Chamber of Senators is renewed by thirds every two years.[6] The Chamber of Senators has the power to:[7]

1) try impeachment cases presented by the Chamber of Deputies;

2) nominate candidates for the offices of archbishop and bishop, the nominations to be presented by the chief executive to the canonical institution;

[1] The *boliviano* is the monetary unit of Bolivia, and is worth about 33 cents in United States currency, under normal exchange rates.

[2] *Constitución política*, p. 29, art. 64.

[3] *Ibid.*, p. 29, art. 65.

[4] *Ibid.*, p. 29, art. 66.

[5] *Ibid.*, p. 31, art. 69.

[6] *Ibid.*, p. 31, art. 70.

[7] *Ibid.*, pp. 31–32, art. 71. In case the Chamber of Senators finds the impeachment well founded, it must suspend the officer impeached and turn him over to the Supreme Court for trial in accordance with the laws which govern such cases. The Chamber of Senators has full power, however, over the impeachment of ministers of the Supreme Court, but the question must be decided by a two-thirds vote of the members present.

3) nominate candidates for the office of member[1] (*vocal*) of the National Tribunal of Accounts, for election by the Chamber of Deputies;

4) restore to citizenship those who have been deprived of it;

5) permit Bolivians to accept honors, employment, titles, or emoluments from other governments, provided these favors do not violate the laws of the republic;

6) elect, by secret ballot, generals and colonels of the army from among those nominated by the chief executive;

7) decree public honors to those who deserve them for great and eminent services rendered to the republic.

The internal organization of each of the two chambers is prescribed in detail. The officers of the Chamber of Deputies—a president, two vice-presidents, and two secretaries—are elected at the first regular session of the Congress.[2] These five officers compose the *mesa* of the Chamber of Deputies. The president has large powers. He speaks for the Chamber in words approved by it. He opens and closes the sessions, but closes them only when instructed to do so by the Chamber. He preserves order in strict accordance with the regulations of the Chamber governing that matter. He announces the subjects for discussion, puts the questions to a vote, and gives preference to pending questions before the Chamber. He supervises the work of the employees and officers of the Chamber, and satisfies himself that the work is done punctually and effectively. He has charge of the attendance of the deputies and may excuse them from the sessions but not to exceed eight days at a time, except by special permission of the Chamber. He orders the payment of the salaries of the secretaries and of the deputies; and he receives the oath of the deputies in public session. The vice-presidents of the Chamber perform the duties of the president in case of his absence or inability to perform the duties of his office. In the absence of the president and vice-presidents, a deputy, elected for that purpose by a majority of the votes cast, presides over the Chamber. The Chamber of Deputies does its work through nineteen permanent commissions.[3]

[1] The members of the National Tribunal of Accounts serve for a term of six years, and may be removed only for cause, the cause to be determined by the Supreme Court (*Constitución política*, pp. 29–30).

[2] Araoz, *Nuevo digesto*, vol. I, pp. 54–55. This is in accordance with the *Reglamento de debates* for the Chamber of Deputies of September 24, 1900, amended in 1928. The deputies must arrive in the city where the sessions are to be held on August 4, to help prepare for the opening of the Congress on the 6th of that month, and to have their credentials examined and approved. A preliminary session is held at which a commission of five members is elected to examine the credentials of all the new members. In case any difficulty arises over the credentials, the question is referred to the regular session of the Congress. The deputy whose credentials are challenged is, of course, not allowed to take his seat until they have been approved.

[3] These commissions are: Comisión de Poderes, de Constitución, de Policía Judicial, de Negocios Diplomáticos, de Hacienda y Contabilidad, de Presupuesto, de Administración Política y Municipal y de Policía de Seguridad, de Justicia, de Instrucción Pública, de Guerra,

The Chamber of Deputies may not begin its sessions unless half of the membership is present. The regular sessions are held daily at two o'clock in the afternoon and last four hours with two or three fifteen-minute intermissions. There are no sessions on Saturdays or on holidays unless there is urgent need for such a session. Secret sessions may be held when requested by the chief executive or by the Chamber itself. Special sessions may be held when the chief executive requests them, or when five members of the Chamber request them in writing.

The ministers of state may attend the sessions of the Chamber of Deputies whenever they so desire. They may take part freely in the debates, but when doing so are subject to the same rules as the deputies. The minister of state, however, has no vote and may not be present in the Chamber when a vote is taken. Any deputy may ask a minister of state for information on any subject connected with his ministry when the minister is in the Hall of Sessions. The minister is not obliged to give any information which he deems prejudicial to the welfare of the state. A minister of state may be requested to attend a session, and is under obligation to attend when so requested. The ministers of state are also obliged to submit to interpellation. They may, of course, resign rather than submit to interpellation. They are given time, however, to prepare for the interpellation. When a deputy desires to interpellate a minister of state he must make a request in writing to the president of the Chamber, formally stating what he desires to have discussed, and must so inform the minister. The Chamber decides the day on which the minister is to appear, and formally informs him of it. If the minister decides to defend himself in the Chamber he may do so, and the whole question may then be discussed at length. When the matter is deemed to have been discussed sufficiently, the Chamber may call for the order of the day pure and simple, or it may decide to vote on the subject discussed. The first procedure has the effect of dismissing the whole subject. The second implies a censure or a vote of confidence, according to the result of the vote. If the motion is on the question of confidence in the national government, an adverse vote means a censure.[1] The right of inter-

de Industria, de Obras Públicas, de Aviación, Vialidad, y Navegación, de Culto, de Peticiones, de Colonias y Agricultura, de Minería, de Higiene y Salubridad, de Reformas Sociales, and de Régimen Interno. The Comisión de Justicia has nine members, those on Constitución, Negocios Diplomáticos, Hacienda, Vialidad, and Presupuesto have eight each, and all the others have five members each. The Chamber may, of course, alter the membership of each of these when it so desires. It may also decrease or increase the number of commissions.

[1] Araoz, *Nuevo digesto*, vol. I, pp. 54–64. No deputy may speak more than once on any subject without permission from the Chamber. No deputy may be interrupted when speaking, unless he is out of order, when the president has the right call to him to order. The speaker may appeal from the decision of the chair. If the decision is against him he may not continue his speech. All matters are decided by a majority of the votes cast, unless otherwise ordered. No deputy may refuse to vote or retire from the Hall of Sessions while the voting is going on.

pellation has been in force in Bolivia from the beginning of its political independence. The practice of interpellation is European in origin, and has been followed in Bolivia for the same reason as in European countries. Its object is to bring an individual minister of state or the whole ministry or a whole party into political disrepute. It is therefore primarily the weapon of a political opposition. It has been used in Bolivia on several occasions with telling effect.

The internal organization of the Chamber of Senators is fully as complicated as that of the Chamber of Deputies.[1] The presiding officer is the vice-president of the republic. He may not take part in the debates, but he has large powers nevertheless. He has the regular duties of a presiding officer. The Chamber of Senators also elects its own presiding officer from among its own membership, to serve for one year.[2] A secretary is also elected from among the members of the Chamber. The vice-president of the republic, the president *pro tempore*, and the secretary constitute the *mesa* of the Chamber of Senators. Like the Chamber of Deputies, the Chamber of Senators has its permanent commissions, of which there are ten.[3] The sessions of the Chamber are public, and are conducted in accordance with rules similar to those in force in the Chamber of Deputies.[4]

The Electoral Law of 1924 is of importance in connection with the election of the members of the Congress. The law is based on the principle that citizenship must be exercised in order to be enjoyed. Citizenship has duties and obligations as well as privileges. The citizen votes and holds office on that principle. Voting is obligatory. The failure to vote is a failure to perform a duty. The citizen must inscribe his name in a civil register kept for that purpose. In order to inscribe his name, the citizen must have the necessary qualifications. He must be at least twenty-one years of age if single, and eighteen if married. He must know how to read and write the Castilian language. He must have an annual income of Bs. 200, or real property which will bring him an annual income of at

[1] Araoz, *Nuevo digesto*, vol. I, pp. 39–51. The senators must arrive in the capital several days before the formal opening of the Congress, for reasons similar to those for the Chamber of Deputies.

[2] The president *pro tempore* performs the duties of the presiding officer whenever the vice-president of the republic is absent or unable to perform the duties of the office. The presiding officer has no vote except in case of a tie.

[3] Araoz, *Nuevo digesto*, vol. I, p. 41. These commissions are: Comisión de Constitución y Policía Judicial, de Negocios Internationales y Culto, de Hacienda y Presupuesto, de Justicia y Peticiones, de Instrucción Pública, de Administración Política y Municipal, de Guerra, de Colonias y Agricultura, de Industria, Navegación, Obras Públicas, y Vialidad, and de Reformas Sociales. Each commission has a president and a secretary elected from its own members. The Senate may not begin its regular sessions without the presence of at least an absolute majority of the total membership of its body. The daily session begins at 1 P. M. There is an official, known as the *oficial mayor*, who keeps the papers of the Senate and the National Congress in order.

[4] *Ibid.*, pp. 39–51. There are a great many details which are not given here.

least that amount. This law is equally definite in precluding men who are not considered fit to enjoy the privilege of the franchise. These include the insane, idiots, and feeble-minded; vagabonds as defined by law; and confirmed drunkards, according to the testimony of three persons of quality. This class also includes those who are legally incapacitated, such as citizens naturalized in foreign countries; those who have lost their citizenship through the acceptance of offices and decorations from foreign governments without permission from the Bolivian government; those who have been exiled; and members of the regular clergy. Another class includes those who are juridically and morally incapable of exercising the franchise, such as those who have been condemned to corporal punishment, or have been dismissed from public service, and who have not been restored to citizenship; those who have been found guilty of bearing false witness, or of electoral crimes, and have not yet been restored to citizenship; those who have been adjudged, by a judicial sentence, to be defrauders of public moneys (*defraudadores de caudales públicos*); and those who have been adjudged bankrupt. The last class also includes those who are engaged in certain professions or services, such as generals, chiefs (*jefes*), officials (*oficiales*), corporals (*cabos*), and soldiers of the line, and members of groups of active or reservist *militares*. Soldiers or *militares* who have been pensioned are not included in this class; but it does include the commissary, the agents of the police, gendarmes, day and night watchmen, and all members of the police force. All these men, however, perform the other duties of citizenship.[1]

[1] Every electoral district has its civil register, in which all citizens, eligible to do so, must have their names inscribed. They must enter their civil residence, place of business, trade, profession, or occupation. Registration in any other place has no value, except in the case of public functionaries, who may register in the district where they exercise their functions. Registration in the civil register is a purely personal matter and cannot be performed by anyone but the person concerned. Only Bolivians who are absent in foreign countries may have the registration performed for them by Bolivian consular agents. Registration in the civil register must be repeated every ten years, *desde su iniciación*. The registration must be made before a notary public, who has been appointed for that purpose by the district courts, and who must give bond for the proper performance of his duties. This bond is in the amount of Bs. 1000 in the capitals of the departments, Bs. 500 in the provinces, and Bs. 200 in the municipal districts (*secciones municipales*). The notary serves for a term of ten years, and may not be removed from office except for cause. He is paid a salary determined by law. The registry contains the full name of the registrant, place of birth, place of residence, status, age, profession, income, color of hair, and bodily defects or blemishes. The civil register is open for inspection by the public. It is closed, however, thirty days before each election, but is opened immediately after election. The civil registers cannot be taken away from their places of deposit. All men born in 1887 and after are required, on registering, to present documents to show that they have met the military requirements. The testimony of one or two men of known honesty is required to witness the signature of the registrant. When the registration has been completed, the voter is given a little booklet, 14 centimeters long and 9 wide, which must contain, on the left, the name of the department and electoral district, the number of the registrant and the number of the *partida y su folio*, and the signature of the registrant. On the right is the name of the voter, the general specifications as given in the civil register, and his signature. Every political party

The Electoral Law of 1924 also specifies the number of deputies to be elected to the Chamber of Deputies. There are two classes of deputies: *propietarios*, or deputies proper, and *suplentes*, or alternates. There are seventy *propietarios* for the whole republic: eight for the Department of Chuquisaca, sixteen for the Department of La Paz, fourteen for the Department of Cochabamba, eleven for the Department of Potosí, six for the Department of Oruro, five for the Department of Tarija, seven for the Department of Santa Cruz, and three for the Department of El Beni. In every instance, of course, the number of deputies from the capital of the department is larger than from any of the provinces. This is only natural, since the rural population of Bolivia is much smaller than the urban population. The city of La Paz alone sends four out of the sixteen deputies from that department.[1] The election of the deputies and alternates is

may have someone to watch over the registering and to see that everything is done correctly. On the other hand, the notaries public may ask to have the party representatives removed if their presence is an inconvenience. In case the registration has been made out fraudulently, the whole process of registration becomes null and void; the registrant involved must pay a fine of Bs. 100, and may also be imprisoned for three months. The notary must also pay a fine of Bs. 300, and may be imprisoned for six months or a year. Infringements of the electoral law are tried by the Supreme Court.

The selection of the jurors who are to constitute the *juntas calificadoras* is an elaborate process, as is also the manner in which they are to exercise their functions. There are also *mesas receptoras*, which receive the votes cast at an election. Members of these *mesas* are elected for that purpose. Their duties are many and very important. It is their business to see that there are no frauds or irregularities in voting. This process is called scrutinizing the election returns, or rather counting the votes cast in the elections. These returns must give an accurate statement of the votes cast, the names of the candidates, and the names of those duly elected. The voting is done in secret, but before the citizen may vote he must present evidence of his right to vote; that is, he must present his book of registration to the *mesa receptora*, which decides whether he may or may not vote. The *mesa receptora* may not, however, question the information in the book of registration. The *escrutinios* must count the votes cast with great care. Any vote that is not clear is thrown out and reasons must be given for such action. The *mesa receptora* decides who has been elected by the number of votes each candidate receives. It certifies the election and presents the successful candidate with a certificate of election. The elections for the officers of state are scrutinized several times, depending upon the number of electoral units involved. The provincial authorities scrutinize the returns of the electoral districts, and the departmental authorities those of the provincial elections. Finally the Congress itself, or rather each of the two chambers, repeats the scrutiny of the election of its own members, of which the chamber concerned is the sole judge, as we have already noted. For the president and the vice-president of the republic, the Congress in joint session scrutinizes the returns and pronounces the results. The Congress alone has final jurisdiction in that matter, and it alone declares the results in a formal law. For these reasons the date on which a president of the republic takes office is a fluctuating one. The president in power at the time the constitutional term expires is not infrequently authorized by the Congress to continue in power until the result of the elections for his successor has been determined.

[1] Araoz, *Nuevo digesto*, vol. I, pp. 226–227, art. 125.

held on the first Sunday in May.[1] The procedure for the selection of the senators is also prescribed in detail in the Law of 1924. There are sixteen senators, two from each department. The selection of the president and vice-president of the republic is also prescribed in detail. The more important of the details will be given in the chapter on the executive branch of the national government.

The electoral guaranties are elaborate and are fully set forth in this Law of 1924. The main purpose is to guard against corrupt practices in the elections. One of the most important precautions is against any display of military force on election day in the municipality where the election is held. This is rational enough. If elections are to be free, why the presence of armed forces? Order can be maintained through the regular police force. All functionaries, except deputies and senators, are strictly forbidden to take part in political demonstrations, or to belong to political clubs. As soon as a functionary acts contrary to this regulation, he automatically separates himself from his office or employment. The police are strictly forbidden to interfere with the *mesas receptoras;* if they do interfere, the elections become null and void. Anyone who takes part in disorders of any kind against elections is liable to a heavy fine. The *mesas receptoras* are also not to have any interference from any functionary, civil, ecclesiastical, or military. No voter may absent himself from an election, or refuse to vote, without incurring the penalty of the law. No person may carry insignia, banners, or other emblems whatever on election day under penalty of fine and imprisonment. All saloons and places where strong drinks are sold, served, or drunk must remain closed on election day. Any person who offers to buy a drink or sell votes is subject to a fine of from Bs. 200 to 250 and imprisonment for three to six months. The fine and prison term are greater for the candidate for office who offers to sell or buy votes, a fine of Bs. 1500 to 2000 and six months imprisonment being prescribed for such an offense. It may be observed that these provisions, on the one hand, are too complicated, and, on the other, do not prevent irregularities, since the fines and the terms of imprisonment are not heavy enough. What is a couple of hundred or even a couple of thousand bolivianos to a Bolivian politico? Something more drastic than these precautions is necessary to clean up politics in Bolivia. There is still one more body provided by the Law of 1924 to preserve the sanctity of elections, and that is the electoral police, the *policía electoral*, or *mediador electoral*. It is the business of this body to preserve order and to see that the rules and regulations governing elections are observed. This body has large powers, and upon the honesty of its members depends, to a great degree, the conducting of decent elections. Finally, it should be noted that the fines that are collected for infringements of this law are put in a special fund, known as the *cajas de fondos*

[1] Holding elections on a Sunday is a common practice in Latin America, as well as in many other countries of the world. Sunday is usually a non-working day. The voters are thus enabled to discharge their electoral duties without interference with their labors.

judiciales, and deposited in the Bank of the Nation (*Banco de la Nación*). The *fondos* are thus used for a worthy cause, the cause of justice.[1]

Constitutionally the national legislature of Bolivia is a parliament rather than a congress. It has more power than an ordinary congress has in a democracy. The constitutional system of Bolivia resembles the British parliamentary system more than it does the French system. The right of interpellation of the ministers of state, already briefly explained, amounts to ministerial responsibility, for no ministry has yet dared to remain in power after it has been censured by the Congress. The executive power of Bolivia is, therefore, as definitely under the control of the legislative power as is the British ministry. It is true, as will appear in the study of the executive power, that the president of Bolivia has the absolute right to appoint and dismiss the ministers of state. But once they are duly installed they become answerable for their acts not only to him but to the Congress, and through it to the people. The Congress has in fact far greater power than the British Parliament in that it serves for its elected constitutional period, a fact which prevents the executive power from appealing, if it should so choose, to the people direct, as the executive power in Great Britain may. It may thus be said that the most powerful single body in the Bolivian government, constitutionally considered, is the national legislature. In that body, the body nearest to the Bolivian people is the Chamber of Deputies, as is the case with the British House of Commons. The Congress of Bolivia has played a powerful rôle, accordingly, throughout the whole history of the republic. As legislative bodies go, it has been conspicuous for the leadership it has displayed. In great political crises, such as those of 1839, 1851, 1861, 1871, and 1880, the Congress showed very great ability, due primarily to the quality of its leadership. The Congress of 1880, meeting, as it did, in one of the darkest periods of the history of the country, was an especially brilliant gathering. It has justly been said that Bolivia really began to live in 1880 through the greatness of the leadership of that body.

[1] Araoz, *Nuevo digesto*, vol. I, pp. 203–237. The act is a long one, having 195 articles and covering, as indicated above, more than thirty pages.

THE NATIONAL GOVERNMENT: THE EXECUTIVE

THE national executive power (*poder ejecutivo*) is vested in a citizen with the title of President of the Republic (*Presidente de la República*). The executive power is exercised, however, only through the medium of ministers secretaries of state (*ministros secretarios del despacho*).[1] The chief executive of the Bolivian state has not always exercised his power in that restricted manner. It is true that he has always been considered as the chief administrative officer of the national government. He was not responsible for the acts of his administration, it will be recalled, under the Bolivarian Constitution.[2] The Constitution of 1831, on the other hand, declared the president of the republic responsible for the administrative acts of his government.[3] The Constitution of 1834 declared that he was responsible for the crimes of treason, of illegal retention of office, and of usurpation of any other constitutional powers.[4] The Constitution of 1839 made him responsible for all the acts of his administration conjointly with the ministers of state, each minister for the acts of his own ministry.[5] It was to be expected that any fundamental change made in 1839 would place definite restrictions upon the powers of the chief executive. The overthrow, in that year, of Andrés Santa Cruz brought about, after all, the end of an era and the beginning of another. The Period of Restoration, as the new era was called, was itself of only short duration. The main personality of the Restoration era was José Ballivián.[6] The Constitution of

[1] *Constitución política*, pp. 37–38, art. 82.

[2] Ordóñez López, *Constitución política*, vol. II, p. 294, art. 80.

[3] *Ibid.*, p. 311, art. 71.

[4] *Ibid.*, p. 330, art. 73.

[5] *Ibid.*, p. 350, art. 65.

[6] José Ballivián was one of the most powerful personalities of his age. He was born in La Paz in 1804 of one of the most distinguished families of Bolivia. By his apologists he is also considered as one of the most notable figures of the republic. He was unquestionably one of the ablest military men of his age, his fame resting primarily on the brilliant victory over the Peruvians, under Gamarra, in the celebrated battle of Ingavi of November 18, 1841. Consult José María Aponte, *La batalla de Ingavi: recuerdos históricos*, for a detailed account of this battle. Ballivián received a good education, but entered the military service while still a young man, fighting against Pedro de Olañeta in 1825 and in the wars of Andrés Santa Cruz against Gamarra and Salaverry in 1835 and 1836. He was also a revolutionary leader from the earliest days of his career, seeking through military service to obtain personal glory and

1839 gave way to that of 1843, an instrument that was primarily aristocratic and centralized. The Constitution of 1843 required the chief executive to give an account of his administration to the Congress, but was silent on the further responsibility for the acts of his administration.[1] The Constitution of 1851

---

advancement. His rôle in the *motín militar* (*coup de main*) resulting in the assassination of Pedro Blanco, January 1, 1829, is still wrapped in mystery. He served Andrés Santa Cruz through the most spectacular years of that man's remarkable career, but was one of the first to turn against him. He did this just as soon as he had assured himself that there was little to lose, and much to gain, by deserting Santa Cruz. Here he gave an example of that sense of loyalty so often exhibited by political leaders of Bolivia: abandon an erstwhile benefactor as soon as he is on his way out. The choice of the former president Velasco to guide the destinies of Bolivia, following the downfall of Santa Cruz, caused Ballivián to turn against Velasco. He was defeated in his efforts to overthrow Velasco, and was exiled. But the effort of Gamarra to reincorporate Bolivia with Peru after the overthrow of the Peru-Bolivian Confederation, in 1841, brought Ballivián back into active service. He was given command of the armed forces of Bolivia to repel the Peruvian invasion under Gamarra, with the result already described.

It was the defeat of Gamarra at Ingavi that made José Ballivián the hero of the hour, for that event is considered a third victory for the independence of the republic. He overthrew Velasco and proclaimed himself provisional president early in 1842. In 1843 he was elected constitutional president. He then caused a new political constitution to be drawn up, which was proclaimed in 1843. Ballivián was but continuing a practice which became common in his country. The man who is successful in a revolution to overthrow the president of the republic usually considers it his duty to incorporate the revolutionary ideology in a new constitution; only in this way do many victorious revolutionary leaders feel that they can truly triumph. But Ballivián wanted, in reality, to be a dictator. He sought to restore the Bolivarian régime, and hoped to bring about the adoption of the aims and ideals of Bolívar and Santa Cruz. He was firmly convinced that the people of Bolivia were not able to govern themselves successfully, and needed a very long period of apprenticeship in the art of self-government. He was an ardent supporter of a highly centralized national government and believed in giving the chief executive a great deal of power. This was done by the Constitution of 1843. The result of the dictatorial activities of José Ballivián was inevitable. Manuel Isidoro Belzu took advantage of the discontent with his rule to lead a successful revolution against him, and Ballivián was forced to take the *via dolorosa* of exile on December 23, 1847. He went to Valparaiso, Chile, and later to Rio de Janeiro, Brazil, where he died on October 16, 1852. His remains were brought back to Bolivia and placed in a beautiful mausoleum in La Paz. Consult José María Santivañez, *Vida del general José Ballivián*, and also the author's chapter on "The dictators of Peru, Bolivia, and Ecuador" in Wilgus (ed.), *South American dictators*, p. 290.

[1] Ordóñez López, *Constitución política*, vol. II, p. 371, art. 52. The makers of the Constitution of 1843, unlike those of the Constitution of 1839, not only were under the control of Ballivián but also represented a very different school of political thought. They believed that Ballivián was the real heir to the mantle of leadership which had been laid down by Bolívar and Santa Cruz. The men of 1839, on the other hand, believed in rule by the people, and not by the aristocracy alone; and they certainly did not want a one-man rule. The Constitution of 1839 which they proclaimed has been declared by many scholars to be the most democratic of all the fundamental laws of Bolivia. It is true that it incorporated most of the democratic features of its age. It is particularly important because of the large attention

made the chief executive, conjointly with the ministers of state, responsible for the acts of his administration. Each minister was also responsible for the acts of his own ministry.[1] The Constitution of 1861, the most radical of all the fundamental laws of Bolivia, made the president of the republic, conjointly

---

which it gave to municipal government; in fact, it was the first instrument to establish a democratic municipal régime in the republic.

Despite these laudable services to democracy, the Constitution of 1839 left much to be desired. In the first place, the great majority of the people of Bolivia were excluded from direct participation in the government of the country. The government was still in the hands of the upper classes. The vast body of the people, the Indians and many of the mixed castes, were still without the franchise. It was the white man's rule that was to be preserved at all hazards. In the next place, it must be said that the framers of this fundamental law failed to realize the great fervor of the people of Bolivia for a veritable new age. This fervor was allowed to cool off, as it has been allowed to do in subsequent periods, because of the ambitious designs of influential political leaders, or mere *caudillos*.

[1] Ordóñez López, *Constitución política*, vol. II, p. 383, art. 66. The Constitution of 1851 was the work of the Belzu régime. Manuel Isidoro Belzu, the leader of a mobocracy the like of which Bolivia had never known before, was born on April 4, 1808, in La Paz. He was of the masses, from which group he received his power, and had but little formal education beyond that received in the barracks. He entered the army early. He fought in the wars of emancipation, distinguishing himself in the battle of Zepita, and in the war against Peru in 1841–1842. In the latter he distinguished himself in the battle of Ingavi. He became an enemy of the dictatorship of José Ballivián, and led the December 1847 Revolution which forced Ballivián out of power. He did not seize the supreme power immediately, allowing Velasco another chance. But in December 1848 he defeated Velasco in the battle of Yampu, and proclaimed himself provisional president of the republic. The "Lion of the North," as he was called, deliberately appealed to the *cholos*, by whom he was considered little less than a god. He urged the *cholos* to rise against the upper classes as the authors of their oppression, declaring that they had been robbed by "los que se dicen nobles. . . . La riqueza de los que se dicen nobles, es un robo que se os ha hecho." Consult Alcides Argüedas, *Historia de Bolivia. La plebe en acción, 1848–1857*, pp. 140 ff. Naturally, very bitter opposition developed against him on the part of the upper classes. He was forced to move his government about from place to place to put down revolts against his rule, and developed, in this fashion, a practice which has been rather common in Bolivia. Most of the important cities of the republic served as the seat of the national government during his dictatorship. The attack upon his life in the Prado of Sucre, December 6, 1850, was seized upon by his supporters as occasion for paying him the honors of a god, and using the most extravagant phrases concerning the importance of Belzu in the regeneration of the Bolivian people.

It was during the rule of Belzu that the question of the opening of the Amazon River was at its height. He responded to the importunities of the diplomatic representatives of the United States by declaring the rivers of Bolivia which flow into the Amazon open and free to all the nations of the world. It was also during his rule that Bolivia again made use of the services of Andrés Santa Cruz, employing him as its diplomatic representative to the governments of Europe. Belzu secured the election of Jorge Córdova, a relative, as president in 1855, and retired to private life. Belzu spent some time abroad, but returned in 1865 to lead a revolt against Mariano Melgarejo. Belzu and Melgarejo met in La Paz. The meeting proved to be one of the most dramatic events in their lives, but with Melgarejo victorious. Belzu lost his life in the encounter, probably at the hands of Melgarejo himself. Belzu remains in the history of Bolivia as one of the most enigmatic figures of the nineteenth century.

with the ministers of state, responsible for the acts of his administration.[1]

[1] Ordóñez López, *Constitución política*, vol. II, p. 396, art. 44. The Constitution of 1861 was the work of the group of men who brought about the overthrow of José María Linares, the man who overthrew Córdova, and who established one of the most absolute dictatorships the country has ever known. No dictator could boast of a more autocratic manner of assuming or exercising power than Linares. This is the more remarkable because of his talents and training. Linares was born on July 10, 1810, in Potosí, of one of the most distinguished families in Bolivia. He was of the nobility, a grandson of the Conde de Casareal, one of the most illustrious gentlemen of his age. Linares received an excellent education, graduating from the University of San Xavier as a doctor of laws. He entered public life while quite a young man, and soon displayed statesmanship of the highest order. He was an ardent supporter of José Ballivián and served under him as minister to Spain. It was in that capacity that he negotiated, in 1846, the treaty by which the Spanish government recognized the independence of Bolivia. Linares was the implacable enemy of Belzu and was able to overthrow Córdova in 1857. He was opposed to the rule of Belzu not because he was opposed to dictatorship *per se*, for he firmly believed in dictatorship, but because Belzu appealed to the wrong group of people. Linares was an aristocrat of the aristocrats, and believed in rule by the *élite*. He was of the opinion that the Bolivian people were utterly incapable of governing themselves and needed to be governed by men with absolute powers. He chose able men to help him. Tomás Frías was his minister of the treasury, and other men of ability served him with distinction.

Linares found relations with Peru unsatisfactory because of the designs of Ramón Castilla upon Bolivia. Castilla, like Gamarra, was a firm believer in the union of Bolivia and Peru, and like Gamarra he believed that Bolivia should be made an integral part of Peru and not a member of a federal union. Fortunately for Linares, Castilla was too much concerned with Juan José Flores and Gabriel García Moreno, of Ecuador, to give Linares much real trouble. The arbitrary rule of Linares became more and more objectionable. He refused stoutly to call the national legislature, and was finally overthrown in 1860. He went into exile in Chile, and died in Valparaiso the next year. A *junta gubernativa* composed of Ruperto Fernández, José María de Achá, and Manuel Antonio Sánchez took over the government. The junta called the national legislature to meet in May 1861, and ordered elections of deputies for that body. The deputies elected were among the ablest men that the Bolivian people have ever chosen for their legislative body. It was this body of men who drafted the Constitution of 1861, which many hold to be the best fundamental law ever adopted in Bolivia.

The contest which developed over the election to the presidency had a sinister effect upon this great reform movement. Achá, who was victorious and who was elected constitutional president, was not a friend of the new constitution. He found the instrument much too liberal and soon took steps to have it radically changed. It was in this crisis that Adolfo Ballivián, *el Chico*, the son of José Ballivián, *el Grande*, gained a great reputation by his support of the Constitution. Ballivián was especially incensed at the decree issued by Achá on November 18, 1862, calling for a meeting of the Assembly to draw up a new fundamental law to displace that of 1861. In a proclamation which Ballivián issued against Achá he declared: "La constitución no es vuestra, general Achá. No se hizo para vos; se hizo para Bolivia. No es el imperio de vuestras pretenciones; es el código de nuestras garantías." Though Achá withdrew his decree, his acts had turned the people against him, and it became a relatively easy matter to stage a revolution. It was in December 1864 that he was overthrown, and had to give way to the greatest of all the dictators of Bolivia, Mariano Melgarejo. Achá escaped and died away from his native land. Consult the *Redactor de la Asamblea Constituyente del año 1861* (two volumes) for a great deal of very valuable information on the drafting of the Constitution of 1861, and more particularly on the rivalry among the leaders. The Constituent Assembly of 1861 is another example of the dire results of leaders' falling out among

The fundamental law proclaimed during the dictatorship of Mariano Melgarejo[1] contained no provision concerning the responsibility of the president of the republic. This is rather remarkable since its makers, at the head of whom was the man who served as secretary general throughout the *sexenio* of Melgarejo,

themselves and prostituting their positions for their own advancement rather than using them for the advancement of a great cause.

[1] Mariano Melgarejo was born on April 13, 1820, in Tarata, in the Department of Cochabamba, the son, so it is claimed by many, of Lorenzo Valencia and Ignacia Melgarejo. He was a love child, a bastard, and became the product of the conditions surrounding bastardy. He is still the subject of much difference of opinion as to his character and abilities. Friend and foe alike are agreed, however, that he was a man of extraordinary talents, more particularly in the arts of war. A child of passion, he early became a slave of passion: of strong drink and of women. The lure of excitement, the insatiable desire for adventure, and the love of the Bohemian life made him a willing slave of those who could supply these. He found adventure in the army, which he entered at an early age, and became in reality a child of the army. The only formal education he received was gotten in the barracks. His valor and audacity won him early fame and promotion. He loved the rôle of the revolutionary and began to play that rôle when he was still quite young. He did very good work in the battle of Ingavi and became a great admirer and supporter of José Ballivián, but turned against him and his dictatorship. He was also very much opposed to Belzu and led a revolution against him in Cochabamba. He was unsuccessful in this venture and was imprisoned, tried, and condemned to death. Belzu saved his life, only to have Melgarejo become, later, one of his bitterest enemies, and the man who more than anyone else was responsible, as we have seen, for his untimely death in 1865.

Melgarejo came into power by the December 1864 Revolution against Achá, immediately seizing the supreme power in the state, and held that power for six years. The *sexenio* of Melgarejo has come to be considered, and justly so, as the very acme of dictatorship, and Melgarejo the dictator *par excellence* of Bolivia. He is usually classed with Juan Manuel de Rosas of Argentina, the Nero of South America, and with his notorious contemporary Francisco Solano López of Paraguay. Melgarejo was under the influence of his mistress, a beautiful woman of La Paz, even more than López was under the influence of Mme Lynch, his French mistress. Both women undoubtedly possessed much ability, and must take much of the blame for the misdeeds of their paramours. Melgarejo was constantly harassed by revolutionists, and moved his government about from place to place in order to put down revolutions. He was able at the height of his power to impress foreign observers with his ability. Hull, United States minister to Bolivia, on March 31, 1866, wrote to Seward from Cochabamba: "Melgarejo's Government is as firmly established as has been that of any of his predecessors in office. For thirty years there has been no *accession* to the Presidency in this country by election. All Melgarejo's predecessors came into power originally by military violence—all save the three first Presidents of Bolivia, Bolívar, Sucre, and Velasco. Velasco was overthrown by Santa Cruz before he had been in office one year. It is utterly vain to hope for, at present, a constitutional Government in Bolivia. . . . I do not believe, for a moment, that Melgarejo out of the way, there would be any other than a military Government established. I believe—I have no doubt whatever—that if he were to die, the country would be immediately plunged into civil war by some three or four, or five or six aspirants for the Presidency." Consult the *Despatches*, *Bolivia*, vol. 2, U. S. Department of State, Washington, for much illuminating material on this man. Melgarejo was finally defeated in the January 1870 Revolution and forced to flee the country. He lived in Lima, Peru, for some time, and was assassinated there in 1875.

Mariano Donato Muñoz,[1] declared that their purpose was to democratize the political government to a degree unknown up to that time. The Constitution of 1868 did require that the acts of the president of the republic be countersigned by a minister of state to be legal.[2] It also required that the chief executive give an account of the state of the republic in a message to the Assembly, at its opening session.[3] The Constitution of 1871, like that of 1861, contained much the same provisions relative to the president of the republic. There were still the same restrictions on the president's leaving the republic,[4] and provisions regarding the joint responsibility of the president of the republic and the ministers of state for the acts of the administration.[5] The Constitution of 1878, an instrument drawn up and promulgated under conditions very similar to those under which the Constitution of 1868 was adopted—for the dictatorship of Hilarión Daza [6] was but little better than that of Melgarejo—could hardly be

[1] Mariano Donato Muñoz must have possessed considerable ability, for he was able to remain the chief servant of Melgarejo throughout his entire rule. That in itself was no mean achievement. It is, on the other hand, very difficult to determine to what extent Muñoz was responsible for the nature and events of the period of the Melgarejo government. To solve this question it will be necessary to have recourse to documentary materials which it may be impossible ever to get. The difficulties of the student of the revolutionary periods in the history of Bolivia are enhanced by the lack of material on these fundamentally important periods. The very nature of revolutionary activities, of course, makes for just such gaps in the evidence, for officials of such régimes have not been above destroying valuable documents or secreting them. There is still much material in family archives. Some day these data may be fully exploited and a fairly accurate account given of the many controversial topics. While Melgarejo and Muñoz have been savagely criticized for the evils of the period over which Melgarejo ruled, much good was also done which has been allowed to go unsung.

[2] Ordóñez López, *Constitución política*, vol. II, pp. 412–413, art. 73.

[3] *Ibid.*, p. 412, art. 70.

[4] *Ibid.*, p. 428, art. 78. This Constitution forbade the president of the republic and the ministers of state to leave the republic while the Assembly was in session (*ibid.*, p. 413, art. 76).

[5] *Ibid.*, p. 426, art. 61.

[6] Hilarión Daza, like Mariano Melgarejo, is regarded by a large majority of the people of Bolivia as the most irrational and the most absolute of all its leaders. The fact that Daza was so largely responsible for the disastrous War of the Pacific, one of the worst wars in which Bolivia has been engaged, accounts for the execration in which this stupid dictator is held. Daza was of humble origin, ill prepared for the rôle of dictator, and unscrupulous in the attainment of his objectives. He was just one more military *caudillo* who, possessed of an insatiable ambition, sought the opportunity to seize the supreme power in the state. Tomás Frías, one of the most learned and cultured rulers of Bolivia, appointed Daza as his minister of war. Frías did not know Daza, and must have forgotten, during the long period of time in which he himself played a very large rôle in the political life of his country, what might happen with such an ambitious man in the ministry of war. Daza seized the supreme power while Frías was too ill to defend himself, and made himself provisional president of the republic on March 4, 1876. In the decree which Daza issued on that date he declared that he had seized

expected to be democratic. Yet under it the president of the republic was responsible, jointly with the ministers of state, for the acts of the administration, though he was not prohibited from leaving the republic immediately at the end of his term of office.[1] The responsibility of the ministers of state was of two kinds: one, under which they were responsible merely for the acts of their own ministry; and the other, under which, by the action of the Council of the Cabinet (*Consejo de Gabinete*), they became jointly responsible with the other members of the ministry for the acts of the Council of the Cabinet.[2] The Constitutions of 1880 [3] and 1931 [4] contain similar provisions. All the constitutions declare that the salary of the president of the republic shall not be increased or diminished during his term of office.[5] All have the same provision about the relationship between the presidency and the captaincy general of the republic, that is, that the captaincy general inheres in the presidency of the republic.[6]

The history of the presidency of Bolivia contains a large number of tragedies. Of the twenty-five presidents between 1825 and 1925,[7] two resigned volun-

the reins of government because the people had urged him to do so. He explained that the people had long clamored for relief from the ills of the rule of Frías; he complained that Frías had ruled tyrannically, playing one faction against another, and that he was lacking in aggressiveness. Daza announced that he would pursue a policy of conciliation and friendship without regard to political parties, and forgetful of past events. His decree was just one more of the camouflage statements inherent, it would seem, in Bolivian political dictatorship. Loyalty to those high in office, who may have befriended a leader, does not seem to mean much among the *caudillos* of Bolivia. In fairness it should be said that this characteristic is not peculiar to the political leaders of that republic. *Caudillos* in Spanish America, as elsewhere, are all susceptible to the contagion of disloyalty.

Daza may have blundered into the war with Chile, but there is just as much reason to conclude that he saw in that war an excuse for strengthening himself in Bolivia. He did not have the power or the ability to conduct the war for Bolivia, and he failed. He was overthrown on December 28, 1879, because of his mismanagement of the war, and left the country. On September 16, 1880, the National Convention declared Daza unworthy of the name Bolivian and ordered him tried for the crimes he had committed against his country. He did not return, however, until 1894, and then only to meet death at the hands of an assassin in Ayuni.

[1] Ordóñez López, *Constitución política*, vol. II, p. 447, art. 93.

[2] *Ibid.*, p. 447, art. 94.

[3] Araoz, *Nuevo digesto*, vol. I, p. 16, arts. 93–95.

[4] *Constitución política*, pp. 37–38, art. 82; p. 47, arts. 101–102.

[5] Araoz, *Nuevo digesto*, vol. I, p. 13, art. 79. Also *Constitución política*, p. 39, art. 86.

[6] Araoz, *Nuevo digesto*, vol. I, p. 15, art. 90. Also *Constitución política*, p. 46, art. 97.

[7] Guillén Pinto and Guillén Pinto, *Geografía-atlas escolar de Bolivia*, pp. 117–118. These authors list the presidents with dates as follows:

Simón Bolívar, August 11, 1825, to January 1, 1826
Antonio José de Sucre, January 1, 1826, to August 1, 1828

tarily, three died while in office, nine were forced to resign, eight were assassinated, but not all while in office, and four died in exile. These were assassinated: Sucre, Blanco, Belzu, Córdova, Melgarejo, Morales, Daza, and Pando. Blanco and Morales were assassinated while in office. These died in exile: José Ballivián, in Rio de Janeiro, Brazil; Andrés Santa Cruz, in Nantes, France; José María Linares, in Valparaiso, Chile; and Tomás Frías, in Florence, Italy.[1] Hernando Siles was overthrown in the Revolution of June 1930, and took the doleful *camino del destierro*, thus adding another figure to that mournful drama so common in the political life of Bolivia.[2]

José Miguel de Velasco, August 12 to December 14, 1828
Pedro Blanco, December 25, 1828, to January 1, 1829
Andrés Santa Cruz, May 24, 1829, to February 20, 1839
José Miguel de Velasco, February 22, 1839, to September 27, 1841
José Ballivián, September 27, 1841, to December 23, 1847
José Miguel de Velasco, January 18 to December 6, 1848
Manuel Isidoro Belzu, December 17, 1848, to August 15, 1855
Jorge Córdova, August 15, 1855, to October 21, 1857
José María Linares, December 19, 1857, to January 14, 1861
José María de Achá, May 6, 1861, to December 29, 1864
Mariano Melgarejo, December 28, 1864, to January 15, 1871
Agustín Morales, January 15, 1871, to November 27, 1872
Adolfo Ballivián, May 6, 1873, to January 31, 1874
Tomás Frías, February 14, 1874, to May 4, 1876
Hilarión Daza, May 4, 1876, to December 27, 1879
Narciso Campero, January 19, 1880, to September 3, 1884
Gregorio Pacheco, September 3, 1884, to August 15, 1888
Ancieto Arce, August 15, 1888, to August 11, 1892
Mariano Baptista, August 11, 1892, to August 19, 1896
Severo Fernández Alonso, August 19, 1896, to April 10, 1899

Certain dates have been changed, others have been supplied in this list. Sucre resigned on August 1, 1828, not on April 18. The dates for Pando, Montes (both administrations), Villazón, Guerra, Saavedra, Siles, and Salamanca are not given. The last named came too late to be included in this book by the Guillén Pintos.

[1] Antonio José de Sucre was assassinated June 4, 1830, on his way from Bogotá, Colombia, in the mountains near La Capilla. His remains were deposited in the crypt in the Monastery of San Francisco in Quito, where they remained until 1900, when they were removed to the Cathedral of Quito. Efforts have been made by the Bolivian government to have the remains brought to Bolivia, but without success. The Venezuelan government has also tried to have the remains of this distinguished son of Venezuela brought to Caracas, but without success. It is fitting that he should rest in Quito near the scene of his first great battle, that of Pichincha. Who killed Sucre? It is believed by many that Juan José Flores, who, like Andrés Santa Cruz, found Sucre an obstacle to his rise to power, was implicated in the crime. Flores was the commander of the Department of the South of Great Colombia in this fateful year of 1830, and may have been more concerned in the disappearance of Sucre than has yet been fully revealed. Alfredo Jáuregui Rosquellas has given much consideration to this and many other phases of the life of Sucre in his work entitled *Antonio José de Sucre: héroe y sabio, mártir y santo.*

[2] Siles was a victim of the Revolution of 1930. This event was one of those upheavals that come about in Bolivia, either through a conviction on the part of the people that a revolution is necessary to put an end to an intolerable situation, or through astute and powerful leadership. The revolution in question was of the former class. A large number of the people be-

The office of vice-president of the republic has likewise undergone several changes since the establishment of a political government in Bolivia. In fact there have been more changes in that office than in the presidency itself. We have already noted the peculiar position of the vice-president in the *Constitución vitalicia*. The Constitution of 1831 became the prototype for the other instruments, as far as the vice-presidency is concerned. That document provided for a vice-president of the republic, an officer with the same qualifications as those of the president of the republic,[1] and elected for the same term of office. The provisions of the Constitution of 1834 [2] were similar to those of the Constitution of 1831. The Constitution of 1839 did not provide for a vice-president, but provided that the president of the Chamber of Senators should be elevated to the presidency of the republic in the event of the death or disability of the president. In case of the absence, death, or disability of the president of the Chamber of Senators, the president of the Chamber of Deputies was to be elevated to that position; and in the absence, death, or disability of the president of the Chamber of Deputies, the president of the Supreme Court was to assume the office of president of the republic.[3]

The Constitutions of 1843, 1851, 1861, 1868, and 1871 also did not provide for a vice-president. That of 1843 provided that, in case of the death, resignation, or disability of the president of the republic, the president of the National Council (*Consejo Nacional*) was to take his place. He was, however, only to serve as acting president, and was to hold the office until a president of the republic had been installed. In case the president had served only two years, there was to be a new election, called by the president of the National Council, who was also to summon the Congress to meet to count the votes for the president of the republic.[4] The Constitution of 1851 provided that in case of death, resignation, or disability of the president of the republic, the Council of Ministers (*Consejo de Ministros*) was to take charge of the administration of the state. The Council of Ministers was to choose from among its members one who was

---

lieved that Siles had become impossible because of his interest in international capitalists, and had to go. Of course the causes are complex and by no means so simple as would appear on the surface. The *junta de gobierno* which was set up did good work in its efforts to renovate and democratize the government. In the election of January 1931 Daniel Salamanca was chosen president of the republic, and took formal charge of his high office in March. In the more than one year which elapsed between the June revolution and the adoption of the Constitution of September 26, 1931, the leaders did much to bring about some very important modifications of the Constitution of 1880, which forms its basis. President Salamanca has begun his administration in a manner that speaks well for the future of Bolivia.

[1] Ordóñez López, *Constitución política*, vol. II, pp. 313–314, arts. 80–84.

[2] *Ibid.*, pp. 332–333, arts. 81–86.

[3] *Ibid.*, p. 351, arts. 69–71.

[4] *Ibid.*, p. 371, arts. 54–55.

to serve as president of the republic. This new officer was then to proceed in the manner prescribed in the Constitution of 1843 for the selection of the president of the republic.[1] The Constitution of 1861 provided that in case of the death, disability, resignation, or removal of the president of the republic, the president of the Council of State (*Consejo de Estado*) was to take his place. The acting president was to call elections for the presidency within a period of ten days.[2] The Constitution of 1868 provided that in case of the death, disability, resignation, or removal of the president of the republic, the place was to be filled temporarily by a person selected by the Council of Ministers. The new officer was required to issue orders for an election of a president of the republic within a period of fifteen days. The election was to be held within four months, and the Congress was to meet within forty days after the election to determine who had been elected president of the republic, and to proclaim that fact within the terms of the law covering that particular matter.[3] The Constitution of 1871 provided that in case of the death, resignation, or disability of the president of the republic, his place was to be filled by the president of the Council of State, who was to serve during the remainder of the constitutional term.[4]

The Constitution of 1878, however, did provide for a vice-president.[5] The vice-president could not be reelected, nor could he be elected to the presidency of the republic until eight years had elapsed. In the absence of the vice-president, the president of the Chamber of Senators was to take the place of the president of the republic in case there was a vacancy in that office.[6] The Constitution of 1880 provided for two vice-presidents.[7] In case of a vacancy in the presidency of the republic, the first vice-president, the second vice-president, the president of the Chamber of Deputies were to become president of the republic in that order.[8] Neither the first nor the second vice-president might be reelected to the vice-presidency, nor might either of them be elected to the presidency.[9] The vice-president has been required, whenever that office has been in existence, to have the same qualifications as the president of the republic. He has served for the same term and has been, generally considered, sub-

[1] Ordóñez López, *Constitución política*, vol. II, p. 384, art. 74.

[2] *Ibid.*, p. 397, art. 53.

[3] *Ibid.*, p. 411, art. 67.

[4] *Ibid.*, p. 426, art. 70. It was under this provision that Tomás Frías became president of the republic immediately after the death of Adolfo Ballivián and served, as we have noted, until forced out of office by Daza in 1876.

[5] *Ibid.*, p. 444, arts. 77, 83.

[6] *Ibid.*, p. 444, arts. 77, 78, 80, 82.

[7] Araoz, *Nuevo digesto*, vol. I, p. 13, art. 81.

[8] *Ibid.*, pp. 12–13, art. 77.

[9] *Ibid.*, p. 13, art. 78.

jected to the same restrictions as the occupant of the higher office. In 1921 the office of second vice-president was abolished.[1] The Constitution of 1931, as already noted, provides for only one vice-president.[2]

The length of the term of the president and vice-president of the republic has also varied considerably. The term of office under the Bolivarian Constitution, it will be recalled, was for life.[3] Under the Constitutions of 1831,[4] 1834,[5] 1839,[6] 1868,[7] 1871,[8] 1878,[9] 1880,[10] and 1931[11] the term of office was four years. Under the Constitution of 1843[12] it was eight years, under that of 1851,[13] five years, and under that of 1861,[14] three years. The manner of electing the president of the republic has changed but slightly, however. Under the Constitution of 1826 the president was elected for the first time by the Constituent Congress, upon nomination by the electoral college.[15] The president chose the vice-president to succeed him in the presidency. Under the Constitution of 1831, the president was elected by the electoral parochial juntas (*juntas de parroquia*).[16] In case the candidate had not received two-thirds of the votes of these juntas, the Congress elected the president from among the three receiving the highest number of votes.[17]

The provision for the election of the president in the Constitution of 1834 was much the same as in the Constitution of 1831.[18] The Constitution of 1839 provided that the president should be elected by a direct vote of the people.

[1] Araoz, *Nuevo digesto*, vol. I, p. 13, note 1. By article 3 of the Law of January 24.

[2] *Constitución política*, pp. 38–39, art. 85.

[3] Ordóñez López, *Constitución política*, vol. II, p. 294, art. 77.

[4] *Ibid.*, p. 311, art. 70.

[5] *Ibid.*, p. 330, art. 72.

[6] *Ibid.*, pp. 351–352, art. 75.

[7] *Ibid.*, p. 411, art. 66.

[8] *Ibid.*, p. 426, art. 69.

[9] *Ibid.*, p. 444, art. 76.

[10] Araoz, *Nuevo digesto*, vol. I, p. 12, art. 76.

[11] *Constitución política*, p. 38, art. 83. The term is constitutional, and not personal.

[12] Ordóñez López, *Constitución política*, vol. II, p. 371, art. 50.

[13] *Ibid.*, pp. 383–384, art. 72.

[14] *Ibid.*, p. 397, art. 52.

[15] *Ibid.*, p. 294, art. 78.

[16] *Ibid.*, pp. 310–311, art. 66.

[17] *Ibid.*, pp. 310–311, art. 66.

[18] *Ibid.*, p. 330, arts. 68–69.

In case there was no election by the people, the election was to be by the Congress in the same manner as prescribed in the Constitution of 1834.[1] The Constitution of 1843 provided that the president should be elected by the people, but made no provision for failure to elect in the general elections.[2] The Constitution of 1851 provided that the president was to be elected by a direct and a secret vote of the citizens in full enjoyment of the franchise. The votes were to be scrutinized by the Congress and the results incorporated in a special law. In case there was no election by the popular vote, the Congress was to elect him.[3] The Constitutions of 1861,[4] 1868,[5] 1871,[6] 1878,[7] 1880,[8] and 1931[9] had similar provisions. The practice which has been and still is common throughout Spanish America is to prohibit the immediate reelection of the president of the republic. This practice has been in force in Bolivia since 1839. The Constitutions of 1826,[10] 1831,[11] and 1834[12] placed no restrictions upon the reelection of the president. The Constitutions of 1839,[13] 1843,[14] 1851,[15] 1861,[16] 1871,[17] 1878,[18] and 1880[19] required that there should be no reelection until an intervening term of office had elapsed. The Constitution of 1868 permitted immediate reelection, but limited such reelection to one term only.[20] The Constitution of 1931 demands, as has already been noted, that eight years, or two

[1] Ordóñez López, *Constitución política*, vol. II, p. 330, art. 70.

[2] *Ibid.*, p. 370, art. 48.

[3] *Ibid.*, p. 383, arts. 68–69.

[4] *Ibid.*, p. 396, art. 46.

[5] *Ibid.*, p. 411, art. 63.

[6] *Ibid.*, p. 426, arts. 63–68.

[7] *Ibid.*, pp. 444–445, arts. 84–88.

[8] José Ignacio Rodríguez, *American constitutions*, vol. II, pp. 434–435, arts. 83–88.

[9] *Constitución política*, p. 40, arts. 90–95.

[10] Ordóñez López, *Constitución política*, vol. II, p. 294, art. 78.

[11] *Ibid.*, pp. 310–311, art. 66.

[12] *Ibid.*, p. 330, arts. 68–70.

[13] *Ibid.*, pp. 351–352, art. 75.

[14] *Ibid.*, p. 371, art. 50.

[15] *Ibid.*, pp. 383–384, art. 72.

[16] *Ibid.*, p. 397, art. 52.

[17] *Ibid.*, p. 426, art. 69.

[18] *Ibid.*, p. 444, art. 76.

[19] Rodríguez, *American constitutions*, vol. II, p. 432, art. 76.

[20] Ordóñez López, *Constitución política*, vol. II, p. 411, art. 66.

terms of four years each, shall elapse between the constitutional end of the four-year term and reelection.[1]

The qualifications of the president and vice-president of the republic have undergone but slight changes. Those qualifications laid down in the Bolivarian Constitution have served for all subsequent constitutions. By that fundamental law the candidate for the presidency had to be a native-born Bolivian, in full enjoyment of the franchise, a believer in the religion of the state, at least thirty years of age, a man who had rendered important services to the state, of known administrative ability, and without a criminal record. The latter requirement was further strengthened by the addition of the words "ni aun por faltas de leyes."[2] By the fundamental laws since 1826 the candidate must be at least thirty-five years of age. Nothing has been incorporated in the constitutions since 1826 concerning administrative ability, or even concerning services rendered the state or its people. The Constitution of 1871 required that the candidate for the presidency of the republic should have only the qualifications of a member of the Chamber of Deputies, although it did require that he be at least thirty-five years of age.[3] The Constitutions of 1878,[4] 1880,[5] and 1931[6] required that the candidate must have the qualifications of a member of the Chamber of Senators. The Constitution of 1843, strangely enough, had no provision concerning condemnation for crime.[7]

The rank of captain general of the republic inheres in the office of the president of the republic, and is, of course, so designated, as has been noted, in the Constitution of 1931.[8] There is also a General Comptrollership (*Contraloría General*), the inspector general (*contralor general*) of which is appointed by the president of the republic upon nomination by the Chamber of Senators. The Contraloría General was created by the Law of May 5, 1928. It is independent of all the ministries and of all other officers of the state except the president of the republic. The term of office of the inspector general is six years, with the right to be reappointed if the president so desires. He is responsible, with his subordinates, to the Congress, but he may not be removed except for just cause. The Contraloría General is the central office of the state for the business

[1] *Constitución política*, p. 38, art. 83.

[2] Ordóñez López, *Constitución política*, vol. II, p. 294, art. 79.

[3] *Ibid.*, p. 426, art. 62.

[4] *Ibid.*, p. 444, art. 79.

[5] Rodríguez, *American constitutions*, vol. II, p. 435, art. 79.

[6] *Constitución política*, p. 39, art. 86.

[7] The Constitution of 1843 was the work of the National Convention which met in Sucre, and with which we have already dealt.

[8] *Constitución política*, p. 46, art. 97.

for which it was created and for which it is maintained. It is really a clearing house for all the financial transactions of the republic. The decisions of the inspector general are final.[1] The Law of May 5, 1928, also provided that the inspector general should have the assistance of a foreign technical adviser. There is also a National Tribunal of Accounts (*Tribunal Nacional de Cuentas*), and an Inspectorship of Bookkeeping (*Inspección de Contabilidad*), independent of the National Tribunal of Accounts. Both of these agencies are primarily concerned with financial matters.[2]

Bolivia has never had, technically speaking, a cabinet. There are ministers of state, who are the heads of ministries. By the *Reglamento* for the Political Administrative Organization of the Republic of January 10, 1903, public administration is under the direct supervision of ministers of state.[3] The Constitution of 1931 provides that the business (*negocios*) of the state is to be directed by ministers of state, the number of whom is to be determined by law.[4] The same fundamental law also prescribes the qualifications of the ministers. A minister of state must have the same qualifications as a member of the Chamber of Deputies.[5] The ministers are responsible, conjointly with the president of the republic, for the acts of their respective ministries (*ramos*).[6] The ministers are also jointly responsible for the acts approved by the Council of the Cabinet, as the ministries taken together are called.[7] All the decrees and orders of the president must be countersigned by the ministers in their respective departments, and have no validity unless so countersigned, nor are they to be obeyed unless so signed. For the appointment and dismissal of ministers of state the signature of the president of the republic alone is sufficient.[8] The ministers of

[1] Araoz, *Nuevo digesto*, vol. II, pp. 28–38. The Constitution of 1931 provides for this agency in art. 98, p. 46. The salary of the inspector general is Bs. 24,000 a year. He is assisted by an assistant inspector general with a salary of Bs. 20,000, a controller general (*interventor general*) with a salary of Bs. 15,000, and an accountant general (*contador general*) with a salary of Bs. 12,000 a year. All are appointed by the president of the republic.

[2] *Supremo Tribunal Nacional de Cuentas: primer centenario de su fundación, 1825–1925*, p. 3. This tribunal was founded by Simón Bolívar by Decree of December 20, 1825, as we have already noted. It was called a *contaduría jeneral de hacienda pública* and was to have its headquarters in the capital of the republic. The Supremo Tribunal Nacional de Cuentas was established by the Law of November 28, 1883. The booklet cited was published in Sucre in 1925 and contains a great deal of interesting information.

[3] Araoz, *Nuevo digesto*, vol. I, pp. 76–99.

[4] *Constitución política*, pp. 46–47., art. 99.

[5] *Ibid.*, p. 47, art. 100.

[6] *Ibid.*, p. 47, art. 101.

[7] *Ibid.*, p. 47, art. 102.

[8] *Ibid.*, p. 47, art. 103.

state may take part, as has already been noted, in the debates in either chamber of the Congress, but must retire before a vote is taken.[1] The ministers of state must make a report to the Congress on the activities of their departments, in the manner prescribed by the Constitution.[2] These reports were originally made orally by the ministers to the Congress. In later years, with the increase in the number of ministers, and more especially in the volume of business and the complexity of modern life, the reports have been made in writing to the president of the republic. The reports are usually published separately. The printed reports of the ministers are of course available to the members of the Congress. The report of the minister of the treasury (*hacienda*) must contain an itemized account of the incomes and expenditures of the previous year, and must also contain the budget for the ensuing year. The budget is the joint product of the whole ministry, and must have the approval of the National Tribunal of Accounts before it can be presented to the Congress.[3] Under no circumstances may the president of the republic, either orally or in writing, excuse a minister from responsibility for the acts for which he is, constitutionally, responsible.[4] Finally, the ministers may be impeached and, if convicted, may be tried by the Supreme Court of the republic for the crimes for which they were impeached.[5]

There are at present six ministries of state in Bolivia. They are the Ministry of Foreign Relations and Religion (*Relaciones Exteriores y Culto*), of Government and Justice (*Gobierno y Justicia*), of the Treasury and Industry (*Hacienda e Industria*), of Public Works and Communications (*Fomento y Comunicaciones*), of Public Instruction and Agriculture (*Instrucción Pública y Agricultura*), and of War and Colonization (*Guerra y Colonización*). Each ministry, it will be noted, is composed of two distinct departments.[6]

The Ministry of Foreign Relations has general charge of the international relations of the country, under the direction of the president of the republic. It has control over the consular and diplomatic service of the national government. It has control over the negotiation of treaties, conventions, and agreements with foreign countries. It also has charge of special conventions and

[1] *Constitución política*, p. 47, art. 104.

[2] *Ibid.*, pp. 47–48, art. 105, in the form prescribed in clause 9 of art. 96 of the Constitution.

[3] *Ibid.*, p. 48, art. 106.

[4] *Ibid.*, p. 48, art. 107.

[5] *Ibid.*, p. 48, art. 108. The ministers of state may be impeached, as we have already noted, by the Congress for crimes committed in the discharge of their duties as ministers. They may also be tried as individuals, separately from their position as ministers of state, for other crimes which they may have committed, by the Supreme Court.

[6] Araoz, *Nuevo digesto*, vol. I, p. 76, note 1. The *reglamento* dealt of course, originally, with five instead of six ministries, the actual number in 1903.

international conferences. It conducts the correspondence of the national government with foreign governments. It has a division of boundaries, and has charge of the archives of the ministry. The Ministry of Religion has general charge of the ecclesiastical affairs of the republic. As such the minister is responsible for the welfare of the people in its relations with religious bodies; and he is likewise responsible for the welfare of these bodies, and especially of the Roman Catholic Apostolic religion as the religion of the state. He negotiates concordats and other agreements with the Holy See, and enforces the laws of the republic on ecclesiastical matters. He also has charge of the missionary work among the uncivilized native peoples of the republic.[1]

The Ministry of Government has general charge of the political administration of the country. In particular, it must preserve law and order throughout the republic, and maintain peace and harmony among the various political divisions. Bolivia has a unitary form of government and hence has neither states nor commonwealths. It has departments and territories, but no federal units within the republic. The ministry has control over all questions arising out of differences over domestic boundaries, investigating them and reporting the findings to the Congress. It has general charge over municipal affairs, especially over the financial affairs of municipalities. It promulgates the decrees convoking and closing the Congress, executes election laws, has control over the police (*policía de seguridad*) and the firemen (*bomberos*), and decrees amnesties for political crimes, in accordance with the laws on that subject. It has charge of public buildings and of the means of protecting the public health, especially hygienic conditions in industrial and manufacturing establishments and the health of the employees in such plants. The Ministry of Government has full charge of the postal and telegraph systems of the republic. It appoints the employees of the postal and telegraph stations, and is charged with the establishment and upkeep of postal routes and post-offices. It collects the taxes due to the national government from the operations of the postal and telegraph systems.

The Ministry of Justice has general supervision over the judicial system of the republic. It is charged with the duty of bringing about reforms in civil and penal legislation, supervises the administration of justice, issues certificates of appointment to its employees in accordance with the constitutional provisions on that subject, and has charge of the prisons and penal and correctional institutions of the republic. It grants, or refuses to grant, commutation of the death penalty, enforces the decisions of judicial tribunals, and establishes, improves, and conserves prisons, penitentiaries (*presidios*), and houses of correction. Finally, it builds and maintains judicial offices and determines the amount of revenues to be used for that purpose.

[1] The legislation which established religious toleration in Bolivia will be dealt with in the section on "The Church and the State."

The Ministry of the Treasury has general charge of the different systems of taxation. Bolivia has long had the system of farming out the collection of taxes. Companies are given the concession for collecting the taxes, receiving a certain percentage of the taxes collected. The Ministry has charge of the urban and the rural censuses, which are the basis for determining the rate of taxation. It supervises the collection, administration, and use of departmental funds. It has charge of the public lands, their general use, sale, and rental.[1] It determines the funds to be used by the prefects, and has general charge of the customs system of the republic. It has charge of the ports, and inspects financial establishments, banks, stock companies, insurance companies, and houses of credit in general. It has charge of the surveys of lands. It appoints all employees of the ministry. It keeps an inventory of the properties of the republic, and has charge of the purchase and sale of the same, but such purchases and sales must always have the approval of the Congress to be binding.

The financial history of Bolivia is obviously a comprehensive one.[2] The wealth of the republic is to be found primarily in the regions of which the cities of Cochabamba, Potosí, Sucre, and La Paz are the centers.[3] One of the main sources of wealth is the much hated *tributo*, which has already been discussed in this study, and which is still among the taxes to be paid.[4] Obviously a system that has meant so much to Bolivia has been well worked out. In the first place, a census of all the Indians is taken in order to find out who are the *tributo*-payers. This means that the country is divided into small and well-defined units. The cantons are divided into *ayllus*, *haciendas*, and *fincas* for the purpose of keeping better control of the *tributo*-paying Indians. The Indians themselves are divided into four classes: *reservados*, *niños*, *solteros*, and *casados*. Of these the *casados* (married Indians) are the only ones who pay the *tributo*. In the earlier

[1] The public land question is discussed under the subject of colonization.

[2] Casto Rojas, *Historia financiera de Bolivia*, pp. 1–4. Rojas has done an excellent piece of pioneer work, and deserves much credit for having been able to turn the attention of scholars to this field for fruitful exploitation. This should mean that there will be many others who will be able to do good work in this field. It is one of the most important fields for scientific investigation in the whole history of the republic. Rojas divides his book into three parts. The first deals with the finances of the colonial period, the second with the finances of the period of the republic, and the third with the finances from Belzu to Daza.

[3] It was Simón Bolívar who started the new republic, as we have seen, on its independent financial career. He established its credit by the Law of December 1, 1825, by pledging the national properties as securities for that credit. On December 28, 1825, he decreed the creation of the Economic Society of Chuquisaca.

[4] Rojas, *Historia financiera de Bolivia*, pp. 34 ff. The *tributo* was a very rich source of income in the colonial period. Rojas declares: "La renta más considerable que se recaudaba en provecho de S. M. Católica, era el tributo. Como su nombre lo dice, tenía por fundamento el derecho de conquista, en cuya virtud los súbditos del extinguido reino de los incas debían pagar tributo al monarca español, dueño y señor absoluto" (*ibid.*, p. 34).

period of the republic, the classification varied somewhat from the above. There were *forasteros* and *yanaconas* who paid the *tributo*, while the *ausentes*, *proximos*, and *niños* were exempt from the payment of the *tributo*. The *yanaconas* were also obliged to work in the *mita* two times each year. In the year 1858, for example, the Canton Laja had twenty-eight estates: twenty-four *haciendas* and four *ayllus*. Each of these estates had its name, and each had a detailed record of the *tributo* paid.[1] Rojas declares that the Indians who owned lands paid from 8 to 10 pesos, those who rented lands from 4 to 6 pesos, and the *forasteros* up to 3 pesos a year. The machinery for taking care of the financial affairs of the republic was established, as has been noted, by Bolívar. Juan de Bernabé y Madero, the first minister of the treasury, organized the revenue system in 1826. In that year the total income was a little over 2,000,000 pesos, as compared with about 1,500,000 pesos in 1825. The population in 1826 was about 1,000,000.[2] The budget system was really put into operation in 1827, and called for an expenditure of 2,349,763 pesos. The principal sources of revenue were the *tributo* paid by the Indians, the tithes (*diezmos*), the duty on metals (*derecho metálico*) or the fifth (*quinte*), the sales tax (*alcabala*), the sale of the properties of the suppressed convents and of the exiled Jesuits, the sale of minerals, the income on ecclesiastical properties (*temporalidades*), and the import

[1] These data were gathered by the author from the materials in the archives of the Supreme National Tribunal of Accounts in Sucre. The Canton Laja was located in the Province of Omasuyos in the Department of La Paz. The manuscripts consulted gave these data for the year 1858: 2130 baptisms, 667 marriages, 1222 deaths, and 161 *entierros de párbulos*. There were 260 *tributarios*. There were also 135 *forasteros* who paid 5 pesos a year and 72 *yanaconas* who paid the same amount. Information about the Hacienda Reñaplanta, Hacienda Rechocollo, Hacienda Ticuyo, and Hacienda de Santa Rosa was equally detailed. For the twenty-eight properties there were 6193 inhabitants, of whom 1709 paid the *tributo*, in the amount of 8830 pesos. Of these *tributo*-payers, 667 were *forasteros* and 982 *yanaconas*. The total number serving in the *mita* for that year was 8790. The document giving this particular information was signed in Laja on May 28, 1858. The Canton Collocollo had a population of 2468, of whom 451 were *forasteros* and 729 *yanaconas*. The total amount of the *tributo* paid in 1858 was 3840 pesos. The Canton Aigachi had 4896 inhabitants, of whom 1493 paid *tributo*, amounting to 7500 pesos. The Canton Copacabana had a population of 5357, of whom 1894 paid *tributo*, amounting to 9830 pesos. The Canton Pucarani had a population of 5875, of whom 1722 paid *tributo*, amounting to 9170 pesos. And so on for the whole republic.

[2] José María Dalence, *Bosquejo estadístico de Bolivia*, estimates that the population in 1846 was about 1,373,896 as compared with about 1,000,000 in 1825. Neither of these figures includes the savage Indians of the Oriente, of whom Dalence thinks there were over 700,000 in 1846. The number of natives of this class in 1825 was estimated at about 600,000. The increase in the total of the first group was less than 100,000. According to the census of 1846, such as it was, the Indian population constituted 51.6 per cent and the whites and *mestizos* 48.4 per cent of the total. On that basis there must have been 482,000 whites and *mestizos* and 514,000 Indians in 1825. Consult Rojas, *Historia financiera de Bolivia*, pp. 79–80.

duties.[1] For the period up to the beginning of the War of the Pacific, as the footnote has explained, there was not much fluctuation in the annual receipts. The Casa de Moneda coined, between 1825 and 1827, 4,561,827,7 silver pesos. The minting of gold coins did not begin until 1831. During the three years 1828, 1829, and 1830, 4,708,689 pesos were coined, or about 1,500,000 a year.[2] During the first four years of the rule of Andrés Santa Cruz the country experienced a vigorous growth in its economic life owing to his very able leadership.[3] Few men have done more for Bolivia than Santa Cruz. Following his

[1] Rojas, *Historia financiera de Bolivia*, p. 412. Rojas declares that Bolivia began her independent existence with financial resources amounting to about 1,500,000 pesos and at the end of the first half-century received about the same amount. He gives the following table:

Year		Income (*ingresos*)	Expenditures (*egresos*)
1825	Pesos	1,500,000	1,800,000
1826–1829		2,000,000	2,349,763
1830		1,537,702	1,537,702
1833–1835		2,033,577,3½	2,033,577,3½
1840–1841		1,810,253,5½	1,810,253,5½
1845–1846		1,977,139	2,076,505
1847–1848		2,131,298	2,293,979
1850–1857		2,093,016	1,919,984
1860		2,224,286,5	2,339,704,1
1865		2,136,808	2,505,615
1869–1870	Bs.	2,190,888,5	2,854,666,02
1872		2,136,808	2,505,615
1873–1874		2,929,573,85	4,825,361,37
1878–1879		1,870,383	1,870,383

Rojas observes: "De 1825 a 1879, el desarrollo de los recursos fiscales fué insignificante. El país entregado a continuas revueltas que esterilizaron las más importantes reformas hacendarias, no avanzó mucho en su organización financiera ni en el crecimiento de la riqueza pública y privada." Then he gives the above table with this comment: "He aquí un cuadro de los ingresos y egresos nacionales de ese período, que no necesita comentario."

[2] *Ibid.*, pp. 76–77.

[3] Between 1826 and 1833 the national government set aside a sum of 2,000,000 pesos yearly for the expenses of the government. In 1833 the sum of 2,033,577 was set aside for that purpose. The same amount was set aside in 1835. The allocation of the money was as follows:

Servicio Legislativo	Pesos	57,809
Servicio del Supremo Gobierno		71,200
Servicio de Relaciones Exteriores		100,000
Servicio del Consejo de Estado		22,600
Servicio de la Corte Suprema		34,100
Servicio de la Contaduría		18,800
Servicio del Crédito Público		2,899
Departamento de Chuquisaca		153,458,2½
Departamento de La Paz		198,786,1½
Departamento de Potosí		166,930,1
Departamento de Cochabamba		86,278,2
Departamento de Oruro		101,746,7
Departamento del Litoral		16,054,6
Departamento de Tarija		16,503,3½
Gastos extraordinarios (Cobija)		100,000
Ejército: 4 batallones, 2 regimientos, y una brigada de artillería		746,192,4
Importe del servicio nacional	Pesos	1,891,358,3½
Servicio de Instrucción		142,219
Total	Pesos	2,033,577,3½

downfall the financial condition of the republic grew worse up to and through the War of the Pacific. It was not until the beginning of the twentieth century that Bolivia again began to improve her economic condition.[1]

See Rojas, *Historia financiera de Bolivia*, p. 141. Rojas finds that the era of *restauración*, following the downfall of Santa Cruz, was largely unsatisfactory financially, declaring: "El gobierno de la Restauración pasó breve como una llamarada de patriotismo, sin dejar huella de su acción en las finanzas públicas. Como todo régimen provisional y de transición, abundó en buenos propósitos, pero no tuvo tiempo de ponerlos en práctica" (*ibid.*, p. 153). It was Andrés María Torrico who in 1848, by his *reglamento* for the Casa de Moneda de Potosí, laid the basis for the monetary system of Bolivia (*la carta orgánica de la moneda*) and fixed the weight and fineness of the gold and silver coins. In 1848 the *caudillaje* began its disastrous attack upon the financial and economic system. At the end of the fiscal year 1845–1846 the income was 1,977,139 pesos and the expenditures amounted to 2,076,505 pesos, with a deficit of 129,366 pesos, including the 30,000 pesos claimed by the *recaudación aduanera*, or the fees for collecting the taxes. The deficit at the end of the fiscal year 1847–1848 was 162,681 pesos. The period beginning with Manuel Isidoro Belzu and ending with Hilarión Daza was a very dismal page in the financial affairs of Bolivia. Rojas declares:

"Un raro socialismo desenvolvió en su política el gobierno, ejerciendo actos de adulación peligrosa de las clases populares en detrimento de la unidad social del país. Más propiamente pudiera llamarse 'populacherismo' el sistema implantado por Belzu y seguido, aunque con menos suerte, por su sucesor el general Córdova.—La manía de Belzu de echar monedas al populacho y de arengarle en tono indigno de un jefe de Estado, halagando las más perversas pasiones de la canalla contra los pretendidos 'aristócratas' de partido rojo, no sólo abrieron un abismo social, sino que causaron un grave daño al desarrollo de la riqueza pública y privada, por la holgazanería y el vicio fomentados, por las constantes amenazas de saco y pillaje, por las hostilidades al comercio y, en fin, por los despilfarros y desaciertos financieros del poder.—Degeneración de todas las democracias ha sido y es el culto de populacho" (*ibid.*, p. 199).

He has much more to say about the mania of the leaders for the support of the mob, adding: "Estos sistemas de fraudo político no pueden conducir sino a la retardación del progreso económico y financiero de un país.

". . . El artesano no es un ente miserable que necesite de la caridad política para vivir. . . . Su porvenir está asegurado y no depende sino de su propia voluntad. . . .

"El populacherismo de Belzu y el militarismo de Ballivián, han sido dos obstáculos igualmente funestos al desarrollo de la riqueza privada y fiscal. . . " (*ibid.*, pp. 200–201).

[1] Rojas, *Historia financiera de Bolivia*, pp. 326–327. Rojas has a great deal more to say about *caudillaje* and finance in the history of Bolivia. He deals with "Repairing the disaster" ("*Reparando el desastre*") in a whole chapter (*ibid.*, chap. VI, pp. 323–343). He describes the efforts of the Assembly of 1871 to rectify the wrongs done during the *sexenio* of Melgarejo to the financial affairs of the republic, especially in the matter of lands seized from the Indians. The Law of July 31, 1871, declared that the lands which had been taken from the Indians were taken illegally because the Indians had a legal right to the lands held in common by them (*de origen y las comunidades*). But it was one thing to declare the measures of Melgarejo null and void, and quite another to bring about the proper readjustment. The Assembly of 1872 did not improve matters by taking measures which would withhold the right of the Indians to the lands until they had learned how to read and write Castilian. This means of further educating the Indian may have been, in itself, a very good plan, but it tended merely to continue a practice established by old Spain, and left Bolivia in a position to continue to levy and collect the *tributo*. Rojas declares that the plan "reconocía y consagraba la injusticia que desde la época española venía pesando sobre la raza indígena" and permitted the national government to collect "el tributo sin más razón que la que invocó la corona de España."

This discussion of the Ministry of the Treasury would be incomplete without a brief treatment, at least, of the legislation known as the banking laws (*leyes bancarias*), dealing with the banking system of the country. On July 11, 1928, the General Law of Banks (*Ley General de Bancos*) was passed. It is a measure which goes into the subject in great detail.[1] On July 20, 1928, a law was passed making the Bank of the Bolivian Nation (*Banco de la Nación Boliviana*) the Central Bank of the Bolivian Nation (*Banco Central de la Nación Boliviana*).[2] The central idea is that a banking institution is a public and not a private institution, and should have the attributes of a public institution. It should be more than that: it should be a state institution in which the people have a right, as composing the state, to contribute to its funds for specific purposes, no less than to use the funds for specific purposes. The greatest concern is, of course, that the state should protect the funds in the banks. In the reorganization of the banking system of Bolivia, for it was nothing less, the Central Bank of the Bolivian Nation was made the central banking agency of the republic. This meant that the National Bank, the Mercantile Bank, and the Bank of the Nation, the three largest banks in Bolivia, were merged into the Central Bank of the Bolivian Nation. This bank is located in La Paz.

There was also a reform in the monetary system of the country. The Monetary Reform Law was enacted on July 11, 1928.[3] The legal coin is the gold boliviano, containing 0.54917 grams of fine gold (*gramos de oro fino*). The coins are in two denominations, the ten- and twenty-boliviano pieces. The ten-boliviano coin is known as a Bolívar and the twenty-boliviano coin is called a doble Bolívar. The alloy used in these gold coins is copper. Only the national government and the Central Bank of the Bolivian Nation have the right to purchase gold for these coins, and the purchase is to be made through the National Mint (*Casa Nacional de Moneda*) of Potosí. This law also provides that English, Peruvian, and United States gold coins may be accepted in payment of all national and private debts and in all payments made by the national government. There are also silver coins in three denominations, the boliviano, the medio boliviano, and the quinto de boliviano.[4] Copper is also the alloy for these silver coins. Then there are nickel coins, or *monedas menores*, in two denominations, the ten-centavo and five-centavo pieces. Any coin that is clipped or other-

[1] Araoz, *Nuevo digesto*, vol. II, pp. 210–262. Several efforts had of course been made long before this law was passed to improve the banking system of the country. Important legislation had been passed in 1886, 1889, 1890, 1891, 1892, 1894, 1902, 1911, 1914, 1919, and 1921.

[2] *Ibid.*, pp. 262–285. This law has 90 articles, while that of July 11 of the same year has 232 articles. There is obviously no room in this study for the detailed treatment that this whole matter deserves.

[3] *Ibid.*, pp. 48–51. Consult also the *Revista de la Universidad de Chuquisaca* for October 1928.

[4] The boliviano is worth about 33 cents in United States currency. The medio boliviano is half of that, and the quinto boliviano a fifth of it.

wise mutilated ceases to be a legal coin and may be legally refused. The Decree of August 20, 1928, established the Central Bank of the Bolivian Nation and the Superintendency General of Banks (*Superintendencia General de Bancos*).

The taxation system of Bolivia is a complex one. The tax on land, known as the *catastro*, is probably the most important. The law governing this tax was enacted on August 15, 1880, and modified by the Laws of October 16, 1906, and April 27, 1928.[1] This law abolished, in the first place, the taxes known as the tithe (*diezmos*), the first fruits (*primicias*), the twentieth part (*veintenas*), and those known as taxes on rural and urban lands (*la denominada de predios rústicos y urbanos*), and substituted for them the land tax (*catastro*). The tax is paid semiannually by all realty owners. The tax on metals is also important. There are the mining fees, or *patentes*, paid on gold, tin, coal, sulphur, lignite, petroleum, and other mineral substances.[2] There is a tax on the production and sale of alcohol, tobacco, and matches, which are state monopolies.[3] The Law of

[1] Araoz, *Nuevo digesto*, vol. II, pp. 56–68. In each province of the republic there is a commission to administer this law. The members of this body are appointed for one year by the national government. This is provided for in the Decree of March 8, 1888, which is a by-law for the land tax (*reglamento del catastro*). The execution of this decree is in the hands of the officials of the cantons, supervised by the commission referred to above. The cantonal officers are to be assisted in the collection of this tax by the ecclesiastical officers of the cantons. The realty owners are to be urged from the pulpits to respect the obligations resting upon them to see that this law is honestly and quickly enforced. Indians are especially to be urged from the pulpits to declare their real properties before the proper cantonal officers (art. 15). All lands of the republic are subject to the operations of these commissions, known as Central Commissions (*Comisiones Centrales*). The commissioners have a heavy job, at least from the clerical angle. They are to keep seven different books. There is also another body to help in the proper enforcement of this law, known as Appellate Land Tax Court (*Juzgado de Apelaciones Catastrales*). The owners of estates (*fincas*) may appeal to this tribunal for changes in the tax evaluations, and in regard to other matters connected with the levy of the land tax. The Laws of March 3 and May 3, 1928, govern the tax on the public lands (*impuesto sobre tierras baldías*), or the public lands granted to private individuals for a nominal price. The Law of September 17, 1917, imposed a tax of one centavo per hectare, the proceeds to be used for the construction of the Cochabamba–Santa Cruz Railway.

[2] Abdon Calderón, *Codificación de leyes y disposiciones referente a minería*, gives a good account of these matters and others connected with mining. The annual *patente* on land containing metallic substances is Bs. 4 per hectare. On gold and tin placers the *patente* is Bs. 2 per hectare. For other mineral substances the *patente* is B. 1 per hectare. For coal, sulphur, and lignite the *patente* is one-half boliviano per hectare. The *patentes* are paid semiannually. The Laws of December 7, 1906, December 12, 1916, February 9, 1920, and June 16, 1921, all bear on this subject. The *patente* on petroleum is based on the concessions from the state (*concesiones en sociedad con el Estado*).

[3] A Law of January 23, 1918, prohibited the importation of alcohol and distilled liquors. The state alone has the right to import these. By the contract of February 13, 1914, the state entered into an agreement with the Tobacco Administrative Company (*Compañía Administradora del Estanco de Tabacos*) for the manufacture of cigars and cigarettes and for the importation of manufactured tobacco. This company secured the monopoly of this work for

April 27, 1928, authorized the president of the republic to enter into a contract with a stock company (*compañía anónima*), which he was to create, to take over the collection (*recaudación*) of all the taxes (*impuestos*), rents (*rentas*), and incomes (*ingresos*) provided for in the national budget (*presupuesto nacional*), and all such contributions which might be demanded in the future. The company was to be known as the National Collection Company (*Compañía Recaudadora Nacional*). This concern, which was recommended by the Kammerer Mission, is really a process of farming out the taxes for collection on a percentage basis. The money collected by the company is to be deposited by it in the Bank of the Bolivian Nation.[1]

The customs system of the country was reorganized by the Law of April 1, 1929. This law is known as the Organic Law for the Administration of Customs (*Ley Orgánica de Administración Aduanera*), and deals with the whole subject in great detail. For the purpose of collecting customs duties the republic is divided into eleven customs districts, which are under the jurisdiction of the customs officials in La Paz, Oruro, Uyuni, Villazón, Charaña, Villa Bella, Guayaramerín, Cobija, Abuná, Yacuiba, and Puerto Suárez. These officials have charge of the importation and exportation of goods whether in transit, in storage (*depósito*), or in reembarcation (*reembarque*), and of goods that are exchanged between the ports of the republic, or in *cabotaje*,[2] as it is termed. There is a director general who has general charge of the administration of the customs.[3]

---

the period ending January 1, 1934. On August 29, 1916, a contract was let by the state to the National Match Company of Bolivia, Ltd., for the monopoly of the manufacture, importation, and sale of matches. The contract was renewed on April 7, 1919, to run until May 12, 1929, and was again renewed on February 17, 1928. Consult Araoz, *Nuevo digesto*, vol. II, pp. 163–164.

[1] Araoz, *Nuevo digesto*, vol. II, pp. 6–10. The Compañía Recaudadora Nacional has full powers to use such means as may be necessary to collect the different taxes, but is of course under the control of the national government. The company is especially charged with minute control over the duties to be paid at the frontiers, and has a right to such papers and such information as consular agents may have at their offices dealing with these matters. The company was to be formed with a capital of Bs. 2,500,000, and is obliged to pay to the national government at least Bs. 2,000,000 each month to defray the public expenses of the government. By *Resolución* of August 14, 1928, the contract with the Collection Company (*contrato de la Compañía Recaudadora*) was incorporated. It stated that the proposal of Jorge Sáenz, José Mendieta, Casto Rojas, Ernesto García, Héctor Lorini, and José Salmón B., president and members of the provisional directorate of the National Collection Company, had been accepted, and further declared that these men were authorized to continue to perfect the organization of the company, and to perform the business for which it was established.

[2] The term *cabotaje* means traffic between the ports of the country, as phrased in the law itself: "El tráfico entre puertos de Bolivia con mercaderías nacionales ó nacionalizadas, en lastre; y el transporte de pasajeros entre dichos puntos."

[3] Araoz, *Nuevo digesto*, vol. II, pp. 291–385. This law contains 613 articles and a transitory article, giving in great detail the whole customs system of the country. The main purpose

By the Decree of March 24, 1928, the importation of arms, munitions, and explosives was allowed only to the national government, and definite penalties were prescribed for any infringement of the decree.[1] The Decree of May 19, 1928, regulates the commerce in drugs and opiates.[2]

The two Laws of May 3, 1928, increased the taxes on immovable and movable property. The Law of Immovable Property created a Permanent Fiscal Commission (*Comisión Fiscal Permanente*) which was to have general charge of the administration of the provisions of this law. The Ministry of Agriculture was also to aid in the enforcement of the law. There were also to be Commissions of Estimates (*Comisión de Avalúo*), one for each department of the republic, and a group of patrons (*padrones*) who were to assist in the administration of this law.[3] The second law provided for an increase in the *rentas global* and *mobiliaria*. The Permanent Fiscal Commission was also to have charge of the administration of this law under the immediate supervision of the Ministry of the Treasury.[4]

The National Treasury was organized by the Law of April 27, 1928, and placed under the direct control of the Ministry of the Treasury. It was to have a treasurer nominated by the Chamber of Senators and appointed by the president of the republic. He was to serve for a term of six years and might be reappointed. He was to make an annual report on the condition of the treasury, and a monthly report to the minister of the treasury.[5] On the same date, April 27, 1928, the Law of the Budget (*Ley Organica de Presupuesto*) was enacted. The executive power was directed by it to lay the budget before the Congress, on the first day of the regular session. It is to contain an estimate of the receipts and expenditures for the ensuing fiscal year. It must include the estimate for the departments as well as for the general government. The estimate must be in the form of a project for a law and is to be presented to the president of the Chamber of Deputies. When it is approved by that body it must be presented to the Chamber of Senators for its approval. The budget consists of three parts. The first contains an estimate of receipts and expenditures of the national govern-

---

of the law is to control the importation and exportation of goods at the various frontiers: the lacustrine, riverine, and land boundaries.

[1] Araoz, *Nuevo digesto*, vol. II, pp. 393–395.

[2] *Ibid.*, pp. 395–401.

[3] *Ibid.*, pp. 83–93. The tax was fixed at Bs. 4 for each Bs. 1000 worth of property above the value of Bs. 3000 (art. 2). Exempt from this tax were the *tierras de originarias* that paid a territorial tax; churches, temples, convents, and parochial buildings; cemeteries; and schools, colleges, hospitals, *hospicios*, orphan asylums, and other charitable institutions.

[4] *Ibid.*, pp. 93–109. This was an income tax and was graduated, increasing with the increase in the income. No tax was to be paid on an income under Bs. 3000. An annual income of Bs. 6000 paid Bs. 60 a year, and an income of more than Bs. 30,000, Bs. 1750 a year (art. 6).

[5] *Ibid.*, pp. 18–19.

ment and of the departments for the fiscal year. The second is a detailed statement of the receipts expected. The third is a detailed statement of the proposed expenditures. The fiscal year begins on January 1 and ends on December 31. The budget, as has been noted, is made by the ministers of state, severally and collectively, with the assistance of the presidents of the two chambers of the Congress, assisted by a third party, representing the national government, if that is considered necessary. Then the inspector general makes up the budget from the estimates of these bodies.[1]

The Law of February 8, 1911, ordered that the public debt should be paid.[2] The Decree of October 4, 1913, ordered that an inventory should be made of all immovable properties of the state, departmental as well as national. In the future such surveys were to be made every four years.[3]

The Ministry of Industry has general charge of the industrial and commercial life of the republic. It seeks to encourage domestic and foreign commerce, agriculture, mining, and industry in general. It seeks to improve industry by inviting new methods and means of constructing and developing public industrial institutions, or by introducing into Bolivia new methods and improvements from foreign countries. It has charge of industrial expositions, national as well as departmental in scope. It seeks to encourage industry by introducing new industries, capital, and talent. It grants monopolistic privileges in conformity with law.[4] It grants patents to inventors, grants trademarks (*marcas de fábrica*), studies reforms in commercial legislation, and maintains relations with private concerns interested in developing the industries of the country. It codifies legislation affecting industrial and commercial activities, and collects statistics and geographical and technical data throughout the world, with a view to increasing trade and commerce and industry in Bolivia; and in general aims to promote the industrial and commercial life of the republic. The Law of December 12, 1916, prescribed the manner of bringing about these objectives.[5] The Law

[1] Araoz, *Nuevo digesto*, vol. II, pp. 19–27. The national government is strictly forbidden to contract any debt not provided for in the budget. This law repealed that of October 24, 1913, and such other laws as conflicted with it.

[2] *Ibid.*, pp. 42–45.

[3] *Ibid.*, p. 55.

[4] The Law of December 12, 1916, authorized the national government to grant to Richard Levering and Company the right to develop oil resources in the republic, the "derecho de explotar y reconocer" for three years in "todas las zonas petrolíferas reservadas para el Estado" in the "departamentos de Chuquisaca, Santa Cruz y Tarija." The Standard Oil Company of Bolivia became the successors to this company. By the contract with the national government the Standard Oil Company of Bolivia acquired some 1,000,000 hectares in the east and southeast of the republic (*en el Oriente y Sueste de la República*).

[5] Araoz, *Nuevo digesto*, vol. II, pp. 408–418. The law deals with *privilegios industriales*. It declares that all commercial and industrial inventions and discoveries may be patented,

of January 15, 1918, prescribed in detail the regulations for obtaining trademarks (*marcas de fábrica*).[1] The Decree of March 8, 1860, authorized the organization of stock companies, as provided in the Civil Code. Such companies must be incorporated as juridical personalities before they are entitled to operate as independent concerns.[2] The Law of November 20, 1895, provides that none but members of the directorate of companies are entitled to the rights guaranteed by that law. The Law of February 23, 1927, requires that stock companies engaged in mining must have their headquarters in the republic.[3] The Decree of July 31, 1902, requires that such companies must conform to the rules and regulations of that document.[4] The Decree of June 11, 1921, requires that such companies file with the national government a statement of the moneys used by them in foreign countries.[5]

The Law of September 27, 1904, authorizes the establishment of life insurance companies (*compañías de seguros*) in the republic; but no insurance company may operate in the country without express permission from the national government.[6] As early as 1879 the control of the fluvial waters was established by the Decree of September 8 of that year. This included control of the surface as well as the subsurface waters and their uses.[7] The Law of November 21, 1924, regulates the hours of labor and the guaranties to employees in commerce and other industries. It established an eight-hour day, medical care for occupational accidents and diseases, protection from dismissal without cause, annual vacations, and protection from loss of employment because of absence during the period of military service.[8] It also provided for pacific settlement of disputes

---

and when so patented they are the exclusive property of their author and his legal heirs. The Law of November 13, 1909, authorized copyrighting of intellectual, literary, and artistic productions. The Law of November 20, 1895, had done the same for scientific discoveries.

[1] Araoz, *Nuevo digesto*, vol. II, pp. 418–426. The term *marcas* is defined in this manner: "Se entiende pro marca, todo signo, emblema ó denominación característica y peculiar, con que se quiera especializar los artefactos de una fábrica, los objetos de un comercio, los productos de la tierra y de las industrias agrícolas, forestral, ganadera y extractivas."

[2] *Ibid.*, pp. 426–432.

[3] *Ibid.*, p. 432, note.

[4] *Ibid.*, pp. 433–434.

[5] *Ibid.*, p. 434.

[6] *Ibid.*, pp. 434–435. This law covers insurance in all its known forms.

[7] *Ibid.*, pp. 436–474. Naturally the control of the waters of the republic is important. The drinking waters are controlled by the Decrees of June 26, 1896, and February 17, 1902. This Decree of September 8, 1879, was incorporated in the Law of November 28, 1906.

[8] *Ibid.*, pp. 475–482. The working day must be divided into two parts, separated by at least one hour. Increased wages must be paid for overtime work. The annual vacation was to be for a month and with pay. Notice of dismissal must be given three months before becoming effective.

between employers and employees through conciliation and arbitration. Occupational accidents were further taken care of by the Law of January 19, 1924.[1] The Law of March 18, 1926, created the Department of Labor.[2] The Law of February 12, 1927, divided the republic into four labor districts. There were to be headquarters for the National Labor Department in La Paz, Oruro, Potosí, and Uncía.[3] The Decree of June 7, 1926, ordered an account opened in the National Treasury for funds for the Caja de Garantía del Departamento Nacional del Trabajo to pay the damages from occupational accidents.[4] The Law of May 28, 1927, made it obligatory upon the owners and operators of mines to prevent accidents to their employees. The National Body of Mining Engineers (*Cuerpo Nacional de Ingenieros de Minas*) was to constitute a commission to study means for preventing accidents in mines, under the supervision of the National Department of Labor.[5] The Supreme Resolution (*Suprema Resolución*) of August 13, 1926, exempted students in industrial schools from the benefits of the Law of January 19, 1924.[6] The Law of April 18, 1928, prescribed the damages to be paid to those suffering from occupational diseases.[7] The Decree of October 7, 1920, created the Institute of Social Reforms (*Instituto de Reformas Sociales*), and the Decree of April 13, 1927, created the Commission of Studies (*Comisión de Estudios*) for the study of social laws.[8] The Law of January 25, 1924, made it obligatory upon employees in mines, the street-car system, and other transportational systems to carry accident insurance. The employer and the employee each were to pay an equal amount, 5 per cent of the wage, to cover such insurance.[9] On July 7, 1928, a decree was issued prescribing the nature of the obligation of employers for the safety of their employees.[10] It may be concluded from this brief statement that

[1] Araoz, *Nuevo digesto*, vol. II, pp. 482–496.

[2] *Ibid.*, pp. 497–498.

[3] *Ibid.*, p. 498. The District of La Paz included also the Department of El Beni; that of Oruro, the Departments of Cochabamba and Santa Cruz; that of Potosí, the Departments of Chuquisaca and Tarija; and that of Uncía, the Provinces of Bustillo, Charcas, Alonso de Ibáñez, and Chayanta.

[4] *Ibid.*, p. 500.

[5] *Ibid.*, pp. 500–502.

[6] *Ibid.*, p. 482, note.

[7] *Ibid.*, p. 496.

[8] *Ibid.*, p. 497, note.

[9] *Ibid.*, p. 502. The exact words are: "trabajadores mineros, tranviarios, ferroviarios y asalariados en general."

[10] *Ibid.*, pp. 507–508. The National Department of Labor was to make a study of the whole situation and to see that the decree was enforced.

Bolivia has done much for the social security of her people, and that she is well to the front in this matter.

One of the most important industries of Bolivia, if not the most important, is mining. It is natural, therefore, that the national government should desire an ever increasing control over it. The Law of January 14, 1928, created the National Superintendency of Mines, at the head of which was to be a national superintendent of mines. This officer was to be nominated by the Supreme Court and the district courts and appointed by the president of the republic. His term of office was six years, and he could not be removed without just cause, but might be reappointed.[1] On January 28, 1928, the *reglamento* was issued prescribing the nature, powers, and duties of the National Superintendency of Mines. It was to have its headquarters in the *de facto* capital of the country. There was also to be a secretary.[2] The Law of March 21, 1928, created the Fiscal Office (*Fiscalía*) of the National Superintendency of Mines.[3] The Decree of March 30, 1928, created the General Superintendency of Mines and Petroleum. This was a consolidation of the General Directorate of Mines and the General Directorate of Geology. It was to have its headquarters in the city of La Paz, with a head to be known as the director general of mines and petroleum.[4] The Decree of November 26, 1927, obliged the concessionaires of mines to register with the General Superintendency of Mines and Petroleum in La Paz within thirty days after the decree has been published. The period was changed from thirty to sixty days by the Decree of December 26, 1927.[5] The Decree of February 2, 1928, authorized the Mining Police (*Policía Minera Obrera*) to operate in every city where there was a labor bureau (*jefatura del trabajo*). These police agents were to work with the National Department of Labor. There were to be seven such agents, including a chief of police. They were to help maintain peace and order in the mines in their districts.[6] The Law of November 24, 1911, ordered the creation of the office of assayor of minerals

[1] Araoz, *Nuevo digesto*, vol. II, pp. 508–509.

[2] *Ibid.*, pp. 509–511. The *reglamento* states that the headquarters are to be in "el asiento del Supremo Gobierno," which may be taken to mean the *de facto* capital, that is, the city of La Paz. Of course, that is not the interpretation to be put upon it literally and legally, for the phrase means the city in which the supreme government has its seat.

[3] *Ibid.*, p. 511.

[4] *Ibid.*, pp. 511–512. As early as 1911, by a law of November 16 of that year, the National Body of Mining Engineers (*Cuerpo Nacional de Ingenieros de Minas*) was created, and on May 2, 1912, it had been formally organized (*ibid.*, pp. 512–513, 513–523). The Law of December 20, 1917, created the National School of Mining Engineers, to be located at Oruro (*ibid.*, p. 525). On November 24, 1927, a decree was issued which declared that mines without *patentes* were to be considered as *terrenos francos*.

[5] *Ibid.*, pp. 528–529; note on p. 528.

[6] *Ibid.*, pp. 533–534.

(*ensayador fiscal de minerales*) for the capital of each of the departments of Potosí, La Paz, and Oruro.[1] His duties were prescribed in a Decree of December 26 of the same year.[2] The Law of June 20, 1921, prescribed in detail the conditions under which the exploitation of petroleum lands might be carried on in the republic. It declared that the exclusive right to grant concessions for such exploitation inhered in the state.[3] The Chief Executive of the state was fully authorized to set aside such lands as he saw fit, for exploitation by the state itself. The companies formed to exploit the oil lands must have their legal residence in the republic and must be operated under the laws of the state. The Supreme Decree of May 17, 1929, amended article 27 of the Mineral Code (*Código de Minería*) to include provisions governing the General Superintendency of Mines and Petroleum.[4] The Decree of May 31, 1929, prescribed the wages to be paid the engineers who were to survey mining claims.[5]

The Ministry of Public Works and Communications has general charge of all public works in the republic, and of the means of communication, the drinking waters, and the activities of the geographical surveys. It has charge, more particularly, of the construction, capitalization, and management of the railways, and of means of transportation in general throughout the country. It has control over projects for fluvial routes and for canals, and over ways and means of improving them. It has charge of the public credit in so far as this affects its own particular fields. It builds legislative and other government buildings, theaters, hospitals, hospitals for the insane, and houses of refuge. It allocates the money to be used for these purposes and for the purpose of keeping up repairs on public buildings. It protects the rights of the state in international relations affecting its particular fields, and especially in the relations between state-owned and privately owned means of communication and transportation. By the Decree of June 28, 1926, the General Directorate of Public Works and the National Association of Engineers were united in a single office, with a director general of public works and chief of the National Association of Engineers. The administration and development of the railways are under the director general of public works. Nothing may be done without the formal permission of this officer in matters over which he has jurisdiction.[6] The construction and development of railways are subject to the provisions of the Law of October 3, 1910, known as

[1] Araoz, *Nuevo digesto*, vol. II, p. 534.

[2] *Ibid.*, pp. 534–535.

[3] *Ibid.*, pp. 538–549. This law is known as the Ley de Adjudicaciones de Yacimientos Petroleros, also as the Ley de Petroleros.

[4] *Ibid.*, pp. 567–568.

[5] *Ibid.*, p. 568.

[6] *Ibid.*, vol. III, pp. 1–2. Railroads are to be constructed in compliance with the resolutions adopted by the Pan American Congress of Highways (*Congreso Panamericano de Carreteras*).

the General Law of Railways (*Ley General de Ferrocarriles*). No railway may be constructed in the republic without formal permission from the national legislative power. Request for permission must be made to the Ministry of Public Works. When permission has been formally granted, the persons to whom it has been granted must establish a legal residence in the republic, and must operate the railroad in conformity with the laws of the state governing such matters. The authorities operating the railroad are obliged to carry the mails, and such officials and persons as have been given passes, without cost. The national government has direct control over the rates to be charged passengers and for the goods carried. There is an inspector who is charged with the careful supervision of the whole railway system.[1]

The General Regulation for Railways (*Reglamento General de Ferrocarriles*) of July 20, 1911, prescribed in detail the general management of the railways.[2] The Decree of November 24, 1928, required all persons entering the republic, whether nationals or foreigners, to present their passports on the international trains over the Villazón–Atocha, the Antofagasta–Oruro, the Arica–La Paz, and the Guaqui–La Paz lines.[3] The Law of December 1, 1911, dealing with riverine and lacustrine navigation, provided that no person might engage in such navigation except by formal permission and under the supervision of the national government.[4] The Decree of January 30, 1912, prescribed in detail the nature of this navigation.[5] The Decree of August 2, 1927, prescribed the

1 Araoz, *Nuevo digesto*, vol. III, pp. 5–14.

2 *Ibid.*, pp. 15–38.

3 *Ibid.*, pp. 38–39.

4 *Ibid.*, pp. 44–45.

5 *Ibid.*, pp. 45–54. At the time this decree was issued Bolivia had the following ports (the name of the river on whose bank the port, or ports, are located is given first, followed by the name of the port, or ports):

Piray: Cuatro Ojos
Guapay: Puerto Velardo
Chapare: Todosantos
Mamoré: Guayaramerín
Villa Bella
Exaltación
Nuevo Berlín
Ibara: Puerto Ballivián
Yacuma: Santa Ana
Iténez: Meteguá
Blanco: Bella Vista
Baures
El Carmen
Itonama: Magdalena
Machupo: San Joaquín
San Ramón
Madera: Manoa
Grande y Piray: Puerto Rojas
El Beni: Rurrenabaque
Salinas
Riberalta
Cachuela Esperanza
Madre de Dios: El Fortín Heath
Ortón: Porvenir
Puerto Rico
Acre: Cobija
Santa Cruz
El Sacado
Bolpebra
Tiahuamanu: Bella Flor
Porvenir
Abuná: Villa Rica
Santa Rosa
Lake Titicaca: Yampupata
Titicachi
Santiago de Huata
Chua

The following were made free ports for fifteen years by the Law of December 9, 1926: Puerto

manner in which both private and public roads were to be constructed. The construction of these roads was, of course, to be under the supervision of the General Directorate of Public Works. No roads might be legally constructed without special permission from this body.[1] The Law of December 9, 1905, and the Decree of January 19, 1906, ordered that all men over the age of eighteen years must work on the public roads or pay a poll tax. No exemptions were to be allowed.[2] The Decree of April 28, 1924, compelled the owners of real property to keep the public roads in repair. The penalty for failure to keep the roads in good shape was severe.[3] The Law of April 8, 1922, required that all buildings in the urban communities be provided with the necessary sanitary equipment. The Bureau of Drainage Inspection (*Inspección Fiscal del Alcantarillado*) was to supervise the enforcement of this law. Further details were given in the Decree of July 27, 1927.[4]

The Ministry of Public Instruction and Agriculture has general charge of the educational activities of the republic. It seeks to increase learning and to develop wisdom. It inspects and protects scientific and literary institutions, and organizes and seeks to improve libraries and museums, especially those that belong to the state.[5] It publishes textbooks and provides apparatus for use in educational institutions. It encourages the study of the sciences and the arts. It is particularly interested in geography in all its phases, and gives aid to geographical societies through appropriations of moneys for that purpose. It encourages the scientific study of agriculture, viniculture, and stock breeding (*ganadería*), and in general seeks to keep pace with the cultural activities of the age.

The present educational system of Bolivia is based upon the Law of November 22, 1872, and explained in detail in the Decree of January 15, 1874. Public instruction is divided into three sections: popular, collegiate (*media*), and professional. Popular instruction is divided into primary, elementary, and second-

---

Suárez, Puerto Sucre, those on Lake Gaiba, and the Pueblo de San Matías. Most of these ports are located in the region of the Oriente and Noroeste of the republic (*ibid.*, p. 47, note).

[1] Araoz, *Nuevo digesto*, vol. III, pp. 54–64.

[2] *Ibid.*, pp. 64–69.

[3] *Ibid.*, pp. 69–70. Land owners are responsible only for the upkeep of roads that either cross or run alongside their property.

[4] *Ibid.*, pp. 70–72, 72–90. The number of such details can be judged from the amount of space the Decree of July 27, 1927, actually occupies, for it has 122 articles.

[5] *Ibid.*, vol. I, p. 69, note. The National Museum of La Paz is one of the best in Latin America. It is housed in a palace built in the Tiahuanaco style of architecture, which is, in itself, a very commendable thing, and a splendid tribute to the great people of the Lake Titicaca valley. It has an excellent collection of anthropological materials and an unusually good collection of specimens of the natural resources of the country.

ary. Collegiate instruction is intrusted to the *liceos*, colleges, and universities. Professional instruction is given in professional institutions, and prepares for careers in the applied sciences, the arts, and the trades. Primary instruction is under the exclusive control of the state. It is free and obligatory, and is based upon the principle that every individual is entitled to an education. The only limitation upon the educative process is found in the individual himself, for he must be physically, mentally, and morally capable of education. Instruction in the intermediate grades is given in the elementary schools. Instruction in the secondary schools is given to those who are prepared to enter such institutions, and extends over a period of four years.[1] It is the business of the national government to establish, or to see to it that there are established, secondary and normal schools wherever they may be thought necessary. The courses in the professional schools are prescribed in detail, especially in the medical schools, the schools of law and jurisprudence, of agriculture, and of mining, and the schools of the arts and the trades.

The school year is divided into ten months, beginning on December 1 and ending on September 30. Promotion from one grade to another is determined by formal examinations. The Decree of March 21, 1910, prescribes these examinations in detail.[2] The decree provided that examinations were to be given in the period between October 15 and November 1 of each year. These dates could not be changed except by action of the national government. The Decree of May 29, 1915, modified the above decree by ordering that the period in which examinations should be given was to begin on October 1 and end on October 31. The regulations concerning examinations were further modified by the Decree of January 2, 1929, by exempting those who had received the grades of excellent

[1] The Law of December 17, 1904, was of course amended after the enactment of the Law of August 15, 1906, establishing religious toleration in the republic. Prior to that time, a course in the New Testament had been required in these schools.

[2] Araoz, *Nuevo digesto*, vol. III, pp. 162–163. The results of the examinations are announced on November 1. The examinations in the intermediate schools are held between October 1 and October 10, in the secondary schools between October 10 and October 20, and those for the professional schools between October 20 and October 31. The examinations for the bachelor's degree (*bachillerato*) are held between December 15 and December 31. The regulations for admission to the universities were changed by the Decree of January 10, 1929. Admission to the university is by certificate of completion of the work in the four years of the secondary schools or by an examination in the studies of those four years. The Decree of December 26, 1923, changed the regulations for the examinations. Those who had failed in an examination were permitted to take a second examination. But under no circumstances is promotion to be made without passing these formally prescribed examinations. By the Decree of October 21, 1927, written examinations were substituted for the oral examination in the schools of law and jurisprudence. The Law of November 21, 1907, required formal written examinations in the schools of medicine and pharmacy. The regulations for these examinations were explained in detail in the Decree of May 23, 1910.

(*sobresaliente*) and good (*bueno*) in their studies for the year.[1] The state also issues evidences of achievement to those individuals who have satisfactorily completed a given course or courses of instruction. A graduate of a school of law and jurisprudence, or of a school of the political and social sciences, receives the degree of lawyer (*abogado*) or doctor; a graduate of a school of medicine, the degree of doctor; a graduate of a school of theology or of the ecclesiastical sciences, the degree of *licenciado;* and a graduate of a teachers college, the degree of Bachelor of Letters or of the Sciences. The state also issues certificates to those who desire to establish art or trade schools and who are technically prepared to conduct such institutions. Finally, the state requires that professors who come from foreign countries, or those from Bolivia trained in foreign countries, must present evidence of training equivalent to that required of persons trained in her own institutions.[2]

The Decree of November 6, 1922, provided a new plan of studies for the schools of law and jurisprudence, or, as it is called, the Facultad de Derecho y Ciencias Sociales de la República. It provides a five-year course for lawyers, and a two-year course for *notarios y procuradores*, and for the doctorate in the political and social sciences. The emphasis upon the study of sociology is in keeping with the tendency in other parts of Latin America. The decree also provided that after the year 1925 the degree of *Doctor en Ciencias Sociales* would be required of those who desired to enter the diplomatic service or to teach in the schools of law and jurisprudence. The degree of *Doctor en Ciencias Sociales* was not to be required, however, of those who had had seven years of successful work in the diplomatic service or teaching in schools of law. The decree also required that after the year 1926 the degree of *Licenciado en Derecho* would be given only to persons who had practiced law successfully for eight years, unless they held the degree of Doctor of Law from a recognized school of law. The same decree also required that students in the schools of law and jurisprudence take the prescribed examinations. It also gave the faculties of these schools the right to elect their own deans and secretaries, who were to serve for one year, and could be reelected. The Decree of November 10, 1922, reorganized the courses of study, as well as the internal organization, of the medical schools. The Decree of February 18, 1924, provided for an Escuela de Odontología, and prescribed its course of studies. The Decree of November 29, 1922,

[1] Araoz, *Nuevo digesto*, vol. III, pp. 164–166. These are the highest grades given in the Bolivian schools. The other grades are *regular* (average), *malo* (poor), *pésimo* (passing), and *nulo* (failure). By an earlier decree, that of December 6, 1923, good conduct of the student was recognized as an element in promotion; conduct disapproved by teachers and administrative officers is to count against the student in questions of promotion.

[2] The national government is also under obligation to found normal schools for the preparation of teachers for the primary and secondary schools. The act also provided for the establishment of a normal school for both sexes in the capital of the republic.

reorganized the courses of study in the Instituto Nacional de Comercio. The Law of December 9, 1905, regulated the professional practice of *ingenieros, arquitectos, y agrimensores*.[1] The minister of public instruction has general supervision over these several institutions. He is assisted by the councils of education and inspectors. There is a council of instruction in the capital of each of the departments of the republic.[2] The names of the universities, other than the University of San Francisco Xavier, have been changed. The University of Santa Cruz was given the name of University of Gabriel René Moreno by the Law of December 9, 1911; the University of Potosí, that of University of Tomás Frías by the Law of December 2, 1924; the University of Juan Misael Saracho, that of University of Tarija by the Decree of May 13, 1927; and the University of La Paz, that of University of the Mariscal Andrés de Santa Cruz by the Decree of May 27, 1927.[3] The financial support for the Ministry of Public Instruction is provided by legislative appropriations, by the sale of public lands,[4] by the produce of the *estancaminas* of the state, by fines for failure to serve in the National Guard, and by fines for engaging in public education without the necessary legal qualifications. Also by the sale of the products of the arts and trade schools and by the fees for certificates and diplomas.

There is no phase of the public life of Bolivia which has received greater attention during the past quarter of a century than public education. The forces of democracy have been giving special attention to this all-important matter. The movements have been in the direction of a more modern type of education. There has been a powerful, but numerically small, group of leaders in the Youth Movement in Bolivia which has taken the initiative in the movement to democratize and to modernize the whole educational system. The students have been very active in this movement, for the Bolivian university student, in common with his fellows throughout Latin America, takes these matters more seriously than does the university student in the United States of America. The students of Bolivia are organized under able leadership. The Federación de Estudiantes de Cochabamba (Federation of Students of Cochabamba) has made its power felt in this movement. It issued a booklet in 1928 entitled *Primera Convención Nacional de Estudiantes Bolivianos* (First National Convention of Bolivian Students), which contained a statement of the principles supported by the

[1] Araoz, *Nuevo digesto*, vol. III, pp. 181–185.

[2] *Ibid.*, p. 99. The council is divided into two sections. In the first section are the inspector general, two members chosen by the colleges, two appointed by the council, the directors of the *liceos*, and two members chosen by the Municipal Council. In the second section are the inspector of primary instruction, the *directores* of the higher schools, the *directores de las escuelas de asilo*, two members appointed by the Municipal Council, and the *directores* of the schools of arts and crafts.

[3] *Ibid.*, p. 99, note.

[4] The amount is placed at a sixth of the total amount received from the sale of the land.

Federación, and the organic statute and regulations for the debates of the Federación Universitaria Boliviana (Bolivian University Federation). The call for the convention emphasized the need of perfecting the organization of the students of Bolivia, for the welfare of the university students of the country can best be attained through a union of the laboring classes and the students.[1] The

[1] *Primera Convención Nacional de Estudiantes Bolivianos*, pp. 1–2. The Federación de Estudiantes in each of the departments of the republic was invited to send three delegates to this convention. The national government gave its support and provided free transportation on the railways to and from the convention. The purpose of the convention was declared to be twofold: (*a*) "Declaración de principios en lo referente a las cuestiones internacional, económica y principalmente universitaria"; (*b*) "Organización de la Federación Universitaria Boliviana." The booklet also contained the *proyecto* for the *estatuto orgánico de la Federación Universitaria* by Dr. José Antonio Arze. Dr. Arze declared that the Federación "será organismo que tienda a unificar las aspiraciones ideológicas de la clase estudiantil de la República, y que tienda a encarnar en la vida institucional esas aspiraciones." The ideologies of the students should be made known, Dr. Arze maintained, in order to enable the students to play their part in the life of the *nueva generación*. Among the purposes of the Federación were a union of the students of Latin America, and a union between the students and the manual and intellectual proletariat, the Liga Pro-Indio and other organizations being formed for that purpose. Dr. Arze has been one of the most intelligent and one of the hardest-working leaders for the improvement of the lot of the Indian. He has sought to arouse an interest in the welfare of the native people, and has had commendable success.

Another purpose of the Federación was to indorse the idea of the complete autonomy of the university and to urge the introduction of reforms "sobre las bases de la Autonomía y la Reforma Universitaria" in order that "los planteles de instrucción se adapten, en lo metodológico, a las normas más modernas de la Pedagogía." The project declared definitely that the "Federación de Estudiantes Bolivianos no tiene carácter de Partido Político." Dr. Arze also drew up, in this same booklet, the "programa de principios de la Federación Universitaria Boliviana." The Federación was distinctly opposed to the "sostenedores del Privilegio Económico, de la Tiranía Política y del Oscurantismo" and in favor of "los partidarios del Bienestar Colectivo, de la Libertad y de la Verdad Científica." It was in favor also of a "Renovación, es decir, el partido que busca el imperio del altruismo, de la Paz, de la emancipación del espíritu." The Federación, as we have already observed, was to make common cause with the youth that was free, the proletariat, and the "pensadores imparciales y altivos del orbe entero." Universities which do not take up in detail the *cuestión social* were declared, of course, to fail to do what they were organized to do for the general good of humanity. Above all else, the students were declared to have a right to air their "inquietudes y sus orientaciones" in the universities. The Federación also took up the more important educational questions before the republic for solution. It declared that education was the most important problem before the Bolivian people, and urged the decentralization of the whole educational system. Bolivian teachers should be substituted for foreigners teaching in Bolivian universities. Bolivian teachers should be given a more comprehensive education, especially through a plan to send teachers to foreign countries for study. The educational institutions should be taken out of politics. The Federación also favored two vacation periods of forty-five days each in the year. New types of examination were to be substituted for the old. It also favored the harmonious development of the physical, the mental, and the moral capabilities of the individual.

The Federación also took up the larger problems of the country. It favored a pacifist internationalism and a rational nationalism, and the abolition of all racial and class distinc-

students were urged to unite with labor, for only in that way could they hope to attain their objectives. The Convention met during the Fiesta de los Estudiantes, August 17 to 20, 1928, in Cochabamba.

---

tions. It declared that the universities should be given greater financial support and believed that the best way to take them out of politics was to make them autonomous. Under "Política territorial" it advocated the "reintegración de la soberanía marítima de Bolivia, en toda extensión del Pacífico" and the "reivindicación de la costa que le fué arrebatada por la violencia guerrera y por la presión diplomática." It recommended the "defensa de las fronteras de la Nacionalidad." It also wanted an "intensificación de la vialidad," in order to secure an outlet to the Atlantic from the north and from the Oriente, and in the southeast through the Río de la Plata. It declared further that "la Juventud Universitaria cree que el Estado debe desplegar el máximum de sus esfuerzos financieros para resolver estos magnos problemas de la vialidad boliviana." It favored the expropriation of private monopolies of transportational facilities without indemnification in order to get from under such a monstrosity as private ownership of public utilities. It favored the conservation of natural resources for the good of the people of Bolivia. It was also gravely concerned about the population of the country. It urged immigration on a large scale, and more intelligent training and a more humane treatment of the Indians so as to increase the Indian population. It urged the incorporation of the Indian into civilized life after the fashion of Mexico, and held that such incorporation was only possible through the abolition of the feudal agrarian system. The education of the Indian would have to be something more than an effort to make him into a white man. On this head the Federación declared that *castellanización* was not the solution of the Indian problem, and that the plan "debe orientarse hacia su habilitación técnica para la vida económica, mediante una intensa difusión de métodos y maquinaria para los trabajos rurales, por cuenta del Estado." It also held that it was necessary to free the Indians from the *propaganda oscurantista* of the clericals. The *mestizo* should be reformed—the "moralización del mestizo" is the way Dr. Arze phrased it—and emancipated from "el alcoholismo y la politiquería, funestamente estimulados por la política partidista, al través de toda nuestra historia política."

The Federación would give intelligent scientific attention to public health, urging the establishment of a ministry of public health (*salubridad pública y previsión social*). It also urged a definite limitation upon privileges, personal and economic. It was equally emphatic in its attitude toward *política interna*, favoring a decrease in regionalism and a more powerful nationalism, and believing that federalism was the best way of increasing national unity and decreasing regionalism. It was even more emphatic in urging a reform in the *orden económico*. It held that true democracy and capitalism were incompatible, declaring, accordingly, that "la única salvación de Bolivia está, pués, en la progresiva socialización de la riqueza privada." It urged an extensive and intensive program of nationalization to attain that end. In regard to the *orden financiero* it was less drastic. It did not favor the complete overthrow of the capitalistic system, but urged reforms in it. With regard to the *régimen constitucional*, it urged a new fundamental law to displace the old one. In the *cuestión religiosa* it demanded the absolute separation of Church and State. As regards the *cuestión militar*, it urged a new army for the Nueva Causa. It pointed out that both Russia and Mexico had been forced to develop an army in order to protect themselves against the states of the world that are still unregenerated. As regards Bolivian militarism it declared: "Si en la tumultuosa historia de Bolivia ha sido frecuente el tipo del militarismo caudillista y parasitario, bien pudiera el porvenir prometernos el tipo del militarismo identificado con la causa de Emancipación Social." On the *cuestión internacional* it was also pacific, urging the "solidaridad de las Repúblicas Latinoamericanas," the creation of *la Liga de Naciones Latinoamericanas* with a view to the ultimate establishment of one state for the whole of Latin America, the

Much of the progress of recent years in the educational development of Bolivia has come about through the able and intelligent efforts of Daniel Sánchez Bustamante. A direct result of his activities was the Decree of July 30, 1921, reorganizing the university councils. A university council was set up in the capital of every department of the state. It was composed of the rector of the university, who was its president, the deans of the schools of law and medicine, the director of the institute or normal school, the director or directress of the superior, the secondary, or the technical schools, the director or directress of the primary schools, the director of the private schools, and a representative of the student body, elected by, but not necessarily a part of, that body. The university council meets weekly, or oftener if necessary. Its membership is renewed every year. The council does not have the power to choose the officers of administration or instruction, but it has considerable influence in their selection.

The Decree of January 21, 1929, was a further effort to modernize the educational system. It was largely concerned with the introduction of new subjects in the curricula and new methods of determining promotion.[1] The Decree of February 2, 1929, ordered that January 6 of each year be set apart as the Día del Niño and be observed as an official holiday. It is to be observed in an appropriate manner, emphasizing a healthy and beautiful childhood.[2] The Decree of March 25, 1926, created the General Directorate of Public Instruction. At its head is the general director, with a salary of Bs. 12,000 a year. There are also a general inspector of secondary and special instruction, with an annual salary of Bs. 7200, and a general inspector of primary instruction, with an annual salary of Bs. 6000. The General Directorate has

---

repudiation of the principle of conquest of territory by armed force, substitution of the principle of *solidaridad latinoamericana* for the principle of Monroeism and Panamericanism, which has been in the service of Yanqui imperialism, and the prevention of Yanqui imperialism from intervening in inter-Latin American disputes and in the internal affairs of the Latin American countries, and from exploiting the natural resources of the Latin American states. As one means of bringing about all these desired reforms the Federación urged a Confederación de Universitarias Latinoamericanas in order to bring it about that "la vigorización de este nuevo sentido de patriotismo racial, será obra de la Nueva Generación Universitaria y del Proletariado consciente de todos los pueblos latinoamericanos, coordinados para combatir las fuerzas reaccionarias de sus respectivos Estados." Finally, it urged the youth of the United States to fight against its oligarchic imperialism and to work for a conquest of *un Panamericanismo verdadero* and for the *Patria Universal* "sin dioses en Cielo ni amos sobre la Tierra." We have purposely incorporated these ideas because of their importance in the Youth Movement of Bolivia. It is true that the ideology was presented by one man, but it was approved by the convention. It is hardly to be expected that the ideals set forth by Dr. Arze will ever be fully realized. The New Age of which he speaks so stoutly is still a great way off, and may never come into being.

[1] Araoz, *Nuevo digesto*, vol. III, pp. 515–519.

[2] *Ibid.*, p. 519.

extensive powers, having general supervision, under the Ministry of Public Instruction, of the educational activities of the republic.[1] The Law of December 17, 1904, modified in 1908, 1919, 1923, 1924, and 1927, described in detail the right of the exercise of the *profesorado*. No person may exercise that right who has not been duly certified by the Ministry of Public Instruction.[2] The Decree of July 31, 1928, placed the teachers of the state in the class of public employees, thereby depriving them of the right to strike or to assemble in undisciplined and subversive ways. Any teacher who joins a union, engages in a strike, or indulges in undisciplined and subversive assemblages, or who is an accomplice in such activities is immediately suspended from his position, with loss of pay until his case has been disposed of.[3] The Decree of November 12, 1928, placed further restraints upon the activities of the teachers in public schools. The *sobresueldos* (bonuses) were abolished, but this was not to apply in case a teacher had taught for twenty years. The decree also ordered that the teaching load be apportioned among the teachers so as to give them as many working hours as possible.[4] The Decree of April 2, 1906, made registration of the teachers of the state compulsory.[5] The Law of December 11, 1905, amended by the Law of March 31, 1921, provided for *jubilaciones* (pensions) for teachers, to be paid out of the national public treasury.[6]

The Normal School of Sucre was established by the Decree of January 3, 1909, modified by the Decree of January 5, 1922. It was limited to the preparation of teachers for the primary grades.[7] The Superior Normal Institute of La Paz was created by the Law of December 10, 1916. A Department of Physical

[1] Araoz, *Nuevo digesto*, vol. III, pp. 122–123. In addition there was to be a general secretary, with a salary of Bs. 4500 a year. The total expenses for the year were not to exceed Bs. 40,000.

[2] *Ibid.*, pp. 123–128.

[3] *Ibid.*, pp. 128–129.

[4] *Ibid.*, pp. 131–132.

[5] *Ibid.*, pp. 132–133. The teachers were required to register in a special book, called the *libro de matrícula nacional de profesores*, and in another to be known as the *libro de inscripciones*. A certificate of registration was necessary for a certificate to teach and for eligibility for a pension. Teachers who were dismissed from the service were to be dropped from the registration books. The Decree of January 21, 1923, increased the registration requirement to include the teachers in all the schools of the republic, private as well as public.

[6] *Ibid.*, p. 133. These pensions were for teachers in the public schools only, who had taught twenty-five years continuously, or thirty years with interruptions.

[7] *Ibid.*, pp. 140–142. The decree limited the number of students admitted from each department: five for Chuquisaca, five for La Paz, four for Potosí, four for Santa Cruz, four for Oruro, three for Tarija, and two for El Beni.

Education was added to the institution by the Decree of December 28, 1918.[1] By the Law of December 11, 1905, modified by the Circular of January 17, 1918, and by the Decree of August 23, 1927, all individuals who establish schools with their own private funds for teaching Indians are to be paid Bs. 20 for each Indian receiving instruction in their institutions. The teachers in these schools are eligible for pensions from the state.[2] The Supreme Decree of June 4, 1921, requires that teachers in the public schools shall give two public lectures a year on a subject in which they are giving instruction, or on an allied subject.[3] The school holidays are enumerated by the Decree of June 9, 1923.[4] The Decree of November 24, 1910, made it obligatory upon all Bolivians who receive their degrees in foreign countries to secure formal permission from the national government to practice their profession in the republic.[5] The Law of October 7, 1915, and the Decree of April 15, 1920, established the position of director of school hygiene, to have charge of public school sanitation and hygiene. There was to be such an officer in each department of the republic, although the Dirección General de Sanidad Escolar de la República is under the supervision of the director in La Paz. The whole is, however, under the direct control of the Ministry of Public Instruction.[6]

The Bolivian government has also provided other means of advancing the education of its people. An exposition is held at the end of each school year which is national in scope. Its purpose is to give the people an idea of the work of the schools, to encourage the culture of personality and conserve its powers, to develop initiative, and to nurture the spirit of ingenuity and invention. All

[1] Araoz, *Nuevo digesto*, vol. III, pp. 142–143. The Institute was placed under the supervision of the rector of the University of San Andrés in La Paz.

[2] *Ibid.*, pp. 144–146.

[3] *Ibid.*, p. 146. These lectures are organized and conducted by the rectors and general inspectors of the districts, and attendance of teachers as well as students is compulsory. The lectures must be written and a copy of each sent to the Ministry of Public Instruction. The lectures are given a great deal of publicity in order to get the most out of them. At least such is the letter of the decree.

[4] *Ibid.*, p. 152. The holidays are: Sunday; the first, second, and third of January; Monday, Tuesday, and Wednesday of Carnival week; Thursday, Friday, and Saturday of Holy Week; Corpus Christi; May 26; the Feast of the Passover; the fifth, sixth, and seventh of August; the *efemérides patrias;* the eighth of September; and the Feast of the Nativity (*Fiesta de la Navidad*). To this list must be added, very naturally, the days of great occasions. By the Decree of May 28, 1924, the vacations are made to come in the months of June and December in the cold zones of the republic, that is, in the Departments of La Paz, Oruro, and Potosí; and in the months of November and December in the temperate zones, that is, in the Departments of Chuquisaca, Cochabamba, Santa Cruz, Tarija, and El Beni.

[5] *Ibid.*, pp. 171–178.

[6] *Ibid.*, pp. 179–181. Among the provisions of these measures are those providing for a dental service, and a department of childhood (*puericultura*).

the school authorities must help to prepare for this exposition and take charge of its management.[1] The folklore of Bolivia was ordered collected by the Decree of August 3, 1928. The president of the republic is charged with the direct control of this work. All the professors in the country are obliged to help collect, arrange, and classify the folklore of the nation. The minister of public instruction must organize committees to aid in this work and to further its completion by any means within their power.[2] The Law of October 10, 1910, ordered that October 12, or Columbus Day, should be celebrated throughout the republic in a suitable manner, in commemoration of the discovery of America.[3] The Decree of July 29, 1924, requires all the students in all the educational institutions of the country to take the oath to defend and protect the flag of the country against all its enemies, even to the extent of sacrificing their lives, if that be necessary. The oath must be taken each year, on August 6, at the schools in the departmental capitals.[4] The Decree of July 30, 1924, designated August 17 of each year as Flag Day (*Día de la Bandera*),[5] in commemoration of the date of the adoption of the flag of the republic.[6] The day is to be fittingly celebrated in the schools throughout the country. It is to be used to inculcate patriotic principles and to nurture a love of country among

[1] Araoz, *Nuevo digesto*, vol. III, p. 186.

[2] *Ibid.*, pp. 186–187. In collecting the folklore special attention is to be given to narratives and traditions, traditional and existing customs and manners, the popular languages, beliefs and superstitions, popular songs, popular life and art, and the popular sciences and achievements of the people of Bolivia. This measure is an excellent one, and places Bolivia in the front rank of nations which are interested in this commendable type of work. In this wise the heritage of a rich past, as well as the life of the present, will be preserved.

[3] *Ibid.*, p. 187. The day is to be known as the Day of the Race (*Día de la Raza*).

[4] *Ibid.*, p. 187. The form of the oath is as follows: "¿Juráis por Dios y por la Patria respetar vuestra bandera, cubrirla siempre con vuestro amor, seguirla en su camino de gloria y defenderla de sus enemigos cuando la Nación solicite vuestros sacrificios y vuestra sangre?" "Sí, juramos."

[5] León M. Loza, *Historia de la bandera*. This is a pamphlet which gives a good brief account of the flag. As we have already noted, the flag was adopted by the General Assembly on August 17, 1825. Dr. Loza declares that the flag had been agreed upon as early as August 5, but that the General Assembly did not adopt it until August 17, and that it was not until April 5, 1831, that the national flag was consecrated. This was done by order of Andrés Santa Cruz, at the head of the national government at the time. The *Voce nacional*, La Paz newspaper, gave a detailed account of the ceremonies in the Templo de San Francisco in its issue of April 7, 1831. This paragraph is illuminating: "S. E. que experimentaba en aquel momento mil transportes de jubileo, tomó los estandartes, y habiendo cual otro Napoleón dirigido a los nacionales una enérgica y majestuosa alocución, les entregó expresándoles eran el depósito más sagrado que debían conservar, y al pronunciar si juraban sostenerlos, levantaron todos la voz, y se escuchó hasta en el empiero el grito de los libres por su independencia."

[6] Araoz, *Nuevo digesto*, vol. III, p. 187.

the people. The Decree of November 8, 1927, designated May 27 of each year as Mother's Day (*Día de la Madre*), when maternal virtues are to be extolled.[1] The Decree of November 11, 1909, forbade excavations in Tiahuanaco and the islands of Lake Titicaca, belonging to Bolivia, without special permission from the national government.[2]

The Constitution of 1931 has a special article on the universities of the republic. It provides that rectors, other university authorities, and professors are to be appointed by the universities themselves, which also have the power to determine their rank and titles. The universities also have the right to receive legacies and donations, administer their funds, and prepare and present to the Congress the budget for the year. With the approval of the Congress the universities may make loans, guaranteed by their own funds, in order that they may be autonomous and support their own institutes and faculties.[3]

The Ministry of Agriculture has general supervision over the cultivation of the soil and over the allied arts and sciences. The Law of August 26, 1907, divided Bolivia into five agricultural zones, in order to improve agriculture and stock raising in the several zones.[4] The Decree of June 17, 1924, created a National Bureau of Agricultural Statistics (*Oficina de Estadística Nacional de Agricultura y Ganadería*) in the Ministry of Public Instruction.[5] The Decree of July 11, 1924, created departmental agricultural juntas in the capital of each department of the republic, which were to have direct charge of the interests of the Ministry of Agriculture in their respective localities.[6] The Decree of Febru-

[1] Araoz, *Nuevo digesto*, vol. III, pp. 187–188.

[2] *Ibid.*, p. 188. No materials or objects of any kind may be taken from the ruins of these places, and no materials or artistic objects removed from these ruins may be used for any purpose whatsoever without permission. The Law of March 8, 1927, declared that all the national monuments and objects of historical value were the possession of the nation, and were to be preserved as such (*ibid.*, pp. 188–189).

[3] *Constitución política*, p. 54, art. 116. The incorporation of this whole matter in the Constitution, and placing it in a section by itself, further demonstrates the effects of the movement supported by the Federación Universitaria Boliviana, for the article includes some of the most cherished provisions of its *nuevo credo*.

[4] Araoz, *Nuevo digesto*, vol. III, pp. 279–280. Zone A included the Departments of Santa Cruz and El Beni, with Santa Cruz de la Sierra as the center; Zone B, the Departments of Chuquisaca and Tarija, with the city of Tarija as the center; Zone C, the Department of Cochabamba, with the city of Cochabamba as the center; Zone D, the Departments of Oruro, Potosí, and La Paz, with the exception of the Province of Caupolicán, with the city of La Paz as the center; Zone E, the Territorios de Colonias and the Province of Caupolicán, with the center wherever the national delegate resides. The first four zones were to have experimental agricultural stations.

[5] *Ibid.*, p. 280. It was in this decree that provision was made for the agricultural juntas (*juntas agrícolas*), some of which were established according to the Decree of July 11, 1924.

[6] *Ibid.*, pp. 281–282. The Decree of November 13, 1924, ordered the cultivation of the cotton plant; that of October 22, 1925, established a school of agriculture at Villa Alianza,

ary 26, 1920, further enlarged the activities of the Ministry of Agriculture by providing a more scientific control of farming and stock raising.[1] The Decree of January 24, 1919, ordered the cultivation of the silk industry in Bolivia through a school for the study of silk culture in Cochabamba.[2] The Law of November 19, 1912, established a meteorological service for Bolivia.[3] From this brief statement it will be seen that the Bolivians are not neglecting agriculture, the most important single industry within their land. But while they are giving scientific attention to farming in its different aspects and phases, they still have a great way to go. They are much too largely dependent upon the Indians to attain the degree of success which that industry promises. This means that they will have to make agriculture attractive to an ever increasing number of non-Indian peoples. When they shall have developed their agricultural resources fully, they will have unlocked a source of wealth far greater than that to be expected from the old established professions.

The Ministry of War has general charge of the armed forces under the immediate control of the president of the republic, who is also the captain general of its armies. At the head is the minister of war. There is also a chief of the General Staff (*jefe del Estado Mayor General*), and several other officers to assist him. It is the duty of the Ministry of War to preserve and defend domestic tranquillity and to defend the state from dangers from without. The powers, duties, and organization of the Ministry are prescribed in the Organic Law of the Army enacted on January 22, 1927.[4] The law placed heavy responsibilities upon the men in the armed forces. The great emphasis is upon obedience. The army may not be, under any circumstances whatsoever, a deliberating body.[5] The army is completely subject to this law and its rules and regulations. All able-bodied men between the ages of nineteen and forty-nine are obliged to perform military service. The period of service is, in time of peace, two years; and in time of war as long as may be necessary. The men of the line may not engage in any political activity and have no right either to vote or to hold political office. They may hold no political administrative position except in case of international war or of war within the country.

---

in the Department of La Paz; the Law of February 3, 1926, ordered the forestation of the Andean region; the Decree of June 29, 1926, established an agricultural experimental station in Tarija; the Law of December 23, 1926, established a veterinary school in Santa Cruz.

[1] Araoz, *Nuevo digesto*, vol. III, pp. 282–291.

[2] *Ibid.*, pp. 291–292.

[3] *Ibid.*, p. 292.

[4] *Ibid.*, pp. 190–213. The Reglamento Interno del Ministerio de Guerra was issued on November 14, 1927.

[5] *Ibid.*, pp. 190–191, art. 2. The exact words are: "La fuerza armada es esencialmente obediente y en ningún caso puede deliberar. Está en todo sujeta a la presente ley y sus reglamentos." Consult *Constitución política*, pp. 5–6, art. 10.

The standing army consists of those in active service, those in the *depósito*, and those in the reserve, as well as those who are in the training organizations of the army, such as the Superior Military School, the War College, and the School of Music. The territorial army consists of the special reserves and the territorial guard. There are several different bodies to assist the minister of war in the performance of his duties: the Supreme War Council, which has charge of the military judicial tribunals; the Ecclesiastical Military Service, which has charge of the chaplains, under the orders of the *vicario castrense;* the General Staff; the War Arsenal; the Sanitary Service; and the financial inspector of the army. The military command of the army resides in the president of the republic and in the minister of war. In time of peace, the command of the army is under the chief of the General Staff.[1]

Bolivia is divided into military zones, each zone with its own commander.[2] There is also a divisional organization separate from the military zonal divisions. At the head of the divisional organization is the division commander (*comandante de división*). Mobilization may be either partial or complete, and can be ordered only by the president of the republic. The officers of the army are divided into three classes. The first class includes the men of the rank of general, such as major general, general of division, and general of brigade. The second class includes the *jefes*, such as colonel, lieutenant colonel, and major. The third class includes the subalterns, such as captain, lieutenant, and sublieutenant. These officers receive a salary determined by law. Promotion from one class to another is made according to fixed rules and regulations. Promotion to the rank of general or colonel is made by the Chamber of Senators upon nomination of the president of the republic. In case of a foreign war, however, the captain general may promote, for extraordinary gallantry in the

[1] In time of war it is necessary, as we have noted before, for the president of the republic to divest himself of his office as chief executive if he desires to take over the command of the armed forces in person. He is not permitted to resume his office as president of the republic until he has relinquished the command of the armed forces.

[2] Araoz, *Nuevo digesto*, vol. III, pp. 225–226. The Decree of December 24, 1918, referred to above, divided the republic into three zones: Zone I contained the Department of La Paz and was known as Zona del Norte; Zone II contained the Departments of Oruro and Cochabamba and was known as Zona del Centro; and Zone III contained the Departments of Potosí and Chuquisaca and was known as Zona del Sud. The Law of November 22, 1924, created the military colony of La Horquilla and that of Mateguá in the Province of Iténez. The Departments of Tarija, Santa Cruz, and El Beni, and the Territorios de Colonias were to constitute three military commands (*tres comandancias militares*). The officers in command of zonal divisions were to reside in La Paz, Oruro, and Potosí, respectively, and for the Military Command of the North (*Comandancia Militar del Norte*), comprising the Territorios de Colonias and the Department of El Beni, at Riberalta; of the Oriente, comprising the Department of Santa Cruz, in the city of Santa Cruz; and of the Sudeste, comprising the Department of Tarija and the Gran Chaco, at Villa Montes. The *reglamento* for the division was issued in the form of a Decree of March 18, 1919.

face of the enemy, from the lower to the higher ranks on his own authority, as authorized by the Constitution of the state. In time of peace, the president of the republic may only promote, on his own authority, officers from the lower ranks up to and including that of lieutenant colonel.[1]

Discipline throughout the army demands that the officers and soldiers shall attend strictly to their duties as military men. There are, accordingly, restrictions upon their private rights. No army officer may belong to a political organization, or a secret organization of any kind, no matter what may be its purpose or aim. He may write nothing for publication without special permission of a superior officer. Marriage is permitted to army officers but only with the formal permission of the minister of war; the marriage ceremony must be performed in compliance with the civil law. No army officer has a right to communicate with the president of the republic except through the minister of war.

There are compensations, however, to offset these restrictions. The profession of arms is still one of the most popular in Bolivia. It is, in many respects, the most respectable profession, not even on a plane inferior to that of service in the Church. Excellence in military service is rewarded not only by promotion in rank, but by elevation to membership in the order known as Al Mérito Militar. A pension is granted at the end of the period of service, provided the man has served for a certain period of years. The shortest period is fifteen years of consecutive service, or twenty years with interruptions. The pension received is then equivalent to one-half of the salary received at the time the pension goes into effect. A man who has served thirty consecutive years, or thirty-five years with interruptions, is entitled to full pay for the remainder of his life.[2] The Decree of March 26, 1926, created an aviation service for the army. The service has its own school, with a director of the School of Aviation (*director de la Escuela de Aviación*) at the head.[3] The Decree of January 9, 1928, made it compulsory for men in the reserve who are physically able and between the ages of twenty-five and thirty-five to enroll in courses of instruction in

[1] Araoz, *Nuevo digesto*, vol. III, pp. 199–213. Law of January 22, 1927. Promotion is almost exclusively conditional upon fitness for the higher position. Article 97 declares in part: "La primera condición para ser promovido al grado inmediato, . . . será la aptitud de la persona para el desempeño del grado inmediato. En estes sentido, serán más decisivas la competencia y la moralidad." Other factors are of course to be taken into consideration. Meritorious work in the *profesorado de los "cursos de clases"* is to be given due credit. Promotion to the rank of major general is made only when the extraordinary qualifications of an officer are recognized by the national government and approved by the Chamber of Senators.

[2] *Ibid.*, pp. 208–209. The scale of pensions is of course graduated according to the age at which the pensions begin. Article 210 gives this matter in full detail. Article 211 declares that the heirs *forzosos* of those who die in the service are to receive a pension for life. Those who are wounded in the service are also to receive pensions in accordance with the nature of the wounds.

[3] *Ibid.*, p. 232.

military science and tactics. The instruction covers a period of five months, with two hours a week devoted to the work, and entitles those who complete the course satisfactorily to a commission in the army.[1]

The Law of December 21, 1928, protects reservists in their employment to the extent that it prohibits any employer from refusing to permit a reservist to return to the work he had before he did reserve duty.[2] The Decree of February 6, 1929, forbids lieutenants and sublieutenants to contract matrimony while in the army.[3] The Decree of March 7, 1929, incorporated the Lloyd Aéreo Boliviana in the army of the republic.[4] The Law of March 7, 1929, ordered that men, civil and military, who had been declared well-deservers of the country (*beneméritos de la patria*) for services rendered in the campaigns in Acre should be paid a bonus of 50 per cent of the amount which they had received for their services in those campaigns. The law also included the Veterans of the Pacific (*veteranos del Pacífico*).[5] This was a very generous act on the part of the people of Bolivia. It showed an intelligent gratitude for the services rendered in two very important crises in their history. This was not the first time that Bolivia had shown her gratitude to the veterans of these wars. The Law of December 22, 1908, recognized the *veteranos del Pacífico* and the *beneméritos del Acre* as defenders of the integrity of the national territory of the republic and as entitled to further monetary compensation. The *veteranos del Pacífico* were those who had defended Bolivia in the War of the Pacific from Calama to Alto de la Alianza and were to be paid a pension by the state, depending upon the rank and length of service in that war, but in no case to exceed Bs. 20,000. The Law of December 15, 1909, declared that those who served in the campaigns in Acre were to be given the title of *beneméritos de la patria* and were to receive a bonus of a year's salary. The national government had recognized, as early as October 7, 1901, in a *resolución* of that date, the services of Lucio Pérez Velasco, Ismael Montes, and Andrés S. Muñoz for services rendered in the Acre campaigns.[6] Further notice was taken of the services of the men in the Acre campaigns by *Resolución* of December 28, 1903,[7]

[1] Araoz, *Nuevo digesto*, vol. III, p. 520. The hours of instruction are to be arranged so a not to interfere with the regular civilian work of the reservists.

[2] *Ibid.*, p. 521.

[3] *Ibid.*, p. 521.

[4] *Ibid.*, p. 521.

[5] *Ibid.*, p. 523.

[6] *Ibid.*, p. 271. The three men were given gold medals 45 by 25 millimeters in size with these inscriptions: on one side, "A los pacificadores de los territorios del Acre, en al año 1900"; on the other side, "Delegado del Gobierno" and "El Senado Nacional de Bolivia, 1901."

[7] *Ibid.*, p. 272.

by *Resolución* of October 12, 1916,[1] by *Resolución* of October 13, 1916,[2] by Law of December 16, 1909,[3] by Decree of February 24, 1911,[4] by Law of November 18, 1914,[5] by *Resolución* of February 3, 1919,[6] by Law of December 4, 1923,[7] by Law of October 7, 1926,[8] by Law of October 10, 1928,[9] by Law of January 27, 1926,[10] by Law of December 13, 1926,[11] by Decree of December 17, 1926,[12] and by Decree of May 30, 1927.[13] The Decree of March 26, 1929, set aside the third Sunday of December of each year as the Reservist Day (*Día del Reservista*). All the reservists of the republic were to meet on that day in the military headquarters of their respective localities to be duly registered. One of the main purposes of this decree was to take a census, in this way, of the reservists throughout the whole country.[14] The Decree of September 12, 1927, created the Bureau of Transportation and Colonization (*Oficina Técnica de Vialidad y Colonización*) in the Ministry of War.[15] The Decree of July 22, 1927, created the Superior Council of National Defense (*Consejo Superior de Defensa Nacional*).[16]

The health and the morals of the soldiery are carefully guarded. The Decree

[1] Araoz, *Nuevo digesto*, vol. III, p. 272.

[2] *Ibid.*, p. 272.

[3] *Ibid.*, pp. 272–273.

[4] *Ibid.*, pp. 274–275.

[5] *Ibid.*, p. 276.

[6] *Ibid.*, p. 276.

[7] *Ibid.*, p. 277.

[8] *Ibid.*, p. 277.

[9] *Ibid.*, p. 277.

[10] *Ibid.*, p. 277.

[11] *Ibid.*, pp. 277–278.

[12] *Ibid.*, p. 278.

[13] *Ibid.*, p. 278.

[14] *Ibid.*, pp. 525–526. Article 1 declared: "Se crea el 'Día del Reservista,' destinado a ejercer el control y leventar un censo de los reservistas de toda la República." All the reservists during the past twelve years were to register. There was a penalty for failure to register, and careful note was to be taken of each and every registrant in order to have a full and complete account of the man power of the country for military purposes. There were to be no expenses for the reservists, since the officers who were designated to take the census were to serve "ad honorem, sin que ningún ciudadano pueda rehusar su concurso a este trabajo de importancia para la defensa nacional." The administration of this decree was placed in the hands of the Estado Mayor General.

[15] *Ibid.*, p. 213.

[16] *Ibid.*, p. 213, note.

of November 9, 1923, prohibited the sale and consumption of alcoholic spirits, with the exception of beer and wine, the use of which must be moderate. The military officers are charged with the enforcement of this decree, infringements of which must be severely punished.[1] The Law of January 16, 1907, made military service obligatory. The service was divided into four grades. The first, from the age of nineteen to twenty-five, must serve in the troops of the line. The second, from the age of twenty-five to thirty-two, must serve in the reserves. The third, from the age of thirty-two to forty, must serve in the special reserves. The fourth, from the age of forty to forty-nine, must serve in the National Guard. The military year begins January 1 and ends December 31. While physical disability alone excuses a man from this military service, there is a rather large number of exemptions. Those who have university degrees, those who are in religious orders, those who have a trade (*maestro de taller*), and those who are employed by the state or by the municipality are exempt from military service. The insane, idiots, and the feeble-minded are, of course, also exempted. Registration in the military register (*registro militar*) is obligatory, and must be completed before the man has reached his nineteenth year. The period of registration begins on December 15 and continues to the end of the month.[2] The Decree of December 19, 1928, further enlarged the list of exemptions from the Law of January 16, 1907.[3] Service in the more distant military posts was given preferential treatment. The Decree of April 3, 1916, limited service in the garrisons of the Norte, Noroeste, Puerto Suárez, San Matías, and El Pilcomayo. Conscripts for other distant points were also given careful consideration.[4] The War College (*Escuela de Guerra*) was reorganized by the Decree of November 12, 1923, so as to provide special courses for majors and captains in the regular army.[5] The tendency has been, accordingly, to lay greater rather than less emphasis upon the military in Bolivia. The peculiar geographical location of the country demands that its people and government be prepared for any and every eventuality. There may be other means of protecting the national interests, but until these have been evolved, military preparedness is necessary for Bolivia.

The Ministry of Colonization has general charge of the administration of the territories and settlements outside the departments, but within the republic. Bolivia has no colonies outside its own national territory. The term "colony" (*colonia*) has thus a meaning all its own, a settlement outside the departmental limits. The *colonia* is usually located in a delegation (*delegación*) which is under

[1] Araoz, *Nuevo digesto*, vol. III, pp. 232–233.

[2] *Ibid.*, pp. 234–253.

[3] *Ibid.*, pp. 254–256.

[4] *Ibid* , p. 257.

[5] *Ibid.*, p. 259.

its own administration, or under the general administration of the national government. The *colonia* is usually composed of settlements of immigrants from foreign countries. There is a large section of the republic not yet included within departmental jurisdictions. The most important of the group of *colonias* is, of course, the region called the Territorios de Colonias.[1] The term *territorio* has much the same meaning that "territory" has in the United States, a district out of which, some day, a department or departments can be created. Before taking up the work of the Ministry of Colonization it will be necessary to give a brief account of the development of the colonial policy of the republic during the republican period.

The national government was faced, from the very beginning of the republic, with the problem of how to encourage immigration. The problem is still largely unsolved. Much has been done, of course, as this review of the history of colonization will reveal. A considerable body of legislation has been enacted on the subject.[2] The first law regulating colonization was that which declared certain lands of the republic public lands and prescribed the manner in which these might be disposed of for settlement purposes. The Law of October 30, 1833, opened certain public lands (*tierras públicas*) to settlement, and the Law of November 5 of the same year laid the basis for the settlement of public lands by foreigners. Public lands might be granted in an amount ranging from 2000 to 12,000 square rods (*varas en cuadro*) to founders of colonies, with the requirement, however, that the lands be settled within two years. This became the basis for the public land policy of the republic. It should be noted in this connection that this law paved the way for inroads upon the communal lands (*tierras de*

[1] Eduardo Diez de Medina, *Bolivia: breve resumen histórico, físico y político*, gives (p. 73) the areas of the several divisions of the country, illustrating the relative size of these divisions. According to his figures, the Territorios de Colonias has an area of 72,380 square kilometers, the Department of Cochabamba 65,513, the Department of Oruro 53,518, the Department of La Paz 105,406, the Department of Potosí 116,662, the Department of El Beni 247,033, the Department of Santa Cruz 275,763, the Department of Chuquisaca 94,125, and the Department of Tarija 81,778 square kilometers. The Chaco Boreal, with 120,626 square kilometers, is also outside of the departmental set-up. There are in reality three national territories (*territorios nacionales*) in Bolivia: Territorio del Noroeste, Territorio del Gran Chaco, and Territorio del Oriente.

[2] J. Lavadenz, *La colonización en Bolivia durante la primera centuria de su independencia*, p. 2. The first bit of legislation on this subject was that issued by the Liberator as a decree of December 14, 1825. We have dealt with much of this in the earlier parts of this study. Sucre issued the Decree of May 24, 1826, and the Law of October 13 of the same year, dealing with this subject. The Decree of February 16, 1830, also sought to give concrete form to the ideas that the national government had for the solution of the land problem. The *Orden* of August 25, 1832, and the *Resolución* of September 27 of the same year granted large areas of land to Francisco Burdett O'Connor, who was to settle the lands granted to him within a period of five years (*ibid.*, pp. 4–5).

comunidad) belonging to the Indians.[1] José Ballivián issued a decree on November 22, 1841, detailing the organization of military colonies to be founded on the frontiers, in the valleys of navigable rivers, on the prairies, and in the sparsely settled valleys of the country.[2] Ballivián also issued a decree on August 6, 1842, separating the Province of Mojos from the Department of Santa Cruz, and providing for the settlement of that region. The lands were to be sold for 2 pesos per hectare.[3] The Law of June 14, 1861, was largely responsible for the settlement of large sections of the District of Cordillera, the District of Tomina, and the District of Salinas, now called the Province of the Chaco, the Province of O'Connor, and the Province of Arce, respectively.[4] The *orden* issued by Melgarejo on March 19, 1865, granted lands in Caupolicán and El Beni to army officers, with the result that large regions were reduced to settlement. Melgarejo also issued a decree on March 20, 1866, which declared that the lands belonging to the Indians (*tierras de comunidad*) were open to the public for sale; and a decree on September 28, of the same year, in which he declared that these *tierras de comunidad* were public lands and that the state had the right to offer them for sale.[5]

The Law of December 1, 1874, authorized the granting of public lands to builders of roads and railways.[6] The Law of February 23, 1878, granted lands to those who should be the first to explore the Inambati, Beni, Madre de Dios, Purús, Pilcomayo, and Bermejo Rivers.[7] The *Resoluciones* of August 9 and 22, 1878, authorized the founding of fortlets (*fortines*) in the Oriente.[8] The War of the Pacific also had its effect upon the public land policy of the national government. The Law of October 12, 1880, authorized the president of the republic to grant lands to those who had lost their property in the war with

[1] J. Lavadenz, *La colonización en Bolivia, etc.*, p.3.

[2] *Ibid.*, p. 4.

[3] *Ibid.*, p. 4. The Law of August 21, 1851, gave to Carlos Bridoux 12 square leagues of land in the District of the Yuracarés (*Comarca de los Yuracarés*). The law also authorized the president of the republic to offer public lands for sale to foreigners as well as nationals, but on condition that an equal amount be sold to both groups, and on the future condition that the lands should be settled within a period of five years.

[4] *Ibid.*, p. 5.

[5] *Ibid.*, pp. 6–7. The *Ordenes* of January 19 and February 24, 1871, declared the acts of Melgarejo null and void. Melgarejo granted lands for colonization purposes to A. D. Piper and Orestes Mendoza, and to others. These acts of Melgarejo, especially his treatment of the Indians, together with his liberal cessions to Chile and Brazil, have made his name infamous in Bolivia.

[6] *Ibid.*, p. 7.

[7] *Ibid.*, p. 8.

[8] *Ibid.*, p. 8.

Chile. The Law of October 16, 1880, and the *Resolución* of October 25 of the same year, authorized the national government to accept the plan of Francisco Javier Brabo for navigating the rivers and for colonizing the eastern section of the republic. The grant of land included some of the best lands of the Departments of Chuquisaca, Santa Cruz, and El Beni, and the District of Chapare, and what is now the Territorios de Colonias. The contract between Brabo and the national government authorized him to sell the lands within his grant provided he reserved a tenth of the lands thus sold to the republic. The contract laid great emphasis upon the settlement of this whole region. At the end of the first ten years a population of 100,000 inhabitants was required, at the end of twenty years, 200,000, at the end of thirty, 400,000, and at the end of forty years, 500,000. Brabo was to pay 2,000,000 pounds sterling to the national government for this concession. But this rather grandiose scheme failed, and the contract was annulled.[1]

The Law of November 24, 1883, declared that the Indians were the owners of the communal lands, and entitled to the full rights of such ownership.[2] The most important piece of legislation, however, dealing with the land question was the Law of November 13, 1886, laying down the principle that the public lands should be carefully surveyed before being thrown upon the market for sale. The act also authorized the president of the republic to grant free of charge or to sell the more desirable lands of the republic in amounts of three lots of 25 hectares each to the head of a family, and another lot to every son of the family over fourteen years of age, with the understanding that at least a sixth of that land should be under cultivation by the end of the fourth year. If these conditions were not met, the lands were to be forfeited to the state. But this law had only partial success. The Law of March 10, 1890, declared that the only public lands open for settlement and colonization were those in the Departments of Chuquisaca, La Paz, Cochabamba, Tarija, Santa Cruz, and El Beni, but excluding the communal lands belonging to the Indians.[3]

The present public land system of Bolivia is based on the Law of October 26, 1905, as amended by the Law of September 14, 1915. The latter law suspended the sale of public lands, with the exception of such lands as the Congress might want to dispose of. The act outlawed the measurement known as the *estrada* and substituted for it the hectare (*hectárea*). The Law of October 26, 1905, provided that any person, national or foreign, might buy lands from the state

[1] J. Lavadenz, *La colonización en Bolivia, etc.*, p.8.

[2] *Ibid.*, p. 9. An important forward step in the management of the sale and settlement of public lands was taken in 1886. The Law of February 22 of that year created the Office of Public Lands and Colonization (*Oficina de Tierras y Colonización*) to take over that part of the business of the national government.

[3] *Ibid.*, pp. 12–14.

in an amount not to exceed 20,000 hectares, at 10 centavos per hectare, if the lands were to be used for farming and stock raising; and at B. 1 per hectare for lands that had rubber trees on them. The purchaser was to settle at least one family on every thousand hectares. The national government also reserved to itself the right to set aside such lands as it might need for colonization purposes. The Decree of June 20, 1907, was the *reglamento* for the administration of the public lands.[1]

The Decree of August 24, 1922, made provision for the establishment of colonies in the Department of Santa Cruz, and ordered that a grant of 25 hectares be made to each colonist for that purpose.[2] The Law of December 27, 1926, provided for the free entry into Bolivia of foreign laborers, agricultural as well as industrial, under the age of sixty. It also required that they be of good moral character and aptitude. Public lands were to be sold to them at the rate of 10 centavos per hectare. The immigrant and his family were to be

[1] Araoz, *Nuevo digesto*, vol. III, pp. 292–304. The period between 1890 and 1905 was an important one. The *Resolución* of April 28, 1894, granted lands to Miguel María Velarde for building a road between Santa Cruz and Trinidad. The Law of November 5, 1895, granted lands to Weneslao Añez for the exploration of the Verde River. The *Resolución* of December 7, 1895, granted lands to Víctor Mercier for building a road from Sayuba on the Beni River to Tumupasa. The Law of December 12, 1895, regulated the sale of lands containing rubber trees and other plants from which commercial products might be made. The law declared that such lands were the property of the state and that the disposal of them was a right of the state (*ibid.*, pp. 314–325; also the Decree of June 30, 1896). It was in this period that José Vicente Ochoa and others did much to acquaint the world with the riches of Bolivia. The Law of January 9, 1900, granted lands to Deves and Company, constructors of a railroad for communication with the Beni, Madre de Dios, Aquiri, and Purús Rivers. The Law of January 19, 1900, granted lands to Arnold Jacoby and Company for building a road between Cochabamba and the Chimoré. The *Resolución* of April 9, 1900, granted lands to the Orton Bolivia Rubber Company, Ltd., for building a road from Florida del Beni to Guayaramerín. The *Resolución* of May 17, 1901, granted lands to the Bolivia Trading Company for colonists whom they might bring to Bolivia. The *Resolución* of May 31, 1901, and the Law of December 3 of the same year granted to Jesús Mansilla and Maurice Frochot lands for building a road from Riberalta to Guayaramerín and from Puerto Pérez to Guanay. The Law of December 13, 1901, granted L'Africaine Company lands for establishing a port at Bahía Negra on the Paraguay. The Law of December 21, 1901, granted lands to the Bolivia Syndicate for aid in the Separatist War in Acre. The *Resolución* of October 4, 1902, granted lands to Reginaldo Emanuel for building a railroad between Oruro and Cochabamba. The *Resolución* of July 28, 1905, granted lands to the Bolivia Corporation, Ltd., of London, for building a railroad between Lake Gaiba and Santa Cruz. On April 25, 1905, a decree divided Bolivia into colonization zones. There were eight of these: Zone A, comprising Territorios de Colonias; Zone B, the Department of La Paz; Zone C and Zone D, the Department of El Beni; Zone E, the Department of Cochabamba; Zone F, the Department of Santa Cruz; Zone G, the Department of Chuquisaca; and Zone H, the Department of Tarija (*ibid.*, pp. 329–330).

[2] *Ibid.*, p. 325, footnote. Colonies were to be established in Monte Grande, Tres Cruces, Poso del Tigre, Guarayitos, Libertad, and Puquios.

given free transportation, with his property, to his lands.[1] Despite all the efforts to solve the problem of the sale and settlement of the public lands, only relatively small progress has been made. Of the 500,160.96.15 hectares of public lands in the republic, only 16,248.89 hectares have been disposed of.[2] The lands of Oriente Boliviano are rich and should attract a larger number of immigrants than they have attracted up to the present.[3] The great difficulty is the lack of means of transportation, for little progress can be made until that problem has been solved.

The national executive has also had other powerful departments. The most important of these has been the body known as the Council of State. This body first came into existence by the Constitution of 1831. The Bolivarian Constitution made no provision for such a body. The Council of State as established by the Constitution of 1831 was composed of seven members and elected by the Congress by an absolute plurality of votes. Each department of the republic and the Provinces of the Litoral and Tarija had a counselor of state (*consejero de estado*). The president and the vice-president were also members of this Council. The counselor of state was to have the same qualifications as a member of the Chamber of Senators, and he was to serve for four years. He might be reelected but only after the expiration of another four-year term. The Council of State gave advice to the president of the republic upon all matters which he might lay before it. In addition, it had the right to convoke

[1] Araoz, *Nuevo digesto*, vol. III, pp. 335–339. This law laid especial emphasis upon the need of wide publicity for the opportunities afforded immigrants in Bolivia. The consular agents, and more particularly the consular offices (*oficinas consulares*) in Hamburg, Vienna, Antwerp, Barcelona, Paris, Bordeaux, Le Havre, Marseilles, Lyons, London, Liverpool, Genoa, Naples, Rome, Turin, Milan, Lisbon, Stockholm, Bern, and Geneva were ordered to induce immigrants to come to the republic.

[2] Lavadenz, *La colonización en Bolivia, etc.*, pp. 40–41. The distribution of the lands by departments, in hectares, is: Chuquisaca, 14,656.25.00; La Paz, 53,980.00.00; Cochabamba, 525.92.64; Santa Cruz, 23,302.25.08; Tarija, 10,663.87.50; Beni, 207,473.94.63; Noroeste, 167,905.00.00; Gran Chaco, 6,212.39.02; and Oriente, 15,441.32.28. The Ministry of Colonization, created by the Law of November 13, 1886, has done much good work. It was not until 1905, however, that the present Ministry of Agriculture and Colonization was organized, in accordance with the provisions of the Law of October 18, 1904. Important grants of land, in addition to those already listed, are: to the Antofagasta and Bolivia Railway (granted first to the National City Bank of New York and Speyer and Company) in 1905 for construction of that railroad; to the Bolivia Development Corporation for construction of railroads in 1912; to the Jewish Colonization Association in 1921; and to Dionisio Foanini for a factory for cotton goods in 1924.

[3] *Ibid.*, pp. 87–108. This was the view expressed by Cristián Suárez Arana in an address read by him before the Sociedad Geográfica de Santa Cruz on March 12, 1923. Lavadenz reproduces this paper in his work, on pp. 87–108. The work by Ciro Torres López on *Las maravillosas tierras del Acre* (*en la floresta amazónica de Bolivia*) contains much interesting material of a varied character, even though colored marvelously by the patriotic fervor of the author.

the national legislature whenever the president of the republic failed to do so. It could also convoke the electoral juntas whenever they had not been called by the president of the republic. It also had the power to see that the Constitution was enforced and to inform the Congress of any failure to enforce that instrument; and it had the power to nominate for the several ecclesiastical positions in the republic. The counselors of state could not be removed without just cause, and were responsible for the acts of their administration. Finally, the president of the Council of State succeeded, in the event that there was no president, vice-president, or minister of state, to the presidency of the republic.[1]

The Constitution of 1834 also provided for a Council of State in terms similar to that of 1831.[2] The Constitution of 1839 failed to provide for such a body. The Constitution of 1843 provided for a National Council (*Consejo Nacional*), composed of two senators, two representatives, the ministers of state, two ministers of the Supreme Court, a general of the army, an ecclesiastic of dignity, and a chief of one of the divisions of the Ministry of the Treasury. The senators and representatives were elected by their own chambers, while the president of the republic appointed all the others. The term of office was four years. At the end of his term of office the president of the republic became a life member of the Council. The powers and duties of the Council were similar to those of the Council of State under the constitutions of 1831 and 1834, but much restricted in fundamentals.[3] The Constitution of 1851 did not provide for a Council of State. The Constitution of 1861 provided for a Council of State composed of fifteen members, at least seven of whom were to be elected by the Assembly and the others from those citizens who were not members of that body.[4] The membership was renewed by thirds every two years, with no restriction upon reelection.[5] This Council had extensive powers. It prepared legislative measures and presented them to the Assembly, and selected two of its members to represent it in the Assembly when these measures were discussed. It made suggestions to the president of the republic for the execution of the laws. It approved or disapproved the proposals presented to it by the ministers of state. It tried accused members of the Supreme Court and of the General Tribunal of Appraisal (*Tribunal General de Valores*). It decided whether papal bulls, briefs, and rescripts were or were not in opposition to the Constitution and laws of the republic. It had jurisdiction in matters relating to differences between the *patronato nacional* and the national government, but only in conformity with the wishes

[1] Ordóñez López, *Constitución política*, vol. II, pp. 314–315.

[2] *Ibid.*, p. 334.

[3] *Ibid.*, pp. 371–372.

[4] *Ibid.*, p. 396.

[5] *Ibid.*, p. 395.

of the Supreme Court. It decided the legality of the financial transactions of the municipalities. It granted naturalization papers to those whom it believed entitled to them. It received, during the recess of the Assembly, accusations against the president of the republic and the ministers of state, and presented them to the Assembly when the latter resumed its session. A commission of seven members of this Council formed a supreme tribunal *contencioso-administrativo*.[1]

The Council of State under this fundamental law was thus, in many respects, the most powerful body in the republic. The Constitution of 1868 did not provide for a Council of State. The Constitution of 1871 provided for a Council of State of nine members elected by a two-thirds vote of the Assembly. The membership was renewed every two years, and there was no restriction upon reelection. The powers of this body were similar to those under the Constitution of 1861.[2] The Constitutions of 1878, 1880, and 1931 failed to provide for a Council of State. It will thus be seen, by way of repetition, that the Council of State was provided for only in the Constitutions of 1831, 1834, 1843, 1861, and 1871.

[1] Ordóñez López, *Constitución política*, vol. II, p. 396.

[2] *Ibid.*, p. 425.

THE NATIONAL GOVERNMENT: THE JUDICIARY

THE national judiciary (*poder judicial*), like the two other coordinate branches of the national government, has undergone important changes at the hands of the makers of the Constitution of 1931. Justice is administered in the name of the nation through the Supreme Court (*Corte Suprema de Justicia*), the district courts (*cortes de distrito*), and the inferior tribunals and courts established by law. The regular judges have supervision over litigation between individuals and between individuals and the exchequer. They decide the legality of popular elections, irrespective of the offices involved. The courts also take cognizance of all acts or resolutions of the functionaries of the state which are not of a public character.[1] The administration of justice is free; the functionaries who administer justice, and who receive a regular fixed salary for such services, are prohibited from demanding fees.[2] The administration of justice has not always been free in Bolivia. The Bolivarian Constitution was silent on the subject, despite the fact that Simón Bolívar, its author, was always much concerned with the manner in which justice should be administered. The Constitution of 1839, article 90, declared that justice should be administered free as soon as a special law could be enacted for that purpose.[3] The Constitution of 1851 had a like provision,[4] while the Constitutions of 1871,[5] 1878,[6] and 1880[7] declared that justice was to be administered free. The other fundamental laws were silent on the subject.

The Supreme Court of Bolivia is composed of a president and eight ministers, and is divided into two chambers (*salas*). The president and the ministers of the Supreme Court are elected by the Congress. A two-thirds vote of the members present in the joint session is necessary to such election. The qualifications of the ministers of the Court are set forth in detail in the Constitution itself. To be eligible for election to the Court a man must have been born in the republic,

[1] *Constitución política*, pp. 54–55, art. 117.

[2] *Ibid.*, p. 55, art. 118.

[3] Ordóñez López, *Constitución política*, vol. II, p. 355, art. 90.

[4] *Ibid.*, p. 387, art. 91.

[5] *Ibid.*, p. 428, art. 80.

[6] *Ibid.*, p. 448, art. 109.

[7] Araoz, *Nuevo digesto*, vol. I, p. 17, art. 109.

or be a naturalized citizen with five years' residence in the country. He must be over forty years of age, and must have been a justice in a district court or a district attorney for five years, or have practiced law creditably for ten years. In addition he must be able to give evidence that he has never been condemned to corporal punishment by a competent judicial tribunal.[1] The Supreme Court represents and exercises the judicial power of the national government. It appoints the justices of the district courts and the other justices in conformity with the laws. The president of the Supreme Court presents the credentials of office to these officials. The Supreme Court prepares the annual budgets for the several courts and judicial bodies under its jurisdiction, and presents them to the national treasury. This latter body then determines the budget for the year in accordance with the law on the national budget. The Supreme Court takes cognizance of writs of error in accordance with the laws, and decides at the same time the principle of the law in question. It also takes cognizance of writs of abrogation of cases which deal with, or are contrary to, the Constitution begun in the inferior courts; of all cases over which it has original jurisdiction; of the impeachment of diplomatic and consular agents, national commissioners, justices of the superior courts, district attorneys, members of the National Tribunal of Accounts, and prefects, for offenses committed while in the exercise of their official functions; of claims arising out of alleged breaches of contracts, negotiations, and concessions made by the executive power of the state, and of claims against the national government for injuries sustained by the claimants through a governmental agency or measure; and of all matters subject to litigation in the exercise of the national patronage, vested in the national government. It also takes cognizance of conflicts of jurisdiction between municipal councils or political authorities and the municipal boards of the provinces; of impeachments of public officials accused of crimes against the laws or of crimes committed upon members of the Congress, whatever may be the position of the individuals directly concerned; and, finally, of problems concerning boundaries between the departments, or any matters at issue between the several departments of the republic.[2]

The ministers of the Supreme Court take the oath of office before the Congress in joint session.[3] The president of the Court is the presiding officer of the two tribunals.[4] He supervises the administration of justice throughout the

[1] *Constitución política*, pp. 55–56, art. 119.

[2] *Ibid.*, pp. 56–58, art. 120.

[3] When the Congress meets in a place other than the capital of the republic, the Congress intrusts to the ecclesiastical *cabildo* of Sucre the administration of the oath of office to the ministers of the Supreme Court. This provision serves again to call attention to the fact that Bolivia has two capitals: the *de jure* in Sucre, where the Supreme Court is located; and the *de facto* in La Paz, where most of the governmental branches are located.

[4] *Constitución política*, pp. 55–56, art. 119.

republic, and issues to all the functionaries of the Department of Justice, with the advice and consent of the Supreme Court, the observations, admonitions, or suggestions he may have to make to them. He also has the power to order the attorney general (*fiscal general*) of the republic to institute prosecutions, or to issue such instructions as he shall deem necessary in such matters in accordance with the Constitution and the laws.[1] The attorney general is appointed by the president of the republic from three names submitted to him by the Chamber of Deputies. The term of office is ten years, and he may be reappointed. He may be removed from office only for due cause and by a decision of the Supreme Court.[2]

The district courts have jurisdiction, in addition to the duties and powers given them by law, over offenses committed by officials of the municipalities in the exercise of their functions, individually or collectively. The subprefects are also subject to this same jurisdiction.[3] The judges of the inferior courts are appointed, as has already been noted, by the Supreme Court from the lists of three names submitted by the district courts.[4] The district attorneys and their agents and subordinates are appointed by the president of the republic from the lists of three names submitted by the attorney general.[5] The ministers of the Supreme Court hold office for a term of ten years, the justices of the district courts for six years, and the justices of the district (*partido*) and the justices of instruction for four years. The members of these judicial bodies may be reelected or reappointed, as the case may be. The length of the term of office, however, is personal and not constitutional. No justice or judge can be removed or suspended from office except for just cause and in conformity with the laws, nor can any official of this group of officers be transferred from one locality to another without his consent.[6] Publicity is an essential element in the administration of justice in Bolivia. All trials of cases at law must be held in public except where the nature of the trial may offend good morals.[7] The tribunals or the courts must not permit justices or judges not appointed in conformity with the law to discharge judicial functions.[8] The secretaries and subordinate officers of the judiciary are appointed by the district courts from the lists of

[1] *Constitución política*, p. 59, art. 122.

[2] *Ibid.*, p. 59, art. 123.

[3] *Ibid.*, pp. 59–60, art. 124.

[4] *Ibid.*, p. 60, art. 125.

[5] *Ibid.*, p. 60, art. 126.

[6] *Ibid.*, p. 60, art. 127.

[7] *Ibid.*, p. 61, art. 128.

[8] *Ibid.*, p. 61, art. 130.

names submitted to them by the judge under whom they are to serve. The Supreme Court appoints its own secretaries and inferior officers.[1]

The judiciary of Bolivia has undergone important changes since its establishment in 1827.[2] The fundamentals, however, have remained the same. In the first place, the Court has had different names. It was called the Supreme Court of Justice (*Corte Suprema de Justicia*) in the Constitutions of 1826,[3] 1831,[4] 1834,[5] 1839,[6] 1843,[7] 1851,[8] 1878,[9] 1880,[10] and 1931.[11] It was called the

[1] *Constitución política*, p. 61, art. 131.

[2] Luis Paz, *La Corte Suprema de Justicia de Bolivia: su historia y su jurisprudencia*, pp. 23–26. The Supreme Court of Bolivia was inaugurated by Sucre on July 16, 1827. Manuel María Urcullu, Mariano Guzmán, Juan de la Cruz Monje y Ortega, and Casimiro Olañeta, the newly chosen ministers of the Court, were formally inducted into office on that occasion. The ceremony took place in the Sala de la Corte in Chuquisaca. Sucre delivered a famous address. He declared that the installation of the high court was the last act in the definite establishment of the Republic of Bolivia as a sovereign and independent nation. The following statement was of special significance: "La vida, la fortuna, el honor de los Bolivianos quedan depositados en vosotros, que como apóstoles de la ley, que como sus magistrados, veréis que al recinto de este templo se acercan desde los Ministros de Estado hasta el último de los ciudadanos, con la confianza de que la justicia tiene aquí sacerdotes incorruptibles, y que la distribuyen corazones inspirados por la rectitud de Dios mismo; vuestra misión es sagrada; su fiel desempeño os traerá las bendiciones de vuestra patria." The oath of office taken by the ministers of the Supreme Court was: "¿Juráis a Dios nuestro Señor, y estos Santos Evangelios guardar la Constitución de la República, ser fiel al gobierno que ella establece, observar las Leyes, y administrar imparcialmente la justicia? Contestó: Sí juro.—Si así lo hiciéres Dios os ayude, y de lo contrario El y la Patria os lo demanden." The president of the Supreme Court took his oath before the president of the republic, and then he, in turn, administered the oath to his colleagues. Manuel María Urcullu, as president of the Supreme Court, then delivered an address. Consult also the two publications issued at the time of the one hundredth anniversary of the founding of the Supreme Court: *Corte Suprema de Justicia de Bolivia: jurisprudencia y doctrinas expuestas en correspondencia y circulares de sus presidentes;* and *Discursos de los presidentes de la excma. Corte Suprema de Justicia de Bolivia: homenaje en el primer centenario de su fundación*. The former was published in Sucre and the latter in La Paz in 1927.

[3] Héctor Conte Bermudez, *La creación de Bolivia y la Constitución bolivariana en el istmo de Panamá*, p. 78, art. 102.

[4] Ordóñez López, *Constitución política*, vol. II, p. 316, art. 111.

[5] *Ibid.*, p. 335, art. 113.

[6] *Ibid.*, p. 355, art. 91.

[7] *Ibid.*, pp. 372–373, art. 72.

[8] *Ibid.*, p. 386, art. 82.

[9] *Ibid.*, p. 448, art. 108.

[10] Araoz, *Nuevo digesto*, vol. I, p. 17, art. 108.

[11] *Constitución política*, p. 54, art. 117.

Court of Cassation (*Corte de Casación*) in the Constitutions of 1861[1] and 1871.[2] The influence of French political philosophy was responsible for the change in the name as well as the nature of the Court. In the Constitution of 1868 it was called by still another name, Supreme Tribunal of Justice (*Supremo Tribunal de Justicia*).[3] The length of the term of office of the members of the Supreme Court has also varied. Up to 1888 the term was for life, or during good behavior. The Law of November 20, 1888, limited the term to ten years, and this has been continued to the present day. The law placed no restrictions upon re-election.[4] The number of the members of the Supreme Court has also varied. The Constitutions of 1826[5] and 1831[6] provided for six members, a president, and an attorney (*fiscal*). The Constitution of 1834 provided for six members and an attorney.[7] The Constitution of 1839 provided for seven members and an attorney.[8] The Constitution of 1843 left the number to be determined by law.[9] The Constitutions of 1851,[10] 1861,[11] and 1868[12] provided for seven members and an attorney, as in the Constitution of 1839. The Constitutions of 1871,[13] 1878,[14] and 1880[15] provided for seven members; and the Constitution of 1931[16] provided for a president and eight members, as already noted.

The qualifications for membership in the Supreme Court have also varied from time to time. The Constitution of 1826 required that a member should be at least thirty-five years of age, a citizen in the exercise of the full rights of the franchise, and that he should have had practical experience fitting him for the position.[17] The Constitution of 1831 required that the member should be at

[1] Ordóñez López, *Constitución política*, vol. II, p. 399, art. 62.

[2] *Ibid.*, p. 428, art. 79.

[3] *Ibid.*, p. 413, art. 78.

[4] Araoz, *Nuevo digesto*, vol. I, p. 18, art. 19.

[5] Ordóñez López, *Constitución política*, vol. II, p. 297, art. 108.

[6] *Ibid.*, p. 316, art. 111.

[7] *Ibid.*, p. 335, art. 113.

[8] *Ibid.*, p. 355, art. 91.

[9] *Ibid.*, p. 373, art. 73.

[10] *Ibid.*, p. 386, art. 83.

[11] *Ibid.*, p. 399, art. 63.

[12] *Ibid.*, p. 413, art. 78.

[13] *Ibid.*, pp. 428–429, art. 81.

[14] *Ibid.*, p. 448, art. 110.

[15] Araoz, *Nuevo digesto*, vol. I, p. 17, art. 110.

[16] *Constitución política*, pp. 55–56, art. 119.

[17] Ordóñez López, *Constitución política*, vol. II, pp. 297–298, art. 109.

least thirty years of age, that he should have had experience as a law reporter, a *fiscal* agent, a judge of letters, an auditor, or an advocate of the army, or that he should have practiced law successfully for eight years, and that he should have a good moral character.[1] The Constitution of 1834 reduced the age to twenty-five years, and required that the member should have served in a district court, but without specifying the length of such service.[2] The Constitution of 1839 raised the age requirement to forty years, and required that the member should have served as an employee of the judicial service for ten years, or have practiced law creditably for twelve years.[3] The Constitution of 1843 was silent on the age requirements; while the Constitution of 1851 returned to the age requirement laid down in the first Constitution. The Constitution of 1851 required that the member should have been a member of a superior court or have practiced law creditably for ten years.[4] The Constitution of 1861 raised the age requirement to forty years.[5] In addition the member was required to have had practical legal experience either as a member of a district court or as a *fiscal* of such a court. The Constitution of 1868 merely provided that a special law should be enacted by the national legislature prescribing the qualifications for membership in the Supreme Tribunal of Justice.[6] The Constitutions of 1871,[7] 1878,[8] 1880,[9] and 1931[10] followed the Constitution of 1861.

[1] Ordóñez López, *Constitución política*, vol. II, p. 316, art. 112.

[2] *Ibid.*, p. 337, art. 121.

[3] *Ibid.*, p. 356, art. 97.

[4] *Ibid.*, p. 386, art. 86.

[5] *Ibid.*, p. 399, art. 64.

[6] *Ibid.*, p. 413, art. 78.

[7] *Ibid.*, pp. 428–429, art. 81.

[8] *Ibid.*, p. 448, art. 110.

[9] Araoz, *Nuevo digesto*, vol. I, p. 17, art. 110.

[10] *Constitución política*, pp. 55–56, art. 119. The functions of the Supreme Court have also undergone important changes. The Constitution of 1831 included the president of the republic among the officials against whom criminal charges might be made by this Court. Among the duties of the Supreme Court as laid down in the Constitution of 1839 was that of advising the president of the republic on the question of calling the Congress in special session. The president of the republic was also required to take his oath of office before the Supreme Court. The Constitution of 1843 held the members of the judiciary responsible for any infraction of the laws committed by them in the performance of their official duties. The same provision was included in the Constitution of 1851. The latter fundamental law also laid great emphasis upon publicity of trials in the courts and forbade any and every attempt of a judge or justice to alter or omit the forms of law. Only the Congress, it was declared by this Constitution, could change the laws. The statement of the functions of the Court of Cassation in the Constitution of 1861 varied considerably from the preceding fundamental laws. Emphasis was laid

The Law of December 12, 1914, divided Bolivia into judicial districts. These districts were again divided into *partidos*, and the *partidos* into seats (*asientos*). The Judicial Districts of Chuquisaca, La Paz, Cochabamba, Potosí, and Oruro each have a court of five judges (*vocales*) and a district attorney. The Judicial Districts of Santa Cruz, Tarija, and El Beni each have a court of three members and a district attorney.[1] The courts of the *partidos* are located in the places assigned to them by the head of the judiciary, and the courts of instruction in the places assigned as judicial seats.[2] The *partidos* and the judicial *asientos* of the republic are located as follows: four courts of *partido* and three judicial *asientos* in the Judicial District of Chuquisaca,[3] six courts of *partido* and six judicial *asientos* in the Judicial District of La Paz,[4] five courts of *partido* and five judicial *asientos* in the Judicial District of Cochabamba,[5] seven courts of *partido* and seven judicial *asientos* in the Judicial District of Potosí,[6] three courts of *partido* and three judicial *asientos* in the Judicial District of Oruro,[7] two courts of *partido* and two judicial *asientos* in the Judicial District of Tarija,[8] and three courts of *partido* and three judicial *asientos* in each of the two remaining judicial districts.[9]

The national judiciary of Bolivia has had a very interesting history. Justice has been predicated upon the principle that there is much of the divine in it. The celebrated Luis Paz considered justice a great attribute of God (*gran atributo de Dios*).[10] The venerable Saturnino Sanjinés declared in 1881, when

upon the right of this Court to pass upon the constitutionality of a law, to conduct trials for the crimes of treason and extortion, and criminal acts of the president of the republic and the ministers of state, and to suggest reforms in the codes to the Council of State. The Court was not given this latter right by the Constitution of 1868. The Constitution of 1871 did not make any important changes in the powers of the Court. The Constitution of 1878 not only changed the name to Supreme Court of Justice but gave it the right to take cognizance of all cases in which the Constitution had granted special jurisdictions. The National Tribunal of Accounts and the prefects of the departments of the republic were included among the public officials to be tried by the Supreme Court.

[1] Araoz, *Nuevo digesto*, vol. I, p. 293, art. 1.

[2] *Ibid.*, p. 293, art. 2.

[3] *Ibid.*, p. 293, art. 3.

[4] *Ibid.*, pp. 294–295, art. 3.

[5] *Ibid*., pp. 295–296, art. 3.

[6] *Ibid.*, pp. 296–297, art. 3.

[7] *Ibid.*, pp. 297–298, art. 3.

[8] *Ibid.*, p. 298, art. 3.

[9] *Ibid.*, pp. 298–299, art. 3.

[10] Paz, *La Corte Suprema de Justicia de Bolivia*, p. 6.

formally opening the session of the Supreme Court: "Señores jueces, asimilaos á la Divinidad, al ejercer ministros tan augusto, *Deus estis super terram*."[1] While Sucre and Bolívar did much for the development of the judicial system in Bolivia, it was rather the men who have served the Supreme Court as presidents that have caused its growth. Urcullu laid the foundation, and has had very able successors. The greatest problem before the builders of the Court has been to give it an independence of action comparable with that of the other coordinate branches of the national government. The real friends and supporters of the Court have had to contend with the older Spanish spirit, which is a heritage of the colonial period. This was particularly true of the earlier years of the republic. The colonial spirit continued in Bolivia, as elsewhere in the Indies, long after the power of old Spain had been overthrown in Spanish America.[2] Bolivia was, in the first place, too closely associated with Peru to get away from the contest between the old aristocracy of the nobility and the supporters of the ideology of the new age. Bolivia was, in the second place, created by the conservative aristocratic groups, and remained under their control for fully a quarter of a century after achieving independence. Under these circumstances the problem of developing institutions required by progressive peoples of the nineteenth century was a very difficult one. Another problem of even greater importance was that of preventing attacks upon the law and legal security by the dictator *caudillos*. No country has been the prey of a militant and revolutionary *caudillaje* in a more detrimental way than Bolivia. It has been the peculiar aim of the Bolivian dictator *caudillos* to make themselves the sole power in the state. Her greatest problem is that of ridding herself of this type of *caudillismo*, a problem which she has not yet solved.

The fight to keep the Supreme Court independent has been, accordingly, a very formidable one. It was the celebrated Casimiro Olañeta, with all his strange conduct as a political leader, who worked intelligently, fearlessly, and forcefully to keep the judiciary independent and yet coordinate with the two other branches of the national government. It was he who gave the Supreme

[1] Paz, *La Corte Suprema de Justicia de Bolivia*, p. 6.

[2] Jorge Basadre, *La iniciación de la república*, vol. I, pp. 78–85. Basadre emphasizes the fact that it took Peru about half a century to emanicipate herself from the colonial nobility. The point to have in mind in this connection is that Bolivia as well as Peru was dominated by "la clase aristocrática," which "durante algunos años después de Ayacucho mantuvo . . . el dominio social." Basadre further declares: "El liberalismo, el individualismo, el anticolonialismo, la antifeudalidad necesitaban para su advenimiento, de la civilización, de europeización. Pero ellas, por razones geográficas, sociales y económicas llegaron con tardanza" (*ibid.*, p. 84). We have used the terms *caudillo*, *caudillaje*, and *caudillismo* in the sense of political bossism rather than in their primary meaning of leadership. It may be possible to defend the use of these terms as applying exclusively to political leadership of the constructive type, but when applied to the political life of Bolivia, they should be used in the sinister sense of dictatorship; and of dictatorship that knows no law but that of force.

Court its final great and permanent form. Olañeta was a great student of the French judicial system and sought to build the Bolivian system along similar lines. In this effort he very naturally encountered great opposition. Andrés María Torrico, who was president of the Supreme Court from 1863 to 1869, was able to counteract the powerful influence of Olañeta. It was Torrico who founded the school of jurisprudence which was to make the judicial system of Bolivia truly Bolivian. He was followed in this by Basilio de Cuéllar. Cuéllar was president of the Supreme Court from 1869 to 1882. These two men, serving as they did during two of the most powerful dictatorships that Bolivia has ever had, did great work for the independence of the judiciary, and for this valiant championship they deserve the greatest praise and honor. Pantaleón Dalence, who was a great force in the legal profession of his country for more than thirty-four years, was the founder of a new school of jurisprudence, based upon the Constitution of 1880. While he accepted the main principles for which Olañeta, Torrico, and Cuéllar had labored, he insisted upon making the Supreme Court function as a real coordinate branch of the national government. He did this by maintaining the balance of power between the three branches of the government. It was the mature opinion of Luis Paz, himself one of the great jurists of the republic, that all the political constitutions of Bolivia prior to that of 1880 had insisted upon subordinating the Supreme Court to the other branches of the national government. Paz believed that if the judicial branch had been able, as a whole, to function as a real coordinate branch of the national government, the Bolivian people would not have been compelled to endure, for any great length of time, the tyrannical rule of the chief executives who subordinated the judiciary to the executive branch. He also believed that this subordination of the judiciary was peculiarly the result of the great influence of French law and jurisprudence in the republic. He declared that the Supreme Court had been reduced, as the highest court in France had been reduced, to a position of merely applying the law, without the right and power to discuss the merits of the law itself.

Dalence was very greatly impressed with the work of John Marshall, of the United States of America, and, holding a similar position in Bolivia, won a very high place in the legal profession of his country. It was Dalence who finally triumphed over the Galicanos, as those were called who supported the French system of jurisprudence. It was Luis Paz' mature belief that Pantaleón Dalence was the greatest jurisconsult ever to preside over the Supreme Court of Bolivia, and the man who did more than any other to enrich its national jurisprudence; for which reason, among many others, he called Dalence the John Marshall of Bolivia.[1] Belisario Boeto, who served as president of the

[1] Paz, *La Corte Suprema de Justicia de Bolivia*, p. 8. The following excerpt from the annual address of Dalence in 1882 will illustrate his view: "Las reformas reintegraron al Poder Judicial en la plenitud de sus funciones que son de su esencia. Relegando los resabios y preocupaciones

Supreme Court for eight years, followed very closely in the footsteps of Dalence. Then came Luis Paz himself, who served with conspicuous success in the same rôle as his famous predecessors, becoming president of the Court in 1920. Paz

de una viciosa organización monárquica que heredamos, y después de ensayado el sistema francés, las reformas, a ejemplo de la Gran República, sometieron al Poder Judicial, el conocimiento de todas las cuestiones sobre aplicación de la ley, cualquiera que sea la calidad o la jerarquía oficial de las partes; le sometieron igualmente la soberana potestad de aplicar o no en los litigios, los actos de los otros altos Poderes del Estado, en relación con la ley fundamental. El Poder Ejecutivo que antes compartía con el Judicial el ejercicio de la judicatura . . . eran una monstruosa superfetación en nuestra forma de Gobierno." Few men have had a larger hold upon the judicial life of Bolivia than Pantaleón Dalence. He became a member of the Supreme Court for the first time in 1855, serving, according to the Constitution of 1851, as a member for the Department of Oruro. He was reelected in 1864 and again in 1882. He was a member of this high court for thirty-four years, and was its president from 1871 to 1873 and from December 1882 until his death on November 16, 1889. Paz declares: "Ningún presidente del supremo tribunal ha tenido un reinado más largo que el señor Dalence, y ninguno ha tenido una autoridad superior en la dirección y disciplina de la justicia, de tal manera que se debiera distinguir en la historia de la corte suprema con el título de 'jefe de la justicia de Bolivia,' como se designa al cuarto y más ilustre presidente de la corte federal de Norte América, cuyo reinado fué de 34 años, de 1801 á 1835, 'John Marshall, jefe de la justicia de los Estados Unidos' " (*ibid.*, p. 173).

The Supreme Court of Bolivia has done much to uphold the dignity of the Constitution and the laws. Some of the more important instances may be given to prove that fact. In the celebrated case of Pedro Señavilla, a Negro, who was claimed by Ramón Alvarado, an Argentine, as his slave, and who had come to Bolivia, the Supreme Court held that Alvarado had no legal claim upon the Negro because the Bolivian Constitution declared that slavery did not exist in Bolivia. The case came before the Court because of a crime committed by Señavilla. The Court held that Señavilla had attained his freedom the moment he stepped upon Bolivian soil. Alvarado was informed that Señavilla had to answer for his crime since he was a free man and not his slave. In 1840, when the invasion from Peru loomed large and dangerous, especially since the ambitious designs of Chile threatened to aid Peru, the Supreme Court took note of the gravity of the situation and gave its support to José Miguel de Velasco as president of the republic. In the same year, the Supreme Court took measures to discipline one of its own members. Casimiro Olañeta, a member of the Supreme Court at the time, had declared, during the carnival season, that he wished that President Velasco were dead. On March 23, 1840, the Supreme Court took formal note of this declaration by Olañeta and censured him. Olañeta immediately presented his resignation, which was promptly accepted. The Supreme Court also gave its support to the municipalities. The early period of Bolivia was a very trying one for the municipalities, a fact which has previously been noted in this study. The Supreme Court, in its efforts to democratize the national government, was naturally interested in giving to the municipalities their proper place in the life of the nation. The Court also came to the support of law and order in the period of the persecution of Andrés Santa Cruz, that is, between 1839 and 1843. The president of the republic, Velasco, ordered the prefect of the Department of La Paz to seize the property of Santa Cruz. The Congress of Bolivia, in a moment of gratitude for the services of the Mariscal de Zepita, had granted him two estates which were acquired at the expense of the state: the *haciendas* of Chincha and Anquioma. The Law of August 27, 1839, ordered that these two estates be seized on the account of the state. Manuela Santa Cruz, daughter of Mariscal Santa Cruz, took the case to the Supreme Court, which decided in her favor and ordered the two estates returned to her. On the other hand, the Court refused to be drawn into the political contest over the protest of Velasco

very naturally believed, and firmly defended the thesis, that it has been the Supreme Court that has fought hardest and most intelligently for the conservation of an ordered political constitutional government, and this in the face of strenuous efforts on the part of the politicos to govern the Bolivian state without the restraining force of the Court.[1] The great services of the national judiciary in behalf of a stable government in Bolivia deserve, accordingly, high praise. The added fact that Bolivia was the first country in Spanish

---

after his overthrow in 1841. In an *Acta* of October 25, 1841, the Supreme Court exhorted the Bolivian people to defend the republic against the attacks of Gamarra and to defend and preserve the independence and territorial integrity of the country.

The beginning of the rule of Manuel Isidoro Belzu in 1848 was also the beginning of great trials and persecutions for the Supreme Court. On December 16, 1848, Belzu ordered that the Supreme Court should cease to function because of lack of funds for its upkeep. The Decree of February 24, 1849, however, ordered the Supreme Court to resume its activities. Cuéllar, Rengel, and Maldonado, members of the Supreme Court, were exiled for refusing to do the bidding of Belzu. José María Linares gave the Supreme Court a much more intelligent position in the national government than had Belzu, even though Linares was fully as dictatorial in his rule as Belzu. It was during the rule of Linares that Olañeta did most of his greatest work for the Supreme Court. He became its president in 1858 and at once sought to restore the Court to its proper position in the state. Paz was greatly impressed with the work of Olañeta in this period and speaks of him as the "ilustre Americano, de política y polemista, de gran diplomático y de incomparable tribuno" and as an incorruptible judge; "el tribunal supremo guardará su memoria con veneración, como uno de los apóstoles de la justicia y uno de sus más ilustres presidentes. . . . Es indudable que el señor Olañeta dió majestad y brillo a la corte suprema con su presidencia." It was during the presidency of Olañeta that the great debate took place between him and Andrés María Torrico on the real nature and position of the Supreme Court. The nature of the difficulties before the Supreme Court during the *sexenio* of Melgarejo can be easily understood. It was on December 1, 1868, that Torrico, Juan José Ameller, Dalence, Fernández, and Carvajal resigned from the Court as a protest against his despotism. The Supreme Court was reorganized on April 3, 1871, after the overthrow of Melgarejo, and was composed of Félix Valdivieso, Saturnino Sanjinés, Mariano Ramallo, José María Calvo, Pedro H. Vargas, Rudesindo Carvajal, and Pantaleón Dalence. The last named became president of the Court. Then came the ill-fated dictatorship of Hilarión Daza. On September 7, 1882, the Supreme Court was composed of Basilio de Cuéllar, Pantaleón Dalence, Saturnino Sanjinés, José María Calvo, Manuel Ignacio Salvatierra, Melchor Terrazas, and Juan Crisóstomo Corrillo. Dalence was elected, as we have already noted, president of the Court, and continued his great work.

It remains to be noted that the Supreme Court took another very important step in 1893. This was the first time that an ex-president of the republic was ordered to return to the country to stand trial before the Supreme Court. Daza returned that year but did not appear before the Court because he was assassinated at Ayuni on his way to Sucre. Perhaps the most remarkable decisions of the Court have been those upholding the legislation enacted under the rule of a dictator. The position taken by the Court has been that such legislation can only be repealed by the national legislature, or by a dictator; and that until such legislation has been repealed it will remain the law of the land, so far as the Supreme Court is concerned.

[1] Paz was president from 1920 to 1928. His work on the *Constitución política de la República de Bolivia: su texto, su historia y su comentario* (Sucre, 1912) is excellent.

America to codify its laws [1] should enable her friends to look with pride upon her achievements.

[1] The honor of having given this code to Bolivia belongs to Andrés Santa Cruz. It was he who ordered the codes made and who proclaimed them in 1832 and modified them in 1834. The fact that he permitted the codes to bear his name should not be criticized too harshly. The Codes Santa Cruz, like the Code Napoleon, had their place in the development of the legal institutions of Bolivia, and great honor is due Santa Cruz for this piece of constructive legislation. The day has come when this great son of Bolivia should be given the honors that are justly due to him. This opinion is expressed, not in condonation of the wrongs and evils of his dictatorship, for many of these deserve severe condemnation, but in appreciation of the constructive work that Andrés Santa Cruz performed for his beloved Bolivia.

LOCAL GOVERNMENT

Bolivia is divided into departments, provinces, and cantons. It will be recalled that Sucre divided Upper Peru into departments, provinces, and cantons in 1825. These terms have, therefore, remained in force to the present time. The superior political, administrative, and economic government of the department is vested in the national government, which acts through a magistrate with the title of prefect. This officer is appointed by the president of the republic for a term of four years, and may be removed by him at any time. The prefect is therefore under the supervision of the president of the republic, whose representative he is. He performs his duties under the immediate supervision of the ministers of state, who are the intermediaries between him and the president. The prefect has control over the functionaries of the department. His duties are numerous and important, since he is in general the ruler of the department, and also has extensive financial and military duties.[1]

The government of each province is in the hands of a subprefect, appointed by the president of the republic upon nomination of the prefect. He, too, serves for a term of four years, or during the pleasure of the president. His duties also are many and important, for, like the prefect, the subprefect is charged with the government of the political division over which he is placed.[2]

The government of the canton is intrusted to a *corregidor*, who is appointed by the prefect upon nomination of the subprefect. This office, too, has many and important duties.[3] The office of the *corregidor* has been carried over bodily from the colonial period, or rather from old Spain herself. The duties of the *corregidor* are still much the same as they were under the rule of Spain. No officer has a more unsavory reputation, largely because of the heritage from the colonial period. To the critical observer of the political government of Bolivia, the *corregidor* seems the very opposite of what an official ought to be. In no vital part of the whole political government is there more urgent need of reform. In common with many of the other officials, the *corregidor* receives a salary that is much too small to insure honesty in government. The temptation

[1] Araoz, *Nuevo digesto*, vol. I, pp. 92–95. Nineteen of the duties of the prefect are enumerated in the *Reglamento* of January 10, 1903.

[2] *Ibid.*, p. 96.

[3] *Ibid.*, pp. 96–97. The *reglamento* declares that: "El cargo de corregidor es concejil y nadie puede excusarse sin causa legal."

to increase the income not infrequently leads to bribery and corruption. This objectionable feature of the corregidoral régime is in the practice and not in the theory of the system. For there is, unfortunately, the same discrepancy between theory and practice in the republican régime that there was in the colonial period. In fact, there is even more, because of the laxity of the supervisory system under the independent republican régime. After all, politics is politics, the world over. There is another class of officials, the *alcaldes de campo*, under the immediate direction of the *corregidores*. These *alcaldes* serve for only one year; they may be reelected, but only after the lapse of one year from the expiration of the term of office.[1]

The Constitution of 1931 made important changes in the government of the departments. It created the departmental assemblies (*asambleas departamentales*), composed of representatives known as *procuradores*. The *procuradores* are elected by a direct and secret vote of the people of the department. The people thus have a large degree of self-government. This reform was, in many respects, the most important achievement of the Revolution of June 1930. Prior to that time the people had had no such share in the government of the department. The members of the Congress are also members of the departmental assemblies, with a right to speak and vote in those bodies. They have, in fact, the same powers and duties as the *procuradores* themselves. The participation of the senators and the deputies of the Congress in the departmental assemblies can only take place, however, when they are in the capital of the department.[2] The departmental assemblies have the power to:[3]

1) elect senators from the department to the Congress;
2) enact ordinances for the welfare of the department and the provinces of the department;
3) levy departmental taxes and prescribe the purposes for which they are to be used;
4) make loans for public works and for the general development of the department and the provinces;
5) establish and maintain a system of police protection;
6) organize or support institutions of public instruction, and develop means of communication and transportation in the department and its provinces.

The consent of the Chamber of Deputies is necessary, however, for contracting loans for departmental purposes, or for the sale or mortgage of immovable property.[4] The national government may intervene in purely depart-

[1] Araoz, *Nuevo digesto*, vol. I, p. 97.

[2] *Constitución política*, pp. 49–50, art. 109.

[3] *Ibid.*, pp. 50–51, art. 110.

[4] *Ibid.*, pp. 50–51, art. 110.

mental matters when the national laws are not enforced, or are actually opposed, or when judicial sentences are not enforced or are opposed. Any differences that may arise between the departments and the national government may be adjusted by the Supreme Court.

Municipalities are organized in accordance with the Organic Law of November 21, 1887.[1] The cities of Sucre, La Paz, Cochabamba, Potosí, Santa Cruz, Oruro, Tarija, and Madrid each have a municipal council (*consejo municipal*) composed of twelve members. There are also twelve alternates for each. The capitals of provinces and the several ports each have a municipal junta of five members. The cantons have three municipal agents, each dependent upon the provincial juntas. The members of these several bodies are elected by a direct and secret vote. They serve for a term of two years, half of them being renewed every year. The alternates are those who receive the next highest votes, and serve in case the councilmen (*concejos*) are unable to do so. To be a member of these municipal bodies it is necessary to be in the enjoyment of full citizenship rights, and to be a resident of the municipality which one represents. No public employees except attorneys at law and medical men may be elected to membership in these bodies. The same applies to clerics, and to blood relations. That is, no two men who are related by blood up to the second degree may occupy a seat in the municipal body at the same time. In the case of an election of two who are related in that degree, one must resign and give way to the alternate. No citizen may refuse to serve as an elected representative in one of these municipal bodies. The number of exceptions to this rule is large, however.[2]

The municipal council and the provincial junta elect their own officers, such as president, vice-president, secretary, and treasurer, from among their own membership, and by a secret vote. The same is also true of other employees of these bodies. A majority vote is necessary to election.[3] In case of an infraction of the rules concerning the qualification of the members elected, the question is referred to the district court, which has full power to act in such cases.[4] The office of secretary is held for three months. It rotates among the members,

[1] Araoz, *Nuevo digesto*, vol. I, pp. 263–272. This law was modified by those of October 28, 1898, and November 17, 1927.

[2] *Ibid.*, p. 264, art. 13. This includes: (1) those appointed to some public office; (2) those over seventy years of age; (3) those afflicted with an illness that would interfere with their regular performance of their duties; (4) those engaged in some labor in a public institution; (5) those living at a distance of more than two leagues from the capital in which the municipal body to which they are elected has its permanent headquarters. Those who fail to comply with this regulation are fined from 25 to 100 bolivianos.

[3] *Ibid.*, p. 265, art. 19.

[4] *Ibid.*, p. 265, art. 18.

and carries no salary.[1] The duties of the councils and municipal juntas are many and varied, and are prescribed in detail.[2] The duties of the several officers are also set down in detail.

The meetings of the *ayuntamiento* of each municipality shall be public, but may be held in secret when the morals or honor of any person may be affected by a public meeting. There are both regular and special meetings of this body. The regular meetings are held twice a week, the hours and the days being

[1] Araoz, *Nuevo digesto*, vol. I, p. 265, art. 21.

[2] *Ibid.*, pp. 265–267. The duties are given as follows:

a) elect the officers of the municipality in the manner prescribed by law;
b) have general management of the municipal funds;
c) assign in annual budget the several sums to be used during the year, which may not be increased, diminished, or modified during that period;
d) remove public employees from office when the good of the municipality demands it;
e) appoint parochial *alcaldes*, from among the nominees presented by the judges of instruction;
f) appoint suburban and rural *alcaldes*, proposed by the cantonal agents, in conformity with the law;
g) appoint jurors for trial of crimes committed by the press;
h) levy and abolish municipal taxes, but only with previous approval of the Chamber of Senators;
i) receive legacies and gifts and negotiate loans for the promotion of works of charity and material improvement;
j) approve the renting and subletting of the *fincas* and lands of each locality under their jurisdiction;
k) collect, administer, or invest their funds;
l) construct establishments for primary education and manage them, administer their funds, dictate their regulations, appoint the teachers and pay their salaries (does not include state schools);
m) take the personal and property census of the municipality; the Supreme Decree of April 1, 1900, regulates the census throughout the republic;
n) collect the departmental statistics;
o) encourage industrial expositions, when considered advisable, and grant prizes, voting the funds for such purposes;
p) exercise a diligent supervision over the prisons and the other houses of correction and detention;
q) promote and watch over the construction of public works within their districts;
r) look after the charitable institutions;
s) grant licenses for raffles, lotteries, *casas de martillo*, and amusements;
t) establish a police system in its various forms;
u) watch over the sale of foodstuffs, but only on the basis of freedom of trade;
v) look after the activities of pharmacies and hold them to a compliance with the laws regulating their activities;
w) oblige physicians to render services to people who are not treated by the hospitals, and to do so free of charge;
x) visit the establishments of apothecaries and inform the Ministry of Government of infractions of the laws committed by them;
y) establish means of public lighting and watch over its care and improvement;
z) provide grounds for the armed force which has its headquarters in their midst, in accordance with the Law of Conscription, January 16, 1907;
aa) prohibit the sale or the deposit of materials injurious to the public health or safety of the inhabitants, in the heart of the municipality;
ab) enforce and regulate the execution of the Law of October 27, 1908, regarding cemeteries and places of interment; and the Law of August 26, 1914, forbidding the taking of corpses into the portico or main body of religious temples;
ac) issue the certificates of *vita et moribus* in cases where this is required by law;
ad) call upon the militia to aid them in enforcing the law whenever necessary.

determined by the *ayuntamiento* itself. The special meetings may be held whenever necessary, but with the proviso that no business shall be transacted which was not specified in the call for the meeting. No business may be transacted in any meeting of the *ayuntamiento* which has not been announced to the public at least one day in advance of the meeting.[1]

The property of the municipalities consists of four different kinds: (1) the public lands or municipal lands within their boundaries; (2) unclaimed lands and forfeited lands; (3) such lands as have been acquired by any legal means whatever; (4) lands secured by them through some process of law and at their expense.[2] There are seven sources of income for the municipalities: (1) the produce or rentals from their property; (2) income from lotteries, licenses, and taxes on diversions and public amusements; (3) rentals from mausoleums and cemeteries; (4) fines imposed for crimes of the press, and other fines imposed by the tribunals and courts of justice; (5) fines imposed for infractions of their rules or ordinances; (6) all the taxes which they collect which have not been definitely allocated; (7) all the funds (*fondos*) recognized as such by existing laws.[3] In addition there are the grants made to the municipalities by the Congress in the national budget.[4] The manner of administering the municipal funds is prescribed in detail.[5]

Finally, it should be noted that the office of the members of these municipal bodies is hedged about with many restrictions. The councilors, juntas, and municipal agents are strictly forbidden to take part in political activities of any kind. They may not even serve on electoral boards.[6] They are all strictly responsible for the performance of the duties of their office, and are held to account for any failure to perform these duties, and those in connection with the observance of the laws of the republic in general.[7]

There are also important changes in the Constitution of 1931 in the matter of rights and guaranties. Emphasis is laid upon the treatment of persons accused of crime. Such persons are to have the opportunity to prove their

[1] Araoz, *Nuevo digesto*, vol. I, p. 268, art. 30.

[2] *Ibid.*, p. 269, art. 32. This whole matter is further regulated by the Resolution of the Senate of December 2, 1905, and the Supreme Resolution of the Congress of April 23, 1907. Consult *ibid.*, p. 269, note 2.

[3] *Ibid.*, p. 269. These matters are also regulated by the Supreme Decree of October 15, 1845, dealing with lotteries; the Law of December 4, 1912, dealing more particularly with judicial fines and the disposition to be made of them; and the Law of December 5, 1906, dealing with the taxes explained or referred to in article 33.

[4] *Ibid.*, p. 269, art. 34.

[5] *Ibid.*, pp. 270–271, arts. 37–51.

[6] *Ibid.*, p. 271, arts. 52–55.

[7] *Ibid.*, p. 272, arts. 56–60.

innocence in the courts of the republic in such a manner as to insure justice to all concerned. Justice is to be made less expensive and less complicated, and it is also to be more certain.[1] The Constitution of 1931 also made important changes in the economic system of the republic. This is dealt with more particularly in the section dealing with the economic and social régime. The first article modifies the power of the chief executive in economic matters by providing that before any recommendation in economic matters is made it must have been approved by the National Economic Council (*Consejo de Economía Nacional*). This Council is composed of representatives of the mining industries and of the commercial, manufacturing, banking, transportational, and agricultural groups, as well as of the labor groups. There must be equal representation from these different groups. Any labor legislation, or any legislation of economic and social importance, must have the support of labor. Labor is also to have a representative in the Congress who is to have the right to take part in the debates on such proposed legislation, but he is to have no vote. Labor has also the right to initiate legislation.[2] The far-reaching effect of this provision can hardly be overestimated. Through it labor has secured a power in legislation which may prove to be of very great usefulness. Although labor is at present hardly in a position to play an important rôle, this provision does give labor an entering wedge and may ultimately prove an important political weapon.

Article 28 of the Constitution of 1931 provides that all concessions for the exploitation of natural resources shall be considered national and therefore under the control of the people. The exploitation must be carried on in conformity with the laws which are to be enacted for that purpose.[3] Article 29 provides that labor shall be entitled to one day of rest in seven.[4] Article 30 provides that working conditions must be hygienic. The employer will be held responsible for the health of his employees, who must be safeguarded by the methods demanded by the nature of the employment in each industry.[5] The chief executive is given full power to protect the people from undesirable foreigners. He may expel foreigners who have proved themselves undesirable, and he may forbid the entry of a foreigner whom he judges undesirable. He also has the power to prevent the entry into the republic of those who are suffering from an infectious or contagious disease or diseases.[6] It will be observed that the framers of the Constitution of 1931 had caught some of the

[1] *Constitución política*, pp. 2–9, arts. 3–26.

[2] *Ibid.*, pp. 10–11, art. 27.

[3] *Ibid.*, p. 11.

[4] *Ibid.*, p. 11.

[5] *Ibid.*, p. 11.

[6] *Ibid.*, p. 11, art. 51.

spirit of the age concerning the "common man," and have laid the foundations for a safer and a saner life for the people of the republic.

The Constitution of 1931 also makes provision for the state of siege, the notorious *estado de sitio*. The president of the republic has the power to declare, with the previous approval, however, of the Council of Ministers, the whole of the republic, or a part of it, in a state of siege, whenever grave dangers from within or from without the country demand such action. The article provides that in case the Congress is called in regular or in special session in the part of the country under a state of siege, the continuance of such a state of siege shall be subject to the wish of the Congress, and cannot be enforced without the special permission of that body. Such authorization from the Congress is necessary even though the district has already been declared in a state of siege by the president of the republic. Without such authorization the decree of the president of the republic shall be without force. In no case, except in the instance of an international war or a civil war, may the state of siege be in force more than ninety days. Any person who receives an injury or who suffers damages because of the state of siege has the right to redress for such grievances. If he has been imprisoned during a state of siege he must be set free at the end of the siege, unless he has been tried and found guilty by a competent tribunal during the state of siege. The president of the republic may not prolong the state of siege for more than ninety days, nor declare another state of siege in the same year, without the special permission of the Congress, called in a special session for that purpose, in case the president of the republic has decreed the state of siege during the recess of that body.[1] The president of the republic may increase the standing army, and he may call the National Guard into active service during the state of siege. He may negotiate for an increase of the financial resources of the state, as well as an increase in the national income, through loans, in such amounts as he may deem necessary to meet the crisis that has arisen. Under no circumstances may he use the regular funds for such purposes. In case money is to be raised through forced loans, the president of the republic shall apportion the amount to be loaned by the municipal councils, having in mind that the loans are to be in proportion to the ability to loan such moneys. He may reduce the salaries of civil, ecclesiastical, and municipal employees in such amounts as may be necessary to finance the military operations. Under no circumstances shall such reductions be more than 50 per cent of the salary. The guaranties and rights established by the Constitution shall in no wise be affected by the declaration of a state of siege. The president of the republic may place such persons as he deems responsible for the disorder, and dangerous to the tranquillity of the country, in a position where they can do the country no further harm, but all this must be done in conformity with the laws. The legitimate

[1] *Constitución política*, pp. 12–13, art. 32.

authorities must cause the arrest of such person or persons, but the person or persons so arrested must be taken before an established tribunal within seventy-two hours after such arrest, for trial in accordance with the established procedure. If the preservation of the public order demands the removal of the accused, he shall be ordered removed to confinement in the capital of a department or of a province. The place to which he is removed must be in a healthful condition, *que no sea malsana*. There shall be no expulsion from the country for purely political reasons. The person arrested, prosecuted, and confined for political reasons may ask for passports for a foreign country, which request may not be refused under any circumstances. The public authorities must act to enforce the rights of such persons to the constitutional guaranties. All public authorities who refuse to enforce the laws or who interfere with the enforcement of the laws are to be treated, at the expiration of the state of siege, as criminals, without any exception whatsoever. The president of the republic also has the right to prevent or suspend the guaranties against the inviolability of the mails, but without violating the mails; and he must put into operation the rules which require passports for travel from one place to another within the republic, particularly from and to the territory under the state of siege.[1]

Under the head of local government should also come the political units called *delegaciones nacionales*, or national delegations. The Law of October 28, 1890, created two national delegations, that of Madre de Dios and that of the Río Purús. These delegations are located in the northeastern and eastern part of the republic. A delegate was placed at the head of each, whose business it was to encourage settlements in the delegation under his charge. The delegate was appointed by the national government and had large powers. He was to make two formal reports a year to the national government, one in May and the other in December.[2] By the Decree of March 8, 1900, the administrative duties of the National Delegation for the Northeast were defined. The decree incorporated the idea of religious toleration, as laid down in article 2 of the Constitution of 1871, but reiterated the fundamental idea that the state recognized only the Roman Catholic Apostolic religion. This was of course changed by the Law of August 27, 1906, which established religious freedom in Bolivia. The delegation might choose its own headquarters, locating it at such place as might seem most important or convenient. The national delegate, representing the president of the republic, was to have the power to issue decrees and make agreements, but was to be responsible to the national govern-

[1] *Constitución política*, pp. 13–15, art. 33. The detailed manner in which the *estado de sitio* is dealt with in the Constitution is evidence of its importance. It would be hard to point out any single feature of the political government of Bolivia which has been of more concern than the *estado de sitio*. Throughout the history of the independence of the country this power has been misused with a regularity that becomes monotonous in the telling. Every effort to abolish this power has failed.

[2] Araoz, *Nuevo digesto*, vol. III, pp. 344–348.

ment for his administration. His term of office was four years, but he might be removed by the president of the republic whenever that official should deem it necessary.[1]

The Law of December 27, 1905, created the National Delegation of the Gran Chaco, which was to confine its activities to the Gran Chaco, located in the Department of Tarija. This delegation was short-lived, for it was abolished by the Law of November 29, 1913.[2] The Law of January 11, 1911, created the National Delegation of the Oriente, which was to continue in existence for three years, and was not to infringe upon the rights of the Department of Santa Cruz.[3] The Law of April 4, 1928, created the National Delegation of the Parapeti River and the Llanos de Manso. It was created for the purpose of protecting the interests of Bolivia in that part of the national territory, and was to continue in existence as long as it was needed.[4] The Law of December 5, 1916, required that the delegations in the Oriente, the Noroeste, and the Gran Chaco should make annual reports of the moneys handled by them to the national government.[5] The Decree of December 23, 1905, defined the purposes of the religious missions, and prescribed the manner in which they were to be conducted. The main purpose of the religious missions was to prepare the nomadic Indians for civilized life, and for the settlement of the country in which they were established. The missions were to be under the jurisdiction of the Ministry of Colonization. The neophytes of these missions were to enjoy the civil rights guaranteed by the Constitution. These rights were to be exercised through the medium of the *padres* (priests).[6] By the Decree of June 8, 1928, the Franciscan missions of San Antonio, San Francisco, and Itatique del Parapeti were established;[7] and by the Decree of January 23, 1929, the missions of the Propaganda Fide of Tarairí, Tigüipa, Macharetí, Santa Rosa de Cuevo, and San Buenaventura de Ivo were abolished.[8] The religious services in these former missions were to be continued by the Franciscan *padres*. The lands were to be made into settlements.[9]

[1] Araoz, *Nuevo digesto*, vol. III, pp. 348–354. The national delegate was to be a native-born or naturalized citizen, and at least thirty years of age. There was an *intendente*, who was to serve in case of absence or disability of the national delegate.

[2] *Ibid.*, pp. 354–355.

[3] *Ibid.*, p. 355. The Decree of December 17, 1912, described the duties of the National Delegation. The Delegation was created, in the first place, to build and improve a port on the Paraguay River (*ibid.*, pp. 355–356).

[4] *Ibid.*, pp. 356–358.

[5] *Ibid.*, p. 358.

[6] *Ibid.*, pp. 358–361.

[7] *Ibid.*, pp. 361–362.

[8] *Ibid.*, p. 362.

[9] *Ibid.*, p. 362.

THE CHURCH AND THE STATE

No account of the political organization of Bolivia would be complete without a brief history of the rôle of the Church. The ecclesiastical history of the republic is almost exclusively the history of the Roman Catholic Church. Roman Catholicism has been the predominant religion since its introduction. It is still the religion of an overwhelming majority of the Bolivian people today. Prior to the Law of August 27, 1906, when religious toleration was established, it was the only religion the public worship of which was tolerated, except in the colonies, where religious toleration was established in 1871.[1] Hence there has been a close relation between the political and ecclesiastical forces throughout the period of white domination. This must not be taken to mean that there has been no opposition to the Roman Catholic Church. The conversion of the Indians has not always been an easy task, for they have been, and still are, tenacious of their old religious beliefs. It is a question whether the Indian ever really became a good Roman Catholic. There are those who maintain that the Christianity of the Bolivian Indians is an Indian Christianity; in other words, that Christianity has been adapted by the natives to meet their own religious views. There is thus a Bolivian Church distinct from the Roman Catholic Church in other countries, even in old Spain herself. Nor have the Bolivian people, whites as well as Indians, been free from the onslaughts of "isms" peculiarly antagonistic to the Roman Catholic Church. There were those who desired the separation of Church and State even during the period when the republic was being established. Casimiro Olañeta, whom we have met frequently in this study, was among those who supported Bolívar in his desire to omit all reference to the Church in the fundamental law. The project presented by Bolívar to the General Constituent Assembly of 1826 for a constitution did not provide for either a state religion or a state church. It was not to be expected that such a radical step would succeed at that time. Protestantism has also come in opposition to Roman Catholicism, particularly since the establishment of the republic, but it has never been a very serious problem to the Roman Catholic Church. There are Protestant educational and charitable institutions operating in the country, but the number is not large. And there are only a few non-Roman Catholic religious organizations in the country.

Roman Catholicism was introduced by Gonzalo Pizarro on his march into

[1] Ordóñez López, *Constitución política*, vol. II, p. 417, art. 2. The article read: "El Estado reconoce y sostiene la Religión Católica, Apostólica, Romana. Se prohibe el ejercicio público de todo culto, excepto en las colonias que se formaren en lo sucesivo."

southern Peru in search of the fabled "Land of Cinnamon." One of the duties with which he was charged by his half-brother Francisco Pizarro was that of converting the Indians. He took with him several priests, and was thus the first man to have mass sung in Bolivia in accordance with the rites of the Roman Catholic Church. The Pizarro brothers were, of course, merely carrying out a well-laid plan of the Crown of Spain to Christianize and civilize the natives of the Americas. It must be remembered that the Crown of Spain had received large rights and privileges from the popes. It had been given powers not only in its possessions in Iberia but also in the lands which it was to discover and colonize outside the Peninsula. Pope Alexander VI, the notorious Rodrigo Borgia, born a Spaniard near Valencia, was merely following in the footsteps of his illustrious predecessors in conferring rights upon the rulers of Spain. The celebrated bull of May 3, 1493, was only one of several such instruments issued by him in favor of the Spanish Crown, authorizing not merely the propagation of the Roman Catholic faith but also further territorial conquests. Both Spain and Portugal had appealed to Alexander VI to arbitrate their differences over the boundaries of newly discovered lands. The decision of the pope was not acceptable to either party, and had to be settled in other ways, as we have noted before. Despite the large emphasis laid upon the ecclesiastical phase of the reduction of the New World, the economic and political aspects of that work were also highly important. The bull *Eximae* of Alexander VI gave the Crown of Spain the same rights which had been given to Portugal by Pope Nicholas V in 1454 and confirmed by Pope Calixtus III on March 7, 1456.[1]

The claims of Spain were also upheld by men in her political and legal life. Juan de Solórzano y Pereira, the famous judge of the Royal Audiencia of Lima, and later a member of the Council of the Indies, declared in book IV of his great work on *La política indiana* that there could be no question about the right of the king of Spain to govern the territorial as well as the spiritual affairs of the Indies.[2] Francisco Rojas, ambassador of Queen Isabella of Castile at the Vatican, was instructed to request of Pope Alexander VI the right of the patronage of the Church in the Americas. He was instructed to call attention to the fact that the rulers of Spain had full control over ecclesiastical matters in their

[1] Dalmacio Velez Sarsfield, *Derecho público eclesiástico. Relaciones del estado con la iglesia en la antigua América española*, pp. 26–29. The author concludes: "Quedó, pues, establecido desde la primera erección de Catedrales en América que los Reyes de España tendrían el patronato de todas las Iglesias del Nuevo Mundo, y que podrían presentar personas dignas para todos los oficios eclesiásticos."

[2] Consult Mary Wilhelmina Williams, "The Roman Church in the Indies," *in* A. Curtis Wilgus (ed.), *Modern Hispanic America*, vol. I, pp. 57–69. Consult also Juan de Solórzano y Pereira, *La política indiana*, bk. IV. He declares: "... que el Papa hizo sus delegados á los Reyes de España, y les concedió el gobierno espiritual y temporal de las Iglesias de Indias, añadiendo: que en ésto no cabe duda alguna" (quoted by Velez Sarsfield, *Relaciones del estado con la iglesia en la antigua América española*, p. 25).

territories according to the provisions of the *Siete Partidas*.[1] On July 28, 1508, Pope Alexander VI granted the right of patronage to the rulers of Spain, and this became one of their most cherished as well as most important rights, in the Indies as well as in the mother country.[2] Of the utmost importance here is the fact that this right has been carried over into the laws of the republics of Spanish America.

The right of the patronage was very comprehensive. It included the absolute right not only to select persons for all the offices of the Church in the Indies, but to govern ecclesiastical affairs in those colonies. The right to fill a vacancy lay in the right of the king to nominate to all those offices whomsoever he chose. No right was guarded with greater care and jealousy, or more religiously enforced. The same can be said of the right of the patronage exercised by the national governments in Spanish America. The rights of the monarchs of Spain in ecclesiastical affairs were restated by Philip II on June 1, 1574. The first paragraph of this famous decree (*cêdula*) is worthy of incorporation here:[3]

> . . . As you know, the right of the ecclesiastical patronage belongs to us throughout the realm of the Yndias—both because of having discovered and acquired that new world, and erected there and endowed the churches and monasteries at our own cost, or at the cost of our ancestors, the Catholic Sovereigns; and because it was conceded to us by bulls of the most holy pontiffs, conceded by their own accord. For its conservation, and that of the right that we have of it, we order and command that the said right of patronage be always preserved for us and our royal crown, singly and *in solidum*, throughout all the realm of the Yndias, without any derogation therefrom, either in whole or in part; and that we shall not concede the right of patronage by any favor or reward that we or the kings our successors may confer.

The wars of emancipation brought about a crisis in the relations between the Church and the State throughout the whole of Spanish America. The

[1] *Los códigos españoles, concordados y anotados* (Madrid, 1848), vol. II, p. 82. This passage is taken from *Las Siete Partidas*, which code is given in this volume. Law Eighteen deals directly with the rights of the king of Castile to fill vacancies in any bishopric. In this law King Alfonso el Sabio, the author of the *Siete Partidas*, proceeded on the assumption that there could be no election of a bishop without the express permission of the king. King Alfonso based his laws upon the ancient usages of his realm, as well as upon the rules and regulations governing the life of its people.

[2] Velez Sarsfield, *Relaciones del estado con la iglesia en la antigua América española*, pp. 27–28. The king had built the cathedral in the island of Española in accordance with the terms of the bull of 1504. By the additional authority of the bull of July 28, 1508, he established the two bishoprics of Santo Domingo and the one in San Juan, Puerto Rico.

[3] Blair and Robertson, *The Philippine Islands, 1493–1898*, vol. XXI, pp. 19–31. Also in Cleven, *Readings in Hispanic American history*, pp. 250–258. The decree here given was sent to the viceroy of New Spain, or to those in charge there. It is safe to say that few documents were guarded with greater care by the civil authorities in Spain and the Indies. It has been of great importance to the civil authorities of Bolivia, for it lays down in no uncertain terms the rights which the civil rulers have over ecclesiastical authorities of the republic.

ecclesiastical authorities were naturally eager to regain the rights and privileges which the popes had surrendered to the State during the colonial period. Simón Bolívar had no doubt whatever as to the position of the ecclesiastical authorities in the state. The state was supreme. This was the one great principle from which he never deviated. Those among the ecclesiastics who opposed the wars of emancipation and the plans and the measures adopted for the political government of the newly created states were given firmly to understand that there could be no interference whatsoever in the affairs of state. No choice was given the ecclesiastical authorities in the matter. They were either for or against the emancipatory movements; and those who were against them had to choose between supporting them and exile. Nor did Bolívar hesitate either to conscript the funds of the Church whenever he considered such funds necessary to the success of his undertaking, or to demand reforms in the policy of the clergy toward the Indians. Examples have already been given to show the use which Bolívar made of his powers during the tour of inspection in Upper Peru in 1825.

Antonio José de Sucre also brooked no interference from the ecclesiastical authorities during his rule in Bolivia. An excellent example of his policy in this matter is found in the *orden* issued by him on February 11, 1826, in which he ordered the *curas* to treat the Indians more humanely.[1] Bolívar's attitude is shown in his famous plan (*proyecto*) for a political constitution for Bolivia in 1826, which has already been analyzed. He deliberately omitted any provision for a state religion or a state church. Religion to him was purely and definitely a personal matter and should not be, by its very nature, the subject of legislation.[2] His views were not accepted by the Fathers of the Republic, and a new

[1] *Colección oficial, años 1825 y 1826*, pp. 124–125. The *orden* was addressed to the ecclesiastical governors from the Palacio de Gobierno in Sucre (then Chuquisaca), and was countersigned by Facundo Infante. The document was in these terms: "Á S. E. el Gran Mariscal de Ayacucho han llegado quejas contra varios curas, que abusando de su ministerio y contra lo mandado, exigen á los indígenas cantidades para fiestas de iglesia ó funciones de algunos santos. S. E. no puede tolerar el que, no respetándose la propiedad de aquella clase hasta ahora tan abatida, se le obligue á actos que por su voluntad, de ningún modo pueden ser aceptos á los ojos de Dios y los santos, por más que sean útiles á sus ministros, mucho menos cuando para tales fiestas dejan arruinada una familia de indígenas, según y todos tienen la experiencia. Con presencia de todo, y deseando S. E. el que la religión recobre su dignidad, y que los indígenas no sean vejados bajo pretextos de ninguna especie, me manda diga á U. S., que el cura a quien se le pruebe que ha exigido cantidad alguna á éstos para fiestas de iglesia, sin que ellos quieran voluntariamente darla, pagará irremisiblemente quinientos pesos aplicados á favor del que diere la queja."

[2] John Miller, *Memoirs of General John Miller in the service of the Republic of Peru*, vol. II, pp. 404–415. Consult also the work of John Lloyd Mecham on *Church and State in Latin America*. The views of the great Liberator on this subject are explained by him in his celebrated address to the General Constituent Assembly of 1826, which he sent along with the project for the constitution. These four paragraphs, though long, are given here because of

article was added to the Constitution in which it was declared, as already noted, that the state religion was the Roman Catholic Apostolic to the exclusion of all other kinds of public worship.[1] And this remained the position of that

---

their importance to a right understanding of the position of Bolívar on this all-important subject:

"Legislators! I shall make mention of an article, which in my conscience I ought to have omitted. No religious creed or profession should be prescribed in a political constitution; for according to the best doctrines concerning fundamental laws, these are the guarantees of civil and political rights; and as religion touches none of these rights, she is, in her nature, not to be defined in the social order, and belongs to intellectual morality. Religion governs man at home, in the cabinet, and in his own bosom, within himself; she alone has a right to examine his most secret conscience. The laws, on the contrary, consider and view the exterior of things; they govern only out of doors, and not within the houses of the citizens. Applying these considerations, how can the state rule the consciences of its subjects, watch over the fulfilment of religion, and reward or punish, when the tribunals of all those matters are in heaven, and when God is judge? The inquisition alone could replace these in this world; and is the inquisition, with its incendiary faggots and piles, to return amongst us?

"Religion is the law of conscience. Every law on this subject annuls religion, as, by imposing necessity upon duty, it would take away the merit of faith, which is the basis of religion. The precepts and sacred dogmas are useful and luminous; they rest on metaphysical evidence; and we ought to profess them; but this is a moral, and not a political duty.

"On the other hand, what are the rights of man with regard to religion in this world? They are in heaven. There is the tribunal which recompenses merit, and renders justice according to the code dictated by the Legislator. As all this belongs to divine jurisdiction, it strikes me, at first sight, as sacrilegious and profane to mix up our ordinances with the commandments of the Lord. It therefore belongs not to the legislator to prescribe religion; for the legislator must impose penalties on the infringement of the laws, to avoid their becoming merely expressions of counsel and advice. When there are neither temporal penalties, nor judge to inflict them, the law ceases to be law.

"The moral development of man is the first intention of the legislator. As far as this development has taken place, man supports his morality by revealed truths, and professes it *de facto*, which is more efficacious, the more he has acquired it by his own investigations. Besides, fathers of families cannot neglect their religious duties towards their children. The spiritual shepherds are bound to teach the knowledge of heaven; the example of the true disciples of Jesus is the most eloquent lesson of his divine morality; but morality is not commanded, . . . nor ought force to be employed in giving counsel. God and his ministers are the authorities of religion which operates by means exclusively spiritual; but by no means is the national body a religious authority, that body having solely the direction of the public power to objects purely temporal." Consult Miller, *Memoirs of General John Miller*, vol. II, pp. 493–494. Also Cleven, "The dictators of Peru, Bolivia, and Ecuador," in Wilgus (ed.), *South American dictators*, pp. 283–284.

[1] Ordóñez López, *Constitución política*, vol. II, pp. 285–286. It forms a title by itself and is the Second Title (*Título Segundo*) of the Constitution of 1826. The article is the sixth, and reads: "La Religión Católica, Apostólica, Romana, es la de la República, con exclusión de todo otro culto público. El Gobierno la protegerá y hará respetar, reconociendo el principio de que no hay poder humano sobre las conciencias." The same identical article was inserted in the Constitution of 1831 (*ibid.*, p. 304), and in that of 1834 (*ibid.*, p. 323). In the Constitution of 1839 it was placed in the first section in article 3. The wording, but not the meaning, was slightly changed, the statement about the law and conscience being omitted (*ibid.*,

religion until 1906. The one exception, as already noted, was in the Constitution of 1871, which established religious toleration in the colonies.

The patronage (*patronato*), however, has always been exercised by the national government, which has proceeded on the assumption that the right of the *patronato* inheres in sovereignty itself and is, accordingly, to be exercised by the people through their legally constituted authorities.[1] So important is this principle that it has been established as a part of the constitutional law of the republic. The president of the republic is the national patron (*patrono nacional*), and has exercised the functions of that office since the beginning of the independence period. There have, of course, been important controversies between the national government and the Roman Catholic Church over the ecclesiastical rights claimed by the former. On July 24, 1835, Andrés Santa Cruz as the *patrono nacional* nominated José María Mendizábal for the position of archbishop of La Plata. Though there was opposition to this proceeding, the pope appointed Mendizábal to that office.[2] On November 30, 1835, the

p. 342). The Constitution of 1843 contained the same ideas as that of 1839 but the wording is somewhat different. It became article 4 instead of 3 (*ibid*., p. 364). The Constitution of 1851 placed the statement on religion under that on the public rights of the citizens, and in article 3 (*ibid*., p. 377). The Constitution of 1861 included the same idea, but placed it in article 2 (*ibid*., pp. 389–390). The Constitution of 1868 again placed the statement regarding the Church in article 4 (*ibid*., p. 404). The Constitution of 1871 changed it, as noted before, providing for religious toleration in the colonies (*ibid*., p. 417, art. 2). The Constitution of 1878 restored the Roman Catholic religion to its supreme place (*ibid*., pp. 433–434, art. 2). The Constitution of 1880 reverted to the statement in the Constitution of 1871 (Araoz, *Nuevo digesto*, vol. I, p. 1). Finally, the Constitution of 1931 made article 2 read: "El Estado reconoce y sostiene la religión católica, apostólica, romana, permitiendo el ejercicio público de todo otro culto" (*Constitución política*, p. 2). All the constitutions contain the expression "En el Nombre de Dios," or words to the same effect.

[1] The right of the *patronato* is a privilege given by the Roman pontiff out of gratitude for conspicuous services to the Church. This right undoubtedly represents a limitation upon ecclesiastical authority and was so intended. The tendency within recent times has been to refrain from granting the right of the *patronato*, if not wholly to abolish it. In point of fact, canon law does not recognize this right.

[2] The archbishops of La Plata since 1835 have been: José María Mendizábal, who served from 1835 to 1856; Miguel Angel de Prado, 1856 to 1862; Pedro José Cayetano de la Llosa, 1862 to 1898; Miguel de los Santos Taborga, 1898 to 1905; Fray Sebastián Píffieri, 1905 to 1924; and Fray Francisco Pierini, 1924 to the present (1932). The archbishopric includes Argentina, Paraguay, and Uruguay in addition to Bolivia. In this connection it should be noted that the *patriarcado* of the Indies, which was in existence in the reign of the King-Emperor, was created anew in 1572 at the request of Philip II. But the Patriarcado de Indias never had any jurisdiction in the Indies because the Indies never had an *iglesia patriarcal*. It was a title of honor "del primer capellán del Rey, al cual se dió el Vicariato que se extendía de mar y tierra de España," but which never was extended to America. As early as 1545 the whole of the Church in the Americas was divided into three parts, the third division including "todas las Iglesias del alto y bajo Perú."

patrono nacional issued a *pase* permitting the entry of certain papal documents. On May 19, 1837, the *patrono nacional* nominated Francisco León de Aguirre, a native of Santa Cruz de la Sierra, for the office of bishop of La Paz. On March 12, 1840, the *patrono nacional* announced the formalities to be observed in the publication of the bulls of the Santa Cruzada in Bolivia.[1]

The question of the form of the oath for ecclesiastical authorities was discussed with no little concern throughout the earlier period of the republic. It was especially acute in the case of the bishop-elect of La Paz, José Manuel Indaburú. The whole question was discussed with much warmth in the Chamber of Senators in 1844. The debate was caused by the action of the Holy Father, who held that Indaburú had been elected bishop by the people of La Paz and not by the national government. The bull which the Roman pontiff issued in connection with the consecration of Bishop Indaburú contained the oath to be taken by the newly chosen bishop. This oath was contrary to that required by the laws of the Republic of Bolivia. This act of the Holy Father aroused considerable opposition, and was variously interpreted. It was believed by many that the pope had failed to recognize the political independence of Bolivia, and that he had deliberately exempted the bishop-elect from the obligations imposed upon ecclesiastical officials by the laws of the country. If such was the case, His Holiness was only following the example of Spain, which had not up to that time recognized the independence of Bolivia. The debate in the Congress was a brilliant one. Torrico, in the Senate, took the position that the *pase* was a real law, and should be recognized as such.[2] For this reason, he maintained, the Congress had the right to impose such restrictions or conditions on the action of the pope as that body might deem necessary. He held that these restrictions or conditions could be laid down in the *pase* itself.

The result of the discussion was the passage of the Law of November 11, 1844, by which all ecclesiastical officials were obliged to take the civil oath

[1] On February 2, 1841, the archbishop of La Plata, in conformity with the papal *breve* of June 21, 1836, and with the permission of the national government, declared certain days of the year feast days. These were: all the Sundays, the day of the Circumcision of the Savior, Epiphany, Ascension, Corpus Christi, Christmas, Purification, Assumption, the Immaculate Conception, St. John the Baptist, St. Peter and St. Paul, All Saints, and the Patriarch St. John. In addition there were of course the saint's days of the patron saints of the departments, the provinces, the cantons, and the municipalities, all of which were also to be commemorated by those directly concerned. The number of days was reduced in the interest of industry, especially agriculture.

[2] *Redactor del H. Senado Nacional del año 1844*, pp. 26–32. Torrico declared in part: "No señor, el pase es una verdadera ley. Sabemos que ninguna autoridad extranjera puede ejercer jurisdicción en la República sin voluntad de ella. Esta voluntad se expresa por el poder legislativo al conceder el pase, . . . el pase que es una ley, . . . la Representación Nacional tiene facultad para imponer las condiciones o restricciones que le parezcan convenientes, al dictar la ley que concede el pase a las bulas."

required of all other public officials.[1] Again on October 18, 1846, the same restrictions were enforced in the case of the newly consecrated Bishop Miguel Angel de Prado of Santa Cruz de la Sierra. This law also provided that the president of the republic could name the place and designate the official before whom the oath was to be administered. By these two laws it was made perfectly clear that the national government would brook no interference from ecclesiastical authorities. It was made equally clear that the ecclesiastical authorities were public functionaries and were under the same obligations as other public functionaries; and that they would have to take an oath not to accept an office that required them to perform activities that were contrary to the Constitution and laws of Bolivia. In the course of this debate in the Congress it was repeatedly stated by the defenders of ecclesiastical privileges that the archbishops and bishops preferred to take an oath to the pope alone so as to be exempt from the irksome restrictions placed upon them by these laws. In every case, the reply was that the state could not afford to tolerate any power within its borders exercising functions as agent of another sovereign power to whom alone it would be responsible. Thus with the passage of each new *pase* the churchmen, many of whom were members of the Congress, made attacks upon the limitations imposed by that *pase*. The result was inevitably the same, a victory for the civil power.

The death on September 30, 1846, of Archbishop Mendizábal[2] gave José

[1] Article 4 of the law contained the following: "Juramento civil del Arzobispo y Obispos para entrar en el ejercicio de sus respectivos cargos. El Arzobispo, Obispos y cualesquier otros eclesiásticos seculares, o regulares que obtuvieron del Romano Pontífice dignidad, beneficio, honor, jurisdicción, o cualesquier otro encargo, o comisión espiritual o temporal, con renta o sin renta, no podrán aceptar ni proceder al ejercicio de sus funciones sin prestar antes el juramento civil a que están obligados todos los funcionarios públicos, prometiendo ser fiel a la Constitución de Bolivia y a las leyes de la República, y a no aceptar, ni ejercer funciones que sean opuestos a ellas."

[2] The death of the archbishop of La Plata brought to an end the life of one of the most important public men in Bolivia. He had a long and an honorable public career, that began with the birth of the republic itself. He was a member of the Deliberative Assembly from La Paz and was vice-president of that body at the time of the adoption of the Declaration of Independence. He was commissioned by that same body, as we have already noted, to offer the life presidency to Simón Bolívar. Later he was also commissioned to go to the government of Argentina (then the United Provinces of Río de la Plata) to urge it to recognize the independence of Bolivia. In this he was successful. He was also a very active supporter of Andrés Santa Cruz, especially in the efforts to form a union of Peru and Bolivia. He was a firm supporter of the plan to organize a Peru-Bolivian Confederation, and was largely responsible for its creation. Santa Cruz appointed him one of the three Bolivian representatives to the Assembly of the Peru-Bolivian Confederation at Tacna in 1837. He took an active part in the Assembly and helped to produce the Pacto de Tacna, which was the constitution of the Peru-Bolivian Confederation. As early as 1830 he had been made bishop of La Paz through the nomination of his powerful friend Andrés Santa Cruz, and in 1835 he was raised to the position of archbishop of La Plata, again through the act of Santa Cruz. He had become, by that elevation, the

Ballivián, as *patrono nacional*, the opportunity to appoint to that high office a man acceptable to the national government. Miguel Angel de Prado, whom he nominated, was duly consecrated and formally installed as archbishop of La Plata in accordance with the laws of the republic. There was really nothing new in these proceedings, for Ballivián was merely giving rugged adherence to the traditional policy inaugurated by the great Liberator himself. He was, of course, giving support to a movement that had for its ultimate goal the separation of the Church and the State.

The national government had sought, on several occasions, to induce the Holy Father to negotiate a concordat, but it was not successful in its efforts until Andrés Santa Cruz was commissioned to represent it. It was Belzu who made use of this celebrated exile as minister to the European governments and to the Vatican. Santa Cruz was able to negotiate a concordat in 1851. So important was this instrument that Belzu called the Congress in extra session to consider it. He sent a message to the National Convention, as the national legislature was called then, in which he dealt with the concordat in some detail, emphasizing the significance of the negotiations which had resulted in a friendly agreement between the republic and the Holy See.[1] The National Convention took up the entire question of the relationship between the two governments. The instrument was found, however, to infringe upon the sovereignty of the state in several particulars. In the first place, the Holy Father, Pope Pius IX, reserved the right to limit the president of the republic in the exercise of the *patronato nacional*. This was, of course, contrary to article 76 of the political Constitution and could not be tolerated. The majority of the members of the National Convention held that this provision in the concordat was a new species of recognition of papal power which Bolivia could not tolerate.[2] The net result was that the concordat was approved only upon con-

first archbishop of La Plata to be selected during the period of the republic. He is justly considered one of the ablest churchmen that Bolivia has produced. The fact that he had such a large share in the formation of the republic made his career as the ecclesiastical leader of the nation a most important one. This accounts in a large measure also for the important rôle he played in the life of the country from the very outset of its existence. He was a zealous son of Bolivia as well as of the Church, and believed that the greatness of the two lay in close cooperation, not in rivalry. A rivalry between them could only end in the loss of power and prestige by both, as he understood it.

[1] *Redactor de la Convención Nacional de 1851 y de sus sesiones extraordinarias en el mismo año*, pp. 203–206. The message bore the date of October 27, 1851, and contained this statement about the negotiations: "Estaba reservado para nuestros tiempos y para la ilustración de Pío IX, el Concordato que ha celebrado con la Nación Boliviana. Este tratado honrará tanto la memoria de aquel digno sucesor de San Pedro, como a la Representación Nacional que lo apruebe. El hábil negociador boliviano General Santa Cruz, es digno de la gratitud pública, que la Convención sabrá expresar debidamente."

[2] It was during the course of the debate on the concordat that Torrico and Comacho defended with great power the right of the national government to exercise the *patronato nacional*.

dition that the objectionable provisions should be changed so as to conform to the Constitution and laws of the republic. This, of course, meant the defeat of the concordat, because the Holy See would not agree to these conditions.[1] On October 4, 1860, an *oficio* was issued by the national government which ordered that the different concordats which had been agreed to between Spain and the Holy Father were to be in force in Bolivia from that date forward, or until a concordat had been adopted incorporating the desired provisions.[2]

Comacho called attention to the fact that several concordats had been agreed to between Spain and the Holy See, namely, those of 1564, 1569, 1585, 1753, and 1814; and that Bolivia was only following in the footsteps of old Spain. He urged the members of the Convention to bear in mind that they were living in the nineteenth century, and that Bolivia had rights that she should defend. He contended that the new age required new points of view. The position of the Holy See was no less ably defended by its supporters, and the debates rose to the heights of eloquence aroused by a subject about which there was such depth of feeling.

[1] The concordat placed restrictions upon the rights of the *patronato nacional* in the control of the monasteries and in the management of the ecclesiastical synods. In regard to the latter, the pope demanded that they should be taken from under the control of the national government. The national government of Bolivia refused to concede this right to the Holy Father, and insisted that it had the right to exercise direct control over these synods, and that it would continue to exercise that right. No synods could be called without the express permission of the national government and no subjects could be considered which were deemed objectionable by it. The national government also had no idea of surrendering its control over monasteries. No religious order could enter Bolivia or operate therein except by the express permission of the national government, and in conformity with its wishes. Bolivia was not disposed to permit any religious organization to operate in its domain which was responsible to a foreign sovereign power. There was nothing new in these views. The thing to note is that the control over ecclesiastical matters in Bolivia had been too well established to be surrendered at this time. Consult the *Redactor de la Convención Nacional de 1851 y de sus sesiones extraordinarias en el mismo año*, p. 288, for the reservations to this concordat.

[2] These concordats, including, as we have already noted, those of the years 1564, 1569, 1585, 1753, and 1814, had all been incorporated in the *Recopilación* and in the *Leyes de Castilla*. The national government also ordered in the same *oficio* that Ley 35 of the *Recopilación* should be put into effect in Bolivia. Consult the *Colección oficial, año 1860*, vol. V, pp. 66–67, for this *oficio*. Other measures were taken to show the control of the national government over ecclesiastical affairs. The *Resolución* of October 14, 1868, granted a *pase* to the bulls to Francisco María del Grande, *obispo auxiliar* of Cochabamba. On February 13, 1868, Melgarejo abolished the Ley de Secularización of August 23, 1826. Consult the *Anuario administrativo de 1868* (*Anuario de leyes y supremas disposiciones, 1855–1919;* La Paz, 1856–1919), pp. 12–13. Melgarejo was interested in the Vatican Council of 1869–1870, and sent representatives to that august body at the expense of the national government of Bolivia. In his message to the Constitutional Assembly, as the national legislature was then called, of 1870 he declared: "Existen actualmente en Roma, como miembros del Concilio Vaticano, nuestro mui Reverendo Arzobispo Doctor Don Pedro Puch, y el Iltmo. Obispo de La Paz Dr. D. Calixto Clavijo. Interesado el Gobierno en que la Iglesia boliviana tuviera sus representantes en tan augusta y universal Asamblea, les felicitó el abono de sus sueldos, y que la penuria fiscal no le permitió ofrecerles otros recursos que su viático." Consult Melgarejo's *Mensaje que el presidente provisorio de la República dirije a la Asamblea Constitucional de 1870*. In a

The relations between the Church and the national government have not always been friendly. The differences between the archbishop of La Plata and the national government in 1877 were of a rather serious nature. The main issue was the right of the *patrono nacional* to fill vacancies in the curacies. The crisis came on May 18, 1877, when the archbishop denied the right of the *patrono nacional* to fill such vacancies, and claimed the right to do so. The minister of religion, in turn, declared that the *patrono nacional* could not admit the contention of the archbishop; that the right of *patronato* inhered in the sovereignty of the nation, and that this right resided, according to the Constitution and the laws of Bolivia, in the president of the republic. The president, therefore, had an unquestioned right and power to intervene in the external government of the Church, including the right to fill the vacancies in question. The minister reminded the archbishop of the power of the president of the republic to refuse or to permit the entry into the republic of any and all papal documents. The minister concluded that the national government could not permit innovations in its control over ecclesiastical affairs in the republic.[1] The archbishop of La Plata, however, continued his opposition. On July 13, 1877, the national government ordered the prefect of the Department of Chuquisaca to withhold payment of the salaries (*temporalidades*) of the ecclesiastical authorities because of the failure of the archbishop of La Plata to conduct the government of the archbishopric in accordance with the Constitution and the laws of Bolivia. The salary of the archbishop was also to be withheld until such time as the president of the republic should authorize the prefect to pay it.[2] On August 27, 1880, the president of the republic suggested to the archbishop of La Plata that the Monastery of Santa Monica in Sucre should be closed, and it was closed. On February 17, 1881, the president of the republic suggested to the Bishop of La Paz that the Convent of La Merced should be closed, and it was closed. On September 16, 1881, the president of the republic, as *patrono nacional*, suggested to the archbishop of La Plata that he make a visit of inspection of his ecclesiastical dominions in order to note how many of

---

Resolución of February 4, 1879, a *pase* was granted for the papal bulls creating Juan José Baldivia bishop of Santa Cruz de la Sierra. It also prescribed the oath to be taken by him and the person before whom the oath was to be taken. The document used the term *patrono nacional* and stated that the *patrono nacional* had nominated Baldivia for that office. Consult the *Anuario de leyes y supremas disposiciones de 1879*, p. 23. Of interest, too, in these codes is the material in connection with the elevation of Juan de Dios Bosque to the bishopric of La Paz. On July 3, 1873, the *patrono nacional* nominated Dios Bosque to that position. On August 20, 1874, the papal bulls of May 9, 1874, arrived appointing him bishop of La Paz. The language used was that Juan de Dios Bosque had been "presentado al Santo Padre para esta dignidad por el gobierno de la república, como patrono nacional de la iglesia boliviana." And so on down through the whole of the subsequent history of the republic.

[1] *Anuario de leyes y supremas disposiciones de 1877*, vol. II, pp. 419–420.

[2] *Ibid.*, p. 420.

the benefices were vacant.[1] On April 27, 1882, the *patrono nacional* again suspended the *temporalidades* of the archbishop of La Plata for failure to recognize the rights of the president of the republic in ecclesiastical matters. On January 15, 1883, the pope gave his approval, or *accessit*, to the regulations concerning the abolition of the *diezmos* in Bolivia. On November 22, 1883, the Fourth Diocesan Synod began its sessions, with the previous consent of the national government, in La Paz.[2] On August 25, 1886, the *patrono nacional* authorized the sale of the house which formed the Monastery of the Remedios in Potosí.[3] On June 9, 1889, the La Platan Provincial Council (*Concilio Provincial Platense*) met in Sucre, with the approval of the national government.[4] Archbishop Pedro José Cayetano de Llosa called this Council and acted as its presiding officer. The Law of November 25, 1897, declared that the salaries of the archbishop and the members of the Cabildo Metropolitano of La Plata were henceforth to be national in character, and were to be voted in the regular annual budget of the national government. The sum allowed for this purpose at the time was Bs. 40,000.[5]

The movement for religious freedom, however, had made only slight progress in Bolivia by the end of the nineteenth century. The efforts of Guillarte in 1843 to secure religious freedom for the colonists in El Beni failed.[6] The failure of the national government to ratify the concordat of 1851 was a victory for a more liberal ecclesiastical policy. The question of the relation between Church and State was discussed in detail in the Constituent Assembly of 1861. The opposition to the degree of control over education exercised by the Church was pronounced. The supporters of the movement for religious freedom took the position that the national government and not the bishops should select the *curas*, because the *curas* had such a powerful influence over education in their

[1] *Anuario de leyes y supremas disposiciones de 1881*, vol. II, p. 565.

[2] The First Diocesan Synod was held in 1619 and was called by Bishop Pedro de Valencia. The second was held in 1638 by Bishop Feliciano de la Vega, and the third met in 1731 under Bishop Agusto Rodríguez Delgado.

[3] On September 18, 1889, Pope Leo XIII appointed José Belisario Santiestevan bishop of Santa Cruz de la Sierra, the nomination having been made in due form by the *patrono nacional*. On November 7, 1889, the *patrono nacional* nominated Juan José Baldivia bishop of La Paz, and he was duly appointed by the pope to that office.

[4] The First La Platan Provincial Council was held in 1629 by Archbishop Fernando Arias de Ugarte. The second was held in 1771 by Archbishop Pedro Miguel de Argondoña. The Council of 1889 was the first to be held under republican rule. The point to be borne in mind in regard to all these ecclesiastical gatherings is that they were held only after the supreme national civil power had given its consent. This again illustrates the great power of the civil over the ecclesiastical authorities in the colonial as well as in the independent republican period.

[5] *Colección oficial, año 1897*, p. 25.

[6] Hernando Siles, *Derecho parlamentario de Bolivia*, vol. I, pp. 62, 65. Siles devotes pp. 59–182 to a discussion of article 2 of the Constitution of 1880, dealing with religion.

dioceses. They demanded that education should be taken out of the hands of the clergy and placed in the hands of men and women scientifically trained for the work.[1] The subject was again discussed in the Constituent Assembly in 1871,[2] and again in 1880.[3] The only concrete victory was the reincorporation

[1] *Redactor de la Asamblea Constituyente del año 1861*, pp. 188 ff. The debate was both lengthy and brilliant. Natalio Irigoyen, from Cochabamba, fought valiantly for the modernization of the whole educational system of Bolivia. He held that his country was far behind the European countries in that the clergy in those countries received a far better education than those in Bolivia. The European clergy were able to readjust religious activities in conformity with the demands of the time. He explained: "Este poder novador eleva la inteligencia del educando religiosa a la superficie del mando intelectual, en cuyos horizontes tiene que caminar el sacerdote con la sociedad a que preside; y, o ha de pertenecerla si es capaz de comprenderla, o está fuera de ella, y apartado de toda influencia, sino llega a cancebirla. En la babel del progreso, el sacerdote debe hablar todas las lenguas, si ha de conservar la alta importancia que merece. Que se niegue al Estado la acción directiva de la enseñanza religiosa; que esto se llegue a hacer en Bolivia, y no tardaremos en ver aparecer la escolástica por sistema de filosofía, falseada la historia, mutilada la ciencia y la inteligencia de una clase entera, lanzada en una retroacción que la lleve arriba de la corriente de los siglos, para detenerse en la edad media. En nombre de la instrucción del clero es que defiendo la dirección del Estado." Irigoyen also opposed the plan to negotiate with the Ab-legado Apostólico Monseñor Ignacio V. Eyzaguirre because the latter was the representative of Pope Pius IX, who had offered them the concordat of 1851. It was useless to hope for better terms than in 1851.

[2] *Redactor de la Asamblea Constituyente del año 1871*, pp. 870 ff. The incorporation of the provision for religious freedom in the colonies was undoubtedly the greatest victory achieved by the religious reformers up to that time. This was the beginning of the end of the monopoly of the Roman Catholic Church on public worship.

[3] *Redactor de la Convención Nacional del año 1880*, pp. 56 ff. It was in this session that Miguel de los Santos Taborga again played an eminent rôle, as he had in the Constituent Assembly of 1871. He was a staunch champion of the rights of the Church and felt that it was an insult to her to have to accept the restrictions placed upon her by the State. Despite his strenuous efforts to prevent such restrictions, the two legislatures incorporated the principle of the *patronato nacional* in the political constitutions adopted by them. It was too late for even a Taborga to secure the reversal of an ecclesiastical policy which the temporal power had practiced for more than three centuries. Because of the position occupied by Taborga in the public life of Bolivia, a brief biographical sketch of him will not be out of place here. He was born in the city of Sucre (then Chuquisaca) on July 5, 1833, and died there on December 12, 1905. He received an excellent education, and began to prepare himself for the priesthood at an early age. While still a young man he organized the Sociedad Católico-literaria, in which organization he had the support of Mariano Baptista, el Gran Tribuno, as he came to be called in later years. From the first Taborga fought the irreligiosity of his age, with a vehemence and a power matched only by that of his distinguished contemporary Gabriel García Moreno, of Ecuador. Taborga held, according to Luis Paz (in his *Colección de escritos de Luis Paz. Biografías*, pp. 151–229) that: "El clero es institución militante, y tiene el deber de combatir el error de la doctrina, la mentira y la impiedad, donde que se presenten." Like García Moreno, Taborga early became a writer and used his talents for the furtherance of religion. Like him, too, he made use of the press. He was also a great organizer. In 1852 he organized El Amigo de la Verdad, which was a power among the younger men. He represented Chuquisaca in the Congress for many years, and in 1887 he became minister of religion and did

of the principle of religious freedom in the colonies, which had been omitted from the Constitution of 1878. In 1893 Antonio Quizarro urged that Bolivia should free herself from dependence upon the Church. He declared in the Chamber of Deputies that the large power exercised by the Church in Bolivia was a heritage of the Spanish colonial period. It was necessary, he held, to separate the Church and the State in order to enable the Bolivian people to work out their own destiny.[1]

The movement for religious freedom did not gain any real momentum, however, until the Liberal Revolution of 1898–1899 overthrew the power of the conservative groups.[2] As soon as the revolution was well under way, the Liberals began to agitate for religious freedom with great earnestness. There are two leaders who stand out with considerable prominence, and who had to bear the brunt of the opposition forces. In the Chamber of Senators José D. Barrios sought to have that body pass legislation for religious freedom in 1901. In the same year, in the Chamber of Deputies, León M. Loza sought to secure the necessary legislation.[3] Both of these men failed at the time. The bill which

much good work for the Church. In 1898 he was elevated to the high position of archbishop of La Plata and continued in it until his death. He lived to see the *fuero eclesiástico* abolished, but was spared the mortification of the establishment of religious freedom. The *jacobinismo* which he had fought so strenuously to defeat was gaining its objectives, and is still marching on in his beloved Bolivia.

[1] Siles, *Derecho parlamentario de Bolivia*, vol. I, pp. 103–104.

[2] The Revolution of 1898–1899 was primarily the work of General Pando, who assumed command of the armed forces and attacked the national government. He received his support, at first, from the people of the North of the republic, but gradually the other parts of the country joined him. On May 11, 1899, he defeated the government forces and established a provisional government. By the end of that year the constitutional régime had been reestablished. The Liberal Revolution, however, was a failure, because it failed to set up a federal republic, which was one of the objects for which it was fought. The question of the form of the national government was discussed with great power and much warmth at the time, but the supporters of the unitary form were again victorious. The main argument of the Federalists was that the unitary system had failed, thus far, to bring about real unity in the republic and to establish genuine political democracy. The Unitarians countered with the argument that Bolivia was in no sense prepared for a federal form of government, because of the great size of the country, its sparse and heterogeneous population, the lack of the necessary means of communication and transportation, and more especially the great and keen sectionalism of its people. These arguments are still advanced whenever the question of a federal form of government for Bolivia is discussed, and the Federalists, of whom there is a rather large number, have never been able to achieve their objective. One of the main causes of the Revolution of 1898–1899 was the dissatisfaction of the people of the western section with the unwillingness of the people of the eastern sections to agree to the removal of the national capital from Sucre to La Paz. The effort of the Unitarians, however, failed, and the result has been, as we have noted in several places in this study, the strong emphasis upon the importance of La Paz as the *de facto* capital of the country.

[3] León M. Loza, to whom the author is greatly indebted for many courtesies extended to him while in La Paz and also for a great deal of information, had two purposes clearly in

Loza offered in the Chamber of Deputies was killed in committee. But the end of the power of the Roman Catholic Church in politics was approaching, for it was only a matter of a short time before the forces of religious freedom were to win. In the session of the Congress in 1904 the friends of this reform were powerful enough to demand serious respect. In the meantime the movement for religious freedom had assumed a more militant form. The leaders charged the Church with responsibility for the lack of morality, as well as for the large degree of illiteracy, among the Bolivian people. These leaders believed that many of the political and social ills of the country were due to these defects in the national character. Hence the Church became the object of very serious attacks, which it was not adequately prepared to meet successfully.

The movement for religious freedom had very strong support in the session of the Congress in 1905. In the discussions of the subject a great deal was made of the need of separating Church and State because of the bearing the ecclesiastical situation in the country had upon immigration. It was held that the economic life of the republic demanded immigrants, and these could only be attracted to Bolivia by assurances that their religious views would be legally protected. The minister of religion, Claudio Pinilla, favored religious freedom not because he was opposed to Roman Catholicism or the Roman Catholic Church, but because he believed that the welfare of the country demanded the separation of Church and State. Finally the measure for religious freedom won handsomely in the Chamber of Deputies, only five votes being cast against it. In the Chamber of Senators opinion was evenly divided, and feeling was more

---

mind in this reform movement. He wanted to deprive the Roman Catholic Church of Bolivia of its title and position as the official church of the state, and to establish complete religious freedom in the republic. Much of the honor, therefore, must go to Loza for the success of the movement. The measure introduced by him in the Chamber of Deputies was referred to the Constitutional Commission, composed of Antonio E. Pizarro, Carlos V. Romero, Daniel Salamanca, Angel Díaz de Medina, Luis Sainz, Francisco Anaya, and José M. Comacho. The Commission defeated the measure, as already noted, maintaining the strict orthodox view that the state has no power over religion. This paragraph explains its views: "Para la minoría informante, el estado social y político de Bolivia, no está convenientemente preparado a esa evolución; las clases sociales, casi en su totalidad, no aspiran a la reforma; el establecimiento del culto público de otras religiones, al lado o en contraposiciones al católico, produciría sacudimientos y resistencias, que el poder público mismo, encargado de hacer ejecutar la ley, sería impotente para dominarlas. Cuando menos la innovación sería impolítica y los desórdenes sociales tanto más profundos, cuanto que ellos nacerían del fondo de las conciencias y de las creencias religiosas tan difíciles de desarraigar, sino por el desarrollo lento y progresivo de las ideas, en todas sus manifestaciones." Consult Siles, *Derecho parlamentario de Bolivia*, vol. I, p. 72. The Commission on Religion, composed of C. Cornejo, N. Rivero, Antonio J. Espinosa, Gerónimo Otazo, and José Orias, approved the measure. Consult *Proyectos e informes*, pp. 204, 206, for the precise form of the reports of these commissions. Thus, while Loza did not achieve his objectives, the Roman Catholic Church being still the state church, he did achieve a very great victory and deserves high honor for the part he took in this famous contest.

intense. In the debates in that body, the opponents of the reform declared that the overwhelming majority of the Bolivian people were members of the Roman Catholic Church, and that probably not more than 25,000 were not members of that Church. The opponents also belittled the view of the supporters of the movement for religious toleration that immigrants and other aliens deserved to have their religious views respected. The foreigners who came to Bolivia, it was declared, came for the primary purpose of accumulating wealth, and could hardly be in a position to ask privileges in matters of religion. One of the most powerful men in the Chamber of Senators in favor of the reform was José Carrasco. He made a great deal of the fact that out of the fifty-six members of the Chamber of Deputies all but five had voted for the reform measure. Arrieto urged that the Roman Catholic Church of Bolivia should break away from Rome and establish an independent church body in the republic. When the vote in the Chamber of Senators was finally taken on the measure, nine votes were cast in favor and five against it. The Chamber decided that the nine votes constituted a two-thirds vote of the Senate, which was necessary to pass the bill.[1] The Law of October 27, 1906, was the result. It abolished the *fuero eclesiastico* as well as all other *fueros* (privileges), and declared that the law would henceforth recognize no *fuero* whatsoever in civil and penal matters.[2]

Another question which gave the non-Roman Catholics a great deal of concern was that of marriage. Under the old régime a marriage must be solemnized with the approval of the Church, and by a person designated by it. The result was the enactment of the Law of October 11, 1911, on civil marriage. The law declared that the only marriage that would be considered legal in Bolivia was the civil marriage.[3] On March 19, 1912, the Reglamento del Matrimonio

[1] Paz, *Constitución política de la república de Bolivia*, p. 40, note 1. Paz declares that the "reforma del art. 2° de la constitución fué sancionada con violación de las garantías establecidas por ella." Earlier he had declared: "La fe es hija de la persuación. Imponerla por la persecución y la fuerza es atentar a una de nuestras esenciales libertades. La libertad de conciencia sufre y se anonada con la cocrción." To which the supporters of the reform movement replied that no question of conscience was involved. It was a question of giving to all the people a right to decide for themselves the religion they wanted. Under the established régime there had been no such freedom of choice, and hence coercion had been practiced upon the non-Roman Catholics by the Roman Catholics. Paz could not understand how nine could be two-thirds of thirteen, the number of senators voting on the bill. It certainly was not two-thirds of the total membership of the Chamber of Senators, or fourteen.

[2] Siles, *Derecho parlamentario de Bolivia*, vol. I, p. 121. At about the same time the number of Church holidays was reduced. The Law of December 19, 1905, was in accordance with the wish of Pope Gregory XVI, who approved of the law because it gave more time for labor. The only holidays were to be such as had been designated by law (*ibid*., pp. 166–167, 170–171, 174–175).

[3] *Ibid*., pp. 175–177. The measure was discussed a long time before it was passed. The Roman Catholic Church fought it bitterly, but was unable to prevent its passage. The fina

Civil was issued, and prescribed in detail the marriage procedure according to that law.[1] The Decree of August 31, 1920, exempted Indians from the civil marriage law. They were to be married according to the canonical law alone, and the marriage was to have the force of that by civil law.[2] The Decree of August 11, 1921, provided for a register for the marriage of Indians and dissidents.[3] The Circular of August 30, 1921, provided that Indians who were not

---

vote was fifty-three to twenty-two in the Chamber of Deputies, and five to five in the Chamber of Senators, the president casting the deciding vote for the measure.

[1] Araoz, *Nuevo digesto*, vol. I, pp. 328–330. The canonical or religious marriage ceremony may be performed only after the civil ceremony has been performed. No civil marriage can legally take place without the proper license. The contracting parties must furnish specific information. They must have resided three months in the community in which they are to be married. Both must present evidence to show that there are no impediments or prohibitions against contracting the marriage. The marriage ceremony must be performed within twenty days after the license has been issued. The date and place of the marriage must be publicly displayed in the office of the *oficial del registro*. Any person may object to the marriage and the charges must be fully investigated. There can be no marriage until the truth or falsity of the accusation has been determined. A marriage certificate is supplied to those who have been married by the proper authorities. Consuls and consular agents may perform the marriage ceremony of Bolivians in foreign countries. The marriage of first cousins is prohibited. The Reglamento sobre la Formación de Legajos y Registros Matrimoniales was issued on November 17, 1916. Again the whole procedure was prescribed in detail. The *reglamento* made the securing of a license for the marriage ceremony more difficult. A baptismal certificate was required, or proof of such a document. There must be written consent of the parents or the guardians of the contracting parties. A widow must furnish evidence that she is a widow. Indians and those who are too poor to meet the expense of these documents need not have them, but may produce proof of the information required in lieu of them. The monetary cost of the marriage ceremony is such as to deter many from contracting matrimony legally, and cause them to enter marital relations without the benefit of such civil sanction (*ibid.*, pp. 335–337).

[2] *Ibid.*, p. 334. The Indians have not always been treated humanely even by the Catholic Church. The Roman Catholic Church is a powerful and a complex institution, and the requirements for its upkeep are exacting, and bear heavily on the people financially. Unfortunately the burden falls, in Bolivia as elsewhere, upon those who are least able to bear it. It is here that the Indians often come in for very unfair treatment. In addition to regular contributions, they are frequently called upon to bear expenses other than those required of the average person. One of the most common, and at the same time one of the most natural, is that connected with the visits of the *curas*. The visit is often, almost always, an expensive affair for the poor Indians. The *cura* must, of course, be properly received, hence his visit must be adequately prepared for. An *alferesado* is appointed to have charge of the preparations. He must secure the necessary provisions, such as potatoes, *chuño*, eggs, lambs, etc. These are presents for the *cura*, and they grow in amount by the time he has concluded his visit. The *cura* may, and often does, sell the surplus at a very high price. There are many *curas* who will not tolerate such elaborate preparations, but on the whole the number who do tolerate and even encourage them is much too large. The practice is one that has grown with the times and has become a part of the life of the clergy and the Indians. But that should make the reform of such practices all the more necessary.

[3] *Ibid.*, p. 334.

members of the Roman Catholic Church should be married according to civil law, and that this service might be performed by the *curas*.[1] The *Resolución Suprema* of May 10, 1923, provided that the civil marriage law should also apply to laborers, muleteers (*arrieros*), farm hands (*estancieros*), and country laborers (*campasinos*) in the Apostolic Province of Gran Chaco.[2]

This concludes, in the large, the account of the movement for religious toleration in Bolivia. It is possible to say that the law which gave religious freedom to the Bolivian people was not enacted in strict conformity with constitutional procedure, as Luis Paz contended; and that ill feeling and hatreds were created that will hamper the movement for an enlightened administration of the ecclesiastical affairs of the republic. On the other hand, it should be borne in mind that such a reform of the political Constitution was long overdue. Moreover, it may be, in the long run, best for the Roman Catholic Church itself. It must be distinctly borne in mind that the attack upon the exclusive power of that Church was not an attack upon Roman Catholicism or upon religion *per se*. It was primarily an attack upon a clericalism that had come to be an obstacle in the path of the larger progress of the Bolivian people. After all, the purpose of the anticlericals of Bolivia has been only that of the anticlericals of other countries: the separation of the temporal from the spiritual power. Roman Catholicism in Bolivia is in no immediate danger from any other religion. Its people are steeped in the tenets of Roman Catholicism, and are likely to continue so for many years. In the meantime, a reform in certain practices of the Roman Catholic Church, especially in the way of better preparation of its clergy, may come about, to the grandeur and glory of the Church itself as well as its people. For in spite of its defects the Roman Catholic Church has done an infinite amount of good. No one, not even its greatest critic, will deny that fact. The future of the Roman Catholic Church in Bolivia lies largely with that Church itself.

[1] Araoz, *Nuevo digesto*, vol. I, p. 335.

[2] *Ibid*., p. 334, note.

APPENDIX A

POLITICAL CONSTITUTION OF THE REPUBLIC OF BOLIVIA (1931)[1]

SECTION ONE
THE NATION

ARTICLE 1. Bolivia, free and independent, constituted as a unitary Republic, adopts the democratic representative form of government.

ART. 2. The State recognizes and supports the Roman Catholic Apostolic religion, permitting the exercise of all other public worship.

SECTION TWO
RIGHTS AND GUARANTIES

ART. 3. Slavery does not exist in Bolivia. When a slave sets foot upon the territory of the Republic he becomes free.

ART. 4. Everyone has the right to enter the Republic, remain therein, travel in it, leave it, without any other restrictions than those established by international law; to work and engage in any lawful business; to publish his ideas through the press without previous censorship; to teach, under the supervision of the State, without any other conditions than those of ability and morality; to enter into associations; to assemble peaceably, and to petition individually or collectively.

Primary instruction shall be free and compulsory.

ART. 5. No one shall be arrested, detained, or imprisoned, except in the cases and in accordance with the forms established by law. No warrants of arrest shall be obeyed which have not been issued by the competent authorities. The warrant shall be in writing.

ART. 6.[2] Everyone believing himself unlawfully detained, persecuted, or imprisoned shall have the right to appear in person or through someone else, with or without notarial power, before the superior court of the district, or before the judge of the partido, as he may choose, to demand the protection of the law. The judicial authorities shall immediately order such person to appear before them, such order to be obeyed without objection or excuse, by those in charge of the prisons or the houses of detention. When the authorities have been informed of the charges against

[1] Promulgated September 26, 1931. This Constitution is given here, instead of that of 1938, for the reason explained in the foreword, page iv. It is the Constitution adopted on October 27, 1880, with the amendments of October 3, 1910, and those of the referendum authorized by the Decree-Law (*Decreto-Ley*) of February 27, 1931.

This translation is based upon the translation of the Constitution of 1880, with the amendments up to 1907, in Rodríguez, *American constitutions*, vol. II, pp. 413–452. Many changes have, however, been made throughout the document. The amendments made in 1930–1931 have been duly noted.

[2] Article 6 was added in 1931.

the accused they shall order his release, if innocent, or his detention, if guilty. In the latter case they shall order him tried by a competent tribunal. The decision of the tribunal may be appealed to the Supreme Court of Justice, but such appeal shall not suspend the execution of the verdict.

Public functionaries or individuals who resist judicial decisions, as explained in this article, shall be considered criminals against the constitutional guaranties, at all times, and shall not be excused on the ground that they acted on instruction from superior officers.

ART. 7. Every offender caught *in flagrante delicto* may be arrested by any person, even without a warrant, if this is done for the purpose of taking him before the proper authority, who must examine him within a period not to exceed twenty-four hours.

ART. 8. The wardens of prisons shall admit only those who have been legally arrested, imprisoned, or detained, and shall enter the warrant for such arrest, imprisonment, or detention upon the register. They shall retain those who have been arrested for the purpose of bringing them before the proper judge. In such cases they are under obligation to report the fact to the judge within twenty-four hours.

ART. 9. All who make attacks upon the rights of personal security shall be held responsible. The fact that such attacks were ordered by a superior authority shall not be accepted as an excuse.

ART. 10. No one shall be tried by special commissions, or by other courts than those established previously to the time of the offense. Only those who are under military jurisdiction may be tried by military tribunals.

The military privilege (*fuero militar*) is abolished except in the case of the military in war, in accordance with article 26 of the Constitution.

Military officers in active service shall be tried by their chiefs and authorities in conformity with their regulations and ordinances.[1]

ART. 11. No one shall be compelled to testify against himself in a criminal cause, nor shall a blood relation up to the fourth degree inclusive, or of the second degree of affinity, be bound to testify against him.

In no case shall torture of any kind be used.

ART. 12. Confiscation of property shall never be made as a punishment for political offenses.

Private correspondence and papers are inviolable and may not be seized except in cases determined by law and by written order of the competent authority. Intercepted letters and private papers seized in violation of this provision shall have no legal effect.

ART. 13. The domicile is an inviolable asylum. It may not be entered at night without the consent of those inhabiting it, and it may be entered in the daytime only by means of a written order of the lawful authority, except in cases of *in flagrante delicto*. No soldier may be billeted in a private house in time of peace without the consent of the owner; nor in time of war except in the manner prescribed by law.

ART. 14. Private property is inviolable. It may not be condemned except for public use and in accordance with law. The property seized must in every case be paid for in advance.

ART. 15. No tax shall be collected unless levied by the authority of the Legislative

[1] The last two paragraphs of article 10 were added in 1931.

Power and in conformity with the provisions of this Constitution. Any person may apply to the proper judicial authorities for claims against illegal taxation.

Municipal taxes must be paid when levied in accordance with the principles established by this Constitution.

ART. 16. No money shall be withdrawn from the national, departmental, municipal, or educational treasuries unless the expenses have been authorized in the respective appropriations. A quarterly account of the public expenses shall be published within sixty days, at the latest, after the expiration of the quarter.

The minister of the treasury shall publish the accounts of the national expenses, and the superintendents those of their respective departments.

ART. 17. Equality is the basis of taxation and of all public obligations. No personal service shall be required of anyone which is not in accordance with the law or judicial verdict.

ART. 18. The landed property belonging to the church and the property of charitable, educational, and municipal establishments or religious corporations shall enjoy the same guaranties enjoyed by the property of private individuals.

ART. 19. The public debt is guaranteed. All obligations contracted by the State in conformity with law are inviolable.

ART. 20. Everyone enjoys civil rights in Bolivia, the exercise of which shall be regulated by the civil law.

ART. 21. The Legislative Power alone has the authority to alter or amend the codes or to enact rules or provisions concerning judicial procedure.

ART. 22. The death penalty is abolished, except in cases of assassination, parricide, and treason. Treason to the country means complicity with the enemy in time of a foreign war.

ART. 23. The penalities of infamy and civil death are abolished.

ART. 24. The acts of those who usurp public functions are null and void, as are also the acts of those who exercise jurisdiction or power not emanating from the law.

ART. 25. The principles, guaranties, and rights recognized in the foregoing articles shall not be changed by the laws intended to regulate their exercise.

ART. 26. Those guilty of violating constitutional guaranties and rights shall enjoy no jurisdictional privileges, and shall be subject to the regular jurisdiction.

SECTION THREE
THE ECONOMIC AND SOCIAL ORDER[1]

ART. 27. The right of the Executive Power to make contracts, loans, and concessions to railroads and guaranties and other acts which compromise the credit of the Republic, which affects the economy that the government must bring about by legislative action, must first receive the approval of the National Economic Council (*Consejo de Economía Nacional*), established in conformity with the laws which define and regulate this institution. The said Council shall be composed of representatives from the mining, manufacturing, banking, and transportational industries, from organized bodies and others having economic capacity, and from the laboring classes. The representation in the Council shall be equitably proportionate.

All projects and modifications in the laws on work and social economy shall be

[1] This entire section was added in 1931.

submitted to this Council for approval. The Council shall have the right to defend its decisions in the Legislative Power through a representative, who shall have no vote but shall have the right to take part in its deliberations. The Council shall also have the power to initiate laws for that purpose in the two chambers of the legislature.

ART. 28. All concessions for exploitation, improvements, or businesses of the country shall be considered national, and shall be subject to the sovereignty, laws, and authorities of the Nation.

ART. 29. The laws shall guarantee to manual laborers the maximum working hours in a day and a day of rest in a week of seven days.

ART. 30. All employers are obliged to maintain conditions that will protect the life and health of their employees, in accordance with the nature and circumstances of each industry.

ART. 31. The Legislative Power shall enact laws which shall prohibit the entry into, and the expulsion from, the country of criminal and foreign agitators, and those who have infectious and contagious diseases.

SECTION FOUR

PRESERVATION OF PUBLIC ORDER

ART. 32. The Chief Executive may, in cases of grave danger to the Republic from internal commotion or foreign war, with the approval of the Council of Ministers, declare such portions of the country as may be necessary in a state of siege, which shall be continued as long as necessary.

If the Congress convenes in regular or special session during the state of siege of the whole or a part of the Republic, the state of siege can only continue through a special act of the Congress. Such authorization shall be necessary even though the Chief Executive has decreed the state of siege.

The state of siege shall automatically cease at the end of ninety days, even though it has not been terminated by the Chief Executive, except in case of an international or civil war. Those who have been prosecuted during the state of siege are to be set at liberty at the end of the same, unless they shall have been condemned by competent judicial tribunals.

The Chief Executive may not continue the state of siege by decree for more than ninety days, nor declare another state of siege within the same year without express permission of the Congress, called for that purpose either in a regular or a special session, if in the recess of that body.[1]

ART. 33. The declaration of the state of siege shall have the following effects:

1. The Chief Executive shall have the power to increase the standing army and may call out the national guard for active service.

2. The Executive shall have the power to collect in advance such portions of the national taxes and revenues as may be necessary, and to raise, in the form of a loan, a sufficient sum of money in case the expenses cannot be met by the ordinary revenues.

The Executive shall fix, in case of forced loans, the quota required of each Department. It shall be the duty of the municipal councils to distribute this contribution among the property owners in their respective districts.

3. The Executive may reduce the payment of the civil and ecclesiastical lists, and

[1] The last three paragraphs of article 32 were added in 1931.

of the sums allowed to the several municipalities, this reduction to be made in such proportion as may be required to cover the necessary military expenses caused by the disturbance in the public order. The said reduction shall not exceed fifty per cent of the amounts fixed in the appropriations law.

4. The guaranties and rights established by this Constitution shall not be suspended *de facto* in general through the declaration of the state of siege. They may be suspended in regard to individuals charged upon good grounds with conspiring against the tranquillity of the Republic. This suspension shall take place in the manner set forth in the following paragraphs:

5. The legitimate authority may issue summonses or orders of arrest against the persons mentioned in the foregoing paragraph; but the persons arrested shall be placed at the disposal of a competent court, within seventy-two hours, if possible, from the moment of the arrest, and all the documents that have given authority for the arrest and the record of the judicial investigations made shall be forwarded to the court. If the proceedings cannot be instituted within the said time, the case may be postponed until public order is established; but in no case, except that of amnesty, shall the proceedings be omitted.

Should the maintenance of public peace necessitate the transportation of the suspected persons to some place, the authorities may order it, provided it is not to a greater distance than fifty leagues or to an unhealthy locality. The banishment or arrest can only take place in the event that the suspected or accused person does not prefer to leave the Republic.

Exile for political reasons is abolished; but a request by the person confined, prosecuted, or arrested for political reasons for a passport to a foreign country may not be refused for any reason whatsoever; and the authorities shall provide the protection required by the law.

Functionaries who shall act contrary to these guaranties shall be punished, after the state of siege has expired, as criminals against constituted authorities.[1]

6. The Chief Executive may also withhold or retain private correspondence, without tampering with it, and reestablish the use of passports for those entering or leaving the territory declared in a state of siege.

ART. 34. The Government shall submit to the Congress at its next session a report on the reasons why the state of siege was declared and the use made by it of the powers vested in it by Section Four of the Constitution, setting forth the result of the judicial proceedings instituted during the same, and suggesting the measures indispensable to meet the debts incurred, whether in the shape of direct loans or in that of reduction of the indebtedness for taxes or payment of the same in advance.[2]

ART. 35. The Congress shall devote its first meetings to the examination of the reports referred to in the preceding article, and either approve them or fix the responsibility incurred by the Executive Power.

The Chambers shall have the power to make all the necessary inquiries concerning the matters referred to in the above paragraph, and ask the Executive for an explana-

[1] The last paragraph was added in 1931.

[2] As amended by the Law of December 2, 1902.

tion of its acts in connection with the state of siege, even if the said acts are not mentioned in the reports presented to the Congress.[1]

ART. 36. Neither the Congress nor any association or public gathering shall have authority to grant to the Executive extraordinary faculties, or complete power, or give to it supremacy by which the life, honor, and property of the Bolivian people should be at the mercy of the Government or of any person whatever.

Deputies who initiate, favor, or carry out these acts shall become, by so doing, unworthy of the confidence of the Nation.[2]

The personal inviolability and the immunities established by this Constitution in favor of the representatives of the Nation shall not be suspended during the state of siege.[3]

SECTION FIVE

BOLIVIANS

ART. 37. Bolivians by birth are:

1. Those born in the territory of the Republic.

2. Those born in a foreign country of a Bolivian father or mother who was in the service of the Republic, or who emigrated for political reasons. These shall be held to be Bolivians even in case a special law may require actual nativity.

ART. 38. The following are also Bolivians:

1. Children of Bolivian fathers or mothers, born in a foreign country, by the simple fact of acquiring domicile in Bolivia.

2. Foreigners who, having resided one year in the Republic, shall declare before the municipal authorities of the place where they live their desire to become Bolivians.

3. Foreigners who, as a concession, have obtained letters of naturalization from the Chamber of Deputies.

SECTION SIX

CITIZENSHIP

ART. 39. To be a citizen it is necessary:

1. To be a Bolivian.

2. To be twenty-one years of age if unmarried, or eighteen if married.

3. To be able to read and write, to own real estate, or to have an income of two hundred bolivianos, provided that this amount does not represent wages received for work as a domestic.

4. To be inscribed in the civil register.

ART. 40. Citizenship confers the right to:

1. Concur in the Constitution or in the exercise of public powers, either as an elector, or as an eligible candidate.

2. Be eligible for all public functions, with no other requisite than that of fitness, with the exceptions established by this Constitution.

[1] As amended by the Law of December 2, 1902.

[2] The first two paragraphs of article 36 constitute an amendment by the Law of December 2, 1902.

[3] The last paragraph was added by the Law of December 2, 1902.

Art. 41. The rights of citizenship are lost by:

1. Naturalization in a foreign country.

2. Judicial sentences passed by a competent tribunal inflicting any form of corporal punishment, until rehabilitation is obtained.

3. Declaration of fraudulent bankruptcy.

4. Acceptance of employment, office, or decorations from a foreign government without special permission from the Senate.

Art. 42. The rights of citizenship are suspended and shall remain *sub judice*, as long as the citizen is under indictment or subject to a writ of execution for debt to the national treasury.

Section Seven
Sovereignty

Art. 43. Sovereignty is vested essentially in the nation, is inalienable and imprescriptible, and its exercise is delegated to the legislative, executive, and judicial powers. The independence of these three powers is the basis of the Government.

Art. 44. The people deliberate or govern only through their representatives and the authorities established by the Constitution. All armed forces or gatherings of individuals assuming the exercise of the rights of the people shall be guilty of sedition.

Section Eight
The Legislative Power

Art. 45. The Legislative Power resides in the Congress, composed of two Chambers, one of Deputies and the other of Senators.

Art. 46. The Congress shall meet in regular session every year in the capital of the Republic on the sixth day of August, even though it has not been previously formally convened. The session shall last for sixty working days, which may be extended to ninety, at the will of the Congress itself, or at the request of the Executive Power.

Art. 47. The Executive may, in case it considers that there exist grave reasons against the Congress' meeting in regular session in the capital of the Republic, cause the Congress to meet in some other place.

Art. 48. The Congress may meet in special session when an absolute majority of the two chambers shall desire it, or when the Executive may desire a special session, in which case the place of meeting shall be determined by the one convoking it.

The Congress must, in either case, occupy itself exclusively with the business for which it was called.

Art. 49. The two chambers of the Congress shall meet at the same time and in the same city, with the attendance of at least an absolute majority of their members. No house shall open or close its sessions on a different day from the other.

Art. 50. A deputy or senator may be made president or vice-president of the Republic, a minister of state, a diplomatic agent, or a military commander in time of war, but shall be suspended from the exercise of his legislative functions so long as he continues in any one of those positions.

The vice-president shall not be suspended from his legislative functions, except when occupying the presidency or any of the other aforesaid positions.

Art. 51. No deputy or senator shall accept a position whose appointment or removal depends upon the Executive, except in cases provided in the foregoing article. Civil, ecclesiastic, and military employees whose appointment and removal depend wholly upon the Executive may not be deputies or senators from any electoral district. Neither may any other paid functionary be elected deputy or senator for the electoral district in which he exercises jurisdiction or authority.

Art. 52. The deputies and senators are inviolable at all times for the opinions expressed by them in the discharge of their duties.

Art. 53. No senator or deputy shall be accused, prosecuted, or arrested from the day of his election to the time he returns to his residence, without the consent of the chamber to which he belongs, except when caught *in flagrante delicto*, and if such an offense renders him liable to corporal punishment. Neither shall a senator or deputy be sued civilly during a period of seventy days prior to the opening of the Congress and during the period necessary for him to return to his domicile. In no case may such arrest take place without the previous order of the chamber to which he belongs, or during the period described above.

The members of the Congress may, during their constitutional term of office, make representations to the Executive Power for the enforcement of the laws and resolutions of the Congress. They may also present the needs of their respective electoral districts and may suggest the manner in which these shall be met.

Art. 54. The sessions of the Congress and of the two chambers shall be public, but they may be held behind closed doors when two-thirds of the members so order.

Art. 55. When a citizen is elected senator and deputy at one and the same time, he shall choose the senate.

Art. 56. When a citizen is elected deputy or senator for two different districts or departments, he shall be free to accept either.

Art. 57. The senators and representatives may resign their positions at will.

Art. 58. The senators and representatives shall receive a regular salary (*dietas*) for each session which they attend. This salary shall be fixed in the regular budget by a special law, changes in which shall go into effect only after two years from the time they are approved.

Art. 59. The Congress shall have power to:

1. Enact laws, and repeal, amend, or interpret them.

2. Levy taxes and imposts of all kinds, abolish those in force, and determine, if necessary, their distribution among the departments and provinces.

3. Fix the expenses of the public administration in each legislative session.

4. Fix also the strength of the armed forces to be maintained in time of peace in each legislative session. The taxes shall be levied only for eighteen months at a time. The armed forces shall continue for the same period of time.

5. Authorize the Executive to contract loans, and provide the funds necessary to pay the interest and the capital. And recognize the debts contracted and provide the means for paying them.

6. Create new departments or provinces, and determine their boundaries. Create ports of entry and establish customhouses.

7. Fix the weight, fineness, value, type, and denomination of the national coins.

Authorize the issue and circulation of bank notes. And regulate the system of weights and measures.

8. Grant subsidies and guarantee the interest for the construction of railroads, canals, post roads, and any other means of communication.

9. Permit the transit of foreign troops across the territory of the Republic, and determine the period of their stay therein.

10. Permit the bodies of the permanent army to be stationed in the place where the sessions of the Congress are held or within a radius of ten leagues.

11. Permit the national troops to leave the territory of the Republic, fixing the time of their return.

12. Create and abolish public offices, determining or modifying their functions and fixing their salaries.

13. Decree amnesties and grant individual pardons after hearing the opinion of the Supreme Court.

14. Approve or reject treaties or conventions of all kinds.

Section Nine
The Congress

Art. 60. Each chamber shall be the judge of the election of its own members, and shall have power to suspend or expel the same, to punish all violations of its rules, to organize the office of its secretary, to appoint all the employees in its service, to make the estimates of its expenses and order the payment thereof, and to attend to everything relating to its internal government and external protection.

Art. 61. The two chambers of the Congress shall meet in joint session to:

1. Open and close their sessions.

2. Examine the certificates of election of the President and Vice-President of the Republic, and scrutinize the votes. And to elect these officers when the electors fail to do so in conformity with articles 91, 92, 93, and 94.

3. Administer the oath of office to the officials named in the preceding paragraph.

4. Accept or refuse to accept the resignation of these officers.

5. Approve or reject treaties and public conventions negotiated by the Executive Power.

6. Reconsider the bills vetoed by the Executive.

7. Declare war upon request of the Executive.

8. Approve or disapprove the accounts of the Public Treasury to the Executive.

9. Determine the strength of the permanent armed force.

10. Decide the conflicts of jurisdiction between it and the Executive or the Supreme Court of Justice, by a two-thirds vote; and by an absolute majority of votes those conflicts of these powers with each other, or between the district courts and the Court of Cassation.

11. Grant pecuniary rewards, but only by a two-thirds vote.

12. Examine the account made by the Executive Power of the use of the state of siege, and the legislative authorization for the same.

13. Elect the president and the ministers of the Supreme Court of Justice.[1]

[1] Clauses 11, 12, and 13 of article 61 were added in 1931.

ART. 62. The Congress may not delegate to one or more of its members, nor to any other power, the functions that are given to it by this Constitution.

SECTION TEN

THE CHAMBER OF DEPUTIES

ART. 63. This chamber shall be composed of deputies elected directly by the citizens, by a simple plurality of votes. A special law shall regulate these elections and fix the number of deputies to be elected.

ART. 64. To be a deputy it is necessary:

1. To be inscribed in the national register.

2. To be twenty-five years of age, a Bolivian citizen by birth, or if by naturalization, to have had at least five years' permanent residence in the Republic, and enjoy an annual income of four hundred bolivianos derived from a profession, industry, or real property.

3. Not to have been condemned to corporal punishment by an ordinary tribunal.

ART. 65. The deputies shall serve for a term of four years, half the membership being renewed every two years. The first Congress shall determine by lot those who will retire at the end of the first two years.

ART. 66. The right to originate legislation in the matters explained in clauses 2, 3, 4, and 5 of article 59 belongs exclusively to the Chamber of Deputies.

ART. 67. The Chamber of Deputies has the power to:

1. Impeach the President and the Vice-President of the Republic, the ministers of state, the ministers of the Supreme Court of Justice, and the diplomatic agents before the Senate for offenses committed in the discharge of their respective functions.

2. Elect the members of the National Tribunal of Accounts. These members shall hold office for a term of six years, with the right of reelection, and may not be removed from office except by a sentence of the Supreme Court of Justice.[1]

SECTION ELEVEN

THE CHAMBER OF SENATORS

ART. 68. The Senate of the Republic shall be composed of two senators from each department.

ART. 69. To be a senator it is necessary:

1. To be a Bolivian by birth, or if by naturalization, to have had five years' permanent residence in the country, and to be inscribed in the national register.[2]

2. To be thirty-five years of age.

3. To be in possession of an annual income of eight hundred bolivianos, derived from a profession, industry, or real property.

[1] The present clause 2 of article 67 was added in 1931. The old clause 2 dealt with the manner of selecting the members of the Supreme Court and was as follows:

"To elect the justices of the Supreme Court upon nomination, three names for each position, made by the Senate."

[2] Clause 1 of article 69 was changed in 1931 to provide for a residential period of from four to five years. The four-year clause was repealed by the Law of December 2, 1902.

4. Not to have been sentenced by the ordinary courts of justice to corporal punishment.

ART. 70. The senators shall serve for six years, and may be reelected indefinitely.

The Senate shall be renewed by thirds every two years. The senators who are to retire at the end of each period shall be determined by lot.

ART. 71. The Chamber of Senators shall have power to:

1. Hear accusations by the Chamber of Deputies against the functionaries named in article 67. The Senate shall, in this case, limit its action to deciding whether or not there is ground for the prosecution. If the decision is in the affirmative, the accused official shall be suspended and placed at the disposal of the Supreme Court, to be tried by it in accordance with law.

The Senate shall have final jurisdiction in impeachment of the ministers of the Supreme Court, and shall exact of them the proper responsibility, whether the accusations proceed from the Chamber of Deputies, from the complaint of injured parties, or from information from a private citizen.

A majority of two-thirds of the votes of the members present shall be required in the cases mentioned in the two foregoing paragraphs.

A special law shall regulate the course of the proceedings and the formalities to be observed in these trials.

2. Submit a list of names of ecclesiastics from which the Executive shall propose to the canonical authorities nominees for archbishop and bishops.

3. Submit a list of names to the Chamber of Deputies from which it shall elect members of the National Tribunal of Accounts.[1]

4. Restore to Bolivian nationality or citizenship, as the case may be, those who have lost it.

5. Permit Bolivians to accept honors, offices, titles, or emoluments from foreign governments, providing this does not contravene the laws of the Republic on that subject.

6. Elect by secret ballot from among a list of three persons nominated for that position by the Executive Power the generals and colonels of the regular army.

7. Grant rewards and public honors to those who may deserve them for services rendered to the Republic.

SECTION TWELVE

ENACTMENT AND PROMULGATION OF LAWS AND RESOLUTIONS

ART. 72. Laws may originate in the Senate or in the Chamber of Deputies, introduced by one of their members, or by a message of the President of the Republic. In the latter case, the measure must be supported in the course of the debate by one of the ministers of state, who shall have no vote.

The cases enumerated in article 66 shall not be included in this provision.

ART. 73. Measures passed in the chamber of origin shall be forwarded immediately to the other chamber for discussion and concurrence during the session.

[1] Clause 3 of article 71 under the old regulations prescribed the manner in which the ministers of the Supreme Court were to be elected. The Senate nominated and the Chamber of Deputies elected the members of the said Court.

Art. 74. Measures rejected in the chamber of origin shall not be reintroduced in either chamber until the next session.

Art. 75. When the measure is rejected in its entirety by the revising chamber, the chamber of origin shall take it up anew. If a two-thirds majority of the members present shall insist upon its passage, it shall be sent again to the revising chamber. The latter chamber must, in order to reject it a second time, disapprove of it by a majority of two-thirds of the members present. The measure shall be considered passed if it is not rejected by this majority of votes.

When the measure is rejected, or when the chamber of origin refuses to insist upon its passage, it shall not be reintroduced the same year.

Art. 76. When the revising chamber confines its action to amending the measure, the chamber of origin shall consider that it has been accepted if the revising chamber concurs in the action by an absolute majority of votes. When the amendment is not accepted or amended, the two chambers shall meet in joint session to debate the subject, under the direction of the president of the Senate. If the measure passes as amended, it shall be sent to the Executive for promulgation as a law of the Republic; if it fails to pass, it shall not again be reintroduced until a subsequent session.

Art. 77. All bills sanctioned by the two chambers may be vetoed by the President of the Republic within ten days from the date on which he receives them, providing the minister of state in whose department the bills belong was not present during the discussion of the bills in the Congress.

Measures which are approved by the President of the Republic within the prescribed period shall be promulgated as laws. If the Congress adjourns before the expiration of the said period, the President of the Republic shall publish the message containing his objections in the official newspaper, in order that they may be taken up for consideration in the next session of the Congress.

Art. 78. Objections to the measure by the Executive shall be addressed to the chamber where the bill originated. If the two chambers concur in the objections and amend the measure in accordance with the objections, the measure as amended shall be returned to the Executive for promulgation.

If the two chambers shall, by a majority of two-thirds of the members present, find the objections of the President of the Republic upon the measure groundless, the President of the Republic shall be bound to promulgate the measure as a law.

When the President of the Republic shall refuse to promulgate the law, the president of the Senate shall do so.

Art. 79. When the subject of discussion in the chambers is merely a resolution of their own exclusive concern, the approval of the two chambers shall be sufficient. The promulgation of the measure shall, in that case, be made by the presidents of the two chambers assisted by their secretaries, and not by the Executive.

The course of the proceedings to be followed in the cases referred to above for the regulation of debates and the decisions concerning the relations between the chamber of origin and the revising chamber shall be the same as those established for regular measures.

Art. 80. The chambers may, on motion of any one of their members, pass a vote of censure on the mere political acts of the Executive, provided that it is addressed to the ministers of state separately or jointly, as the case may be, and provided also that its only purpose is that of obtaining a modification in the political action of the Executive.

For the exercise of this power, the decision of the chamber where the subject was introduced, taken by an absolute majority of votes, shall be sufficient.

ART. 81. The promulgation of the laws shall be made by the President of the Republic in this form:

"Whereas the National Congress has sanctioned the following law:—I hereby promulgate it, and order it to be kept and obeyed as a law of the Republic."

The congressional resolutions shall be promulgated in the following form:

"The National Congress of the Republic decrees:—Therefore this decree shall be observed and obeyed in accordance with the Constitution."

SECTION THIRTEEN

THE EXECUTIVE POWER

ART. 82. The Executive Power shall be vested in a citizen, to be known as the President of the Republic, and this power can only be exercised by him through the ministers of state.

ART. 83. The constitutional term of office of the President of the Republic shall be four years unprorogued (*cuatro años improrogables*), but he shall not be reelected until eight years shall have elapsed from the end of the presidential term.[1]

ART. 84. When the President of the Republic shall fail, during his term of office, to perform his duties, either through resignation, disability, or death, the Vice-President, who shall be elected jointly with him, as provided in the preceding article, shall be called to fill his place until the constitutional term has come to an end.[2]

When the President of the Republic shall place himself at the head of the army, in case of foreign or civil war, he shall also be replaced by the Vice-President.

ART. 85. The Vice-President may not be reelected, nor may he be elected President of the Republic, until eight years have elapsed, in case he has exercised the Executive Power in order to serve out the term of the President of the Republic.

When there is no Vice-President, the president of the Senate or of the Chamber of Deputies shall assume the duties of the President of the Republic, the second in case there is no first.[3]

ART. 86. Only those citizens of the Republic who have the qualifications required of the Senators, and who, in addition, are Bolivians by birth, shall be elected President and Vice-President of the Republic.

The President and Vice-President of the Republic shall receive, during their term of office, an annual salary determined by law. This salary shall not be increased or decreased during their term of office. Neither shall they receive any other kind of remuneration whatever.

[1] Article 83 established a constitutional term of four years for the President of the Republic, and also doubled the period between the end of the constitutional presidential term and re-election of that official, should he seek such reelection.

[2] Article 84 provides for only one Vice-President, whereas the Constitution of 1880 provided for two such officers.

[3] There is no change in article 85 except that the second Vice-President has been removed from the picture.

ART. 87. The President of the Republic shall, upon entering upon the discharge of the Executive duties, take a solemn oath before the joint session of the Congress to fulfill faithfully the duties of his office and to preserve and defend the Constitution of the Republic.

ART. 88. The Vice-President shall take the same oath before the Congress, but after the President has taken it.

When the Vice-President is not exercising the duties of the President of the Republic, he shall be the president of the Senate. The Senate may elect, nevertheless, a president *pro tempore*, who shall serve in his absence.[1]

ART. 89. The salary of the Vice-President shall be the same as that of the President of the Republic, when he is discharging the duties of that office. When he is merely temporarily discharging the duties of the President, he shall receive only the salary belonging to him as Vice-President.

ART. 90. The President and Vice-President of the Republic shall be elected by the direct secret vote of the citizens in the full enjoyment of their rights. The law shall regulate this election.

ART. 91. The president of the Congress shall, in the presence of the latter, open the sealed envelopes containing the certificates of election from the electoral districts. The secretaries, assisted by four members of the Congress, shall proceed immediately to count the votes cast for each candidate. Those having an absolute majority of votes shall be proclaimed President and Vice-President of the Republic.

ART. 92. When none of the candidates for the Presidency and Vice-Presidency of the Republic has obtained an absolute plurality of the votes cast, the Congress shall take three of those having the highest number of votes and conduct an election from among them for the positions under consideration.

ART. 93. This election shall be held in a public and regular session of the Congress. If the first ballot does not result in an absolute majority of the members present, a second ballot shall be taken, with the restriction that only the two receiving the highest number of votes shall be balloted for. When the vote is a tie, the voting shall continue until one of the candidates obtains an absolute majority of the votes.

ART. 94. The scrutiny of the votes for and the proclamation of the election of the President and Vice-President of the Republic shall be made in a public session of the Congress.

ART. 95. The election of the President and the Vice-President of the Republic, made by the people and proclaimed by the Congress, or made by the latter under the above provisions, shall be announced to the Nation by means of a law.[2]

ART. 96. The President of the Republic shall have power to:

1. Negotiate and conclude treaties with foreign nations, ratify and exchange them when approved by the Congress; appoint consuls, consular agents, and diplomatic ministers, admit foreign functionaries of the same character, and conduct foreign relations generally.

2. Conduct the operations of war which has been declared by law, and personally command the forces of the Republic, subject, however, to the provisions of article 84.

[1] Article 88 has been modified to conform with the one Vice-President idea.

[2] The wording of articles 90–95, dealing with the election of the President and the Vice-President of the Republic, has been changed so as to refer to only one Vice-President.

He has command of the regular army and the national guard, in time of peace, in accordance with the laws and ordinances which the Congress may enact on that subject.

3. Assist in the enactment of the laws by means of direct initiative through special messages, with the parliamentary intervention of the respective minister of state, and promulgate them in conformity with this Constitution.

4. Convene the Congress in special sessions whenever urgent affairs of state may require it.

5. Comply, and cause others to comply, with the provisions of the laws, and issue to that effect the orders and decrees that may be necessary, without entering into any definition of the rights or alterations of the rights defined by the law, and without changing or contravening any of their provisions, having in mind the restriction laid down in article 21.

6. Supervise the collection and management of the national revenue and order its disbursement according to law. No disbursement shall be made without his written order, countersigned by the proper minister of state, naming the law authorizing the expenditure.

7. Submit to the Congress annually the budget of the national expenses for the ensuing year, and also the account of the expenditures made from the appropriation of the previous year.

8. Watch over the resolutions enacted by the municipalities, especially in regard to revenue and taxation, and denounce before the Senate those which are contrary to the Constitution and the laws, unless the offending municipality yields to the remonstrances of the Executive.

9. Submit annually to the Congress, at its first session, a written message on the state of the administration during the year, said message to be accompanied by the reports of the ministers of state of the cabinet. In addition, he shall furnish the Congress, through the same channel, all the information which may be needed for specific purposes, but he may omit everything relating to any diplomatic business which, in his judgment, should not be made public.

10. Grant commutation of the sentence of death in conformity with the law.

11. Enforce the decisions of the courts.

12. Grant amnesties for political offenses without detriment to the authority to grant them vested in the Legislative Power.

13. Grant pensions in accordance with the law.

14. Exercise the rights of patronage in the churches and over ecclesiastical persons and benefices.

15. Nominate archbishops and bishops, selecting the candidates from the list of names, three for each position, submitted by the Senate.

16. Appoint canons, prebendaries, and other church dignitaries from among those nominated by the chapters of the cathedrals.

17. Grant or refuse to grant, with the advice of the Senate, the acceptance of the decrees of the councils, or the briefs, bulls, and rescripts of the Supreme Pontiff. A law by the Congress shall be necessary for the acceptance of such documents as may be of a general or permanent nature.

18. Appoint all the employees of the Republic whose appointment or nomination is not reserved to another power by law.[1]

19. Issue in the name of the Nation commissions to all public employees, even if appointed by another power.

20. Appoint *ad interim*, in cases of resignation or death, officers who should be elected or nominated by another power.

21. Attend the opening and closing sessions of the Congress.

22. Preserve and defend the internal order and the external security of the Republic in accordance with the provisions of this Constitution.

23. Send to the Senate nominations for the offices of general and colonel, when such vacancies occur in the army, three names for each position, with a report on the nominees' services and promotions.

24. Confer the ranks of colonel and general of the army, in the name of the Nation, but only on the field of battle in a foreign war.

25. Grant exclusive temporary privileges to inventors, improvers, and importers of processes or methods useful in the arts and the sciences, but only in accordance with the law. And to indemnify the authors in case such processes or methods are secret.

26. Create and organize second-class ports of entry.

ART. 97. The rank of captain general of the army inheres in the office of the President of the Republic.

ART. 98.[2] There shall be a bureau of accounts (*contabilidad*) and statistics (*estadística*) and a fiscal controller, which shall be known as the General Controllership. Laws shall prescribe the rights, duties, and responsibilities of this bureau and its functionaries. The Controller General shall be appointed by the President of the Republic upon nomination by the Chamber of Senators.

SECTION FOURTEEN

THE MINISTERS OF STATE

ART. 99. The business of public administration shall be transacted by the ministers of state, the number of whom shall be determined by law.

ART. 100. To be a minister of state it shall be necessary to have the same qualifications as are required of a member of the Chamber of Deputies.

ART. 101. The ministers of state shall be responsible for acts of administration in their respective departments jointly with the President of the Republic.

ART. 102. The ministers of state shall be jointly and severally responsible for acts agreed upon in the council of ministers.

ART. 103. All the decrees and orders of the President of the Republic must be countersigned by the minister of the proper department; and shall not be obeyed unless so countersigned. The decrees for the appointment and removal of ministers of state require only the signature of the President of the Republic to make them valid.

ART. 104. The ministers of state may take part in the deliberations of either chamber in the Congress, but must retire before the vote is taken.

[1] Clause 18 of article 96 of the Constitution of 1880, dealing with the appointment of members of the National Tribunal of Accounts, which had been amended by the Law of November 20, 1888, to specify the term of its members as six years, was omitted in 1931.

[2] Article 98 was added in 1931.

ART. 105. As soon as the Congress shall begin its sessions the ministers of state shall submit to it their reports on the condition of the business of their respective departments, in the form set forth in clause 9 of article 96.

ART. 106. The account of the disbursement of the revenues, which must be made by the minister of the treasury, carries with it the presumption that it has been examined and approved by the other ministers so far as their respective departments are concerned. The said account shall be submitted to the Congress with a report thereon by the National Tribunal of Accounts.

All the ministers of state shall assist in preparing the general annual budget, each minister to determine the budget for his own particular ministry.

ART. 107. A verbal or written order from the President of the Republic shall not exempt the ministers of state from the responsibilities required of them according to the law.

ART. 108. The ministers of state may be prosecuted before the Supreme Court by private parties for offenses committed by the ministers of state, the trial to be conducted according to law.

SECTION FIFTEEN
LOCAL GOVERNMENT

ART. 109. The superior administration of the government of each department, in political, administrative, and economic matters, shall be vested in a magistrate known as a prefect, dependent upon the Chief Executive and appointed by him from a list of nominees submitted by the Departmental Assembly. The composition, powers, and duties of this Assembly shall be determined by law.

The administration of the department, in matters pertaining exclusively to itself, is the business of this Assembly, the prefect, and the officers who shall be designated for that purpose by law.

The department and its administration shall be subordinated to the Executive and Legislative Powers of the Nation, in all matters of national interest, in matters concerning the military organization, and in all that which pertains to the order and the security of the department. All other matters shall be delegated by them to the prefect and the officers of whatever class and denomination who reside in the territory of the department.[1]

ART. 110.[2] The Departmental Assembly shall be composed of proctors (*procuradores*) elected by the capital and the provinces in the manner and proportion to be determined by law. The Senators and Deputies of Congress shall also have the right to a voice and vote in the Assembly equal to that of the proctors, but only while they reside in the capital of the department.

The Assembly shall have only the powers which are given to it by the laws, but the restrictions upon these powers shall not affect the following rights: (1) To elect the Senators of the department and the provinces. (2) To regulate, by means of ordinances, the collective and individual interests of the department and the provinces. (3) To levy departmental taxes, establish rules for their collection and administration, and arrange the budget for the annual expenditures, in a manner limited by the resources of the de-

[1] All that pertains to the Departmental Assembly in article 109 was added in 1931.

[2] Article 110 was added in 1931.

partment. (4) To contract loans to be used for public works of general utility and creative productivity and authorize public works and concessions for the good of the department. (5) To establish the police system of the department, providing means to defray the expenses of the same and the functionaries necessary for operation of this branch of public service. The number of the agents of the police and the nature of their duties shall be restricted by the Legislative Power in matters pertaining to the national interests. (6) To organize and support public instruction in the department, and to construct and keep in repair the public roads of the department.

The authorization of the Chamber of Deputies shall be necessary for granting concessions or for the sale of immovable property within the department.

ART. 111.[1] The National Executive shall have the power to intervene in purely departmental matters only to have judicial sentences executed, in case there shall be any effort to prevent the execution of such sentences, and when the departmental authorities shall attempt to prevent the execution of the laws of the State, or when the departmental authorities shall fail to perform the duties of their office. In case of conflicts over jurisdiction between the prefect and the Assembly, the same shall be tried before the Supreme Court.

ART 112.[2] The administrator of the treasury, the departmental chief of police, and the subprefects of the provinces who have the character of chiefs of the provincial police shall be appointed by the prefect from among the nominees of the Assembly. The *corregidores* of the cantons shall be elected by the people by a majority of the votes cast at the election [that is, by *propietarios de la circunscripción*].

The prefect may not be removed from office except for crimes, misdemeanors, and abuses committed in the exercise of the duties of his office, for negligence, or for acts which are incompatible with the good administration of the department. The order for his removal shall be made by the Executive Power or by the Assembly before the District Court in the capital nearest the seat of the prefectural government. This Court may pronounce sentence in the case, but the accused shall have the right to appeal the case to the Supreme Court.

ART. 113. To be a prefect one must be a native-born Bolivian or naturalized, with five years' residence in the country; and must be over thirty years of age. To be a subprefect or corregidor it is necessary to be a Bolivian in the enjoyment of citizenship.

ART. 114. The departments may not establish protective or prohibitive systems which interfere with the interests of the other departments of the Republic, nor may they dictate ordinances in favor of the inhabitants of the department, nor against those of other departments.

ART. 115.[3] The Department of el Beni shall be governed like the other departments, and in accordance with the constitutional laws of centralization approved by the Referendum of January 11, 1931.[4] The territories of the colonies shall be under the administration of the National Powers until such time as the Congress shall determine the

[1] Article 111 was added in 1931.

[2] Article 112 was added in 1931.

[3] Article 115 was added in 1931.

[4] This sentence was incorporated in the Law of September 25, 1931.

necessary form for their government, except in the case of the municipalities which are located therein.

SECTION SIXTEEN
THE UNIVERSITY [1]

ART. 116. The universities shall elect their rectors, professors, and functionaries, determining their rank and titles; may accept legacies and donations; shall administer their incomes; shall prepare the annual budget for presentation to the Legislative Power; and may negotiate loans not to exceed their resources but with the approval of the Congress, in order to realize their autonomy and support their institutes and faculties.

SECTION SEVENTEEN
THE JUDICIARY

ART. 117. Justice shall be administered by the Supreme Court, the district courts, and such other tribunals and courts as shall be established by law.

1. To the inferior judges belongs the right to take cognizance of litigation between private parties, as well as conflicts between public and private parties, without any exception whatever.

2. To them belongs also the decision of the validity or invalidity of popular elections, irrespective of the officials involved. The law shall define the jurisdiction and procedures necessary for the application of this guaranty.

3. The right to declare a law null and void shall be reestablished in accordance with article 24 of the Constitution, and against every act or resolution of the public authority, which is not judicial. The tribunals or judges of superior rank shall enjoy a like privilege in the case of functionaries who have abused their powers. The use of this recourse shall not interfere with criminal trial for the transgression of authority.[2]

ART. 118. The administration of justice shall be free; functionaries who receive a salary for exercising jurisdiction are prohibited from exacting fees for their services.

ART. 119. The Supreme Court is divided into two chambers and is composed of a president, who is president of both chambers, and eight ministers. The president as well as the ministers shall be elected by the legislative chambers united in the Congress, by a two-thirds vote of the members present.[3]

To be a minister of the Supreme Court it is necessary:

1. To be a Bolivian by birth, or if by naturalization to have had five years of actual residence, and be over forty years of age.

2. To have been a minister of some superior court or a district attorney for five years, or have practiced law creditably for ten years.

3. Not to have been condemned to corporal punishment by a competent court.

ART. 120. In addition to the powers and duties conceded to it by law, the Supreme Court shall have the following duties:

1. Represent and direct the judicial power of the Nation. Appoint the members of

[1] Section sixteen was added in 1931.

[2] Clauses 1, 2, and 3 of article 117 were added in 1931.

[3] Article 119 here differs from that of the Constitution of 1880 in two respects: in the number of ministers of the Court and in the manner of their selection.

the district courts and the other judges, as prescribed by law, to whom the president of the Supreme Court shall present the necessary credentials of office. Decree the budgets for the department of justice, ordering their payment from the national treasury, which will pay the same in accordance with the terms of the budget law.[1]

2. Take cognizance of writs of errors in all cases in which this can be done in accordance with the law. Decide at the same time also the nature of the subject matter at issue in the controversy.

3. Take cognizance of writs of cassation, when they are presented before the inferior judges (*juzgados*), in cases of unconstitutional procedure.

4. Take cognizance of all cases over which it has original jurisdiction, according to this Constitution.

5. Take cognizance of the impeachment of diplomatic and consular agents, national commissioners, justices of the superior courts, district attorneys, members of the national tribunal of accounts, and prefects, for offenses committed by them in the exercise of their functions.

6. Take cognizance of claims arising out of contracts, negotiations, and concessions made by the Executive Power, and of claims against the government for injuries sustained by the claimants through some government measure.

7. Take cognizance of all matters subject to litigation relating to the national patronage vested in the Supreme Government of the Republic.

8. Settle conflicts of jurisdiction between municipal councils, or between municipal councils and the political authorities, or between municipal councils or political authorities and provincial municipal boards.

9. Take cognizance of crimes against the resolutions of the Legislative Power or of one of the Chambers, when these resolutions affect one or more concrete rights, whether civil or political, irrespective of the persons concerned.

10. Take cognizance of and decide questions which arise between the departments, whether over boundaries or other disputed matters.

ART. 121. The ministers of the Supreme Court shall take an oath of office before the Congress to comply with the Constitution and the laws. Its president, elected by the Congress, shall also be president of the two chambers of the Court, and shall serve in that capacity for ten years, with the right of reelection.

When the Congress meets away from the capital of the Republic, the Court shall delegate to the ecclesiastical chapter of the capital, which shall meet for that purpose in the hall of sessions of the Legislative Body, the power to administer the oath.

ART. 122. The president of the Court shall watch over the strict and full administration of justice throughout the Republic, and shall address to all the functionaries of the judiciary, with the advice and consent of the Court, the remarks, admonitions, or suggestions which he may deem proper, or cause the attorney general to initiate such prosecutions as the Constitution and the laws may allow.

ART. 123. The attorney general shall be appointed by the President of the Republic upon nomination by the Chamber of Deputies.

The term of office of the attorney general shall be ten years, with the option of reappointment. The attorney general shall not be removed except through a decision of the Supreme Court.

[1] Clause 1 of article 120 was added in 1931.

ART. 124. In addition to the duties and powers established by law, the district courts shall have jurisdiction in trials of officials of municipalities for offenses committed in the exercise of their functions, individually or collectively.

The prefects and subprefects shall be subject to the same jurisdiction.

ART. 125. The judges of the inferior courts shall be appointed by the Supreme Court from among three names submitted to it by the district courts.

ART. 126. The district attorneys and their agents and subordinates shall be appointed by the President of the Republic from among three names submitted to him by the attorney general.

ART. 127.[1] The magistrates of the Supreme Court shall serve for a term of ten years; those of the district courts for six years; and the justices of the peace and the judges of instruction for four years, all of whom may be reelected. These terms of office are personal.

During their term of office, no magistrates or judges may be removed from office without a sentence executed, or suspended except in cases determined by law.

Nor may they be transferred without their express permission.

ART. 128. Publicity in trials is an essential condition in the administration of justice, except when public morals may be offended thereby.

ART. 129. The defense of the government which is to be made in the name of the Nation shall be intrusted to committees appointed for that purpose by the Chamber of Deputies, to the attorney general or to any other public functionary established by law for this purpose.

ART. 130. The tribunals or courts shall not, on their own responsibility, allow justices or judges not appointed in conformity with this Constitution to enter upon the discharge of judicial duties.

ART. 131. The secretaries and subordinate officers of the Judicial Power shall be appointed by the district courts from among three names for each position submitted by the judge under whom they are to serve.

The Supreme Court shall appoint its own secretary and subordinate officers.

SECTION EIGHTEEN
THE MUNICIPAL SYSTEM

ART. 132. There shall be a municipal council in the capital of each Department. There shall be municipal boards, the number of which shall be determined by law, in the provinces and their divisions, and in each port. There shall be municipal agents subordinate to these boards in the cantons; these in turn shall be subordinate to the councils.

ART. 133. The organic municipal law shall determine the number of municipal officers in each locality, the manner in which they shall be elected, the qualifications they must possess, the length of their terms of office, and the manner in which they shall perform their duties.

ART. 134. The municipalities shall have the power to:

1. Promote and watch over the construction of public works in their districts.
2. Establish and abolish municipal taxes, but upon previous approval of the Chamber of Senators.

[1] Article 127 was added in 1888 by the Law of November 20 of that year.

3. Establish and supervise primary schools, manage their funds, make rules for their government, appoint teachers and fix their salaries. In regard to the schools supported by the State, they shall have only the right of inspection and vigilance.

4. Make police regulations regarding public health, personal comfort, city ornamentation, and public amusements.

5. Take care of the charitable institutions according to their respective regulations.

6. Take the census of the population and of the wealth of the municipal district.

7. Compile the departmental statistics.

8. Determine, according to the conscription law and the quota ascribed to their respective territories, the number of those who should enter the military service in place of those who have been discharged.

9. Ask for the interposition of the armed force to carry their resolutions into effect whenever necessary.

10. Collect, manage, and distribute their funds.

11. Accept legacies and gifts and negotiate loans to promote charitable work or works of public utility.

12. Watch over the sale of food and provisions but on the basis of freedom of trade.

13. Appoint jurors for the trial of offenses committed by the public press.

14. Appoint, from among three names submitted by the inferior courts, the canton municipal agents, secretary, treasurer, and all other employees in their service.

ART. 135. The municipal councils may enter into contracts and arrangements with each other for the purpose of promoting and constructing roads connecting two or more departments, provided this combination is based upon disbursements made or engagements entered into by the municipal treasurers in the departments interested in the transaction.

SECTION NINETEEN

THE PUBLIC FORCE

ART. 136. There shall be a standing army in the Republic, the strength of which shall be determined by the Congress at each session, provided that this strength does not exceed the limits of absolute necessity.

ART. 137. The armed force is essentially obedient. In no case shall it have the right to deliberate; in everything relating to the service it shall be subject to the military rules and ordinances.

ART. 138. There shall also be a national guard in each Department. Its organization and duties shall be determined by law.

ART. 139. No one shall serve in the army in the capacity of general or chief who is not a Bolivian by birth, or a naturalized citizen with five years' permanent residence in the Republic, without the express consent of the Congress.

SECTION TWENTY

AMENDING THE CONSTITUTION

ART. 140. This Constitution may be amended in whole or in part, but the necessity for the amendment and the determination thereof in a precise manner shall be previously made by means of an ordinary law passed by two-thirds of the votes of the members present in each chamber.

This law may originate in constitutional form in either Chamber.

The law of amendment shall be sent to the Executive for promulgation.

ART. 141. The constitutional amendment shall be considered in the chamber in which the measure originated in the first session of the new Congress, in the body in which the members of the two chambers have been renewed. If the amendment is declared to be necessary by two-thirds of the members present, the subject shall be referred to the other chamber, where it shall also require a two-thirds vote of the members present.

All the other stages through which the measure has to pass shall be the same as those established by the Constitution in prescribing the relations between the two chambers.

ART. 142. The chambers shall discuss and vote upon the amendment, making it conform with the constitutional provisions determined by the law under which it was ordered.

The amendment, once enacted, shall be forwarded to the Executive for promulgation, the President of the Republic having no right to make objections to it.

ART. 143. When the amendment deals with the constitutional term of office of the President of the Republic it shall not be considered until the following presidential period, according to the provisions of the foregoing articles.

ART. 144. The chambers shall have the power to dispel any doubt about the construction to be placed upon one or more of the articles of this Constitution, but such doubts must be expressed by a two-thirds vote of the members present. All the formalities demanded for a regular law shall be observed in all respects.

ART. 145. The colonies shall be ruled by special laws and regulations.

ART. 146. The authorities and tribunals shall give preference to this Constitution over all the laws, and to the laws over all the decrees and resolutions.

ART. 147. The laws and decrees contrary to this Constitution are hereby repealed.[1]

[1] The Constitution used is that authorized by the Chamber of Deputies on September 26, 1931, and published in La Paz.

APPENDIX B

BIBLIOGRAPHY[1]

History

ACOSTA, N. Escritos literarios y políticos de Adolfo Ballivián. Valparaíso, 1894.

ALCÁZAR MOLINO, GAYETANO. Conquistadores y virreyes españoles en América. Madrid, 1931.

——— Los hombres del despotismo ilustrado en España. El Conde de Floridablanca: su vida y su obra. Murcia, 1934. (Instituto de Estudios Históricos de la Universidad de Murcia.)

ALTAMIRA Y CREVEA, E. Historia de España y de la civilización española. Barcelona, 1913–1914.

ALVARADO, PEDRO. La romántica ciudad colonial. La Paz, 1927.

ALVAREZ, AGUSTÍN. Historia de las instituciones libres. Buenos Aires, 1919.

AMUNÁTEGUI Y SOLAR, DOMINGO. Las encomiendas de indíjenas en Chile. Santiago de Chile, 1909–1910.

ANDRÉ, MARIUS. Bolívar et la democratie. Paris, 1927.

ANTEQUERA, JOSÉ MARÍA. Historia de la legislación española. Madrid, 1895.

APONTE, JOSÉ MARÍA. La batalla de Ingavi: recuerdos históricos. La Paz, 1911.

ARAOZ, MARIO C. (ed.). Nuevo digesto de legislación boliviana. La Paz, 1929.

ARGÜEDAS, ALCIDES. Pueblo enfermo: contribución a la psicología de los pueblos hispano-americanos. Barcelona, 1917.

——— Raza de bronce. La Paz, 1919.

——— Historia de Bolivia. La fundación de la república. Madrid, 1920.

——— Historia general de Bolivia (el proceso de la nacionalidad), 1809–1921. La Paz, 1922.

——— Historia de Bolivia. Los caudillos letrados, la Confederación Perú-Boliviana; o la consolidación de la nacionalidad, 1828–1848. Barcelona, 1923.

——— Historia de Bolivia. La plebe en acción, 1848–1857. Barcelona, 1924.

——— Historia de Bolivia. La dictadura y la anarquía, 1857–1864. Barcelona, 1926.

——— Historia de Bolivia. La Paz, 1926.

——— Los caudillos bárbaros, historia—resurrección.—La tragedia de un pueblo (Melgarejo-Morelos), 1864–1872. Barcelona, 1929.

[1] The bibliography here given is not exhaustive. The ground covered in this study is too comprehensive for a complete recital of materials used. Nor is the division into historical and governmental publications a satisfactory one. Newspaper and magazine articles were also found useful, but only a very few have been included in this list; and only the more important governmental publications have been given. Materials on the foreign policy of Bolivia have been omitted, for the most part, since the foreign relations of the republic have only been touched upon.

ARGÜEDAS, ALCIDES. La danza de las sombras (apuntes sobre cosas, gentes y gentezuelas de la América española). Barcelona, 1934.

——— Pueblo enfermo. 3d ed. Santiago de Chile, 1937.

AROSEMENA, JOSÉ. Estudios constitucionales. La Paz, 1911.

ARRECHEA, SANTIAGO JIMÉNEZ. Bolívar y la confederación americana. Cali, 1930.

AYARRAGARAY, JOSÉ MARÍA. La iglesia en América y la dominación española. Buenos Aires, 1920.

BALLIVIÁN Y ROJAS, VICENTE DE (ed.). Archivo boliviano. Colección de documentos relativos a la historia de Bolivia, durante la época colonial, etc. Paris, 1872.

——— Diario de los sucesos del cerco de la ciudad de la Paz en 1781, hasta la total pacificación de la rebelión general del Perú. Por el Sr. Dn. SEBASTIAN SEGUROLA. *In* Archivo boliviano. Paris, 1872.

BARREDA Y LAOS, FELIPE. Vida intelectual de colonia. Lima, 1909.

BARRERA, A. T. Iniciación de independencia en Sud-América. Quito, 1909.

BARRERA, ISAAC J. Simón Bolívar, libertador y creador de pueblos. Quito, 1930.

BARRIOS, CLAUDIO Q. Diccionario de la Constitución política de Bolivia. La Paz, 1898.

BARROS ARANA, DIEGO. Historia jeneral de Chile. 16 vols. Santiago de Chile, 1884–1902.

BASADRE, JORGE. La iniciación de la república: contribución al estudio de la evolución política y social del Perú. Lima, 1929.

BAUZÁ, FRANCISCO. Historia de la dominación española en el Uruguay. 3d ed. Montevideo, 1929.

BELTRÁN Y RÓZPIDE, R. Colección de las memorias o relaciones que escribieron los virreyes del Perú. Madrid, 1921.

BETETE, VIRGILIO RODRÍGUEZ. Ideologías de la independencia. Paris, 1926.

BETRÁN A., MARCOS. Ensayos de crítica histórica. Oruro, 1924.

BILBAO, MANUEL. Historia de Salaverry. Buenos Aires, 1867.

BLAIR, HELEN, and JAMES A. ROBERTSON. The Philippine Islands, 1493–1898. 55 vols. Cleveland, 1903–1909.

BLANCO G., CARLOS. Resumen de la historia militar de Bolivia. La Paz, 1931.

British and foreign state papers. London, 1836.

BULNES, GONZALO. Nacimiento de las repúblicas americanas. Buenos Aires, 1927.

CÁCERES, PÍO BILBAO. El Senado Nacional. La Paz, 1927.

CALVETE DE ESTRELLA, JUAN CRISTÓBAL. Rebelión de Pizarro en el Perú y vida de Don Pedro Gasca. Madrid, 1889.

CALVO, CARLOS. América latina. Colección histórica completa de los tratados, convenciones, capitulaciones, armisticios, etc. Paris, 1869.

CAPPA, R. Estudios críticos cerca de la dominación española en América. 20 vols. Madrid, 1889–1896.

CARDOZA, EFRAÍM. El cholo en el régimen de las intendencias. Asunción, 1930.

CARRASCO, JOSÉ. Estudios constitucionales. La Paz, 1923.

CARVAJAL, ANGEL LEÓN. Bolívar desde los puntos de vista sociológico, político y jurídico. Quito, 1932.

CARVAJAL, GASPAR DE. The discovery of the Amazon (trans. BERTRAM T. LEE; ed. H. C. HEATON). New York, 1934.

CASAS, BARTOLOMÉ DE LAS. *See* LAS CASAS.

CEVALLOS, PEDRO FERMÍN. Resumen de la historia del Ecuador desde su origen hasta 1845. Quito, 1886.

CHÁVEZ S., MEDARDO. Los adelantados del Río de la Plata. La Paz, 1929.

CIEZA DE LEÓN, PEDRO DE. Tercer libro de Las guerras civiles del Perú, el cual se llama La guerra de Quito. Madrid, 1877.

——— The second part of the chronicle of Peru (trans. and ed. CLEMENTS R. MARKHAM). London, 1883.

——— Civil wars of Peru. The war of Chupas (trans. and ed. SIR CLEMENTS R. MARKHAM). London, 1918.

——— Civil wars of Peru. The war of Las Salinas (trans. SIR CLEMENTS R. MARKHAM). London, 1923.

——— La crónica del Perú; con tres mapas. 2d ed. Madrid, 1932.

CLEVEN, N. ANDREW N. Readings in Hispanic American history. Boston, 1927.

——— (trans.). The constitutions of Spain of 1808 and 1812. Pittsburgh, 1932.

COLMEIRO, MANUEL. Memorias. Madrid, 1861.

CONTE BERMUDEZ, HÉCTOR. La creación de Bolivia y la Constitución bolivariana en el istmo de Panamá. Panama, 1930.

CORREA LUNA, CARLOS. Alvear y la diplomacia de 1824–1825 en Inglaterra, Estados Unidos y Alto Perú, con Canning, Monroe, Quincy Adams, Bolívar y Sucre. Buenos Aires, 1926.

CORTÉS, JOSÉ DOMINGO. Diccionario biográfico americano. Paris, 1875.

CUNNINGHAM, CHARLES HENRY. The audiencia in the Spanish colonies as illustrated by the audiencia of Manila (1583–1800). Berkeley, 1919.

DALENCE, PANTALEÓN. Discurso del presidente de la Corte Suprema, año judicial de 1887. Sucre, 1888.

DIEZ DE MEDINA, EDUARDO. Bolivia: breve resumen histórico, físico y político. La Paz, 1926.

DOBRIZHOFFER, MARTÍN. Account of the Abipones. London, 1820.

DONOSO, JUSTO. Instituciones de derecho canónico americano, etc. Paris, 1854.

DUTTO, L. A. The life of Bartolomé de Las Casas. St. Louis, 1902.

ESTRADA, JOSÉ MANUEL. Lecciones sobre la historia de la República Argentina. Buenos Aires, 1925.

FABIA Y ESCUDERO, ANTONIO MARÍA. Vida y escritos de fray Bartolomé de Las Casas, obispo de Chiapas. Madrid, 1879.

——— Ensayo histórico de la legislación española en sus estados de ultramar. Madrid, 1896.

——— (ed.). Documentos legislativos (de Indias). 3 vols. Madrid, 1890–1897.

FERRER DEL RÍO, ANTONIO. Obras originales del conde de Florida Blanca. Madrid, 1867.

FISHER, LILLIAN E. Viceregal administration in the Spanish colonies. Berkeley, 1926.

FREYRE, R. J. Historia del descubrimiento de Tucumán. Buenos Aires, 1916.

FUNES, GREGORIO. Ensayo de la historia civil del 1910–1911. Paraguay, Buenos Aires y Tucumán. Buenos Aires, 1910–1911.

GALDAMES, LUIS. Historia de Chile. La evolución constitucional, 1810–1925. Santiago de Chile, 1926.

GARCÍA CAMBA, JOSÉ. Memorias del general García Camba para la historia de las armas españolas en el Perú, 1809–1820. Madrid, 1916.

GARCILASO DE LA VEGA, EL INCA. Historia general del Perú, ó, Comentarios reales de los Incas. Madrid, 1919.

GÓMEZ ZAMORA, M. Regio patronato, español e indiano. Madrid, 1912.

GUILLÉN PINTO, ALFREDO, and HERIBERTO GUILLÉN PINTO. Geografía-atlas escolar de Bolivia. La Paz, 1918.

GURIDI, ALEJANDRO ANGULO. Temas políticos. Examen comparativo-crítico de las constituciones de hispano América. Santiago de Chile, 1891.

GUTIÉRREZ, ALBERTO. El melgarejismo antes y después de Melgarejo. Paris, 1918.

GUTIÉRREZ, ARGOTE. Constitución política de la república de Bolivia reformada en 1880. Cochabamba, 1886.

GUTIÉRREZ, J. R. Las constituciones políticas que ha tenido la república Boliviana, 1826–1868. Santiago de Chile, 1869.

GUZMÁN, ALCIBÍADES. Libertad o despotismo en Bolivia; el antimelgarejismo después de Melgarejo: controversia histórica sobre política y derecho constitucional. La Paz, 1918.

——— "Los Colorados" de Bolivia . . . historia de nuestras guerras civiles de un cuarto de siglo, desde 1857, que termina con la internacional en el campo de la Alianza, en 1880. La Paz, 1919.

——— Derecho parlamentario: historia, derecho, jurisprudencia, etc. La Paz, 1920.

Harkness Collection in the Library of Congress. Documents from early Peru. The Pizarros and the Almagros, 1531–1578. Washington, 1926.

HERREROS DE TEJADA, LUIS. El teniente general D. José Manuel de Goyeneche, primer conde de Guaqui. Barcelona, 1923.

Hispanic American Historical Review. Duke University, Durham, North Carolina.

ITURRICHA, AGUSTÍN. Historia de Bolivia bajo la administración del mariscal Andrés Santa Cruz. Sucre, 1920.

JAIMES, J. L. La Villa Imperial de Potosí. Buenos Aires, 1905.

JÁUREGUI ROSQUELLAS, ALFREDO. Geografía general de Bolivia; cuatro cursos. 3d ed. La Paz, 1919.

——— La ciudad de los cuatro nombres: cronicario histórico. Sucre, 1924.

——— La España heroica en el Nuevo Mundo. La Paz, 1926.

——— Antonio José de Sucre: héroe y sabio, mártir y santo. Cochabamba and La Paz, 1928.

——— Conferencias didácticas de geografía de Bolivia. La Paz, 1937.

JUAN [Y SANTACILIA], JORGE, and ANTONIO DE ULLOA. Noticias secretas de América, sobre el estado naval, militar, y político de los reynos del Perú y provincias de Quito, costas de Nueva Granada y Chile: gobierno y régimen particular de los pueblos de los Indios: cruel opresión y extorsiones de sus corregidores y curas: abusos escandalosos introducidos entre estos habitantes por los misioneros: causas de su origen y motivos de su continuación por el espacio de tres siglos. Escritas fielmente según las instrucciones del excelentísimo Señor marqués de la Ensenada, primer secretario de estado, y presentadas en informe secreto á S. M. C. el Señor Don Fernando VI. por Don Jorge Juan, y Don Antonio de Ulloa. . . . Sacadas a luz para el verdadero conocimiento del gobierno de los Españoles en la América Meridional, por Don David Barry. London, 1826.

JUAN Y SANTACILIA, JORGE. Noticias secretas de América. Madrid, 1918.

LA FUENTE, MANUEL DE (ed.). Memorias de los virreyes que han gobernado el Perú. Lima, 1859.

LANZAS, PEDRO TORRES. Independencia de América: fuentes para su estudio. Madrid, 1912.

LAS CASAS,[1] BARTOLOMÉ DE. Breve relación de la destrucción de las Indias Occidentales, etc. Seville, 1552.

——— Colección de las obras del venerable obispo de Chiapas, etc. Paris, 1822.

——— De las antiguas gentes del Perú. Madrid, 1892.

——— Historia de las Indias. 3 vols. Madrid, 1927.

LAVADENZ, J. La colonización en Bolivia durante la primera centuria de su independencia. La Paz, 1925.

LEA, C. H. The Inquisition in the Spanish dependencies. New York, 1922.

LECUNA, VICENTE. Documentos referentes a la creación de Bolivia. Caracas, 1924.

——— Cartas del Libertador. Caracas, 1929.

LEGUÍA, JORGE GUILLERMO. Historia de América. Lima, 1928.

LEÓN PINELO, ANTONIO DE. Tratado de confirmaciones reales de encomiendas. Madrid, 1830.

LETURIA, PEDRO. El ocaso del patronato real en la América española: la acción diplomática de Bolívar ante Pío VII (1820–1823). Madrid, 1925.

——— Bolívar y León XII. Caracas, 1931.

——— La emancipación hispanoamericana en los informes episcopales a Pío VII: copias y extractos del Archivo vaticano. Buenos Aires, 1935.

LEVENE, RICARDO. Historia de la nación argentina. Buenos Aires, 1937.

LEVILLIER, ROBERTO (ed.). Antecedentes de política económica en el Río de la Plata. Madrid, 1915.

——— Organización de la iglesia y órdenes religiosas en el virreinato del Perú en el siglo XVI. Madrid, 1919.

——— Chile y Tucumán en el siglo XVI (el conflicto Villagra–Núñez de Prado). Praga [Paris], 1928.

——— Biografías de conquistadores de la Argentina en el siglo XVI. Tucumán. Madrid, 1933.

——— Don Francisco de Toledo, supremo organizador del Perú: su vida, su obra (1515–1582). Buenos Aires, 1935.

LÓPEZ, ISMAEL. Colombia en la guerra de independencia. Bogotá, 1914.

LÓPEZ, MANUEL ANTONIO. Campaña del Perú por el ejército unido libertador de Colombia, Perú, B. Aires y Chile, etc. Caracas, 1843.

——— Recuerdos históricos de la guerra de la independencia. Colombia y el Perú (1819–1826). Madrid, 1919.

[1] In the card catalogue of the Library of Congress this author's name is written more often as Bartolomé de las Casas, and alphabetized under Casas.

LÓPEZ, VICENTE FIDEL. Historia de la República Argentina: su origin, su revolución, y su desarrollo político hasta 1852. 10 vols. Buenos Aires, 1883–1893.

LLORENTE, S. (ed.). Relaciones de los virreyes y audiencias que han gobernado el Perú. Lima, 1867.

LOZA, LEÓN M. Historia de la bandera. Oruro, 1924.

——— Bosquejo histórico del periodismo boliviano. La Paz, 1925.

LOZANO, PEDRO. Historia de las revoluciones de la Provincia del Paraguay (1721–1735). Buenos Aires, 1905.

LOZANO Y LOZANO, FABIO. El maestro del Libertador. Paris, [1913].

MCQUEEN, CHARLES A. The Bolivian public debt. Washington, 1924.

——— Bolivian public finance. Washington, 1925.

MARTÍNEZ, MIGUEL A. Hombres y cosas de América. El general Felipe Santiago Salaverry: ensayo de biografía fisiológica, en el centenario del levantamiento de Salaverry, 23 de febrero de 1835. Lima, 1935.

MARTÍNEZ Y VELA, BARTOLOMÉ. Historia de la conquista del Paraguay, Rio de la Plata y Tucumán. Buenos Aires, 1874.

——— Anales de la Villa Imperial de Potosí. Buenos Aires, 1915.

MATIENZO, JUAN. Gobierno del Perú: obra escrita en el siglo XVI por licenciado Don Juan Matienzo, oidor de la Real Audiencia de Charcas (ed. JOSÉ NICOLÁS MATIENZO). Buenos Aires, 1910.

MEANS, PHILIP A. A study of ancient Andean social institutions. New Haven, 1925.

——— Ancient civilizations of the Andes. New York, 1931.

——— The fall of the Inca Empire and the Spanish rule in Peru, 1530–1780. New York, 1932.

——— The Spanish Main: focus of envy, 1492–1700. London, 1935.

MECHAM, JOHN LLOYD. Church and State in Latin America: a history of politico-ecclesiastical relations. Chapel Hill, 1934.

MEDINA, JOSÉ TORIBIO. Historia del tribunal del Santo Oficio de la Inquisición de Lima (1569–1820). Santiago de Chile, 1887.

——— Historia del tribunal del Santo Oficio de la Inquisición en Chile. Santiago de Chile, 1890.

——— El tribunal del Santo Oficio de la Inquisición en las provincias del Plata. Santiago de Chile, 1899.

——— Francisco de Aguirre en Tucumán. Santiago de Chile, 1896.

——— Juan Díaz de Solís: estudio histórico. Santiago de Chile, 1897.

——— Los viajes de Diego García de Moguer al Rio de la Plata: estudio histórico. Santiago de Chile, 1908.

MENDIBURU, MANUEL DE. Diccionario histórico-biográfico del Perú. 8 vols. Lima, 1874–1890.

MENDOZA, JAIME. La universidad de Charcas y la idea revolucionaria: ensayo histórico. Sucre, 1925.

——— El macizo boliviano. La Paz, 1935.

MERCADO M., MIGUEL. Charcas y el Río de la Plata a través de la historia. La Paz, 1918.

MERRIMAN, J. D. The rise of the Spanish empire in the Old World and in the New. 4 vols. New York, 1918–1934.

MILLER, JOHN. Memoirs of General John Miller in the service of the Republic of Peru. London, 1828.

MONSALVE, J. D. El ideal político del Libertador Simón Bolívar. Madrid, 1916.

MONTEAGUDO, BERNARDO. Escritos políticos; recopilados y ordenados por MARIANO A. PELLIZA. Buenos Aires, 1916.

MONTES DE OCA, MANUEL AUGUSTO. Cuestiones constitucionales. Buenos Aires, 1899.

MOSES, BERNARD. The establishment of Spanish rule in America: an introduction to the history and politics of Spanish America. New York and London, 1898.

——— South America on the eve of emancipation: the southern Spanish colonies in the last half-century of their dependence. New York and London, 1908.

——— The Spanish dependencies in South America: an introduction to the study of their civilization. New York and London, 1914.

——— Spain's declining power in South America. Berkeley, 1919.

——— Spanish colonial literature in South America. London and New York, 1922.

——— The intellectual background of the revolution in South America, 1810–1824. New York, 1926.

——— Spain overseas. New York, 1929.

O'CONNOR D'ARLACH, TOMÁS. Los presidentes de Bolivia desde 1825 hasta 1912. La Paz, 1912.

——— El general Melgarejo: hechos y dichos de este hombre célebre. La Paz, 1913.

——— Rosas, Francia y Melgarejo. La Paz, 1914.

OLIVEIRA LIMA, MANUEL DE. Historia diplomática do Brazil. O reconhecimento do império. 2d ed. Río de Janeiro, 1902.

——— Dom João VI no Brazil, 1808–1821. Rio de Janeiro, 1908.

——— The evolution of Brazil compared with that of Spanish and Anglo-Saxon America. Stanford University, 1914.

——— O movimento da independéncia, 1821–1822. São Paulo, 1922.

——— O império braziléiro, 1822–1889. São Paulo, 1927.

——— Miguel no trono (1828–1833). Coimbra, Brazil, 1933.

ORDÓÑEZ LÓPEZ, MANUEL. Constitución política de la república de Bolivia: leyes y disposiciones mas usuales. La Paz, 1917.

PALMA, RICARDO. Tradiciones peruanas. Chicago and New York, 1936.

PANDIÁ CALOGERAS, JOÃO. A history of Brazil (trans. and ed. PERCY ALVIN MARTIN). Chapel Hill, 1939.

PAREDES, MANUEL RIGOBERTO. Política parlamentaria de Bolivia. La Paz, 1911.

PAZ, JULIO. Historia económica de Bolivia. La Paz, 1927.

PAZ, LUIS. El gran tribuno. Buenos Aires, 1908.

——— La Corte Suprema de Justicia de Bolivia: su historia y su jurisprudencia. Sucre, 1910.

——— Constitución política de la República de Bolivia: su texto, su historia y su comentario. Sucre, 1912.

——— Historia general del Alto Perú, hoy Bolivia. La Paz, 1919.

——— Colección de escritos de Luis Paz. Biografías. Sucre, 1919.

PAZ SOLDÁN, MARIANO FELIPE. Historia del Perú independiente, 1835–1839. Buenos Aires, 1888.

——— Historia del Perú independiente, 1822–1827. Madrid, 1919.

PELLIZA, MARIANO A. Monteagudo: su vida y sus escritos. Buenos Aires, 1880.

PEREZ VELASCO, DANIEL. La mentalidad chola en Bolivia. La Paz, 1928.

PINILLA, CLAUDIO. Estudios comparables de la Constitución boliviana con las de los otros países de América meridional. La Paz, 1927.

PINILLA, SABINO. La vida intelectual en la América española. Buenos Aires, 1910.

——— La creación de Bolivia. Madrid, 1917.

PIZARRO, PEDRO. Relation of the discovery and conquest of the kingdoms of Peru. New York, 1921.

POLO, JOSÉ TORIBIO. Memorias de los virreyes del Perú. Lima, 1896.

PORRAS BARRENECHEM, RAUL. El Congreso de Panamá, 1826. Lima, 1930.

PRADT, DOMINIQUE FREDÉRIC DE RIOM DE PROLHIAC DE FOURT DE. Europe and America in 1821; with an examination of the plan laid before the Cortes of Spain for recognition of the independence of South America. 2 vols. London, 1822.

Primera Convención Nacional de Estudiantes Bolivianos. Programa de principios, estatuto orgánico y reglamento de debates de la Federación Universitaria Boliviana. Cochabamba, 1928.

QUESADA, VICENTE GASPAR. Vireinato del Río de la Plata 1776–1810. Buenos Aires, 1881.

——— Crónicas Potosinas: costumbres de la edad medieval hispano-americana. Paris, 1890.

——— La sociedad hispano-americana, bajo la dominación española. Madrid, 1893.

——— La vida intelectual en la América española durante los siglos XVI, XVII y XVIII. Buenos Aires, 1910.

——— Historia colonial Argentina. Buenos Aires, 1915.

RAMOS MEJÍA, FRANCISCO. El federalismo Argentino. Buenos Aires, 1915.

RENÉ-MORENO, GABRIEL. Anales de la prensa boliviana, 1861–1862. Santiago de Chile, 1886.

——— Últimos días coloniales en el Alto-Perú. Santiago de Chile, 1896.

——— Bolivia y Perú: notas históricas y bibliográficas. Santiago de Chile, 1905.

REPÚBLICA ARGENTINA. MINISTERIO DE RELACIONES EXTERIORES Y CULTO. La gestion diplomática del general Alvear en el Alto Perú (Misión Alvear-Díaz, 1825). Buenos Aires, 1927.

Revista do Instituto Histórico e Geográphico Brasiléiro. Tomo especiál: Congresso Internacionál de História da América. Rio de Janeiro, 1927.

RÍOS, CORNELIO. Bolivia en el primer centenario de su independencia: su participación en la guerra de la emancipación americana; su victimización en la guerra del Pacífico. Buenos Aires, 1925.

RIVAS, MIGUEL. Dictadura Linares. Tacna, 1873.

ROBERTSON, JAMES A. (trans.). Magellan's voyage around the world, by ANTONIO PIGAFETTA. Cleveland, 1906.

ROBERTSON, WILLIAM SPENCE (trans. and ed.). A history of Argentina, by RICARDO LEVENE. Chapel Hill, 1937.

ROJAS, CASTO. Historia financiera de Bolivia. La Paz, 1926.

ROMANA Y PUIGDENGOLAS, FRANCISCO DE. Antigüedad del regionalismo español. Barcelona, 1890.

ROWE, LEO STANTON. The federal system of the Argentine Republic. Washington, 1921.

RUIZ GUIÑAZÚ, E. La magistratura indiana. Buenos Aires, 1916.

SAAVEDRA, BAUTISTA. La democracia en nuestra historia. La Paz, 1921.

SÁNCHEZ BUSTAMANTE, DANIEL. Principio de derecho. La Paz, 1919.

SAN CRISTÓVAL, EVARISTO. Páginas de historia colonial. Sucre, 1920.

SANJINÉS, JENARO. Las constituciones políticas de Bolivia: estudio histórico y comparativo. La Paz, 1906.

SANTA-CRUZ, OSCAR DE. El general Andrés de Santa-Cruz, gran mariscal de Zepita y del Gran Perú. La Paz, 1929.

SANTIVAÑEZ, JOSÉ MARÍA. Vida del general José Ballivián. New York, 1891.

SERNA, JOSÉ DE LA. Manifestación que de la criminal conducta del general Olañeta hace a S. M. el virrey del Perú Don José de la Serna. Madrid, 1894–1898.

SILES, HERNANDO. Derecho parlamentario de Bolivia. La Paz, 1917.

SILVA COTOPAS, CARLOS. Historia eclesiástica de Chile. Santiago de Chile, 1925.

SOLÓRZANO Y PEREIRA, JUAN DE. La política indiana, etc. Madrid, 1648.

SOTOMAYOR VALDÉS, RAMÓN. La legación de Chile en Bolivia. Santiago de Chile, 1867.

——— Estudio histórico de Bolivia bajo la administración del general D. José de Achá. Santiago de Chile, 1874.

SUBIETA SAGÁRNAGA, LUIS. La mita. Potosí, 1917.

——— Bolívar en Potosí. Potosí, 1925.

TORRENTE, MARIANO. Historia de la revolución hispano-americana. 3 vols. Madrid, 1829–1830.

VARGAS, CARLOS CORTÉS. Participación de Colombia en la independencia del Perú. Bogotá, 1924.

VELEZ SARSFIELD, DALMACIO. Derecho público eclesiástico. Relaciones del estado con la iglesia en la antigua América española. Buenos Aires, 1871.

VICUÑA MACKENNA, BENJAMÍN. El Wáshington del Sur—Antonio José de Sucre. Santiago de Chile, 1893.

VILLANUEVA, CARLOS A. La monarquía en América. Paris, 1912.

——— Bolívar y el general San Martín. Paris, 1912.

——— Fernando VII y los nuevos estados. Paris, 1912.

——— El imperio de los Andes. Paris, 1914.

VIVERO, D., and J. A. LAVALLA. Galería de retratos de los gobernadores y virreyes del Perú, 1532–1821. Barcelona, 1909.

WIESE, CARLOS. Historia del Perú y de la civilización peruana. Lima, 1914.

——— Historia del Perú colonial. Lima, 1916.

WILCOCKE, SAMUEL HILL. History and description of the republic of Buenos Aires. London, 1820.

WILGUS, A. CURTIS (ed.). Modern Hispanic America. Washington, 1935.

WILGUS, A. CURTIS (ed.). South American dictators. Washington, 1937.
ZACONETA, JOSÉ VÍCTOR. La democracia de Bolivia en el primer centenario de su gloriosa independencia. Oruro, 1925.
ZAMORA Y CORONADO, J. M. Biblioteca de legislación ultramarina. Madrid, 1844–1849.
ZARATE, AGUSTÍN DE. Historia del descubrimiento y conquista de la provincia del Perú, etc. Santiago de Chile, 1901.

PUBLICATIONS OF THE GOVERNMENT OF BOLIVIA

Constitution

Constitución política de la República de Bolivia: leyes y disposiciones más usuales; contiene además: las constituciones políticas sancionadas desde 1826 hasta 1878 y las leyes de reformas de la legislación civil y criminal. Compilados y concordados por MANUEL ORDÓÑEZ LÓPEZ. La Paz, 1917.
Constitución política del estado y reglamento de debates del Senado y de la Cámara de Diputados. La Paz, 1926.
Constitución política de la República de Bolivia. La Paz, 1931.
Constitución política del estado. Edición autorizada por el H. Senado Nacional. La Paz, 1932.

Laws, Statutes, etc.

Colección oficial de leyes, decretos, órdenes, resoluciones de la República Boliviana, desde 1825 hasta 1926. La Paz, 1928.
Digesto de legislación boliviana por MARIO C. ARAOZ. La Paz, 1920.
Nuevo digesto de legislación boliviana por MARIO C. ARAOZ. La Paz, 1929.
Código de procederes, Santa Cruz, etc. Cochabamba, 1862.
Código penal, Santa Cruz, etc. Corocoro, 1883.
Código civil boliviano explicado y concordado por MELCHOR TERRAZAS. Sucre, 1885.
Código civil boliviano, etc., concordado y comentado con la teoría de autores clásicos y la doctrina y jurisprudencia de la Corte Suprema. Por ENRIQUE MALLEA BALBOA. La Paz, 1906.
Código civil, concordado por HERNANDO SILES. Santiago de Chile, 1910.
Código civil boliviano, compilado por CARLOS MAX DE CASTILLO con autorización del supremo gobierno. 2d ed. La Paz, 1931.
Código de trabajo, nuevo. La Paz, 1929.
Ley electoral. La Paz, 1924.
Legislación integral del Ramo de Colonización. Compiled and annotated by HUMBERTO DELGADO LLANO. La Paz, 1928.
Codificación de leyes y disposiciones referente a minería, por ABDON CALDERON. La Paz, 1928.

Congress

Libro menor de sesiones secretas de los señores diputados que componen la Asamblea General del Alto Perú, instalada en 10 de julio de 1825, y de las sesiones secretas del Congreso General Constituyente instalado en 25 de mayo de 1826. La Paz, 1926.

Redactores antiguos encuadernados y publicados por la Cámara de Diputados. La Paz, 1918–1926.
Redactor de Asamblea General, 1825. Sucre, 1825.
Redactor de la Convención Nacional del año 1843. La Paz, 1926.
Redactor del H. Congreso Constitucional del año 1844. La Paz, 1924.
Redactor del H. Senado Nacional del año 1844. 2 vols. La Paz, 1926.
Redactor de la Cámara de Representantes del año 1844. La Paz, 1926.
Redactor del H. Senado Nacional del año 1850. La Paz, 1850.
Redactor de la H. Convención Nacional de los años 1850–1851. La Paz, 1924.
Redactor de la Convención Nacional de 1851 y de sus sesiones extraordinarias en el mismo año. La Paz, 1925.
Redactor de la Asamblea Constituyente del año 1861. La Paz, 1926.
Redactor de la Asamblea Constituyente del año 1871. La Paz, 1927.
Redactor de la Asamblea Constitucional del año 1872. La Paz, 1927.
Redactor de la Convención Nacional del año 1880. La Paz, 1926.
Senate. Debates en el H. Senado Nacional sobre la concesión de un millón de hectáreas petrolíferas a Richmond, Levering Co. y la Standard Oil Co. Petición del informe del H. Senador por La Paz, Doctor Abel Iturralde. Legislatura ordinaria de 1921–1922. La Paz, 1922.
Senate. Juicio de responsibilidad contra el ex-presidente de la República. La Paz, 1931–1932.
Senate. Discursos pronunciados en el H. Senado Nacional por los ministros de estado en respuesta a la demanda de interpelación que presentaron en la legislatura de 1902, los HH. Señores Ismael Vásquez, Miguel Ramírez y Guillermo Cainzo. La Paz, 1903.
Chamber of Deputies. Comisión de Policía Judicial. Juicio de responsibilidad contra el presidente de la República D. Hernando Siles y sus colaboradores por los delitos de ataque á las garantías constitucionales y malversación de fondos fiscales, cometidos durante su administración. La Paz, 1931.
Historia parlamentaria de Bolivia desde 1825 hasta 1925. La Paz, 1926.

Supreme Court

Corte Suprema de Justicia de Bolivia. Gaceta Judicial. Sucre, 1858–1915.
Corte Suprema de Justicia de Bolivia. Jurisprudencia y doctrinas expuestas en correspondencia y circulares de sus presidentes. Sucre, 1927.
Discursos de los presidentes de la excma. Corte Suprema de Justicia de Bolivia: homenaje en el primer centenario de su fundación. La Paz, 1927.

Miscellaneous

Delegación Nacional en el Noroeste de la República. Informe preliminar de los actos de la Delegación Nacional en el Noroeste de la República, presentado por el delegado Sr. Lisímaco Gutiérrez y el secretario Dr. Román Paz. Sucre, 1895.
Delegación Nacional en el Territorio de Colonias del N. O. Informe presentado por el delegado nacional, Adolfo Ballivián, 1907–1908. Pará, 1909.
Supremo Tribunal Nacional de Cuentas. Primer centenario de su fundación, 1825–1925. Sucre, 1925.

INDEX

C

M